THE NEW
INDUSTRIAL
STATE

John Kenneth Galbraith

**THIRD EDITION,
REVISED**

A MENTOR BOOK
NEW AMERICAN LIBRARY
TIMES MIRROR
NEW YORK AND SCARBOROUGH, ONTARIO

Library of Congress Catalog Card Number: 79-87645

First Mentor Printing, July, 1979

1 2 3 4 5 6 7 8 9

PRINTED IN THE UNITED STATES OF AMERICA

for Andrea Williams

Acknowledgments

THE REVISION of a book such as this is not, for me at least, the most fascinating of tasks. The first time one searches for information, even in the *Statistical Abstract,* there is a moderate sense of discovery. When one goes back for more recent figures or facts, this fades. To find material affirming a point s never as interesting as finding that which originally made or suggested the point. Finding information that casts doubt on a point made in earlier editions is not enchanting at all.

Herein is my debt to David Thomas, for some years my most able assistant in teaching at Harvard, now a lawyer in Denver. In 1976 and 1977, he took many weeks from his practice to give me a hand on material which, from his teaching, he knew better than anyone else. I was not only rescued from drudgery but guided, corrected and stimulated. My debt to David Thomas—and the partners who allowed him leave for the task—is very great.

Emmy Davis, as before, managed my daily routine while the revision was in process. Lynn Feinberg typed and retyped the drafts. And, as for so many earlier volumes, Andrea Williams took charge of my manuscript and saw it through to the present book. To all, much love and more thanks.

Foreword to the Third Edition

THIS BOOK was first published in the spring of 1967, and this is its second revision. In the foreword to the first edition I noted that nearly ten years had passed between initiation and completion so that, with many leaves of absence, I've been involved with this volume for nearly half of my adult life. It is not time I regret, for I consider it the most important thing I have done or, most certainly, am likely to do. And such has been the circulation of the earlier editions—some millions in a score or more of languages extending to the Soviet Union, the Eastern European countries and the distant East—that I allow myself to believe that a fair number of others agree.

2

In the first edition I told a little of the origins of the book, and these are perhaps important enough for me to summarize here. I was completing another book, *The Affluent Society*, when a further and larger world began obtruding itself on my thoughts. This was the world of great corporations—a world in which people increasingly served the convenience of those organizations which were meant to serve *them*. It was a world in which the motivation of those involved did not fit the standard textbook mold. Nor did the relationship between corporation and state. Nor did markets. So far from being the controlling power in the economy, markets were more and more accommodated to the needs and convenience of the great business organizations. Numerous writers had dealt with parts of this reality but without assuming larger change. I became persuaded that these parts belonged to a much greater and very closely articulated process of change.

At first I resisted these thoughts. The book on which I was working was quite obviously a part of this movement and was occasioned thereby. But to tackle the larger task might mean never finishing the book in hand. Friends of mine have gained high professional credit over a long academic career for the perception and scope of their unpublished works and the vividness with which they have described them. But this is a special talent. I went ahead and published *The Affluent Society* and then settled down to try to see what I had only glimpsed.

Two and a half years later, in 1961, I had nearly finished a preliminary draft when President Kennedy asked me to go to India as his ambassador. With some misgivings I put the manuscript away in the vault of the bank. I worried, as I've often said, lest the world were exchanging a somewhat irreplaceable author for a more easily obtainable diplomat. The danger was not as great as I imagined. I returned from India with some new thoughts and, in the end, a better view of the problem. I greatly revised the earlier manuscript. Had it not been for the diplomatic interlude, I might have published a more primitive version. Let every writer, if he cannot arrange a tour as ambassador before publishing, at least take a long reflective holiday.

I would still remind the reader that this book had its origins alongside *The Affluent Society*. It stands in relation to that book as a house to a window. This is the structure; the earlier book allowed the first glimpse inside. Anything that I covered in the earlier book and did not need for the present argument I deleted or dismissed with brief mention in this volume. I thus omitted discussion of the evolution of economic ideas and associated goals, the problem of the balance between the public and private sectors of the economy and the special problem of the poor in an industrial society. But a few of the ideas in the earlier book, notably the accommodation of consumer and public behavior to the needs of producer organization, are indispensable, and on a few other matters I have improved my view. These are here.

The first ten or so chapters lay the foundation for what follows. They are somewhat more demanding than those that come after. I hope they will be found to have repaid the effort. Over all, the argument is progressive. I have thought it useful, at intervals, to remind the reader of what has gone before. This is deliberate. The reader who finds these reminders redundant can take pleasure in reflecting that this is the price of exceptional memory and acuity.

3

In the first revision I corrected the errors, most of them I hope, that had survived the scrutiny of what may be the best staff with which any writer on economics was ever blessed. And I took account of the considerable critical reaction the book provoked. One part of this was rather easily managed. As I said then, whatever the faults of economics as a field of scholarship, it cannot be criticized for failing to foster scholarly self-confidence and ego. One consequence is a sizable group of economists who unhesitantly associate whatever they have been told to believe in their youth with absolute scholarship. Anything alien to such installed belief is deficient. A facility in mathematics or even in theoretical model-building adds alarmingly to this tendency. The resulting criticism, unhappily, tells more of the critic, and the width of the intellectual base from which he operates, than of the faults in the work with which he deals.[1] In the same compassionate vein I would pass over the critics whose reaction is not to error but to the casualness of their own reading. And also those who resort to the oldest of the protective syllogisms of economic orthodoxy. This is to say that there is truth here—sometimes that there is much truth here. But it is not the whole truth. Accordingly, one need not—and in the name of science should not—accept any of it. Better believe and teach as before. This an especially popular escape.

But there were criticisms that any reasonably open-minded writer would take seriously. One such attack was on my methodology. The approved method in economics has come to consist of establishing small points by solid empirical evidence and then proceeding, point by such point, to reassess the structure as a whole. Robert Solow, an energetic defender of this procedure, said, in especially articulate criticism, that economists must be determined "little-thinkers."[2] This book, he complained, was sadly deficient in such determination. It attacks the most central of economic assumptions, that of consumer sovereignty and the ultimate power of the individual in economic life. The individual, it holds, is increasingly

[1] Cf. Scott Gordon, "The Close of the Galbraithian System," *Journal of Political Economy*, Vol. LXXVI, No. 4, Pt. I (July-August 1968), p. 635 et seq.

[2] Robert M. Solow, "The New Industrial State or Son of Affluence," *The Public Interest*, No. 9 (Fall 1967), p. 100.

subordinate to the goals of the producing organization of which he is participant or customer. The relevant facts are arranged within this framework, and, it is held, they fit far better there than in the orthodox neoclassical frame. This— movement from the large assumption to the facts that fit and defend it, not the reverse—is in conflict with the approved procedure. Professor Solow (with others) sorrowed for the established ways.

I would not relish an economic discipline in which everyone was engaged in building big structures. Most of these would then be filled with hot air. But on occasion the effort must be made. The small empirical work, however admirable, never does build up to an assault on or even a view of the larger framework. And if that framework is wrong—if it makes General Motors strictly subordinate to the market, Lockheed to the Pentagon and all other industries subordinate to ultimate citizen will—the approved methodology wonderfully protects and perpetuates error. Such work is not politically neutral; its pedagogy persuades the innocent that they have a power they do not possess and diverts attention from those who do wield power. System-building, to the greatest extent possible, must be the product of ordered thought. It allows of no resort to rhetoric, slogans, indignation or passion. Perhaps it imposes a special obligation in these respects. But when the existing framework is wrong, such systemic treatment cannot be avoided. I believe this to be true of the neoclassical and textbook framework here under attack and which I seek to reconstruct. I find some justification in the fact that what emerges now seems far more commonplace than when I first offered it a decade ago.

A more specific line of criticism, one that still survives, was heavily concerned with my case that the large industrial corporation can manage its consumers—and, by inference, that the defense establishment (the weapons producers and the Pentagon) instructs the public on defense needs and not the reverse. The critics held that no such power could be proven. Accordingly, it does not exist. This is a vital point. If it can be shown that the consumer and the citizen can be managed by those who, nominally, exist to serve him, then the revised sequence—a tendency toward producer instead of consumer sovereignty—becomes possible. If the consumer and citizen cannot be so managed, then the established system is secure. Production responds to his unmanaged decision. I would not

suggest that all my critics, in rallying to the defense of the independent power of the consumer and citizen—to his immunity to persuasion and to his power in the democratic
process—are being tendentious. As always, one must assume
the best of motives, and scholars have a natural respect for
established belief. But that some are seeking to shore up the
established structure of economics at its most vulnerable
point is not in doubt. Their effort reflects an extremely happy
coincidence between scientific conviction and the defense of
intellectual vested interest.

Here one could only stand firm and appeal to the evidence
of the eye. And the evidence of the eye is assuredly there.
The eye sees a vast advertising and sales effort employing
elaborate science and art to influence the customer. It senses
great and subtle effort by the aerospace and like industries to
persuade the armed services to want what they can supply. It
sees a wholly unsubtle process by which the Pentagon instructs the Congress on what it wishes to have.[3] Those who
say that what is so seen cannot be proven are, in effect, saying that nothing can be proven. They are using a pseudo-
scientific syllogism to divert attention from reality.

An almost equally vital point for the established system is
the maximization of profits. If it can be believed that corporations always maximize their pecuniary return, they are ultimately subordinate to the pecuniary commands of the
market. Since the message of more or less money is the
message the market transmits, the market still rules. I here argue that the great corporation maximizes not pecuniary return
but the whole complex of organizational interests of which
pecuniary return is only one part, and that it goes on to ensure
that the goals of the larger community and state will be sym-
pathetic to its own. This involves an exercise of power far
more important than is possible if the firm is confined by its
pursuit of profit.

Here, however, the orthodox attack on my views was less
than full-hearted.[4] The defense of crude profit maximization,
though vital to the neoclassical system, had already crumbled
as regards the great corporation. Numerous scholars, as told

[3] Even the most stalwart defenders of the ultimate authority of the
consumer, as I note herein, jibe when it comes to defending the proposition on weapons and similar public goods.

[4] Cf. Solow, p. 107.

herein, had already rejected it. Much of the objection to the present view—to my contention that the corporation seeks to combine security of minimum return with growth and technical virtuosity for its own sake with profit—is that it lacks symmetry and elegance. This I would readily concede. So, very often, does truth. And it is inherent in this system, as it is not in the neoclassical model, that, within limits, goals may differ as between corporations.

Finally, as I predicted in the first edition, I encountered criticism from the left—passionate from younger radicals in the United States, rather more sedate from the Soviet Union. The system here described associates power with organization—with public and private bureaucracy. This, it is held, obscures or even suppresses the role of the capitalist. Perhaps, some critics averred, this was deliberate and insidious. The capitalist has for long been an embarrassment to those who wish to prove that everything is for the better and eventually for the best. Since no one can defend him, how clever to get rid of him. But, this line of argument continues, no one should be fooled. The capitalist is there, lurking just off stage, pulling the levers that motivate his managerial puppets, and just as powerful and malign as ever. The test of both perception and virtue in economic and political thought is to see this. Truth is tested not by what exists but by courage—and courage is measured by willingness to go down the line with the unvarnished Marx.[5]

To this criticism also I cannot yield. The decisive power in modern industrial society is exercised not by capital but by organization, not by the capitalist but by the industrial bureaucrat. This is true in the Western planning systems. It is true also in the socialist societies. It is why the young American radical is no longer attracted by the Soviet model, for that means exchanging one highly organized bureaucratic system for another highly organized bureaucratic system. It is why he can be attracted to Cuba or to China. These are not bureaucratic—or so bureaucratic. But that is because they are not yet industrialized. When they are, they will be. For organization—bureaucracy—is inescapable in a world of advanced industrial technology—large-volume industrial production.

There was a line of criticism to which I could concede—

[5]Robert Fitch, "A Galbraith Reappraisal: The Ideologue as Gadfly," *Ramparts*, Vol. 6, Nos. 9 and 10 (May 1968), p. 73 et seq.

fortunately, for a too resolute resistance in such matters must surely arouse suspicion. The notion of planning as put forward in the first edition was not satisfactory. Professor James E. Meade pointed out that there can be planning within the framework of the market and there can be planning which subsumes the market.[6] A firm can plan in order to serve the market more efficiently by anticipating market behavior and responding to the resulting prospect—to need for plant, raw materials, labor supply, product design—which will enable it better to meet market preferences. The firm can also plan in the sense of obtaining the prices, costs and consumer and producer response that it wants. There is a vital difference between the two kinds of planning; the first responds more effectively to the market. The second replaces the market. The difference was not clear in the first edition, a fault most readily explained by unclarity in my own mind. The proper correction is, of course, here.

4

A good many critics of the earlier editions were at pains to remind their readers that while my case may hold for the world of the very big corporations, there still remains a world of the market. Farmers, lawyers, cleaners and cobblers, bookstores, musicians and houses of casual pleasure still survive. Here the market still rules; here consumer sovereignty is still inviolate. And no sharp line divides this part of the economy from the smaller of the great corporations which are assimilated to the planning system. With increasing size and corporate power the market gives way to planning but the transition is gradual, not abrupt.

With all of this I agree. Moreover, it is a point I had sought to emphasize in the book. The two thousand or so largest corporations in the United States, the planning system, comprise about half of the economy as measured by their share of total product. In the other advanced industrial countries the giant firms have a roughly similar share. Theirs is the part of the economy where the great organizational and technological change occurs. It is the part that shapes our beliefs and values. But it is not all of the economic system.

[6]James E. Meade, "Is 'The New Industrial State' Inevitable?" *Economic Journal*, Vol. 78, No. 310 (June 1968), p. 372 et seq.

There is the other world of agriculture, service enterprises, artistic endeavor, the penumbra of legal, accounting, advertising, sales and repair enterprises that are brought into existence or sustained by the modern large corporation itself. Firms here approximate in scale and organization, and perhaps also in motivation, the textbook vision of the firm. They do much to sustain the plausibility of the textbook instruction or, in any case, to rescue it from total implausibility. And much that is interesting and important in modern economic life arises from the juxtaposition of the planning system and the surviving market system—the juxtaposition of a few large firms that are infinitely large and many small firms that are infinitely numerous. It is obvious that the relationship between small and large could not be perceived in a book which, as here, dealt only with the large. This, along with further thought on the concept of the household (in conventional economics, a highly fraudulent disguise of the problems of managing consumption in the modern consumer society), on the role of art and aesthetic values in economic development and, most of all, on the problems of public management and policy in a bimodal economy divided between the few large and the many small, led me on to the final volume in this series. This was *Economics and the Public Purpose.*[7] If, as I believe, the present volume is the most important of the three, the third and last was, by a respectable margin, the most difficult to write. That was because I could not ask the reader to return to the two earlier volumes on which it was based. So I faced a heavy task of condensation and summary—but that is another story.

But not entirely so because the writing of the final volume influenced some of the present revision. On numerous matters, large and small, it led to a clearer view, and that is reflected here. It led also to a major change in terminology. In the earlier editions of this book I referred to the part of the economy that is dominated by the great corporations as the *industrial system.* When I came to set this part of the economy in juxtaposition to the world of the small firms—the *market system*—I found it did not serve. Small industrial firms could be subordinate to the market as large industrial firms are not. The phrase *industrial system* has also a connotation applicable to the whole of the modern economy. So, in *Economics and the Public Purpose*, I substituted the more accurately

[7] (Boston: Houghton Mifflin, 1973.)

descriptive term *planning system* to describe the part of the modern bimodal economy that is dominated by the large corporations and where these, as an essential aspect of their planning, take markets under their control. I have now changed the reference in this volume to conform.

The further and more important part of this revision consists in taking account of change and information that have accumulated over the last five years. The volume of both has been great. On occasion they have required that I amend my view, an unwelcome task which I come to only after I have exhausted numerous reasons, spurious and contrived, why I need not do so. But such amendment has not required that I alter the main thrust of my argument in any major respect. More frequently, as well as more agreeably, developments and research since the original writing or the last revision have brought evidence on my side. Reference to this, not surprisingly, is also here.

Material that amends or brings the argument up to date I have generally put in the text. But sometimes the sequence and flow of argument has been better served by footnotes, and this has been especially so of the material that supplements or confirms my case. Every reader has his own habits as regards footnotes; mine is to read them with care and to be a little annoyed when they are put away at the end of a book, something on which some publishers are quite wrongly insistent. I would like to urge attention for at least such of the footnotes herein as go beyond routine citation of author and source.

5

One purpose of the revision, as earlier noted, is to take account of change in the underlying subject matter. In economics, as just implied, this is inconveniently rapid. All economists wish that their subject matter was fixed for all time like the geologist's granite, and many pretend that it is. Were it only so.

And in a revision, even a reasonably comprehensive effort, as I believe this to be, it is difficult to give later change the same aspect of authority and importance the original subject matter had. Two things, I feel, suffer from such absence of original emphasis, and I would like to say a word about each.

Since the first edition of this book, we have seen, especially in the United States, the flowering of the conglomerate enterprise. The takeovers by which these have been built have not affected the very largest corporations of the planning system—Exxon and General Motors are not gravely in danger. They have involved firms of the second order of magnitude, and they have combined some of these into corporations of the first rank. In the combination process there was always, I believe without exception, a motivating entrepreneur. The modern conglomerate is not the creation of a technostructure.

It is a development which, however, affirms both the motivation here urged and also the key role of the technostructure in the corporate operations. No one, I believe, seriously questions the motivation back of the conglomerate movement. It has been growth—empire-building. So far from enhancing profits, this has normally been at the sacrifice of profits. And it seems also fairly certain that the conglomerates improve their performance only as the original architect is supplemented or replaced by, as it is called, an effective management team. In other words, the conglomerate begins to work only as the technostructure takes over.

The other change, a much more subjective matter, concerns our perception of the arms race. Its image in the Cold War years, when I was working on the first edition, was strongly ideological, with a solid further footing in property and pecuniary anxiety and interest. The Communists did not respect personal wealth, income and comfort. And they invited the indignation of liberals on the issue of intellectual and artistic expression, thus bringing liberals into unnatural alliance with conservatives. This was the issue which sustained the arms race.

In more recent times, partly as the result of the initiatives first of Khrushchev and then of Nixon and Kissinger, none figures of deep ideological commitment, I judge the basis of the competition to have changed. More and more people, I believe, see it as a trap—one in which the Soviets do what best stimulates the American military response, we do what most stimulates the Soviet reaction. And in both countries a large military and industrial bureaucracy survives on this interaction. I need scarcely add that the ultimate survival of both systems, whatever their divergent or convergent tendencies, consist in getting this ghastly process under control.

As I observed earlier on, revision is not the most enchanting of tasks. One does discover, with some slight pleasure, how much can be improved; the corollary, alas, is reflection on how much could have been done better in the beginning.

Pleasant or unpleasant, to all work there should be an end. The reader, encountering these words, should know that they are, as it were, the last. The world will continue to change and more rapidly, without doubt, than the economics that interprets and describes it. This revision, nevertheless, I intend to be the final one.

Contents

I

Change and the Planning System

A CURIOSITY of modern economic discussion is the role of change. It is imagined to be very great; to list its forms or emphasize its extent is to show a reassuring grasp of the commonplace. Yet not much is supposed to change. The economic system of the United States is accepted by all but the malcontent as a largely perfect structure. It is not easy to perfect what has been perfected. There is massive change but, except as the output of goods increases, all remains as before.

As to the change there is no doubt. The innovations and alterations in economic life in this century, and more especially since the beginning of World War II, have, by any calculation, been great. The most visible has been the application of increasingly intricate and sophisticated technology to the production of things. Machines have continued to replace crude manpower. And increasingly, as they are used to instruct other machines, they replace the cruder forms of human intelligence.

Eighty years ago the corporation was still confined to those industries—railroading, steam navigation, steel-making, petroleum recovery and refining, some mining—where, it seemed, production had to be on a large scale. Now it also sells groceries, mills grain, publishes newspapers and provides public entertainment, all activities that were once the province of the individual proprietor or the insignificant firm. The largest firms deploy billions of dollars' worth of equipment and hundreds of thousands of men in scores of locations to produce hundreds of products. At the end of 1974, the largest 200 manufacturing enterprises in the United States—one tenth of one percent of all manufacturing firms—had two thirds of all assets used in manufacturing and more than three fifths of all sales, employment and net income. Not only is the concentration great but so is the rate at which it proceeds. At the end of 1974, the largest 200 had a greater share of all manufacturing sales, employment and assets than the largest 500 had in 1955![1]

Eighty years ago the corporation was the instrument of its owners and a projection of their personalities. The names of these principals—Carnegie, Rockefeller, Harriman, Mellon, Guggenheim, Ford—were known across the land. They are still known, but for the art galleries and philanthropic foundations they established and their descendants who are in politics. The men who now head the great corporations are unknown. Not for a generation have people outside Detroit and the automobile industry known the name of the current head of General Motors. In the manner of all men, he must, on occasion, produce identification when paying by check. So with Ford, Exxon and General Dynamics. The men who now run the large corporations own no appreciable share of the enterprise. They are selected not by the stockholders but, in the common case, by a board of directors which, narcissistically, they selected themselves.

Equally it is a commonplace that the relation of the state to the economy has changed. The services of federal, state and local governments now account for between one fifth and one quarter (in 1976, 22 percent)[2] of all economic activity. In 1929, it was about eight percent.[2] This far exceeds the government share in such an avowedly socialist state as India, considerably exceeds that in the anciently social democratic kingdoms of Sweden and Norway and is not wholly incommensurate with the share in Polland, a Communist country which, however, is heavily agricultural and which has left its agriculture in private ownership. A very large part of all public activity (about one third of all government spending on goods and services) is for national defense and (a much smaller item) the exploration of space. These outlays are not regarded even by conservatives as socialism. Elsewhere the nomenclature is less certain.

Additionally, in the wake of what is now called the Keynesian Revolution, the state undertakes to regulate the total income available for the purchase of goods and services in the economy. It seeks to ensure sufficient purchasing power to buy whatever the current labor force can produce. And, more cautiously, sometimes only by incantation or prayer, it seeks

---

[1]William N. Leonard, "Mergers, Industrial Concentration, and Antitrust Policy," *Journal of Economic Issues*, Vol. X, No. 2 (June 1976), p. 356.

[2]*Economic Report of the President, 1977*, p. 187.

to keep wages from shoving up prices and prices from forcing up wages in a persistent upward spiral. By earlier standards the production of goods in modern times has been relatively, though far from completely, reliable.

Previously, from the earliest appearance of capitalism until the beginning of Hitler's war, expansion and recession had followed each other at irregular intervals but in steady procession. The business cycle had become a separate subject of economic study; the forecasting of its course and the explanation of its irregularities had become a modest profession in which reason, divination and elements of witchcraft had been combined in a manner not elsewhere seen save in the primitive religions. In the two decades following World War II, there was no serious depression. In the mid-seventies there was a sharp recession, very severe in such industries as housing. By wide agreement, however, it was the result of a deliberate act of policy to arrest inflation, those holding most vehemently that inflation was still a natural phenomenon being those reponsible for the policy.

Three further changes are less intimately a part of the established litany of accomplishment. First, there has been a further massive growth in the apparatus of persuasion and exhortation that is associated with the sale of goods. In its cost and in the talent it commands, this activity is coming increasingly to rival the effort devoted to the production of goods. Measurement of the exposure, and susceptibility, of human beings to this persuasion is itself a flourishing science.

Second, union membership as a proportion of the labor force is no longer increasing. It reached a peak (of 25.2 percent) in 1956 and has since declined.[3]

Finally, there has been a large expansion in enrollment for higher education, together with a somewhat more modest increase in the means for providing it. This has been attributed to a new and penetrating concern for popular enlightenment. As with the fall in the proportion of workers enrolled by unions, it has deeper roots. Had the economic system need only for millions of unlettered proletarians, these, very plausibly, are what would be provided.

[3]*Handbook of Labor Statistics, 1969* (United States Department of Labor, Bureau of Labor Statistics), Bulletin No. 1630, p. 351; *Handbook of Labor Statistics, 1976* (United States Department of Labor, Bureau of Labor Statistics), Bulletin No. 1905, p. 297.

2

These changes, or most of them, have been much discussed. But to view them in isolation from each other, the usual practice, is greatly to minimize their effect. They are related to each other as cause to consequence. All are part of a yet larger matrix of change. In its effect on economic society this matrix has been more than the sum of its parts.

Thus mention has been made of machines and sophisticated technology. These require, in turn, a heavy investment of capital. They are designed and guided by technically sophisticated men. They involve, also, a greatly increased elapse of time between any decision to produce and the emergence of a salable product.

From these changes come both the need and the opportunity from the large business organization. It alone can deploy the requisite capital; it alone can mobilize the requisite skills. It can also do more. The large commitment of capital and organization well in advance of result requires that there be foresight and also that all feasible steps be taken to ensure that what is foreseen will transpire. It can hardly be doubted that General Motors will be better able to influence the world around it—the prices and wages at which it buys and the prices at which it sells—than a man in suits and cloaks.

Nor is this all. The high production and income which are the fruits of advanced technology, complex and effective organization and the ability of large groups in the society to make effective their claim on income have removed a great part of the population from the compulsions and pressures of physical want. In consequence, their economic behavior has become in some measure malleable. No hungry man who is also sober can be persuaded to use his last dollar for anything but food. But a well-fed, well-clad, well-sheltered and otherwise well-tended person can be persuaded as between an electric razor and an electric toothbrush. Along with prices and costs, consumer demand has become subject to management. This adds an important further element of control over behavior.

When investment in technological development is very high, a wrong technical judgment or a failure in persuading consumers to buy the product can be extremely expensive. The cost and associated risk can be greatly reduced if the state pays for more exalted technical development or guarantees a market for the technically advanced product. Suitable

justification—national defense, national prestige, deeply felt
public need, as for alternatives to petroleum products—can
readily be found. Exemption from the damaging charge that
the action is socialist is automatically forthcoming. Modern
technology thus defines a growing function of the modern
state.

Technology and associated requirements in capital and
time also lead even more directly to the regulation of demand
by the state. A corporation, contemplating an automobile of
revised aspect, must be able to persuade people to buy it. It is
equally important that people be able to do so. This is vital
where heavy advance commitments of time and money must
be made and where the product could as easily come to
market in a time of depression as of prosperity. So there must
be stabilization of overall demand.

Affluence adds to the need for such stabilization of aggregate demand. A man who lives close to the margin of subsistence must spend to exist and what he spends is spent. A man
with ample income can save, and there is no assurance that
what he saves will be offset by the spending or investment of
others. Moreover, a rich society owes its productivity and income, at least in part, to large-scale organization—to the corporation. Corporations also have the option of retaining or
saving from earnings—and can exercise it with the unique
sense of righteousness of men who are imposing thrift on others. There is no guarantee that this personal and corporate
saving will be offset by spending. In consequence, in a community of much well-being, spending and hence demand are
less reliable than in a poor one. They lose their reliability precisely when high costs and the long period of gestation imposed by modern technology require greater certainty of
markets. The Keynesian Revolution occurred at the moment
in history when other change had made it indispensable. Like
the other changes with which this chapter began, it is intimately a cause and consequence of yet other change.

3

In economics, unlike fiction and the theater, there is no harm
in a premature disclosure of the plot: the central purpose of
this book is to see the changes just mentioned and others as
an interlocked whole. I venture to think that modern
economic life is seen much more clearly when, as here, there
is such effort to see it whole.

I am also concerned to show how, in this larger context of change, the forces inducing human effort have changed. This assaults the most majestic of all economic assumptions, namely that man, in his economic activities, is subject to the authority of the market. Instead we have an economic system which, whatever its formal ideological billing, is, in substantial part, a planned economy. The initiative in deciding what is to be produced comes not from the sovereign consumer who, through the market, issues the instructions that bend the productive mechanism to his ultimate will. Rather it comes from the great producing organization which reaches forward to control the markets that it is presumed to serve and, beyond, to bend the customer to its needs. And, in so doing, it deeply influences his values and beliefs—including not a few that will be mobilized in resistance to the present argument. One of the conclusions that follows from this analysis is that there is a broad convergence between industrial systems. The imperatives of technology and organization, not the images of ideology, are what determine the shape of economic society. This, on the whole, is fortunate, although it will not necessarily be welcomed by those whose intellectual capital and moral fervor are invested in the present image of the market economy as the antithesis of social planning. Nor will it be welcomed by their disciples, who, with even smaller intellectual investment, carry the banners of free markets and free enterprise and therewith, by definition, of the free nations into political, diplomatic or military battle. Nor will it be welcomed by those who identify planning exclusively with socialism. The ideas here offered have, in one form or another, been gaining ground. There has been visible movement since they were first offered in the present form in 1967. But they are not yet the ideas of the consensus.

The continuing subordination of belief to industrial necessity and convenience is not in accordance with the greatest vision of man. Nor is it entirely safe. On the nature of this subjugation, and its dangers, I shall also dwell at some length.

4

The boundaries of a subject matter are conventional and artificial; none should use them as an excuse for excluding the important. Nothing so persists in modern social thought as the notion that decisions on public policy should somehow divide along the lines of university departments and curricula.

They do not. In government there are no exclusively economic, political, not even any purely medical judgments. Nor can one be indifferent to the practical consequences of an effort such as this, whatever the tendency to celebrate such indifference as a manifestation of scientific detachment.

Accordingly, in the later chapters I turn to the effect of economic change on social and political behavior, and to remedy and reform. As noted, I am led to the conclusion, which I trust others will find persuasive, that we are becoming the servants in thought, as in action, of the machine we have created to serve us. This is, in many ways, a comfortable servitude; some will look with wonder, and perhaps even indignation, on anyone who proposes escape. Some people are never content. I am concerned to suggest the general lines of emancipation. Otherwise we will allow economic goals to have an undue monopoly of our lives and at the expense of other and more valuable interests. What counts is not the quantity of our goods but the quality of life.

Our present method of underwriting advanced technology by resort to military justification is exceedingly dangerous. It could cost us our existence. Here I suggest alternatives. There is also danger that our educational system will be too strongly in the service of economic goals. Here I suggest safeguards. The analysis leads to conclusions on the relation of the individual to his toil and the community to its planning. These also are discussed. And I deal with the unrealized political opportunities that are inherent in the dependence of the modern economy on trained and educated manpower. This all comes in the later chapters. The man who wants a political platform must obviously work his way up the stairs.

5

Recurrently American business leaders are captured by the thought that if the system is to survive, there must be much better education as to its character. In the mid-sixties and again in the mid-seventies, even suspicion of government was suppressed, and the United States Department of Commerce was brought into the service of the educational effort. The reason is that the public image of economic institutions, based on everyday observation of modern corporate enterprise, does not conform to the executive's accustomed defense of himself. Not surprisingly, he reacts well to the thought that it is the public image, not his own, that should be changed.

The business defense invariably emphasizes the vigorous competition of numerous firms, all subordinate to the market. The resulting education as invariably centers on the small enterprise—in a particularly compelling example from the Department of Commerce, it was on the operation of a lemonade stand conducted by two children under the trees.[4] This economic education holds, in other words, that capitalism can best be understood by examining enterprises with little or no capital, guided by one or two people, without the complications of corporate structure and where there is no union. Part of its appeal is in the way it removes from the corporate executive all power, including the power to do anything wrong. It also has firm historical roots: economic life began with small firms, with small capital, each one under the guiding hand of a single master. Finally, a systematic and internally consistent theory, that of the competitive firm in the market economy, is available for the explanation. This lends itself well to pedagogy.

But this view of the modern economic system is not sanctioned by reality. Nor is it now really sanctioned—a nostalgic, romantic and acquiescent minority apart—by economists. The changes mentioned earlier in this chapter have not spread themselves evenly over the economy. Agriculture, truck mines, painting, musical composition, much writing, the professions, some vice, handicrafts, some retail trade and a large number of repairing, cleaning, refurbishing, cosmetic and other household and personal services are still in the province of the individual proprietor. Capital, advanced technology, complex organization and the other hallmarks of what we have come, not accidentally, to consider modern enterprise are limited or absent.

But this, most now recognize, is not the part of the economy wherein occur the changes just mentioned. Equally it is not the part of the economy which combines advanced technology with massive use of capital and of which the most conspicuous manifestation is the modern large corporation. Nearly all communications, nearly all production and distribution of electric power, banking and insurance, rail and air transportation, most manufacturing and mining, a substantial share of retail trade and a considerable amount of entainment are conducted or provided by large firms. The

[4] *Do You Know Your Economic ABC's? Profits and the American Economy*, United States Department of Commerce, 1965.

numbers are not great; we may think without error of most work being done by a few hundred, at the most a thousand or two, large firms.

This is the part of the economy which, automatically, we identify with the modern industrial society. To understand it is to understand that part which is most subject to change and which, accordingly, is most changing our lives. No exercise of intelligence is to be deplored but to understand the rest of the economy is to understand only that part which is diminishing in relative extent (though it will not disappear) and which is least subject to change.

The two parts of the economy—the world of the technically dynamic, massively capitalized and highly organized corporations on the one hand and of the hundreds of thousands of small and traditional proprietors on the other—are very different. It is not a difference of degree but a difference which invades every aspect of economic organization and behavior, including the motivation to effort itself. It will be convenient, even in advance of more formulation, to have a name for the part of the economy which is characterized by the large corporations. One is readily at hand; I shall refer to it as the *Planning System*. The planning system, in turn, is the dominant feature of the New Industrial State.

II

The Imperatives of Technology

ON JUNE 16, 1903, after some months of preparation which included negotiation of contracts for various components, the Ford Motor Company was formed for the manufacture of automobiles. Production was to be whatever number could be sold. The first car reached the market that October. The firm had an authorized capital of $150,000. However, only $100,-000 worth of stock was issued, and only $28,000 of this was for cash. Although it does not bear on the present discussion, the company made a handsome profit that year and did not fail to do so for many years thereafter. Employment in 1903 averaged 125 men.[1]

Sixty-one years later, in the spring of 1964, the Ford Motor Company introduced what is now called a new automobile. In accordance with current fashion in automobile nomenclature, it was called, one assumes inappropriately, a Mustang. The public was well prepared for the new vehicle. Plans carefully specified prospective output and sales; they erred, as plans do, and in this case by being too modest. These preparations required three and a half years. From late in the autumn of 1962, when the design was settled, until the spring of 1964, there was a fairly firm commitment to the particular car that eventually emerged. Engineering and "styling" costs were $9 million; the cost of tooling up for the production of the Mustang was $50 million.[2] In 1964,

[1]Allan Nevins, *Ford: The Times, The Man, The Company* (New York: Scribner, 1954), p. 220 et seq.

[2]I am grateful to Mr. Walter T. Murphy of the Ford Motor Company for providing these details and the later ones on the Zephyr and Fairmont. In this and subsequent chapters I have also drawn on the earlier help of Robert McNamara, which he gave when he was still an executive of Ford. I wish now, at the outset, not only to concede but to emphasize that one may have planning without precision of result and that there will also be occasional failures. In earlier editions I went on here to note that "the more impulsive critic" would cite another Ford creation, the Edsel, to prove that planning of the sort here

10

employment in the Ford Motor Company averaged 317,000. Assets at that time were approximately $6 billion.[3] In the autumn of 1977, Ford brought out two new models—the Zephyr and the Fairmont. For these the cost was roughly $600 million, although part of the increase reflected the diminution of the dollar. By then Ford's assets were approximately $16 billion, and employment worldwide was around 445,000.

Virtually all of the effects of the increased use of technology are revealed by these comparisons. We may pass them in preliminary review.

2

Technology means the systematic application of scientific or other organized knowledge to practical tasks. Its most important consequence, at least for the purposes of economics, is in forcing the division and subdivision of any such task into its component parts. Thus, and only thus, can organized knowledge be brought to bear on performance.

Specifically, there is no way that organized knowledge can be brought to bear on the production of an automobile as a whole or even on the manufacture of a body or chassis. It can only be applied if the task is so subdivided that it begins to be coterminous with some established area of scientific or engineering knowledge. Though metallurgical knowledge cannot be applied to the manufacture of the whole vehicle, it can be used in the design of the cooling system or the engine block. While knowledge of mechanical engineering cannot be brought to bear on the manufacture of the entire vehicle, it can be applied to the machining of the crankshaft. While chemistry cannot be applied to the composition of the car as a whole, it can be used to decide on the composition of the finish or trim.

Nor do matters stop here. Metallurgical knowledge is brought to bear not on steel but on the characteristics of special steels for particular functions, and chemistry not on

---

described does not work. He would not notice that the Edsel gained its distinction from being an exception to the common expectation of success. I was not disappointed. Such references to the Edsel were, in fact, compulsive.

[3]*Fortune,* July 1964.

paints or plastics but on particular molecular structures and their rearrangement as required.[4]

Nearly all of the consequences of technology and much of the shape of modern industry derive from this need to divide and subdivide tasks, from the further need to bring knowledge to bear on these fractions and from the final need to combine the finished elements of the task into the finished product as a whole. Six consequences are of immediate importance.

First. An increasing span of time separates the beginning from the completion of any task. Knowledge is brought to bear on the ultimate microfraction of the task; then on that in combination with some other fraction; then on some further combination and thus on to final completion. The process stretches back in time as the root system of a plant goes down into the ground. The longest of the filaments determines the total time required in production. The more thoroughgoing the application of technology—in common or at least frequent language, the more sophisticated the production process—the farther back the application of knowledge will be carried. The longer, accordingly, will be the time between the initiation and completion of the task.

The manufacture of the first Ford was not an exacting process. Metallurgy was an academic concept. Ordinary steels were used that could be obtained from the warehouse in the morning and shaped that afternoon. Nothing associated with this basic material required that the span of time between initiation and completion of a car be more than a few hours.

The provision of steel for the modern vehicle, in contrast, reaches back to specifications prepared by the designers or the laboratory and proceeds through orders to the steel mill,

---

[4]The notion of division of labor, an old one in economics, is a rudimentary and partial application of the ideas here outlined. As one breaks down a mechanical operation, such as the manufacture of Adam Smith's immortal pins, it resolves itself into simpler and simpler movements, as in putting the head or the point on the pin. This is the same as saying that the problem is susceptible to increasingly homogeneous mechanical knowledge and its use to improve performance.

However, the subdivision of tasks to accord with the area of organized knowledge is not confined to, nor has it any special relevance to, mechanical processes. It occurs in medicine, business management, building design, child and dog rearing and every other problem that involves an agglomerate of scientific knowledge.

parallel provision for the appropriate metal-working machinery, delivery, testing and use.

Second. There is an increase in the capital that is committed to production aside from that occasioned by increased output. The increased time, and therewith the increased investment in goods in process, cost money. So does the knowledge which is applied to the various elements of the task. The application of knowledge to an element of a manufacturing problem will also typically involve the development of a machine for performing the function. (The word technology brings to mind machines; this is not surprising, for machinery is one of its most visible manifestations.) This too involves capital investment, as does equipment for integrating the various elements of the task into the final product.

The investment in making the original Ford was larger than the $28,000 paid in, for some of it was in the plant, inventory and machinery of those who, like the Dodge Brothers, supplied the components. But investment in the factory itself was minute. Materials and parts were there only briefly; no expensive specialists gave them attention; only elementary machinery was used to assemble them. It helped that the frame of the car could be lifted by two men.

Third. With increasing technology the commitment of time and money tends to be made ever more inflexibly to the performance of a particular task. That task must be precisely defined before it is divided and subdivided into its component parts. Knowledge and equipment are then brought to bear on these fractions, and they are useful only for the task as it was initially defined. If that task is changed, new knowledge and new equipment will have to be brought to bear.

Little thought needed to be given to the Dodge Brothers' machine shop, which made the engine and chassis of the original Ford, as an instrument for automobile manufacture. It was unspecialized as to task. It could have worked as well on bicycles, steam engines or carriage gear and, indeed, had been so employed. Had Ford and his associates decided, at any point, to shift from gasoline to steam power, the machine shop could have accommodated itself to the change in a few hours.

By contrast, all parts of the Mustang, the tools and equipment that worked on these parts and the steel and other materials going into these parts were designed to serve efficiently their ultimate function. They could serve only that function. Were the car appreciably altered, were it shaped, instead of as a Mustang (or a Zephyr), as a Barracuda or a Serpent, Scorpion or Roach, as one day one will be, much of this work would have to be redone. Thus the firm commitment to this particular vehicle for some eighteen months prior to its appearance.

Fourth. Technology requires specialized manpower. This will be evident. Organized knowledge can be brought to bear, not surprisingly, only by those who possess it. However, technology does not make the only claim on manpower; planning, to be mentioned in a moment, also requires a comparatively high level of specialized talent. To foresee the future in all its dimensions and to design the appropriate action does not necessarily require high scientific qualification. It does require ability to organize and employ information or capacity to react intuitively to relevant experience.

These requirements do not reflect, on some absolute scale, a higher order of talent than was required in a less technically advanced era. The makers of the original Ford were men of talent. The Dodge Brothers had previously invented a bicycle and a steam launch. Their machine shop made a wide variety of products, and Detroit legend also celebrated their exuberance when drunk. Alexander Malcolmson, who was Ford's immediate partner in getting the business under way, was a successful coal merchant. James Couzens, who may well have had more to do with the success of the enterprise than Henry Ford,[5] had a background in railroading and the coal business and went on from Ford to be police commissioner and mayor of Detroit, a notable Republican senator from Michigan and an undeviating supporter of Franklin D. Roosevelt. Not all members of the present Ford organization would claim as much reach. But they do have a considerably deeper knowledge of the more specialized matters for which they are severally responsible.

Fifth. The inevitable counterpart of specialization is organization. This is what brings the work of specialists to a coherent result. If there are many specialists, this coordination will be a major task. So complex, indeed, will be the job of organizing specialists that there will be specialists on organization and organizations of specialists on organization. More perhaps than machinery, massive and complex business or-

[5] A case I have argued elsewhere. Cf. "Was Ford a Fraud?" in *The Liberal Hour* (Boston: Houghton Mifflin, 1960), p. 141 et seq.

ganizations are the tangible manifestation of advanced technology.

Sixth. From the time and capital that must be committed, the inflexibility of this commitment, the needs of large organization and the problems of market performance under conditions of advanced technology comes the necessity for planning. Tasks must be performed so that they are right not for the present but for that time in the future when, companion and related work having also been done, the whole job is completed. And the amount of capital that, meanwhile, will have been committed adds urgency to this need to be right. So conditions at the time of completion of the whole task must be foreseen, as must developments along the way. And steps must be taken to prevent, offset or otherwise neutralize the effect of adverse developments and to ensure that what is ultimately foreseen eventuates in fact.

In the early days of Ford the future was very near at hand. Only days elapsed between the commitment of machinery and materials to production and the appearance of the car. If the future is near, it can be assumed that it will be very much like the present. If the car did not meet the approval of the customers, it could quickly be changed. The briefness of the time in process allowed this; so did the unspecialized character of manpower, materials and machinery.

Changes were, indeed, needed. The earliest cars, as they came on the market, did not meet with complete customer approval: there were complaints that the cooling system did not cool, the brakes did not brake, the carburetor did not feed fuel to the engine, and a Los Angeles dealer reported the exceptionally disconcerting discovery that, when steered, "Front wheels turn wrong."[6] These defects were promptly remedied. They did the reputation of the car no lasting harm.

Such shortcomings in the Mustang or now the Zephyr would invite reproach. And they would be subject to no such quick, simple and inexpensive remedy; foresight is necessary to ensure, as far as possible, against such misfortune. The machinery, materials, manpower and components of the original Ford, being all unspecialized, could be quickly procured on the open market. Accordingly, there was no need to anticipate possible shortages of these requirements and take steps to prevent them. For the more highly specialized requirements of the Mustang, foresight and associated action

[6] Nevins, p. 248.

were indispensable. In Detroit, when the first Ford was projected, anything on wheels that was connected with a motor
was assured of acceptance. Acceptance of the Mustang could
not be so assumed. The prospect had to be carefully studied.
And customers had to be carefully conditioned to want this
blessing. Thus the need for planning.

3

The more sophisticated the technology, the greater, in general, will be all of the foregoing requirements. This will be
true of simple products as they come to be produced by more
refined processes or as manufacturers develop imaginative
containers or unopenable packaging. With very intricate technology, such as that associated with modern weapons and
weapons systems, there will be a quantum change in these requirements. This will be especially so if, as under modern
peacetime conditions, cost and time are not decisive considerations.

Thus when Philip II settled on the redemption of England
at the end of March 1587, he was not unduly troubled by the
seemingly serious circumstance that Spain had no navy. Some
men-of-war were available from newly conquered Portugal
but, in the main, merchant ships would suffice.[7] A navy, in
other words, could then be bought in the market. Nor was
the destruction of a large number of the available ships by
Drake at Cadiz three weeks later a fatal blow. Despite what
historians have usually described as unconscionable inefficiency, the Armada sailed in a strength of 130 ships a little
over a year later on May 18, 1588. The cost, though considerable, was well within the resources of the Empire. Matters did not change greatly in the next three hundred years.
The *Victory*, from which Nelson called Englishmen to their
duty at Trafalgar, though an excellent fighting ship, involved
no esoteric and time-consuming problems in design. It was a
standard product, a full forty years old at the time. The exiguous flying machines of World War I, built only to carry a
man or two and a weapon, were designed and put in combat
in a matter of months.

To create a modern fleet of the numerical size of the Ar-

---

[7] Instructions issued from the Escorial on March 31. Cf. Garrett Mat-
tingly, *The Armada* (Boston: Houghton Mifflin, 1959), p. 80. Philip
had, of course, been contemplating the enterprise for some years.

mada, with nuclear-powered aircraft carriers and an appropriate complement of aircraft and missiles, together with nuclear submarines, destroyers, supporting craft and bases and communications, would take a first-rate industrial power a minimum of twenty years. Though modern Spain is rich beyond the dreams of its monarchs in its most expansive age, it could not for a moment contemplate such an enterprise. In World War II, no combat plane that had not been substantially designed before the outbreak of hostilities saw major service. Since then the lead time for comparable matériel has become yet greater. In general, individuals in late middle age stand in little danger of weapons now being designed; they are a menace only to the unborn and the uncontemplated.

4

It is a commonplace of modern technology that there is a high measure of certainty that problems have solutions before there is knowledge of how they are to be solved. It was known in the early sixties with reasonable certainty that men could land on the moon by the end of the decade. Many, perhaps most of the details for accomplishing this journey still remained to be worked out.

If methods of performing the specified task are uncertain, the need for bringing organized intelligence to bear will be much greater than if the methods are known. This uncertainty will also lead to increased time and cost, and the increase can be very great. This problem-solving, with its high costs in time and money, is a recognized feature of modern technology. It graces all present-day economic discussion under the cachet of "Research and Development."

The need for planning, it has been said, arises from the long period of time that elapses during the production process, the large investment that is involved and the inflexible commitment of that investment to the particular task. In the case of advanced military equipment, time, cost and inflexibility of commitment are all very great. Time and outlay will be even greater where—a common characteristic of weaponry—design is uncertain and where, accordingly, there must be added expenditure for research and development. In these circumstances planning is both essential and difficult. It is essential because of the time that is involved, the money that is at risk, the number of things that can go wrong and the magnitude of the possible ensuing disaster. It is difficult because of the number and size of the eventualities that must be controlled.

One answer is to have the state absorb the major risks. It can provide or guarantee a market for the product. And it can underwrite the costs of development so that if they increase beyond expectation, the firm will not have to carry them. Or it can pay for and make available the necessary technical knowledge. The drift of this argument will be evident. Technology, under all circumstances, leads to planning; in its higher manifestations it may put the problems and associated cost of planning beyond the resources of the industrial firm. Technological compulsions, and not ideology or political wile, will require the firm to seek the help and protection of the state. This is a consequence of advanced technology of no small interest to which we shall return.

In examining the intricate complex of economic change, technology, having an initiative of its own, is the logical point at which to break in. But technology not only causes change, it is a response to change. Though it forces specialization, it is also the result of specialization. Though it requires extensive organization, it is also the result of organization. The changes stimulated by technology, slightly reordered for purposes of exposition, are nonetheless the themes of the ensuing chapters. First we shall look more closely at the effect of requirements of time and capital on industrial planning. Thereafter we shall look at the source and role of the capital which it employs in such large amounts. And then we shall examine the role of specialized manpower and its organization. Nor will this be the end. These themes, planning, specialization and organization, like the military symbolism of marching and combat in Protestant hymns and intercollegiate athletics, will recur throughout the book.

III

The Nature of Industrial Planning

UNTIL THE END of World War II or shortly thereafter, planning was a moderately evocative word in the United States. It implied a sensible concern for what might happen in the future and a disposition, by forehanded action, to forestall avoidable disfunction or misfortune. As persons won credit for competent planning of their lives, so communities won credit for effective planning of their environment. It was thought good to live in a well-planned city. The United States government before the war had a National Resources Planning Board. During the war, postwar planning acquired the status of a modest industry in both the United States and the United Kingdom; nothing else, it was felt, would so reassure those who were fighting that they had eventual utility as civilians.

In the Cold War years, however, the work planning acquired grave ideological overtones. The Communist countries not only socialized property, which seemed not a strong likelihood in the United States, but they planned, which seemed more of a danger. Since liberty was there circumscribed, it followed that planning was something that the libertarian society should avoid. Modern liberalism carefully emphasizes tact rather than clarity of speech. Accordingly, it avoided the term, and conservatives made it one of opprobrium. For a public official to be called an economic planner was less serious than to be charged with Communism or imaginative sexual proclivity but it reflected adversely nonetheless. One accepted and cherished whatever eventuated from the untrammeled operation of the market. Not only concern for liberty but a reputation for economic hardihood counseled such a course.

For understanding the economy and polity of the United States and other advanced industrial countries, this reaction against the word planning could hardly have been worse timed. It occurred when the increased use of technology and

19

the accompanying commitment of time and capital were forcing extensive planning on all industrial communities—by firms and of firms' behavior by government. The ban on the use of the word planning excluded reflection on the reality of planning.

This ban is now in the process of being lifted—much has been accomplished in this regard in the eleven years since the first edition of this book appeared. The need for national planning has become a reputable topic for discussion, as also legislation to facilitate it. On a matter such as energy the need is accepted but in circles of the highest repute the term czar is still preferred to that of planner, though not, one judges, because it is deemed more democratic.

However, it is still the instinct of conservatives and those for whom high banking or corporate position serves as a substitute for thought that anything called planning should be resisted. And perhaps there are useful elements of self-interest in the effort. Any discussion of planning by the government will draw attention, inevitably, to the planning by corporations that makes it necessary. Those who now, in the manner of all planners, guide or control the behavior of individuals will no longer be able, on grounds of high principle, to resist public guidance, control or coordination of *their* planning.

2

In the market economy the price that is offered is counted upon to produce the result that is sought. Nothing more need be done. The consumer, by his offer to pay, obtains the necessary responding action from the firm that supplies his needs. By offering to pay yet more, he gets more. And the firm, in its turn, by similar offers gets the labor, materials and equipment that it requires for production.

Planning exists because this process has ceased to be reliable. Technology, with its companion commitment of time and capital, means that the needs of the consumer must be anticipated—by months or years. When the distant day arrives, the consumer's willingness to buy may well be lacking. By the same token, while common labor and carbon steel will be forthcoming in response to a promise to pay, the specialized skills and arcane materials required by advanced technology cannot similarly be counted upon. The needed action in both instances is evident: in addition to deciding what the consumer will want and will pay, the firm must take every feasible step to see that what it decides to produce is wanted by the consumer at a remunerative price. And it must see that the labor, materials and equipment that it needs will be available at a cost consistent with the price it will receive. It must exercise control over what is sold. It must exercise control over what is supplied. It must replace the market with planning.

That, as more time elapses and more capital is committed, it will be increasingly risky to rely on the untutored responses of the consumer needs no elaboration. And this will be increasingly so the more technically sophisticated the product. There is a certain likelihood that even two or three years hence there will be a fairly reliable consumer demand for strawberries, milk and fresh eggs. There is no similar assurance that people will want, so spontaneously, an automobile of particular color or contour or a transistor of particular size or design.

The effect of technology and related change in reducing the reliability of the market for labor or equipment and in making imperative the planning of their procurement is equally clear and can be seen in the simplest case.[1] If men use picks and shovels to build a road, they can be called out on the same morning that the decision is taken to do the job. The picks and shovels serve a variety of purposes; accordingly, the market stocks them in readily available quantities. It will help in getting manpower if, as Marx thought necessary, there is an industrial reserve army of the unemployed. But an equally prompt beginning is possible by raiding the work force of another employer of unskilled labor with the simple market promise of more pay.

When specifications are raised to modern superhighway standards and heavy machinery is introduced, the market no longer works as well. Engineers, draftsmen, drainage experts and those who arrange the elimination of trees, grass, parkland, streams and the other environmental amenities may not be readily available even in response to a substantial advance in pay. Bulldozers and heavy earth-moving equipment cannot be bought with the same facility as picks and shovels. In all

---

[1] In technical terms the short-run supply price of highly specialized materials, components and labor is inelastic. So is the demand for highly technical products. In the first instance large (and punishing) increases in prices will, in the relevant time period, bring no added supply. In the second case large (and equally punishing) decreases will bring no added customers.

of these cases anticipatory steps must be taken to ensure that
the necessary supply is available at an appropriate wage or
price. Market behavior must be modified by some measure of
planning.[2]

For inertial systems engineers, digital circuit design specialists, superconductivity research specialists, aeroelasticity in-
vestigators and radio test and evaluation engineers, as also for
titanium alloys in comparison with steel and space vehicles as
compared with motorcycles, the market is greatly less dependable. Need must be elaborately anticipated and arranged.
The language of both industry and government reflects the
modern fact. Civil War quartermasters went into the local
markets for their needs. So, in turn, did the contractors who
filled these orders. The equivalent procurement would now
have to be programmed months or years ahead.

As viewed by the industrial firm, planning consists in foreseeing the actions required between the initiation of production and its completion and preparing for the accomplishment
of these actions. And it consists also of foreseeing, and having a design for meeting, any unscheduled developments, favorable or otherwise, that may occur along the way.[3] As
planning is viewed by the economist, political scientist or professional sage, it consists of replacing prices and the market
as the mechanism for determining what will be produced with
an authoritative determination by the state of what will be
produced and consumed and at what price. It will be thought
that the word planning is being used in two different senses.
Planning by the firm—its long-range accommodation to the
market influences to which it is subject—is surely different
from exterior planning which stipulates what its prices and
production will be.

[2]That planning is necessary does not mean that it is well done. At
any given time on any particular construction site, as everyone has observed, nothing much is happening. Planning, to anticipate and arrange
material, machinery, manpower and subcontractor requirements, is
necessary. But, in context, it is done with great imprecision or incompetence. Accordingly, something is normally being awaited.

[3]"In practice [business management or planning] . . . aims to minimize uncertainty, minimize the consequences of uncertainty, or both."
Robin Marris, *The Economic Theory of "Managerial" Capitalism*
(New York: Free Press of Glencoe, 1964), p. 232. Similarly, uncertainty that cannot be minimized must be subject to the appropriate
contingent action, which again is to say planning. "Future uncertainty
and change make planning a necessity." Harold Koontz and Cyril
O'Donnell, *Essentials of Management* (New York: McGraw-Hill,
1974), p. 61.

In practice the two kinds of planning, if such they may be called, are inextricably associated. A firm cannot satisfactorily foresee and schedule future action or prepare for contingencies if it does not know what its prices will be, what its sales will be, what its costs, including labor and capital costs, will be and what will be available at these costs. If the market is uncontrolled, it will not know these things. If, with advancing technology and associated specialization, the market becomes increasingly unreliable, as we have seen it does, industrial planning will become increasingly difficult unless the market is also controlled, made part of the planning. Much of what the firm regards as planning consists in minimizing uncontrolled market influences.

3

A variety of strategies are available for dealing with the increasing unreliability of markets. If the item is unimportant, market uncertainty can be ignored. For General Electric it is a matter of considerable interest to know the price at which it will be able to buy high-alloy steel or sell large generators and the quantities that will be forthcoming or that can be sold. No similar urgency attaches to knowledge of the price at which flatware will be available for the plant cafeterias. Something, and perhaps much, can also be learned about the prospective market behavior of consumers by market research and market testing. (Research into what the consumer wants or will want merges into research in how the consumer can best be persuaded.) And, finally, large-scale operations allow some market uncertainty to be absorbed. In 1977, one of the three big Swiss banks, Crédit Suisse, in consequence of what must have been a uniquely massive gap in its management controls, failed to monitor some exceptionally imaginative operations of its Chiasso branch on the Italian border. Losses of several hundred million dollars resulted. So great was the scale of banking operations that these could be absorbed, though not without some promise of improved managerial performance. In the same period, through similar but less inspired incompetence, the large New York banks, Chase Manhattan in particular, had huge losses on speculative real estate and ill-considered foreign loans. These also were absorbed by size, although again not without some need to promise more enlightened future performance. Earlier, in the late nineteen-fifties and early nineteen-sixties, the Convair Division of General Dynamics Corporation lost $425 million on the manufacture of jet transports. Part of this was the result of uncertainties associated with research and development; its 880 and 990 passenger jets cost more to bring into being than expected. But a major factor was the failure of the market— or, more precisely, default on or failure to obtain the contracts that were meant to reduce market uncertainty. The company did not fail (although it was a near thing) because it had annual revenues of around $2 billion from—in addition to aircraft—such diverse artifacts as missiles, building materials, submarines and telephones.[4] None of these was affected by the misfortunes of Convair. For a smaller company, with one product, a $425 million loss would have been uncomfortable. We have here a partial explanation of the origins of one of the more notable corporate developments of recent times, the growth of the conglomerate corporation.[5] It combines great size with highly diverse lines of manufacture. Thus it can absorb the adverse consequences of uncertainty that cannot otherwise be eliminated. Uncontrolled aversion of customers to one product, such as aircraft, is unlikely to affect telephones or building materials. The effects of market uncertainty are thus contained in what will often be a relatively small part of the total planning unit.

But the more common strategies require that the market be replaced by an authoritative determination of price and the amounts to be sold or bought at these prices. There are three ways of doing this:

1. The market can be superseded.
2. It can be controlled by sellers or buyers.
3. It can be suspended for definite or indefinite periods by contracts between the parties to sale and purchase.

[4]Richard Austin Smith, *Corporations in Crisis* (New York: Doubleday, 1963), p. 91 et seq. The company's misfortunes in the sale of aircraft were intimately bound up with the contemporary eccentricities of Howard Hughes at TWA.

[5]In its later development the conglomerate was partly a speculative phenomenon, partly a manipulation of managerial aggrandizement. Firms were acquired by issuing debentures with fixed and tax-deductible interest. Earnings and capital gains of the companies so acquired then greatly inflated the value of the stock of the acquiring company. The common effect was not to increase but greatly to decrease the stability of both the acquiring and the acquired firms. This era of the speculative conglomerate came to an end for the long present with the fall in the stock market in 1969 and 1970. The conglomerate is the subject of later discussion.

All of these strategies are familiar features of the planning system.

4

The market is superseded by vertical integration. The planning unit takes over the source of supply or the outlet; a transaction that is subject to bargaining over prices and amounts is thus replaced with a transfer within the planning unit. Where a firm is especially dependent on an important material or product—as an oil company on crude petroleum, a steel form on ore,[6] an aluminum company on bauxite or Sears, Roebuck on appliances—there is always danger that the requisite supplies will be available only at inconvenient or uncertain prices. To have control of supply—to rely not on the market but on its own sources of supply—is an elementary safeguard. This does not eliminate market uncertainty; rather the large and unmanageable uncertainty as to the price of ore or crude is replaced by the smaller, more diffuse and more manageable uncertainties as to the costs of labor, drilling, ore transport and yet more remote raw materials. But this is a highly beneficial exchange. For an oil company a change in the cost of purchased crude is a serious matter, a change in the cost of drilling equipment a detail.

As viewed by the firm, elimination of a market converts an external negotiation and hence a partially or wholly uncontrollable decision to a matter for purely internal decision. Nothing, we shall see, better explains modern industrial policy—capital supply is the extreme case—than the desire to make highly strategic cost factors subject to wholly internal decision.

Markets can also be controlled. This consists in reducing or eliminating the independence of action of those to whom the planning unit sells or from whom it buys. Their behavior being subject to control, uncertainty as to that behavior is

<hr>

[6] This problem was of importance in the difficulties experienced some years ago by Wheeling Steel, a nonintegrated producer. "Thus under its contracts Wheeling, in the late 1950's and early 1960's, found itself powerless to trim ore supplies as sales fluctuated. . . . Moreover by the early 1960's the operating efficiencies of using beneficiated ores . . . were fully apparent, but Wheeling, tied to outmoded sources of supply, lagged behind many in the industry in using such ores." *Fortune*, June 1965, p. 151. In subsequent years Wheeling experienced further difficulties in this regard.

reduced. At the same time the outward form of the market, including the process of buying and selling, remains formally intact.

This control of markets is the counterpart of large size and large size in relation to the particular market. A Wisconsin dairy farm cannot influence the price that it pays for fertilizer or machinery. Its purchases being small in relation to purchases as a whole, its decision to buy or not to buy has no appreciable signifiance for the supplier. The same is true of its sales. Having no control over its suppliers or its customers, it pays and receives the going prices.

Not so with General Motors. Its decision to buy or not to buy will usually be very important to its suppliers; it may be a matter of survival. This induces a highly cooperative posture. So with any large firm.[7] Should it be necessary to press matters, General Motors, unlike the dairyman, has always the possibility of supplying a material or component to itself. The

[7]Economists, defenders of the orthodox view, were long at pains to disassociate large absolute size from large size in relation to the particular market. ". . . [C]oncentration [i.e., small numbers and hence large size in relation to the market] has nothing to do with size of firms, no matter by what resounding name it is called—big business, colossal corporation, financial giantism, etc. . . . most of my fellow economists would agree that 'absolute size is absolutely irrelevant.' " M. A. Adelman, Hearings before the Subcommittee on Antitrust and Monopoly of the Committee on the Judiciary, United States Senate, Eighty-Eighth Congress, Second Session, Pursuant to S. Res. 262, Part I. *Economic Concentration: Overall and Conglomerate Aspects* (1964), p. 228. This contention, though wrong, served to remove the large firm from the pejorative reputation of the monopoly. It thus rendered the large firm a very considerable protective service. Market power has traditionally been associated by economists not with planning but with monopoly. Market concentration or monopoly in the older orthodoxy was inimical to efficient employment of resources by the market and had strong overtones of illegality. If big business and monopoly power tended to be identical, then all big business was inefficient and presumptively illegal. This, however, given the evident role of large firms in the modern economy was painful as well as absurd. So disassociation of absolute from relative size was important if traditional antipathy to monopoly was to seem sensible and big business was to be legitimate. In fact, large absolute size and large size relative to the market do go together. Great firms—General Motors, Exxon, Ford, United States Steel—are invariably large in relation to their principal markets. This I judge most economists of accessible mind now accept. See the sensible remarks of Carl Kaysen, "The Corporation: How Much Power? What Scope?" in *The Corporation in Modern Society*, Edward S. Mason, ed. (Cambridge: Harvard University Press, 1959), p. 89.

option of eliminating a market is an important source of power for controlling it.[8]

Similarly, size allows General Motors as a seller to set prices for automobiles, diesels, trucks, refrigerators and the rest of its offering and be secure in the knowledge that no individual buyer, by withdrawing his custom, can force a change. The fact that GM is one of a few sellers adds to its control. Each seller shares the common interest in secure and certain prices; it is to the advantage of none to disrupt this mutual security system. Competitors of General Motors are especially unlikely to initiate price reductions that might provoke further and retributive price-cutting. No formal communication is necessary to prevent such actions; this is considered naïve and arouses the professional wrath of company counsel. Everyone knows that the survivor of such a contest would not be the aggressor but General Motors. Thus do size and small numbers of competitors lead to market regulation.

Control of prices is not a part of market control; if uncertainty is to be eliminated, there must also be control of the amount sold. But size also makes this possible. It allows advertising, a well-nurtured sales organization and a careful management of product design which can help to ensure the needed customer response. And since General Motors produces some half of all the automobiles available from domestic sources, its designs do not reflect the current mode but are the current mode. The proper shape of an automobile, for most people, is what the automobile majors decree the current shape to be. The control of demand, as we shall see later, is not perfect. But what is imperfect is not unimportant for reducing market uncertainty.

Finally, in an economy where units are large, firms can eliminate market uncertainty for each other. This they do by entering into contracts specifying prices and amounts to be provided or bought for substantial periods of time. A long-term contract by the Wisconsin farmer to buy fertilizer or sell milk accords no great certainty to the fertilizer dealer or the dairy receiving the milk. It is subject to the capacity of the farmer to fulfill it; death, accident, drought, high feed costs and contagious abortion can all supervene. But a contract

[8]There are similar, although more complex, possibilities for control of the labor market to which I will return.

with the United States Steel Corporation to supply sheet steel or to take electric power is extremely reliable. In a world of large firms, it follows, there can be a matrix of contracts by which each firm eliminates market uncertainty for other firms and, in turn, gives to them some of its own uncertainty.

Outside of the planning system, most notably in agriculture, the government also intervenes extensively to set prices and ensure demand and thus to suspend the operation of the market and eliminate market uncertainty. This it does because the participating units—the individual farms—are not large enough to control prices. Technology and the associated commitment of capital and time require, nonetheless, that there be stable prices and assured demand.[9] But within the planning system similar action is also required where exacting technology, with extensive research and development, means a lengthy production period and a very large commitment of capital. Such has long been the case in the development and supply of modern weapons; it was and remains true in the exploration of space; and it characterizes the development of a growing range of modern civilian products or services, including transport planes, high-speed ground transport, various applied uses of nuclear energy and sundry new sources of energy or forms of energy conservation. Here the state guarantees a price sufficient, with suitable margin, to cover costs. And it undertakes to buy what is produced or to compensate fully in the case of contract cancelation, technical failure or absence of demand. Thus, effectively, it suspends the market with all its associated uncertainty. One consequence, as we shall see, is that, in areas of the most exacting advanced technology, the market is most completely replaced, and planning is therefore most secure. As a further consequence, this has become for the participants a very attractive part of the planning system. The fully planned economy, so far from being unpopular with avowed friends of free enterprise, is warmly regarded by those who know it best.

5

Two things of some interest are evident from this analysis. It is clear, to repeat, that industrial planning is in unabashed alliance with size. The large organization can tolerate market

[9]See Chapters XVI and XVII.

uncertainty as a smaller firm cannot. It can contract out of it as the smaller firm cannot. Vertical integration, the control of prices and consumer demand and reciprocal absorption of market uncertainty by long-term contracts between firms all favor the large enterprise. And while smaller firms can appeal to the state to fix prices and ensure demand, this security is also provided by the state to the big industrial firm when it is most needed. These circumstances—the exacting technology, large commitments of time and capital—make it fairly certain that most of this government work will be done by large organizations.[10]

By all but the pathologically romantic, it is now recognized that this is not the age of the small man. But there is still a lingering presumption among economists that his retreat is not before the efficiency of the great corporation or even its technological proficiency but before its monopoly power. The corporation has superior capacity to extract profits. Therein lies its advantage. "Big business will undertake only such innovations as promise to enhance its profits and power, or protect its market position. . . . [F]ree competitive men have

---

[10]The concentration of industrial research and development expenditure in large firms is, in fact, overwhelming. In 1974, the 126 companies undertaking research and development with employment greater than 25,000 persons reported projects totaling $16 billion. This represented almost three-fourths of all industrial research and development in the United States that year. Included were 35 companies with projects in excess of $100 million. The four companies with the largest R&D programs in 1974 performed 19 percent of all industrial research and development measured in terms of expenditures and accounted for 18 percent of the R&D funds contracted by the United States government to industry. Companies with employment of less than 5000 persons doing research and development numbered over 10,000, or 95 percent of all R&D performing companies but they accounted for just 10 percent of the industrial performance.

Of total industrial R&D expenditures in 1974, 37 percent was financed with federal funds. One hundred large companies received 93 percent of the federal support. *Research and Development in Industry,* 1974 (National Science Foundation, September 1976).

Morton I. Kamien and Nancy L. Schwartz, from a survey of literature on this subject, conclude that while the "vast majority of large firms have, and the vast majority of small firms do not have, sustained R&D programs," it is not clear that among the largest there is an increase in innovational effort with increasing size. ("Market Structure and Innovation: A Survey," *Journal of Economic Literature,* Vol. XIII, No. 1 [March 1975], p. 18.)

always been the true innovators. Under the stern discipline of competition they must innovate to prosper and to survive."[11]

This, by the uncouth, would be called drivel. Size is the general servant of technology, not the special servant of profits. The small competitive firm cannot afford the outlays that innovation demands. An economic system consisting of such firms would require, rather, that we reject the technology which, since earliest consciousness, we have been taught to applaud. It would require that we have simple products made with simple equipment from readily available materials by unspecialized labor. Then the period of production would be short; the market would reliably provide the labor, equipment and materials required for production; there would be neither possibility nor need for managing the market for the finished product. If the market thus reigned, there would be, and could be, no planning. The small firm would then, at last, do very well. All that would be necessary would be to undo nearly everything that, at whatever violence to meaning, has been called progress in the last half century. There may be a case against technical innovation—against supersonic travel and infinitely destructive weaponry and even different automobiles and detergents. There is no case that such innovation will come better from the little man.

The second conclusion is that the enemy of the market is not ideology but the engineer. In the Soviet Union and the Soviet-type economies prices are extensively managed by the state. Production is not in response to market demand but given by the overall plan. In the Western economies markets are dominated by great firms. These establish prices and seek to ensure a demand for what they have to sell. The enemies of the market are thus highly visible, although rarely in social matters has there been such a case of mistaken identity. They are not socialists. The enemies, in both cases, are advanced technology, the specialization and organization of men and process that this requires and the resulting commitment of time and capital. These make the market work badly when the need is for greatly enhanced reliability—when planning is

[11]Horace M. Gray, Hearings before the Subcommittee on Antitrust and Monopoly of the Committee on the Judiciary, United States Senate, Eighty-Ninth Congress, First Session, Pursuant to S. Res. 70, Part III. *Economic Concentration: Concentration, Invention and Innovation* (1965), p. 1164. In the last ten years, although such statements can still be exhumed, they have come, one judges, to be thought exceptional, perhaps slightly eccentric.

essential. The modern large Western corporation and the modern apparatus of socialist planning are variant accommodations to the same need. It is open to every free-born man to dislike this accommodation. But he must direct his attack to the cause. He must not ask that jet aircraft, nuclear power plants or even the modern automobile in its modern volume be produced by firms that are subject to unfixed prices and unmanaged demand. He must ask, as just noted, that they not be produced.

Planning and the Supply of Capital

THE PHYSICAL MANIFESTATION of the planning system is the capital equipment it deploys—the mills, machinery, factories, shops, warehouses, stores, service stations, office buildings with which it covers the landscape. In the manner of all capital goods, and unlike the bread, meat and whiskey that are consumed today, these yield their use only over time. And in the manner of all capital goods they have their source in savings—in the economic resources that individuals and corporations devote not to current consumption but to acquiring or building the equipment that allows of greater or different consumption in the future. All of this has the reassuring ring of the commonplace.

Technology and the associated commitment of time are coupled, we have seen, with large requirements for capital. This is matched in the modern economy by an equal and, on occasion, even greater capacity to provide it. This is also a planned supply; those who make large use of capital have successfully minimized their dependence on the market for what they use.

It is a feature of all planning that, unlike the market, it incorporates within itself no mechanism by which demand is accommodated to supply and vice versa. This must be deliberately accomplished by human agency. Such is true of the supply of savings for capital formation. In the past there was a recurrent tendency for such savings to be excessive, with highly adverse effects on the behavior of the economic system. Further planning, this by the state, was necessary, in consequence, to ensure that what was saved was invested. This step economists have come to denote, perhaps too dramatically, as the Keynesian Revolution. The tendency for savings to be unduly abundant had a further important bearing on the relation of capital to land and to the labor force and to the bargaining position of capital in relation to those who guide or provide technical knowledge to the industrial enterprise. This is a matter for later examination. The present chapter considers the planning that lies back of the capital supply and, in a preliminary way, the resulting need for equating the supply of savings with the demand.

2

The first feature of the planning system which is favorable to a large supply of savings for capital formation is the scale of its production. In 1976, in the United States, $276 billion was saved by individuals and corporations from current product for investment at home and abroad. This would have been difficult to accomplish from a pre-World War II Gross National Product which, in equivalent prices, was about $459 billion. It was easier from a 1976 Product of $1692 billion.[1]

The most obvious effect of large production is that individuals can save more easily from the large personal incomes which this production returns. Consumption has the first claim on income even for the most austere when the alternative is hunger, chill or some other form of physical pain. But when a certain level of well-being is achieved, people can choose to defer consumption in order to cover the needs of old age or a rainy day or to risk the demoralization of unearned income or, an insufficiently noted point, to enjoy having money not for what it will buy but for the mere pleasure of its possession.[2] Poor societies in the past have had a considerable capacity to save, as their surviving monuments attest. But the tourist who gazes on the Great Pyramids, Baalbek, St. Peter's, Chartres, Versailles, Cuzco or the Forbidden City is not looking at the fruits of the voluntary savings of the masses. He is viewing the results of the highly involuntary deprivation of slaves, of the largely lost art of getting tax blood from very dry stones or of insurance taken out against the danger of eternal damnation under conditions of grave discomfort. Or he sees the results of the savings of the minority who were very rich. Only in very recent times has the average man been a source of savings.

[1]*Economic Report of the President, 1977*, pp. 214, 187. The 1976 figures here and elsewhere from the *1977 Report* are subject to minor revision.

[2]A point elegantly made by Wallace C. Peterson in his 1976 presidential address, "Institutionalism, Keynes, and the Real World," to the Association for Evolutionary Economics, *Journal of Economic Issues*, Vol. XI, No. 2 (June 1977), p. 201 et seq.

And he remains a minor source. The approved folk myths of economics have the individual or the household measuring the urgencies and enjoyments of immediate consumption against the foreseen and unforeseeable needs of the future. Allied with this is the calculation that if consumption is deferred and the proceeds are invested with prudence, or possibly courage, the reward will be interest, dividends or capital gains. From this highly rational and admirably individualistic choice come the decision to save and therewith the supply of capital and the growth of the economy. Were it so, the supply of capital would be very small and the growth very slight.

In 1976, personal savings by individuals were $78 billion. Savings by business firms, primarily corporations, were $198 billion, or more than two and a half times as great.[3] And most of the personal saving was by the affluent and rich. A study of saving in the year 1950 showed that households in the lower two thirds of the income range, as measured by after-tax incomes, did no saving at all. On the contrary, they consumed substantially in excess of their income. More than half of all personal savings was supplied by those in the upper-five-percent income bracket.[4] There is no reason to suppose that saving has become appreciably more democratic since that time.

3

The small volume of saving by the average man, and its absence among the lower-income masses, reflect faithfully the role of the individual in the planning system and the accepted view of his function. The individual serves the planning system not by supplying it with savings and the resulting capital; he serves it far more by consuming its products. On no other activity, religious, political or moral, is he so elaborately, skillfully and expensively instructed.

Specifically, along with the production of goods go energetic and no less important efforts to ensure their use. These emphasize the health, beauty, social success and sexual gratification—by common calculation, the happiness—that will result from the possession and use of a particular product. This communication, combined each day with the effort on

[3] *Economic Report of the President, 1977,* p. 214.
[4] Irwin Friend and Stanley Schor, "Who Saves?" *Review of Economics and Statistics,* Vol. XLI, No. 2, Part 2 (May 1959), p. 239.

behalf of countless other products, becomes, in the aggregate, an unremitting argument for the advantages of consumption. In turn, inevitably, this affects social values. A family's standard of living becomes an index of its achievement.[5] It helps ensure that the production and, *pari passu*, the consumption of goods will be the prime measure of social accomplishment. The eloquent reminder, so beloved by guardians of the established ideology, that "no economic system has ever in history provided such a high standard of living" takes for granted that the level of consumption is the decisive measure of social merit. It would be highly inconsistent for a society which so values consumption, and so relentlessly presses its claims, to rely on consumers, through their savings, for its capital. It would be even more incongruous if its need for capital were large. In a society which so emphasizes consumption and so needs capital, the decision to save should obviously be removed from the consumer and exercised by other authority. All industrial societies do so. In the formally planned economies of the Soviet Union and Eastern Europe, income is withheld for investment by the industrial enterprise and especially by the state. In the United States and the Western economies this withholding is performed in largest amount by the corporation. For removing the authority over savings from the individual (and the market) the corporation serves, as on other matters, as the prime planning instrument.[6]

4

Control of the supply of savings is strategic for industrial planning. Capital use is large. No form of market uncertainty is so serious as that involving the terms and conditions on which capital is obtained. Apart from the normal disadvantages of an uncertain price, there is danger that, under some circumstances, supply will not be forthcoming at an acceptable price. This will be at the precise moment when misfortune or miscalculation has made the need most urgent. And unlike suppliers of raw material or labor, the supplier of funds

[5] On this see James S. Duesenberry, *Income, Saving and the Theory of Consumer Behavior* (Cambridge: Harvard University Press, 1949), p. 28 et seq.

[6] In conjunction, as presently to be stressed, with the government, which enters to ensure that the savings generated at high levels of output and employment are all spent.

has traditionally been conceded some degree of power. The provision of credit carries with it the special right to know, and even to suggest, how it is used.[7] This dilutes the authority of the planning unit.

All of these dangers and difficulties are avoided if the firm has a secure source of capital from its own earnings. It no longer faces the risks of the market. It concedes no authority to outsiders. It has full control over its own rate of expansion, over the nature of that expansion and over decisions between products, plants and processes. The last chapter showed that one of the strategies for eliminating market uncertainty is to eliminate the market. This strategy is much used where, as in the case of crude petroleum, iron ore or bauxite, the firm is heavily dependent on a particular raw material and where, as a result, adverse market movements could be very costly. But for all production, capital is an indispensable and expensive ingredient. To minimize dependence on this market is therefore a universal planning strategy.

There is a further advantage in making capital supply fully subject to the power that allows of industrial planning. Capital and labor are partly substitutes for each other. If capital is subject to internal decision, it can be used as a partial substitute for labor. Labor, in the normal case, is subject to the external authority of the union. So, when capital replaces labor, planning authority is enhanced. This is a matter for later attention.

5

In the formally planned economies, although there is some slight reliance on voluntary savings by individuals, the basic decision on how much is to be saved is taken by the state. This decision is implemented in one of two ways. It is made effective by taxation. Or industrial enterprises are encouraged to earn profits for reinvestment and, by the setting of prices and costs in suitable relation, they are enabled to do so. In either case it is the planner's and not the individual's decision

[7] ". . . creditors are likely to take a keen, and indeed a rather insistent, interest in company policies and may well interfere in certain aspects of management. . . . Retained earnings place the capital entirely at management's disposal without any promises or guarantees." Wilbert E. Moore, *The Conduct of the Corporation* (New York: Random House, 1962), p. 227.

that determines the volume of savings. Were it otherwise, consumption would be higher, savings would be smaller and the rate of capital formation and economic growth smaller than the planners believe necessary. It should be noticed that the power of the planners to substitute their view of the desirable rate of savings for that of the individual is not unlimited. In Poland, Hungary and elsewhere in Eastern Europe in past times planners recurrently sought a higher rate of savings than those who saved found tolerable. This has been an important source of unrest, especially so in the Stalinist era.

In the Western economies industrial saving has become, by comparison, nearly painless. A plea for larger dividend payments is occasionally heard at stockholders' meetings. But it is heard respectfully and ignored. And the individual stockholder always has the option of selling his stock and spending his capital gains. Unions cite the level of earnings, including retained earnings, as part of their case for wage increases. It is a bargaining point and not a grievance. If saving by stockholders is pressed too far, there is some chance that their willingness to sell will be exploited by a takeover bid, with a consequent threat to the tenure of the existing management. This may act as a restraint on corporate saving in the less than largest of the large corporations. In the case of General Motors, Exxon, IBM, size is a defense against this threat, and it is not a serious consideration.

The nature of such saving must not, however, be misunderstood. The decisions which provide more than three fifths of the community's supply of savings are made not by individuals but by authority, in the main by the managements of a few hundred corporations. And from these savings comes the major wherewithal for the growth of the economy.[8]

[8]Where the reality does not accord with wish, our practice, as frequently noted, is to devise a myth which then serves as a bridge between evidence that cannot be escaped and the belief that is sought. However, no acceptable myth relates the decisions of the management of the modern corporation on retention or paying out of earnings to the preferences of individuals as to savings and expenditure. It has been suggested that the board of directors, as the chosen representatives of the stockholders, sets the dividend and thus reflects the will of the stockholders. This hardly answers where, as in the common case, the board is selected by, or is otherwise the instrument of, the management. Nor does it serve much better in the cases where the board or some of its members have a measure of independence resulting from stock ownership. For even then the directors normally accept the recommendation of management on retention and investment of earnings. No one familiar with the operations of the modern large corpora-

The parallel with the planned economies will be evident. Neither the Soviet economy nor that of the United States entrusts savings and growth to individual decision. Both entrust them to authority. In social argument to press a strong case too far is to accord the compulsive or motivated critic or the individual who seeks any escape from inconvenient truth the handhold for which he yearns. There are great differences between the systems in the degree of centralization with which savings are planned as well as in the techniques by which they are extracted. But in the supply of capital, as elsewhere, the imperatives of industrialization bring, by whatever differences in path, an inescapable convergence.

6

The most celebrated feature of the market is that it equates supply with demand at a price. If there is an incipient surplus, a falling price encourages buyers, retains sellers and thus eliminates it; if there is a momentary shortage, a rising price attracts suppliers, repels buyers and thus eliminates it. Planning has within itself, as noted, no similar equilibrating mechanism. The planner must deliberately ensure that planned supply equals planned use. If he fails, there will be surpluses or deficits. If the market mechanism is still not used—if prices are not lowered or raised—there will be a disagreeable problem of storing or destroying the surplus or an unseemly scramble for the insufficient supply. These are common results of planning, commonly accompanied by a drastic slump in the reputation of the planner concerned.

The decisions on what will be saved are made, in the main, by a few hundred large corporations. The decisions as to what will be invested are made by a similar number of large firms to which are added those of a much larger number of individuals who are buying dwellings, automobiles and household appliances. No mechanism of the market relates the decisions to save to the decisions to invest. It one of the motives

---

tion would believe that the individual stockholder has a serious voice in this matter, although this does not prevent those who perpetuate the myth from urging it.

The stockholder, as noted, can contract out of the saving to which he is subject by selling his stock and spending capital gains. This does not alter the power exercised by the management over savings by the firm. It does, of course, reduce total saving by the community. The practical effect on aggregate saving of this recourse is not, one judges, very great.

for developing internal sources of savings is to free the firm
from the uncertainties of the interest rate, it is evident that
the decision on this saving will not be affected by the rate of
interest. Having contracted out of the money market, it will
not be much affected by the money market. If, as we shall
see presently, investment is determined also by influences independent of the market—if it too is planned—the rate of interest does nothing to equate supply to demand. Both are
independent of its influence, at least in this part of the
economy. And the interest rate is the price that the market
would presumably rely on to accommodate the supply of savings to requirements.[9]

If savings go unused, that is to say are unspent, demand
for goods in the economy is by this much reduced. Sales of
goods then fall below expected or planned levels and employment falls. Outside of the planning system prices and employment also fall. This will lead to reduction in investment
outside the planning system and, with some delay, to a curtailment of planned investment within. In other words, a
failure to use all that corporations and individuals seek to
save sets in motion the processes of recession and depression.
These will continue until *they* reduce savings to the point
where all are being absorbed by the smaller volume of investment.[10] If, in the opposite case, the economy is functioning
at or near the capacity of its plant or labor force or both,
and corporations seek to invest in the aggregate more than
the equivalent of the current supply of savings, there will be
more spending for investment and consumption than the
economy can accommodate. The result will be a bidding up
of prices, and most markedly of the market prices outside of
the planning system. This is inflation. The lurking threat of
these discomforts thus requires that the planning system have
machinery on the one hand for ensuring that savings are used

[9]This is a brief view of the matter. There are influences both in the
firm and in the economy as a whole which cause investment to increase when savings increase and vice versa. See page 203. But the
large role of industrial saving and investment in the total disposes of
the theoretical possibility that such balancing might take place outside
the planning system. Few economists do, in fact, any longer argue that
savings and investment are responsive (and in the right way) to the interest rate.

[10]More precisely, intended savings. In Keynes's formulation savings are
always offset. The fall in income reduces savings more than it reduces
investment, including that in inventories, and equilibrium is found at a
lower level of output, income and employment.

and on the other for ensuring that use is limited to the savings that are available.

Such machinery has come into being, if in imperfect form, in all industrial countries in modern times. The state uses its power over taxation and expenditure, including borrowing for private investment and spending, to provide the balance between savings and their use that the planning system cannot provide for itself. It supplies the missing element in the planning of savings. This is an integral necessity of modern industrial planning.

7

At first glance it might be imagined that the problem of management of savings and their use—of what is called Keynesian fiscal policy—is symmetrical: there is a danger that savings will be greater than use, and there is a danger that investment (and other use) will exceed supply. There is, accordingly, equal need for measures that will increase use and limit use. In practice the problem changes radically with increasing wealth. In poor countries—India, Pakistan, most of Latin America—the supply of savings, domestic and imported, is exceedingly meager. There the problem is not to ensure use of savings but to limit investment and other claims to what is available, to ensure wise use of savings and to increase the available supply. In the United States, Western Europe and the older British Commonwealth, periods of war and extreme international tension apart, such a preoccupation would seem eccentric. Here the men responsible for economic policy study estimates of intended industrial investment to see whether these, together with the probable government deficit, will absorb net savings. Failure to do so means recession or depression. When Keynes's *The General Theory*[11] was published during the Great Depression and for the two decades following World War II, the essential economic problem was, in fact, to offset savings and thus to maintain the level of output and income. For economists who, like most other people, are most at ease with the comfortable problems of the past this concern became a tradition. It has so remained even though in more recent times inflation has become a major, perhaps the major, source of anxiety.

[11]John Maynard Keynes, *The General Theory of Employment Interest and Money* (New York: Harcourt, 1936).

A steady expansion of output and income is favorable to both corporate and individual saving; depression or recession, by contrast, brings a Malthusian reduction in both. Business savings fell from $11.2 billion in 1929 to $3.2 billion in 1933, the low year of the Great Depression, and did not regain their pre-Depression level until 1941. In 1932 and 1933, savings by individuals were negative, which is to say that individuals, in the aggregate, increased their indebtedness.[12] A lessened rate of expansion in 1959–1960 brought an absolute reduction in individual savings and a leveling off in business savings. In the recession beginning in 1974, private savings again fell drastically—in constant dollars the annual rate of private savings fell from $232 billion in the fourth quarter of 1973 to $184 billion in the third quarter of 1974.[13] Here is the paradox of savings: the steps which ensure that they will be used serve also to increase their supply. The more effectively they are offset by investment, the higher will be the income and the more savings there will be.

Most communities in the past were limited in their progress by the savings they could extract from their meager product to invest in better methods of production. The same is true of poor nations today. The rich nations must also have savings to expand. But what is called economic progress here depends less on the supply of savings than on the effectiveness with which employment of a more than ample supply is ensured. Not a shortage of savings but a recession resulting from the failure to use all available savings is the specter that haunts all policymakers in the affluent countries. For investment to exceed savings, at least in peacetime, is thought exceptional. This tendency of savings and thus of capital to abundance, abundant use notwithstanding, is a matter of penetrating historical and social consequence to which I now turn.

[12]*Economic Report of the President, 1970,* p. 218.
[13]*Economic Report of the President, 1976,* p. 192.

V

Capital and Power

No SUBJECT has been more faithfully explored by economists than the relation between what anciently have been called the factors of production—land, labor, capital and the entre-preneurial talent which brings these together and manages their employment. Until recently the problem of efficiency in production—that of getting the most from the available pro-ductive resources—was envisaged almost entirely as one of winning the best combination of these agents. The elucidation by means of diagrams of the arcane problems inherent in fac-tor combination remains one of the prime pedagogical rites of economics.[1] Economists have been equally concerned with

[1]Changing technology, it is conceded, alters progressively and radi-cally what can be obtained from any given supply of factors. But there is no way by which this intelligence can be developed at length in a textbook. So economic instruction concedes the important and then dis-cusses the unimportant. Thus Professor Samuelson, the most noted of contemporary economists, who more than anyone else has instructed adult Americans in the subject, observes that the output that can be obtained from a given stock of factors "depends upon the state of technology." Then to get back to the teachable minutiae, he adds: *"But, at any time, there will be a maximum obtainable amount of product for any given amounts of factor inputs."* Paul A. Samuelson, *Economics,* 10th ed. (New York: McGraw-Hill, 1976), p. 537. (Em-phasis his.) The problem of factor allocation happens to be the subject on which there is an available doctrine. So having given it such impor-tance as italics provide, this is the subject he discusses. In practice much economic instruction, and notably so in such fields as advanced theory, foreign trade and monetary policy, depends not on the rele-vance of the subject matter but on the existence of an intellectually preoccupying theory. In this case, however, there is a conflict between the technological development, to which Professor Samuelson properly accords the primary role in increasing productivity, and the factor al-location which provides the requisite pedagogical exercise. Technologi-cal development involves, as we have seen, a heavy commitment of capital, organization and time which is safeguarded by planning and companion control over costs, prices and demand. But the approved pedagogical exercise leads to the conclusion that the optimal allocation of factors is obtained by the minimum of such interference with the mark.

42

the way in which the prices of the factors of production—rents, wages, interest and profits—are determined. Indeed, in the classical tradition, the subject was thought of as falling in two parts: the problem of value, having to do with the determination of the prices of goods, and the problem of distribution, or how the resulting income was divided between landlords, workers, capitalists and entrepreneurs.

One aspect of the relationships between the factors of production has, however, been less examined. That is why power is associated with some factors and not with others. Why did ownership of land once convey plenary power over the dominant form of productive enterprise and, therewith, in the community at large? Why, under other circumstances, has it been assumed that such authority, both over the enterprise and in the society at large, should lie with the owner of capital? Under what circumstances might such power pass to labor?

It is a puzzling neglect. On coming on any form of organized activity—a church, platoon, government bureau, congressional committee, a house of casual pleasure—our first instinct is to inquire who is in charge. Then we regularly inquire as to the qualifications or credentials which accord such command. Organization almost invariably invites two questions: Who is the head? How did he get there?

2

One reason the question was slighted was that for a long time in formal economic inquiry no one associated with economic activity was thought to have any worthwhile exercise of power. In the classical economic tradition—that of Adam Smith, David Ricardo, Thomas Malthus, John Stuart Mill and Alfred Marshall—and increasingly, as concepts were better defined, the business enterprise (like the Wisconsin dairy farm today) was assumed to be small in relation to the market supplied. The price it received was impersonally and competitively determined by the market. So were the prices paid to suppliers. Wages were also set by the market. So was the interest on borrowed funds. Profits reduced themselves to a competitive level. Technology was assumed to be stable. Under these circumstances the ideal volume of production for the firm was externally established by the relation of costs to the market price at various levels of output. If the man in charge of the firm has no power to influence prices, costs, wages or interest, and if even his best output is externally determined and his profits are subject to the leveling effect of competition, one can rightly be unconcerned about his power. He has none. Until well into the present century the economics of the textbooks assumed a world of such small and competitive firms. The counterpart neglect of the problem of power was both plausible and inevitable. Other traditions of thought, however, were less handicapped.

In particular there was Marx. In the middle of the last century he brought the subject of power into economic discussion with a vehemence which the world has not yet quite ceased to find alarming. The notion of a system of competitive and hence passive business firms he dismissed as an exercise in vulgar apologetics. Production is dominated by those who control and supply capital—by a "constantly diminishing number of the magnates of capital, who usurp and monopolize all advantages of this process of transformation . . ."[2] Their authority in the enterprise is complete. Prices and wages are set in their collective interest. They dominate the society and set its moral tone. They also control the state, which becomes an executive committee serving the will and interest of the capitalist class. There is no question of power being associated with any other factor of production. At this stage in historical development it belongs unequivocally and totally with capital.

In the classical tradition there was eventually a measure of agreement with Marx. The notion of the competitive market receded; it survives today in formal economic theory but with no serious claim of practical relevance. The business enterprise is routinely assumed to have control over its prices and output—to have the power that is associated with one seller or monopoly, a few sellers or oligopoly, or with some unique feature of its product or service which accords it protection from competition. Only professional defenders of the free enterprise system, members of a lowly and, on the whole, poorly paid craft, still argue for the rule of competition, this being the test their clients are best calculated to fail.[3] There

[2]Karl Marx, *Capital* (New York: Modern Library, 1936), Chapter 32, p. 836.

[3]"To the extent that a price is reached by means that are *not* impersonal—to the extent that either the buyer or the seller can dictate or influence the setting of the price—to that extent our system of controlling the efficient use of resources is not working properly." *Do You Know Your Economic ABC's? Profits and the American Economy*, United States Department of Commerce, 1965, p. 13. This pamphlet

is general agreement that "market power which large absolute and relative size gives to the giant corporation is the basis not only of economic power but also of considerable political and social power . . ."[4]

And the companion point of Marx is assumed. Such power as may be available naturally and inevitably belongs to capital. Its exercise is the prerogative of ownership. The claims of the other factors of production are inherently subordinate. In the assumption that power belongs as a matter of course to capital, all economists are Marxians.

Beyond this, the problem of power is still not much discussed. Prices and wages are fixed, investment determined, dividends declared, production decided, by the owners of capital within the margin of discretion allowed by the market. Influence by business on the state is deemed irregular and illegitimate; such as is nonetheless exercised is in normal and limited pursuit of the interest of the owners of the enterprise. Alternatives to the exercise of power by capital are not seriously considered.

In the last half century there has been a steady accumulation of evidence on the shift of power from owners to managers within the modern large corporation. The power of the stockholders has been shown to be increasingly tenuous. A small proportion of the stock is represented at stockholders' meetings for a ceremony in which banality is varied chiefly by irrelevance. The majority of the stock is voted by proxy for the directors who have been selected by the management. The management, though its ownership is normally negligible, is solidly in control of the enterprise. By all visible evidence it possesses the power. Yet there has been great reluctance to admit of a significant and enduring shift of power from the owners of capital. Some observers have sought to maintain the myth of stockholder power. As in foreign policy and bad marriages it is hoped that incantation may save what the real-

---

was commissioned by the Department of Commerce to promote understanding of (and prove departmental sympathy for) American business. By its test all sizable corporations would, of course, fail. As earlier noted, this effort collided with widely distributed common sense, and the Department (in cooperation with the advertising industry) was led in 1976 to try again.

[4] Carl Kaysen, "The Corporation: How Much Power? What Scope? in *The Corporation in Modern Society*, Edward S. Mason, ed. (Cambridge: Harvard University Press, 1959), p. 99.

ity denies.[5] Others, including Marxians, argue that the change is superficial, that capital retains a deeper and more functional control. Only the naïve react to the obvious. Yet others have conceded a change but have deferred judgment as to its significance.[6] And others still have seen a possibly dangerous usurpation of the legitimate power of capital that should, if possible, be reversed.[7] Comparatively few have questioned the credentials of capital where direction of the enterprise is concerned or suggested that it might be durably in eclipse.

3

Yet, over a longer range of time, power over the productive enterprise—and, by derivation, in the society at large—has shifted radically between the factors of production. The eminence of capital is a relatively recent matter; until about two centuries ago no perceptive man would have doubted that power was decisively associated with land. The comparative wealth, esteem, military position and the sanguinary authority over the lives of the populace that went with land ownership assured its possessor of a position of eminence in his community and power in the state. These perquisites of land ownership also gave a strong and even controlling direction to history. For two centuries, until about two hundred years before the discovery of America, it helped inspire the recurrent military campaigns to the East which are called the Crusades. Succor for Byzantium, which was beset by the infidels, and

[5] "When, for example, John purchased a new issue of stock from the Keim Corporation last year . . . [it gave] him a voice in the decision of 'his' firm's management when he meets with other stockholders at annual meetings." *Do You Know Your Economic ABC's?*, pp. 17-18.

[6] Cf. Edward S. Mason, "The Apologetics of Managerialism," *Journal of Business of the University of Chicago*, Vol. 31, no. 1 (January 1958), p. 1 et seq. And "Comment" in *A Survey of Contemporary Economics*, Bernard F. Haley, ed., Vol. 2 (Homewood, Illinois: Richard D. Irwin, Inc., 1952), pp. 221–222. It is Professor Mason's view that, while the capitalist entrepreneur has lost his power in the modern large corporation, there is no serviceable view of what has taken his place. Accordingly, one can still do best by assuming the entrepreneur and the traditional motivations. ". . . [I] must confess a lack of confidence in the marked superiority, *for purposes of economic analysis*, of this newer concept of the firm, over the older conception of the entrepreneur." Ibid.

[7] Cf. Adolf A. Berle, Jr., *Power Without Property* (New York: Harcourt, 1959), p. 98 et seq.

redemption of Jerusalem, which had been lost to them, served, without doubt, as a stimulant to ardor. But not exclusively. Relations between the eastern and western Christians were always marked by profound mistrust. Jerusalem had been under Islam for 450 years; its redemption had not previously been considered of breathtaking urgency. The younger sons of the Frankish nobility, like the hungry peasants who followed Peter the Hermit, wanted land. Beneath the mantled cross beat hearts soundly attuned to the value of real estate. Baldwin, the younger brother of Godfrey of Bouillon, found himself faced, on the way to the Holy City, with the taxing decision as to whether to continue with the redeeming armies or take up an attractive piece of property at Edessa. He unhesitatingly opted for the latter and only on the death of his brother did he leave his fief to become the first King of Jerusalem.[8]

For three and a half centuries after the discovery of America appreciation of the strategic importance of land gave it an even greater role in history. The Americas were populated, as also the Steppes and the habitable parts of the Antipodes. Once again, religion went hand in hand with real property conveyancing, somewhat disguising the role of the latter. Spaniards considered themselves commissioned by God to win the souls of Indians; Puritans believed themselves primarily under obligation to find a favorable environment for their own. For Catholics and Cavaliers the Lord was believed to favor rather large acreages with the opportunity these accorded for the spiritual custody of aborigines and, as these gave out, of Africans. For Puritans and Protestants spiritual merit lay with the homestead and family farm. But these were details. In the New World, as in the Old, it was assumed that power belonged, as a right, to men who owned land. Democracy, in its modern meaning, began as a system which gave the suffrage to those who had proved their worth by acquiring real property, and to no others.

This eminence of land, and the incentive to acquire it, were firmly grounded in economics. Until comparatively modern times, agricultural production—the provision of food and fiber—accounted for a large share of all production, as it

---

[8]"The opportunity for combining Christian duty with the acquisition of land in a southern climate was very attractive." Steven Runciman, *A History of the Crusades*, Vol. 1. *The First Crusade* (Cambridge, England: University Press, 1951), p. 92.

still accounts for seventy to eighty percent of all output in such economically deprived countries as modern India. Ownership or control of land thus accorded one a position in the dominant form of economic activity; to be landless was to be crowded into what was left.

Meanwhile other factors of production had a much less strategic role. Agricultural technology was stable and uncomplicated; accordingly, slaves apart, it offered small scope for capital, and, as a broad rule, slaves could only be used in conjunction with land. Nonagricultural activity being relatively unimportant, its demand for capital was small and limited further by simple and stable technology. So—a somewhat neglected point—until two hundred years ago a meager supply of capital was matched by an equally meager opportunity for its use. If a man had land in England or Western Europe, he could get the modest supply of capital he needed to till it. Possession of this capital was no guarantee that he could get the land.

Nor was labor difficult to come by. Its well-established tendency was to keep itself in a state of great abundance. David Ricardo, having regard for experience to that time, could hold in 1817 that "no point is better established, than that the supply of labourers will always ultimately be in proportion to the means of supporting them."[9] That was to say that, given a little time, an unlimited supply would be forthcoming at or about a subsistence wage. Enough labor would be used so that, through diminishing returns, the contribution of the marginal worker would be about equal to his subsistence. If he gave up this narrow contest with privation, he could easily be replaced. If a man adds little and can easily be replaced, he will, one can be sure, have small power and small bargaining power.

But no one could doubt the advantage of laying one's hands on an acre, or a hundred acres, or a thousand acres of fertile land. Nor could one doubt the deadly consequences of losing like amounts. This meant that possession of land was strategic, and not even the philosophers whose ideas ushered in the Industrial Revolution could quite envisage a society where this was otherwise. Adam Smith, though he was at odds on most points with his Physiocratic precursors in France who had made land the ultimate source of all wealth,

[9]David Ricardo, *The Works and Correspondence of David Ricardo*, Piero Sraffa, ed., Vol. 1 (Cambridge, England: University Press, 1951), p. 292.

attributed a special bounty to real property, which was returned, as a special mark of grace, to those who owned it.[10] Forty years later Ricardo and Malthus made ownership of land even more crucial. Population would grow in accordance with a biological dynamic of its own. This would make an ever more urgent claim on a much more slowly increasing food supply. In consequence, the relative price of food and the share of income going to landlords would increase insouciantly and without limit. The decisive factor was the scarcity of land. "The labour of nature is paid, not because she does much, but because she does little. In proportion as she becomes niggardly in her gifts, she exacts a greater price for her work. Where she is munificently beneficent, she always works gratis."[11] Nor surprisingly, those who owned this rare resource would exercise full authority in the dominant agricultural economy and be men of prestige and power, the ruling class, in the community at large.

4

In fact, Ricardo wrote at the moment in history when land was being dethroned. That was partly because the scarcity to which he attributed such importance had set in motion a phenomenal search for a new supply. And the two Americas, South Africa and Australia were all found to have large, unused and highly usable amounts. New land could be obtained or lost land could be replaced by going to the frontier. The need now was for capital to pay the passage, to buy seed, livestock and equipment and to tide a man over until the first harvest.

Meanwhile mechanical inventions and the growth of metallurgical and engineering knowledge were prodigiously expanding opportunities for the employment of capital. From this greater use of capital in more advanced technology came greater production. From that production came greater income and more saving. It is not certain that in the last cen-

---

[10]Adam Smith, "Of the Rent of Land," *Wealth of Nations*, Book 1 (New York: Modern Library, 1937), Chapter 11. Cf. Alexander Gray, *The Development of Economic Doctrine* (London: Longmans, 1931), p. 137.

[11]Ricardo, p. 76. Ricardo is, in this passage, taking issue with Adam Smith's suggestion that the return to land was payment for nature's bounty. The detailed point is of no importance here. For both, nature, by way of land, played a large part in determining income.

tury the demand for capital grew more rapidly than the supply. In the new countries, including the United States, capital was usually scarce and the cost was high. But in England, over most of the century, rates of return were low and Englishmen had strong incentive to find more profitable employments for their savings in distant lands. But in Britain coal, iron and steel, railways, locomotives, ships, textile machinery, buildings and bridges were commanding an increasing share of the national product. For producing these, capital was what counted. Agriculture, with its peculiar dependence on land, contributed a diminishing share of total product. The man who owned or controlled capital could now command the needed labor and land. Control of labor or land accorded no reciprocal power to command capital.

So power over the enterprise passed to capital. And so did prestige in the community and authority in the state. At the beginning of the nineteenth century the British Parliament was still dominated by the great landed families. By the middle of the century they were acceding to industrial pressure to lower the price of food, and therewith the level of factory wages, at the expense of their rents. Thus the repeal of the Corn Laws. By the end of the century the premier figure in British politics was the great Birmingham industrialist and pioneer screw manufacturer, Joseph Chamberlain. At the beginning of the century, the United States government was dominated by landed and slave-owning gentlemen of Virginia; by the end of the century, by common agreement, power had passed, depending on point of view, to the men of enterprise or the malefactors of great wealth. The Senate had become a club of rich businessmen and was so described.

The change, a point of much importance for what follows, did not seem natural. George Washington, Thomas Jefferson and James Madison seemed far more appropriate to positions of public power than Collis P. Huntington, J. P. Morgan or Andrew W. Mellon. The former were credited with capacity for action apart from their own interests, as the capitalists were not. And action in their own interest—the defense, for example, of slavery—seemed more gentlemanly, reasonable and legitimate than action by the capitalists in their own behalf. This contrasting impression still survives in public attitudes and the elementary history books. We may lay it down as a rule that the older the exercise of any power, the more benign it will appear, and the more recent its assumption, the more unnatural and even dangerous it will seem.

5

It will now be clear what accords power to a factor of production or to those who own or control it. Power goes to the factor which is hardest to obtain or hardest to replace. In precise language, it adheres to the one that has the greatest inelasticity of supply at the margin. This inelasticity may be the result of a natural shortage, or an effective control over supply by some human agency, or both.[12]

In its age, if one had land, then labor and capital (in the meager amounts required) could readily be obtained. But to have operating capital and the common ability to hire labor did not so readily ensure that a man could get land. There was an admixture here of cause and effect. Because land provided special access to economic and larger power, steps were taken, as through the laws of entail, to confine possession to the privileged or noble caste. And this, in turn, limited the opportunities for acquiring it and further increased the economic power and social authority which, from one generation to the next, land conferred on its owner.

In the ensuing age of capital, land was readily available in the minor amounts required for industrial enterprise, and increasingly so for agriculture. Labor continued to be plentiful. Now possession of land and labor did not allow one to command capital; but with capital, land and labor could easily be obtained. Capital now accorded power in the enterprise and in consequence in the society.

Should it happen that capital were to become abundant, or redundant, and thus be readily increased or replaced, the power it confers, both in the enterprise and in the society, would be expected to suffer. This would seem especially profitable if, at the same time, some other factor of production should prove increasingly difficult to add or replace.

6

The last chapter showed that in the planning system, while capital is used in large amounts, it is, at least in peacetime,

[12]Thus union organization, which accords considerable power to labor in relation to such specific decisions as those affecting wages and working conditions, involves a full control of supply. (In a successful strike the supply price of labor on the plant side of the picket line is infinitely high.) The union power is increased if the supply of labor is not too abundant.

abundantly supplied. The tendency to an excess of savings, and the need for an offsetting strategy by the state, is an established feature of the Keynesian economy. These savings, we have seen, are supplied by the large industrial enterprise to itself as part of its planning. There is a comparatively high certainty as to their availability, for this is the purpose of the planning.

At the same time the requirements of technology and planning have greatly increased the need of the industrial enterprise for specialized talent and for its organization. The planning system must rely, in the main, on external sources for this talent. Unlike capital it is not something that the firm can supply in any comprehensive fashion to itself. To be effective, this talent must also be in an organization. Given a competent business organization, capital is now ordinarily available. But the mere possession of capital is now no guarantee that the requisite talent can be obtained and organized. This being so, one should expect, from past experience, to find a new shift of power in the industrial enterprise, this time from capital to organized intelligence. And one would expect that this shift would be reflected in the deployment of power in the society at large.

This has, indeed, occurred. There has been a shift of power as between the factors of production which matches that which occurred from land to capital in the advanced countries beginning two centuries ago. It is an occurrence of the last fifty years and is still going on. A dozen matters of commonplace observation—the loss of power by stockholders in the modern corporation earlier observed, the impregnable position of the successful corporate management, the dwindling social magnetism of the banker in contrast with that of J. P. Morgan or Andrew Mellon, the air of quaintness that attaches to the suggestion that the United States is run from Wall Street, the energetic search for industrial talent, the prestige of education and educators—all attest the point.

This shift of power had been disguised because, as was once true of land, the position of capital is held to be immutable. That power should be elsewhere seems unnatural, and those who so argue are in search of frivolous novelty. And the shift in power has been disguised because power has not gone to another of the established factors as they are celebrated in conventional economic pedagogy. It has not passed to labor. Labor has won limited authority over its pay and working conditions but none over the enterprise. And it still tends to abundance. If overly abundant savings are not used, one consequence is a substitution of machine processes for unskilled labor and standard skills. Thus unskilled labor and workers with conventional skills suffer, along with the capitalist, from an abundance of capital.[13]

Nor has power passed to the classical entrepreneur—the individual who once used his access to capital to bring it into combination with the other factors of production. He is a diminishing figure in the planning system. Apart from access to capital, his principal qualifications were imagination, capacity for decision and courage in risking money, including, not infrequently, his own. None of these qualifications is especially important for organizing intelligence or effective in competing with it.

Power has, in fact, passed to what anyone in search of novelty might be justified in calling a new factor of production. This is the association of men of diverse technical knowledge, experience or other talent which modern industrial technology and planning require. It extends from the leadership of the modern industrial enterprise down to just short of the labor force and embraces a large number of people and a large variety of talent. It is on the effectiveness of this organization, as most business doctrine agrees, that the success of the modern business enterprise now depends. Were this organization dismembered or otherwise lost, it could not easily be recreated. To create one for a new task is a difficult, costly and uncertain undertaking. As before with land and later with capital, power goes with what is difficult, costly and uncertain of procurement. So it is with organization—organized competence—that the power now lies. Our next task is to examine in some depth this new locus of power in the business enterprise and in the society.

[13]As would be expected, the shift in power is also subject to interruption and even reversal when savings are less than investment demand and when monetary policy—high interest rates and restricted bank lending—is used to curtail investment and thus to control or attempt to control inflation. Although the primary effect is on smaller firms in industries (such as housing) that are heavily dependent on borrowed funds, even the occasional large firm will find difficulty in supplying itself with capital. Under such circumstances its management must defer to banks and other sources of funds and, on occasion, accord them power over some decisions.

VI

The Technostructure

> ". . . the prevalence of group, instead of individual, action is a striking characteristic of management organization in the large corporation."
>
> —R. A. Gordon

THE INDIVIDUAL has far more standing in our culture than the group. An individual has a presumption of accomplishment; a committee has a presumption of inaction.[1] We react sympathetically to the individual who seeks to safeguard his personality from engulfment by the mass. We call for proof, at least in principle, before curbing his aggressions. Individuals have souls; corporations are notably soulless. The entrepreneur—individualistic, ruthless, with vision, guile and courage—has been the economist's only hero. The great business organization arouses no similar admiration. Admission to heaven is individually and by families; the top management, even of an enterprise with an excellent corporate image, cannot yet go in as a group. To have, in pursuit of truth, to assert the superiority of the organization over the individual for important social tasks is a taxing prospect.

Yet it is a necessary task. It is not to individuals but to or-

[1] Writers on management usually feel obliged to apologize before telling of the usefulness of committee action. "Of the various mechanisms of management, none is more controversial than committees . . . Despite their alleged shortcomings, committees are an important device of administration." Paul E. Holden, Lounsbury S. Fish and Hubert L. Smith, *Top Management Organization and Control* (New York: McGraw-Hill, 1951), p. 59.

"Someone has facetiously suggested that a camel is a horse that was put together by a committee. As the tone of the comment suggests, committees have their critics. In spite of their weaknesses, however, the general consensus among administrators is that committees are essential in managing large organizations and often useful in managing smaller groups." Justin G. Longnecker, *Principles of Management and Organizational Behavior*, 3rd ed. (Columbus: Charles E. Merrill, 1973), p. 263.

ganizations that power in the business enterprise and power in the society have passed. And modern economic society can only be understood as an effort, wholly successful, to synthesize by organization a group personality far superior *for its purposes* to a natural person, and with the added advantage of immortality.

The need for such a group personality begins with the circumstance that in modern industry a large number of decisions, and *all* that are important, draw on information possessed by more than one man.[2] Typically they draw on the specialized scientific and technical knowledge, the accumulated information or experience and the artistic or intuitive sense of many persons. And this is guided by further information which is assembled, analyzed and interpreted by professionals using highly technical equipment. The final decision will be informed only as it draws systematically on all those whose information is relevant. Nor, human beings what they are, can it take all of the information that is offered at face value. There must, additionally, be a mechanism for testing each person's contribution for its relevance and reliability as it is brought to bear on the decision.

2

The need to draw on, and appraise, the information of numerous individuals in modern industrial decision-making has three principal points of origin. It derives, first, from the technological requirements of modern industry. It is not that these are always inordinately sophisticated; a man of moderate genius could, quite conceivably, provide himself with the knowledge of the various branches of metallurgy and chemistry, and of engineering, procurement, production management, quality control, labor relations, styling and merchandising which are involved in the development of a modern motorcar. But even moderate genius is in unpredictable supply, and to keep abreast of all these branches of

[2]"The purpose of organization is to exploit the fact that many (virtually all) decisions require the participation of many individuals for their effectiveness." Kenneth J. Arrow, "On the Agenda of Organizations" in *The Corporate Society*, Robin Marris, ed. (New York: Wiley, 1974), p. 224. Professor Arrow uses the term "organization" in a larger sense than do I, and here to embrace the exchange of information through the market. Some of the contributors to Professor Marris's excellent volume conclude (p. 239) "that our entire contemporary society is a 'world of organizations.'"

science, engineering and art would be time-consuming even
for a genius. The elementary solution, which allows of the
use of far more common talent and with far greater predict-
ability of result, is to have men who are appropriately qualified or experienced in each limited area of specialized
knowledge or art. Their information is then combined for
carrying out the design and production of the vehicle. It is a
common public impression, not discouraged by scientists, engineers and industrialists, that modern scientific, engineering
and industrial achievements are the work of a new and quite
remarkable race of men. This is pure vanity; were it so, there
would be few such achievements. The real accomplishment of
modern science and technology consists in taking quite ordinary men, informing them narrowly and deeply and then,
through appropriate organization, arranging to have their
knowledge combined with that of other specialized but
equally ordinary men. This dispenses with the need for
genius. The resulting performance, though less inspiring, is
far more predictable. No individual genius arranged the
flights to the moon. It was the work of organization—bureaucracy. And the men walking on the moon and contemplating their return could be glad it was so. Few things
could more reliably cultivate thought than to be on the moon
and dependent on some single and perhaps eccentric genius
to get you back.

The second factor requiring the combination of specialized
talent derives from advanced technology, the associated use
of capital and the resulting need for planning with its accompanying control of the external factors bearing on this planning. The market is, in remarkable degree, an intellectually
undemanding institution. The Wisconsin farmer, aforementioned, need not anticipate his requirements for fertilizers,
pesticides or even machine parts; the market stocks and supplies them. The cost of these is substantially the same
for the man of intelligence and for his neighbor who, under
medical examination, shows daylight in either ear. And the
farmer need have no price or selling strategy; the market
takes all his milk at the ruling price. Much of the appeal of
the market, to economists in particular, has been from the
way it seems to simplify life. Better orderly error than complex truth.

For complexity enters with planning and is endemic
thereto. The manufacturer of missiles, space vehicles or mili-

tary aircraft, the extreme cases, must foresee the requirements for specialized plant, specialized manpower, exotic
materials and intricate components, and take steps to ensure
their availability when they are needed. For procuring such
things, we have seen, the market is either unreliable or unavailable. And there is no open market for the finished product. Everything here depends on the care and skill with which
contracts are sought and nurtured in Washington or in White-
hall, Paris or Tehran.

The same foresight and responding action are required, in
lesser degree, from manufacturers of automobiles, processed
foods and detergents. They too must foresee requirements
and manage markets. Planning, in short, requires a great variety of information. It requires variously informed men and
men who are suitably specialized in obtaining the requisite information. There must be men whose knowledge allows them
to foresee need and to ensure a supply of labor, materials,
and other production requirements; those who have the
knowledge to plan price strategies and see that customers are
suitably persuaded to buy at these prices; those who, at
higher levels of technology, are so informed that they can
work effectively with the state to see that it is suitably guided;
and those who can organize the flow of information that the
above tasks and many others require. Thus to the requirements of technology for specialized technical and scientific
talent are added the very large further requirements of the
planning that technology makes necessary.

Finally, following from the need for this variety of specialized talent, is the need for its coordination. Talent must be
brought to bear on the common purpose. More specifically,
on large and small matters information must be extracted
from the various specialists, tested for its reliability and relevance, and made to yield a decision. This process, which is
much misunderstood, requires a special word.

3

The modern business organization, or that part which has to
do with guidance and direction, consists of numerous individuals who are engaged, at any given time, in obtaining, digest-
ing or exchanging and testing information. A very large part
of the exchange and testing of information is by word of
mouth—a discussion in an office, at lunch, with alcohol or
over the telephone. But the most typical procedure is through

the committee and the committee meeting. One can do worse than think of a business organization as a hierarchy of committees. Coordination, in turn, consists in assigning the appropriate talent to committees, intervening on occasion to force a decision, and, as the case may be, announcing the decision or carrying it as information for a yet further decision by a yet higher committee.

Nor should it be supposed that this is an inefficient procedure. On the contrary, it is, normally, the only efficient procedure. Association in a committee enables each member to come to know the intellectual resources and the reliability of his colleagues. Committee discussion enables members to pool information under circumstances which allow, also, of immediate probing to assess the relevance and reliability of the information offered. Uncertainty about one's information or error is revealed as in no other way. There is also, no doubt, considerable stimulus to mental effort from such association. One may enjoy torpor in private but not so comfortably in public, at least during working hours. Men who believe themselves deeply engaged in private thought are usually thinking of nothing important. Committees are condemned by those who have been captured by the cliché that individual effort is somehow superior to group effort; by those who guiltily suspect that since group effort is more congenial, it must be less productive; by those who do not see that the process of extracting, and especially of testing, information has necessarily a somewhat undirected quality—briskly conducted meetings invariably decide matters previously decided; and by those who fail to realize that highly paid men, when sitting around a table as a committee, are not necessarily wasting more time than, in the aggregate, they would each waste in a private office by themselves.[3, 4] Forthright and determined administra-

---

[3]Also committees are not, as commonly supposed, alike. Some are constituted not to pool and test information and offer a decision but to accord representation to diverse bureaucratic, pecuniary, political, ideological or other interests. And a particular committee may have some of both purposes. A committee with representational functions will proceed much less expeditiously, for its ability to reach a conclusion depends on the susceptibility of its participants to compromise, attrition and cupidity. The representational committee, in its present form, is engaged in a zero sum game, which is to say what some win others lose. Pooling and testing information is nonzero sum—all participants end with a larger score.

[4]Corporate decision-making is, also, not the expeditious process often imagined. "It is very illuminating to trace the history of an important

tors frequently react to belief in the superior capacity of individuals for decision by abolishing all committees. They then constitute working parties, task forces or executive groups in order to avoid the one truly disastrous consequence of their action, which would be that they would have to make the decisions themselves.

Thus decision in the modern business enterprise is the product not of individuals but of groups. The groups are numerous, as often informal as formal, and subject to constant change in composition. Each contains the men possessed of the information, or with access to the information, that bears on the particular decision, together with those whose skill consists in extracting and testing this information and obtaining a conclusion. This is how men act successfully on matters where no single one, however exalted or intelligent, has more than a fraction of the necessary knowledge. It is what makes modern business possible, and in other contexts it is what makes modern government possible. It is fortunate that men of limited knowledge are so constituted that they can work together in this way. Were it otherwise, business and government, at any given moment, would be at a standstill awaiting the appearance of a man with the requisite breadth of knowledge to resolve the problem presently at hand. Some further characteristics of group decision-making must now be noticed.

4

Group decision-making extends deeply into the business enterprise. Effective participation is not closely related to rank in the formal hierarchy of the organization. This takes an effort of mind to grasp. Everyone is influenced by the stereotyped organization chart of the business enterprise. At its top is the board of directors and the chairman of the board; next comes the president; next come the executive vice president and other viceregal figures; thereafter come the department or divisional heads—those who preside over the Chevrolet division, the large-generators division, the computer division.

---

decision in a major corporation. The length of the process (often a matter of years) and the complexity of its vicissitudes will very likely astonish those who think of the firm as a tightly run autocracy." William J. Baumol and Maco Stewart, "On the Behavioral Theory of the Firm" in *The Corporate Economy*, Robin Marris and Adrian Wood, eds. (Cambridge: Harvard University Press, 1971), p. 139.

Power is assumed to pass down from the pinnacle. Those at the top give orders; those below relay them on or respond.

This happens, but only in very simple organizations—the peacetime drill of the National Guard or a troop of Boy Scouts moving out on Saturday maneuvers. Elsewhere the decision will require information. Some power will then pass to the person or persons who have this information. If this knowledge is highly particular to themselves, then their power becomes very great. In Los Alamos, during the development of the atomic bomb, Enrico Fermi rode a bicycle up the hill to work; Major General Leslie R. Groves presided in grandeur over the entire Manhattan District. In association with his similarly situated co-workers Fermi could, at various early stages, have brought the entire enterprise to an end.[5] No such power-resided with Groves. At any moment he could have been replaced without loss.

When power is exercised by a group, not only does it pass into the organization but it passes irrevocably. If an individual has taken a decision, he can be called before another individual who is his superior in the hierarchy, his information can be examined and his decision reversed by the greater wisdom or experience of the superior. But if the decision required the combined information of a group, it cannot be safely reversed by an individual. He will have to get the judgment of other specialists. This returns the power once more to organization.

No one should insist, in these matters, on pure cases. There will often be instances when an individual has the knowledge to modify or change the finding of a group. But the board rule holds: if a decision requires the specialized knowledge of a group of men, it is subject to safe review only by the similar knowledge of a similar group. Group decision, unless acted upon by another group, tends to be absolute.[6]

[5]He was head of the Advanced Development Division of the Los Alamos Laboratory. His slightly earlier work was central to the conclusion that a self-sustaining chain reaction was possible. Cf. Henry De Wolf Smyth, *Atomic Energy for Military Purposes* (Princeton: Princeton University Press, 1945).

[6]I reached some of these conclusions during World War II when, in the early years, I was in charge of price control. Decisions on prices—to fix, raise, rearrange or, very rarely, to lower them—came to my office after an extensive exercise in group decision-making in which lawyers, economists, accountants, men knowledgeable of the product and industry and specialists in public righteousness had all participated. Alone one was nearly helpless to alter such decisions; hours or days o

5

Next it must not be supposed that group decision is important only in such evident instances as nuclear technology or space mechanics. Simple products are made and packaged by sophisticated processes. And the most massive programs of market control, together with the most specialized marketing talent, are used on behalf of soap, detergents, cigarettes, aspirin, packaged cereals and gasoline. These, beyond others, are the valued advertising accounts. The simplicity and uniformity of these products require the investment of compensatingly elaborate science and art to suppress market influences and make prices and amounts sold subject to the largest possible measure of control. For these products too, decision passes to a group which combines specialized and esoteric knowledge. Here too, power goes deeply and more or less irrevocably into the organization.

For purposes of pedagogy, I for many years illustrated these principles by reference to a technically uncomplicated product, which, unaccountably, General Electric has yet to place on the market.[7] It is a toaster of standard performance, the pop-up kind, except that it etches on the surface of the toast, in darker carbon, one of a selection of standard messages or designs. For the elegant, an attractive monogram would be available or a coat of arms; for the devout at breakfast, there would be an appropriate devotional message from the Reverend Billy Graham; for the patriotic or worried, there would be an aphorism urging vigilance from the late J. Edgar Hoover; for modern painters and economists,

---

investigation would be required and, in the meantime, a dozen other decisions would have been made. Given what is commonly called an "adequate" staff, one could have exercised control. But an adequate staff would be one that largely duplicated the decision-making group with adverse effect on the good nature and sense of responsibility of the latter and even more on the time required for decision. To have responsibility for all of the prices in the United States was awesome; to discover how slight was one's power in face of group decision-making was sobering. President Kennedy enjoyed responding to proposals for public action by saying, "I agree but I don't know whether the government will agree."

[7] Since the first edition of this book appeared, I have been advised by a number of people that they had the same inspiration. A British engineer informed me that he developed the device while on fire watch in London in World War II.

there would be a purely abstract design. A restaurant version
would sell advertising.

Conceivably this is a vision that could come from the
president of General Electric. But the systematic proliferation
of such ideas is the designated function of much more lowly
men who are charged with product development. At an early
stage in the development of the toaster the participation of
specialists in engineering, production, styling and design and
possibly philosophy, art and spelling would have to be sought.
No one in a position to authorize the product would do so
without a judgment on how the problems of inscription were
to be solved and at what cost. Nor, ordinarily, would an adverse finding on technical and economic feasibility be over-
ridden. At some stage further development would become
contingent on the findings of market researchers and mer-
chandise experts on whether the toaster could be sold and at
what price. Nor would an adverse decision by this group be
overruled. In the end there would be a comprehensive finding
on the feasibility of the innovation. If unfavorable this would
not be overruled. Nor, given the notoriety that attaches to
lost opportunity, would be the more plausible contingency of
a favorable recommendation. It will be evident that nearly all
power—initiation, character of development, rejection or acceptance—are exercised deep in the company. It is not the
managers who decide. Effective power of decision is lodged
deeply down in the technical, planning and other specialized
staff.[8]

6

We must notice next that this exercise of group power can be
rendered unreliable or ineffective by external interference.
Not only does power pass into the organization but the quality of decision can easily be impaired by the efforts of an individual to retain control over the decision-making process.

Specifically, the group reaches a decision by receiving and
evaluating the specialized information of its members. If it is
to act responsibly, it must be accorded responsibility. It cannot be arbitrarily or capriciously overruled. If it is, it will develop the same tendencies to irresponsibility as an individual
similarly treated.

[8]". . . the power of the firm's higher officers to enforce a decision
is severely restricted by middle management's ability to delay or to act
only with limited drive and enthusiasm." Baumol and Stewart. Ibid.

But the tendency will be far more damaging. The efficiency of the group and the quality of its decisions depend on the quality of the information provided and the precision with which it is tested. The last increases greatly as men work together. It comes to be known that some are reliable and that some, though useful, are at a tacit discount. All information offered must be weighed. The sudden intervention of a superior introduces information, often of dubious quality, that is not subject to this testing. His reliability, as a newcomer, is unknown; his information, since he is boss, may be automatically exempt from the proper discount; or his intervention may take the form of an instruction and thus be outside the process of group decision in a matter where only group decision incorporating the required specialized judgments is reliable. In all cases the intrusion is damaging. All with experience of large-scale business or government know the amount of time that informed juniors spend on considering how to contend with ill-informed superiors.

It follows from both the tendency for decision-making to pass down into organization and the need to protect the autonomy of the group that those who hold high formal rank in an organization—the president of General Motors or General Electric—exercise only modest powers of substantive decision. This power is far less than conventional obeisance, professional public relations or, on occasion, personal vanity insist. Decision and ratification are often confused. The first is important; the second is not. There is a further tendency to associate power with any decision, however routine, that involves a good deal of money. The most formidable business protocol requires that money be treated with solemnity and respect, and therewith the man who passes on its use. The nominal head of a large corporation, though with slight power and perhaps in the first stages of retirement, is also visible, tangible and comprehensible. It is tempting and perhaps valuable for the corporate personality to attribute to him power of decision that, in fact, belongs to a dull and not easily comprehended collectivity.[9] Nor is it a valid explanation that the boss, though impotent on specific questions, acts on broad issues of policy. Such issues of policy, if genuine, are pre-eminently the ones that require the specialized information of the group.

Leadership assigns tasks to committees from which deci-

[9] I return to these matters in the next chapter.

sions emerge. In doing so, it can break usefully with the routine into which organization tends to fall. And it selects the men who comprise the groups that make the decisions, and it constitutes and reconstitutes these groups in accordance with changing need. This is, perhaps, its most important function. In an economy where organized intelligence is the decisive factor of production, the selection of the intelligence so organized is of central importance. But it cannot be supposed that a boss can replace or even second-guess organized intelligence on substantive decisions.[10]

7

In the past, leadership in business organization was identified with the entrepreneur—the individual who united ownership or control of capital with the capacity for organizing the other factors of production and, in most contexts, with a further capacity for innovation.[11] With the rise of the modern corporation, the emergence of the organization required by modern technology and planning and the divorce of the owner of the capital from control of the enterprise, the entrepreneur no longer exists as an individual person in the mature industrial enterprise.[12] Everyday discourse, except in the economics textbooks, recognizes this change. It replaces the entrepreneur, as the directing force of the enterprise, with management. This is a collective and imperfectly defined entity; in the large corporation it embraces chairman, president, those vice presidents with important staff or departmental responsibility, occupants of other major staff positions and, perhaps, division or department heads not included

[10]Since the earlier editions of this book appeared, my colleague and neighbor, Daniel Bell, has published his important and widely discussed *The Coming of Post-Industrial Society: A Venture in Social Forecasting* (New York: Basic Books, 1973). Proceeding from a quite different departure point in sociology and social theory, Bell concludes, as here, that modern economic society requires extensive planning for which knowledge is the decisive resource.

[11]"To act with confidence beyond the range of familiar beacons and to overcome that resistance requires aptitudes that are present in only a small fraction of the population and that define the entrepreneurial type as well as the entrepreneurial function." Joseph A. Schumpeter *Capitalism, Socialism, and Democracy*, 2nd ed. (New York: Harper, 1947), p. 132.

[12]He is still, of course, to be found in smaller firms and in larger ones that have yet to reach full maturity of organization. I deal with this evolution in the next chapters.

above. It includes, however, only a small proportion of those who, as participants, contribute information to group decisions. This latter group is very large; it extends from the most senior officials of the corporation to where it meets, at the outer perimeter, the white- and blue-collar workers whose function is to conform more or less mechanically to instruction or routine. It embraces all who bring specialized knowledge, talent or experience to group decision-making. This, not the narrow management group, is the guiding intelligence—the brain—of the enterprise. There is no name for all who participate in group decision-making or the organization which they form. I propose to call this organization the Technostructure.

VII

The Corporation

FEW SUBJECTS of solemn inquiry have been more unproductive than study of a modern large corporation. The reasons are clear. A vivid image of what *should* exist acts as a surrogate for reality. Pursuit of the image then prevents pursuit of the reality.

For purposes of scholarly discussion, the corporation has a sharp legal image. Its purpose is to do business as would an individual but with the added ability to assemble and use the capital of several or numerous persons. In consequence, it can undertake tasks beyond the financial reach of any single person. And it protects those who supply capital by limiting their liability to the amount of their original investment, ensuring them a vote on the significant affairs of the enterprise, defining the powers and the responsibilities of directors and officers, and giving them access to the courts to redress grievance. Apart from its ability to mobilize capital and its lessened association with the active life of any individual, the corporation is not deemed to differ functionally from the individual proprietorship or partnership. Its purpose, like theirs, is to conduct business on equitable terms with other businesses and make money for the owners.

Such corporations do exist and in large numbers. But one wonders if the natural interest of the student of economics is the local paving firm or body repair shop. Or is it General Motors, Exxon, IBM and General Electric?

These firms, however, depart sharply from the legal image. In none of these firms is the capital pooled by original investors appreciable; in each it could be paid off by a few hours' or a few days' earnings. In none does the individual stockholder pretend to power. In all four cases, the corporation is far more influential in the markets in which it buys materials, components and labor and in which it sells its finished products than is commonly imagined to be the case with the individual proprietorship.

In consequence, nearly all study of the corporation has been concerned with its deviation from its legal or formal image. This image—that of "an association of persons into an autonomous legal unit with a distinct legal personality that enables it to carry on business, own property and contract debts"[1]—is highly normative. It is what a corporation should be. When the modern corporation disenfranchises its stockholders, becomes gargantuan, expands into wholly unrelated activities, has the powers of a monopsony where it buys and of a monopoly where it sells, something is exceptional and also dubious or wrong.

That the largest and most famous corporations, those whose names are household words and whose heads are accorded the most distinguished honors by their fellow businessmen, should be considered abnormal must itself seem a little dubious.

Additionally, it must be evident that General Motors does not have much in common with the scientists who pool their personal funds and what they can borrow from the banks and their friends to supply some erudite item to the Department of Defense and thus, in their modest way, help to defend their country and participate in capital gains. Their enterprise, created, owned and directed by themselves and exploiting the advantages of the corporate form, clearly approaches the established image. General Motors as clearly does not.

The answer is that there is no such thing as *a* corporation. Rather there are several kinds of corporations all deriving from a common, flexible and highly accommodating legal framework. Some are subject to the market; others reflect varying degrees of adaptation to the requirements of planning and the needs of the technostructure. The person who sets out to study buildings on Manhattan on the assumption that all are alike will have difficulty in passing from the surviving brownstones to the skyscrapers. And he will handicap himself ever more if he imagines that all buildings should be like brownstones and have load-carrying walls and that others are abnormal. So precisely it is with the study of corporations.

[1]Harry G. Guthmann and Herbert E. Dougall, *Corporate Financial Policy*, 2nd ed. (New York: Prentice-Hall, 1948), p. 9.

2

The most obvious requirement of effective planning is large size. This, we have seen, allows the firm to accept market uncertainty where it cannot be eliminated; to eliminate markets on which otherwise it would be excessively dependent; to control other markets in which it buys and sells; and it is very nearly indispensable for participation in that part of the economy characterized by exacting technology and comprehensive planning where the only buyer is the federal government.

That corporations accommodate well to this need for size has scarcely to be stressed. They can, and have, become very large. But because of the odor of abnormality, this adaptation is not stressed. The head of the largest corporation is automatically accorded precedence at all business conventions, meetings and other business rites and festivals. He is the most warmly complimented—for his intelligence, vision, courage, progressiveness and for the remarkable rate of growth of his firm under his direction. But the great size of his firm—the value of its assets or the number of its employees—is not praised, although this is its most striking feature.

Nothing so characterizes the planning system as the scale of the modern corporate enterprise. In 1976, the five largest industrial corporations, with combined assets of $113 billion, had just under 13 percent of all assets used in manufacturing. The 50 largest manufacturing corporations had 42 percent of all assets. The 500 largest had 72 percent.[2]

In the same year corporations with assets of more than a billion dollars, 162 in all, had 54 percent of all assets in manufacturing; corporations with assets of more than $100 million had approximately four fifths of assets; and 3801 firms with assets of more than $10 million had 89 percent of all assets.[3] The largest five manufacturing corporations in terms of employment employed 11 percent of the working force engaged in manufacturing. The largest 15 percent employed one fifth of all workers in manufacturing; these 15 corporations employed more individual workers than the agricultural labor force. Two corporations—American Telephone and

[2] *Fortune*, May 1977. *Quarterly Financial Report for Manufacturing, Mining and Trade Corporations*, Fourth Quarter, 1976 (1977) (Federal Trade Commission-Securities and Exchange Commission), p. 66.
[3] *Quarterly Financial Report*.

Telegraph and General Motors—employed 2 percent of the United States employed civilian labor force.[4]

In 1976, 100 great corporations had 69 percent of all prime defense contracts; the weapons industry is the nearly exclusive preserve of the great enterprise. In 1974, as noted, 126 large firms performed nearly three quarters of all industrial research and development and received 93 percent of all federal support for such work. In the same year four corporations performed nearly one fifth of all such research (the great bulk paid for by the government).[5]

Planning is a function that is associated in most minds with the state. If the corporation is the basic planning unit, it is appropriate that the scale of operations of the largest should approximate that of the government. This it does. In 1976, the three largest industrial corporations, Exxon, General Motors and Ford, had a combined gross income of $125 billion.[6] (This exceeded—by about $20 billion—the total income, including government payments, of all farms in the country.[7]) In 1976, Exxon, with gross revenues of $48.6 billion,[8] had more than a hundred times the revenue of the state of Nevada, more than three times the revenue of the state of New York[9] and about one sixth of the total receipts of the federal government.[10]

There is no evidence of any weakening of the trend either to larger and larger firms or to those having an ever greater share of the total output. One of the leading students of these trends has concluded that in the decade ". . . from 1954 to 1963 there was a moderate trend toward increasing concentration in individual manufacturing industries . . . and that this trend continued and accelerated from 1963 to 1966."[11]

[4] *Fortune*, May 1977 and *Fortune*, July 1977. *Economic Report of the President, 1977*, pp. 218, 224.

[5] *Research and Development in Industry*, 1974 (National Science Foundation, September 1976).

[6] *Fortune*, May 1977, p. 366.

[7] *Economic Report of the President, 1977*, p. 290.

[8] *Fortune*, May 1977. Ibid.

[9] The comparisons to Nevada and New York are estimates based on the total general revenues in those states in 1975. See United States Bureau of the Census, *Governmental Finances in 1974–1975* (Washington: U.S. Government Printing Office, 1976), p. 47.

[10] *Economic Report of the President, 1977*, p. 267.

[11] Joe S. Bain, "Changes in Concentration in Manufacturing Industries in the U.S., 1947–1966: Trends and Relationships to the Levels of 1954 Concentration," *Review of Economics and Statistics*, Vol. LII, No. 4 (November 1970), p. 416.

An examination of these and slightly later years by Willard F. Mueller and Larry G. Hamm has identified a "dramatic increase in market concentration in consumer goods industries"[12] which they associate with the planning gains from large-scale advertising. Concentration in producer goods industries, already high, showed no great change. One subjective indication of this continuing concentration has been the reaction of the motivated academic defenders of the classical market of many small firms. In the past, faced with evidence of increasing scale and concentration, they labored with a manipulative ingenuity and diligence that might, perhaps have been better employed to show that concentration of industry, however great, had not much increased since, say, 1900. This effort, one judges, has now been largely given up. Some truths are beyond even statistical assault.

Concentration of economic activity in a few firms of great size is not an American peculiarity. In Britain in 1909, the hundred largest manufacturing enterprises had an estimated 16 percent of all net manufacturing output. By 1958, the share of the hundred largest had doubled to 33 percent. By 1970, it had nearly tripled to an approximate 45 percent.[13] Fréderic L. Pryor, in an important study, has shown what common observation will suggest. The level of industrial concentration—the broad division as between market system and planning system—is, for all practical purposes, in all mature industrial countries, the same.[14]

Economists have long derived much pleasure from debate over the reasons for the great size of the modern corporation. It is because size is essential in order to reap the economies of modern large-scale production?[15] Is it, more insidiously, because the big firm wishes to exercise monopoly power in its markets? The present analysis allows both parties to the controversy to be partly right. The firm must be large enough

[12]Willard F. Mueller and Larry G. Hamm, "Trends in Industrial Market Concentration, 1947 to 1970," *Review of Economics and Statistics*, Vol. LVI, No. 4 (November 1974), p. 519.

[13]S. J. Prais, "A New Look at the Growth of Industrial Concentration," *Oxford Economic Papers*, Vol. 26, No. 2 (July 1974), p. 273 et seq.

[14]Frederic L. Pryor, "An International Comparison of Concentration Ratios," *Review of Economics and Statistics*, Vol. LIV, No. 2 (May 1972), p. 130 et seq.

[15]Cf. Joe S. Bain, "Economies of Scale, Concentration, and the Condition of Entry in Twenty Manufacturing Industries," *American Economic Review*, Vol. 44, No. 1 (March 1954), p. 15 et seq.

to carry large capital commitments of modern technology. Thus the case for economies of scale. It must also be large enough to control its markets. Thus the case for monopoly as the goal. But the present view also explains what the older explanations do not. General Motors is not only large enough to afford the best size of automobile plant but it is large enough to afford a dozen or more of the best size. This cannot be explained by the economies of scale. It is also large enough to have the market power associated with monopoly. But consumers do not seriously complain of the exploitation classically associated with monopoly. The proper explanation is that General Motors is in the service not of monopoly or the economies of scale but of planning. And for this planning—control of supply, control of demand, provision of capital, minimization of risk—there is no clear upper limit to the desirable size. It could be that the bigger the better. The corporate form accommodates to this need. Quite clearly it allows the firm to be very, very large.

3

The corporation also accommodates itself admirably to the needs of the technostructure. This, to remind, is an apparatus for group decision-making—for pooling and testing the information provided by numerous individuals to reach decisions that are beyond the knowledge of any one. It requires, we have also seen, a high measure of autonomy. It is vulnerable to any intervention by external authority, for, given the nature of the group decision-making and the problems being solved, such external authority will always be incompletely informed and hence arbitrary. If problems were susceptible to decision by individuals, no group would be involved.

One possible source of such intervention is the state. The corporate charter, however, accords the corporation a large area of independent action in the conduct of its affairs. And this freedom is strongly defended. In the American business code nothing is so iniquitous as government interference in the *internal* affairs of the corporation. So strong is the protective convention that even radicals respect it. There is equally vehement resistance to any invasion by trade unions of the prerogatives of management, as, indignantly, they are called.

There is also, however, the danger of intervention by the owners—by the stockholders. Their exclusion is not secured by law or sanctified by custom. On the contrary, either directly or through the agency of the board of directors, their right of intervention is guaranteed. But being legal does not make such intervention benign. Exercise of such power on substantive questions requiring group decision would be as damaging as any other. So the stockholder too must be excluded.

In part this has been accomplished by the simple attrition of the stockholder's power as death and the distribution of estates, the diversifying instincts of trusts and foundations, the distributional effects of property settlements and alimony, and the artistic, philanthropic and social enjoyments of nonfunctional heirs all distribute the stock of any corporation to more and more hands. This process works rapidly, and the distribution need by no means be complete to separate the stockholder from all effective power.

In the mid nineteen-twenties, in the first case to draw wide public attention to this tendency, it became known that Colonel Robert W. Stewart, Chairman of the Board of Directors of the Standard Oil Company of Indiana, had, in concert with some of the men who later won immortality for their association with the Teapot Dome and Elk Hills transactions, organized a highly specialized enterprise in Canada called the Continental Trading Company. This company had the sole function of buying crude oil from Colonel E. A. Humphreys, owner of the rich Mexica field in east central Texas, and reselling it to companies controlled by the same individuals, including Standard Oil of Indiana, at a markup of twenty-five cents a barrel. It was an excellent business. No costs were involved, other than a small percentage to the distinguished Canadian lawyer who served as a figurehead (and went hunting in Africa when wanted for questioning) and for mailing back the proceeds after they had been converted into Liberty Bonds. (If some of these had not been used carelessly to bribe Secretary of the Interior Albert B. Fall and others to pay the deficit of the Republican National Committee, Continental might have forever remained unknown, as was unquestionably intended.) It was Colonel Stewart's later contention that he had always meant to turn over the profit to Standard Oil of Indiana. But, absentmindedly, he had allowed the bonds to remain in his own possession for many years and had cashed some of the coupons for his own use. In 1929, Standard of Indiana was only eighteen years distant from the decree which had broken up John D. Rockefeller's

Standard Oil empire, of which it had been an important part. The Rockefellers still owned 14.9 percent of the voting stock of the Indiana company and were deemed to have the controlling interest. They reacted sternly to the outrage; the elder Rockefeller had, on notable occasions, imposed a somewhat similar levy on his competitors but never on his own company. With the aid of the publicity generated by the Teapot Dome scandal, his own high standing in the financial community, his brother-in-law Winthrop W. Aldrich, who solicited proxies, and a very large expenditure of money, John D. Rockefeller, Jr., was able to oust the Colonel, although not by a wide margin.[16] (The latter had the full support of his board of directors who voted him their confidence. It was fitting, perhaps, that they should do so, for Stewart had selected them.) In the absence of the scandal and his ample resources, Rockefeller, it was realized with some shock, would have had little hope.

In most other large corporations, the chance for exerting such power would have been less, and it has become increasingly less with the passage of time. Professor Gordon's pre-World War II study of the 176 largest corporations showed that at least half of their stock was held in blocks of less than one percent of the total outstanding. In less than a third of the companies was there a stockholder interest large enough to allow of potential control, i.e., the election of a board of directors, and "the number of companies in which any large degree of *active* leadership is associated with considerable ownership is certainly even smaller."[17] That was a third of a century ago; the dispersion of stock ownership, which was then much greater for the older railroad corporations than for newer industrial corporations, has almost certainly contin-

---

[16]Cf. Adolf A. Berle, Jr., and Gardiner C. Means, *The Modern Corporation and Private Property* (New York: Macmillan, 1948), pp. 82–83. Of the 8,465,200 shares represented, Rockefeller got the votes of 5,510,313. Stewart retired on a pension of $75,000 a year. M. R. Werner and John Starr, *Teapot Dome* (New York: Viking Press, 1959), pp. 274–275.

[17]R. A. Gordon, *Business Leadership in the Large Corporation* (Washington: Brookings Institution, 1945), Chapter 2, p. 43. The median holdings of management were 2.1 percent of the stock. In 36 percent of the companies, management owned less than 1 percent; in only 16 of the companies did it own as much as 20 percent of the stock outstanding. A study by Mabel Newcomer, *The Big Business Executive* (New York: Columbia University Press, 1955), showed that by 1952 there had been a further reduction in management holdings.

ued.[18] It means that to change control, more stockholders must be persuaded, against the advice of management, to vote their stock for someone whom, in the nature of the case, they do not know and will not be disposed to trust. The effort must also contend with the tendency of the indifferent to give proxies to management. It is further in face of the requirement that the loser of a proxy battle, if he is an outsider, must pay the cost. And it must contend finally with the alternative, always available to the dissatisfied stockholder, of simply selling his stock. Corporate size, the passage of time and the dispersion of stock ownership do not disenfranchise the stockholder. Rather he can vote but his vote, if for management, is unnecessary and if against, futile. In other words, it is valueless.

4

To be secure in its autonomy, the technostructure also needs to have a source of new capital to which it can turn without having, as a *quid pro quo*, to surrender any authority over its own decisions. Here capital abundance enters as a factor. A bank, insurance company or investment banker cannot make control of decision, actual or potential, a condition of a loan or security underwriting if funds are readily available from another and more permissive source and if there is vigorous competition for the business.

The complexity of modern technological and planning decisions also protects the technostructure from outside interference. The country banker, out of his experience and knowledge of the business, can readily interpose his judgment as against that of a farmer on the prospects for feeder cattle—and does. Not even the most self-confident financier would wish to question the judgment of General Electric engineers, product planners, stylists, market researchers and sales executives on the culturally advanced toaster taken up in the last chapter. By taking decisions away from individuals and locating them deeply within the technostructure, technol-

---

[18]This is explicitly confirmed by a study by R. J. Larner, "Ownership and Control in the 200 Largest Nonfinancial Corporations, 1929 and 1963," *American Economic Review,* Vol. 56, No. 4, Part 1 (September 1966), p. 777 et seq. Professor Larner does not, however, accept the present argument that management control alters the incentives structure of the large firm. See his *Management Control and the Large Corporation* (New York: Dunellen Publishing Company, Inc., 1970).

ogy and planning thus remove them from the influence of outsiders.

But the corporation accords a much more specific protection to the technostructure. That is by providing it with a source of capital, derived from its own earnings, that is wholly under its own control. No banker can attach conditions as to how retained earnings are to be used. Nor can any other outsider. No one, the normally innocuous stockholder apart, has the right to ask about an investment from retained earnings that turns out badly. It is hard to overestimate the importance of the shift in power that is associated with the availability of such a source of capital. Few other developments can have more fundamentally altered the character of capitalism. It is hardly surprising that retained earnings of corporations have become such an overwhelmingly important source of capital.

5

There remains one final source of danger to the autonomy of the technostructure. That arises with a failure of earnings. Then there are no retained earnings. If new plant is needed or working capital must be replenished, there will have to be appeal to bankers or other outsiders. This will be under circumstances, i.e., the fact that the firm is showing losses, where the right of such outsiders to inquire and to intervene will have to be conceded. They cannot be told to mind their own business.[19] Thus does a shortage of capital, though limited in time and place, promptly revive the power of the capitalist. And it is in times of such failure of earnings that the stockholders of the large corporation become a threat to the power of management. The spontaneous stockholder uprising among, say, the 500 largest American corporations is so rare that it can be ignored. And among the very largest it is ignored, partly because, as will be noted presently, among these firms earnings rarely fail.

Below the level of the very largest there is the threat of a takeover bid. If earnings are indifferent, dividends low and stock values in consequence depressed, a controlling share of

[19]Although the habit dies hard. In 1970, when the Penn Central was seeking a government loan to forestall bankruptcy, an executive was asked if this would not mean government control. He replied he did not think the government would presume to interfere with private management decision.

stock can often be obtained by a bid at above current market levels.[20] If this succeeds, it is usually the prelude to some change in the top management or its prerogatives, and avoidance of this threat has, especially in recent times, become a factor in management calculation and incentives. But if revenues are good—they need not be at the maximum, for none will know what this is—and the corporation is safely large, creditors cannot intervene and stockholders cannot be aroused. And the stock will have a unit and aggregate value that places it beyond the threat of a takeover. The most important protection is a secure flow of earnings. Here too the corporation, and the planning system generally, have adapted most effectively to the needs and, in particular, to the protection of the technostructure, although, surprisingly, the nature of the adaptation has been little noticed.[21] The adaptation is, simply, that big corporations almost never lose money.[22] From 1954 through 1976, there were only two years in which as many as five of the hundred largest industrial corporations lost money. In seven of those twenty-three years, all of the hundred showed profits. Similarly, in eight of the twenty-two years from 1955 through 1976, all of the fifty largest merchandising corporations—Sears, Roebuck, A&P, Safeway, et al.—made money. In no year did more than five have losses.

The experience of the mature corporation in the 1974–1975 recession, the most severe economic downturn since the Great Depression, wonderfully underlines this point. Only four of the largest one hundred industrial firms lost money in 1974; only three in 1975.[23] Needless to say, the

---

[20]A management that is financially thus vulnerable will often, also, be in a condition of self-perpetuating mediocrity or obtuseness. A notable case in point was the United Fruit Company takeover by the corporate entrepreneur (or adventurer), Eli Black, which was chronicled in *An American Company: The Tragedy of United Fruit* (by Thomas P. McCann, edited by Henry Scammell [New York: Crown, 1976]). I have commented on this in the *New York Review of Books*, October 14, 1976.

[21]A most distinguished exception is William G. Shepherd, who stresses the high stability of the sales and earnings of the largest corporations and the increase in this stability in recent decades. William G. Shepherd, *Market Power and Economic Welfare* (New York: Random House, 1970).

[22]The railroads, which have not developed either a technostructure or effective planning control of costs, prices charged or market responses of their customers, are an exception among large corporations.

[23]"Directory of the 500 Largest Industrial Corporations"; "Directory of the 50 Largest Retailing Companies," *Fortune*, 1954–1977.

earnings performance of the mature corporations in the planning system was far more stable than that of the entrepreneurial firms on its fringes or outside.

Associated with the stability in earnings and in growth of the mature corporation is a great stability in its position in the planning system. The firms that comprised the largest hundred industrials ten or twenty years ago are, overwhelmingly, those that comprise that list today. Among the largest ten and especially the largest five, changes in membership or even in rank are comparatively rare. The fiction of the "representative firm" growing, aging, falling behind, being replaced by younger, more vigorous specimens, once much beloved by economists is, in this part of the economy, sadly in decline.[24] The great firm is unsparing of even the most agreeable myth.

The American business liturgy has long intoned that this is a profit-and-loss economy. "The American competitive enterprise system is an acknowledged profit and loss system, the hope of profits being the incentive and the fear of loss being the spur."[25] This may be so. But it is not true of that organized part of the economy in which a developed technostructure is able to protect its profits by planning. Nor is it true of the United States Steel Corporation, the employer of the author of the sentence just cited, which, when the lines were inscribed, had not had losses for a quarter of a century.

6

As always, no strong case is improved by overstatement. Among the two hundred largest corporations in the United States—those that form the heart of the planning system—there are few in which owners exercise any important influence on decisions. And this influence decreases year by year. But there are exceptions. The Du Pont and Ford descendants were long active in the firms that bore their name, although, since the early editions of this book, members of these families have ceased to hold the top positions. And in both cases the family members earned influence by being part of the technostructure. Other owners of stock, through their

---

[24]See the very important confirming study by David Mermelstein, "Large Industrial Corporations and Asset Shares," *American Economic Review,* Vol. LIX, No. 4, Part I (September 1969), p. 531 et seq.
[25]United States Steel Corporation, *Annual Report 1958.*

position on the board of directors, have some power in the selection of management—in deciding on those who, in the mature corporation, select those who collectively make decisions. And yet others may inform themselves and intervene substantively on individual decisions—a merger, a plant acquisition or the launching of a new line.

In the last case, however, there must always be question as to how much the individual is deciding and how much has been decided for him by the group which has provided the relevant information; the danger of confusing ratification with decision must again be emphasized. And in all circumstances it is important to realize that corporate ceremony more or less deliberately disguises the reality. This deserves a final word.

Corporate liturgy strongly emphasizes the power of the board of directors and ultimately, thus, of the stockholders they are assumed to represent. The rites which attest this point are conducted with much solemnity; no one allows himself to be cynical as to their lack of substance. Heavy dockets, replete with data, are submitted to the board. Recommendations are appended. Discussion is brief, stylized and superficial. Most of the participants are old men. Given the extent and character of the group preparation, rejection would be unthinkable. The board, nonetheless, is regularly left with the impression that it has made a decision.

Corporate procedure also allows the board to act on financial transactions—changes in capital structure, declaration of dividends, authorization of lines of credit. These, given the control by the technostructure of its sources of savings and capital supply, are frequently the most routine and derivative of decisions. But, as elsewhere noted, any association with large sums of money conveys an impression of power. It brings it to mind for the same traditional reasons as does a detachment of soldiers.

With even greater unction, although with less plausibility, corporate ceremony seeks also to give the stockholders an impression of power. When stockholders are (or were) in control of a company, stockholders' meetings are an occasion of scant ceremony. The majority is voted in and the minority is voted out, with such concessions as may seem strategic, and all understand the process involved. As stockholders cease to have influence, however, efforts are made to disguise this nullity. Their convenience is considered in selecting the place of meeting. They are presented with handsomely printed reports, the preparation of which is now a specialized business. Products and even plants are inspected. During the proceedings, as in the report, there are repetitive references to *your* company. Officers listen, with every evidence of attention, to highly irrelevant suggestions of wholly uninformed participants and assure them that these will be considered with the greatest care. Women stockholders in print dresses, who own ten shares, give votes of thanks "for the excellent skill with which you run *our* company," and these are received by the management with well-simulated gratitude. All present show stern disapproval of critics and especially of those who use the occasion to attack the social, political or military activities of the firm. No important stockholders are present. No decisions are taken. The annual meeting of the large American corporation is perhaps our most elaborate exercise in popular illusion.

In 1956, upwards of 100,000 stockholders of Bethlehem Steel returned proxies to a committee of the management. The management committee voted these routinely for a slate of directors selected by management exclusively from among its own members. The following colloquy occurred in Washington the next year:

> Senator Kefauver: The exhibit shows that the members of the Board of Directors paid themselves $6,499,000 in 1956.
> Mr. Homer (President of Bethlehem Steel Corporation): I wish to interpose there, Senator, we did not pay ourselves. I wish that term would not be used.
> Senator Kefauver: Very well, approved by the stockholders.
> Mr. Homer: That is better.[26, 27]

---

[26]Hearings before the Subcommittee on Antitrust and Monopoly of the Committee on the Judiciary, United States Senate, Eighty-fifth Congress, First Session, Pursuant to S. Res. 57, Part II. *Steel* (1957), p. 562.

[27]In 1966 or early 1967, when the first edition of this book was going to press, the alert editors of *Think,* the house organ of IBM, asked to see and then to publish this chapter—and arranged suitable compensation. It did not appear in the magazine. They later explained that, while the truth of the case was not in question, to inform their stockholders, as would this chapter, that they had no power would not be couth.

VIII

The Entrepreneur
and the Technostructure

THE CORPORATION allows the adaptation of organization to need. As the need is different for different purposes, so is the resulting adaptation. The modern large corporation is adapted to the needs of advanced technology and the large amounts of capital and comprehensive planning which this requires. It reflects the need of its technostructure for freedom from outside interference. It wins this freedom in various ways, including the provision to itself of its own supply of capital.

If technology is simple, the capital supply need not be large. Since markets then function more reliably, there is less opportunity and less need for planning. And for these reasons there is less need for specialized intelligence and associated organization. As a result, the firm can be small. The design and manufacture of jet engines or the design and construction of nuclear reactors are open only to the large firm. But the selling of gasoline at retail or the growing of apples remains available to the relatively small concern.

This firm, as noted, is subject to the market. It cannot influence the prices at which it buys or the quantities that are available at those prices. It cannot much influence the prices at which it sells or the amounts that it sells at those prices. Nothing so effectively economizes effort and intelligence, as distinct from anxiety, as the knowledge that nothing can be done. Decisions concerning production being also simple, the whole process is well within the intellectual competence of a dominant stockholder. Others who have contributed capital can, for the same reason, inform themselves on their investment, and the same remains true if the business is conducted by a hired manager. The firm being small and the number of stockholders being also small, the voting power of the stock remains important. Thus to the comprehensibility of the small corporation is added the power to make this knowledge effective. Given the risks to which the market exposes it, the owners also have need to keep watch on their property. This they can also do. Thus the corporation adapts itself well to the needs of the small enterprise. This adaptation, it will be observed, conforms (as the large corporation does not) to the design that is adumbrated in corporation law and celebrated in the well-regarded textbooks in economics.

With growing size and complexity of operation, smaller or more passive owners tend to lose their power of decision. The number of stockholders usually increases; the share in the voting power of each owner thus declines. More important is the failure of knowledge. Those who are not active in the management of the enterprise have less and less knowledge of what is happening and less opportunity of informing themselves at a time when the increasing size and complexity of the enterprise mean that more and more knowledge is required for intelligent decision. The individual or individuals who are immediately in authority, by contrast, retain the knowledge that goes automatically with such association. This knowledge often accords an individual full authority over the enterprise in the absence of voting control. Others have no alternative but to accept his lead. The one thing worse than the loss of power by the small or passive stockholder would be its uninformed exercise. So the corporation again adapts itself to need—the need at a certain stage in growth to concentrate power in some part of the ownership. This power is concentrated in someone who combines a command of capital with the capacity to exercise command over the enterprise. Thus appears, in classical form, the figure of the entrepreneur.

The entrepreneur can survive a substantial degree of industrial development. Running a large mine may as well be within his reach as a small one. In the early and elementary stages of steel-making he could exercise as much authority over several Bessemer converters as over one. The vital requirement is that both technology and planning remain relatively simple—or limited.

The decline in power of the minority—or possibly even of a sufficiently dispersed majority—also provides the entrepreneur with the opportunity for growth by combination. The possession of a controlling interest gives him access to capital from both within and outside the firm. With this capital other controlling interests in other firms in the same industry can be bought. Only some fraction of the total value of the enterprise must be paid for in cash. Such acquisition, led by an entrepreneur more highly capitalized or more highly motivated than his fellows, has been a feature of virtually every Ameri-

can industry. The process has been invariably regarded with
uneasiness by all except those immediately responsible, and
only the eventual results have been viewed with approval, often as a vigorous manifestation of free enterprise. Petroleum,
steel, tobacco, copper, shipping, meat packing, processed
foods, dairy products, electric and gas utilities, communications, grocery stores, drugstores, even hotels, motels, drive-in
theaters and other places of rest, recreation and assignation
have had their era of consolidation or currently are having
one. Those whose names are linked to such consolidation—
Rockefeller, Morgan, Duke, Harriman, Guggenheim, Durant,
Du Pont, Chrysler, Hartford, Hilton—all united control of
capital with unquestioned authority in the enterprise.[1] In
light of the preceding and following argument, it is worth
noting that no one of equal notoriety ever followed these pio-
neering entrepreneurs. The names of their successors in office
are lost to history or were never known.

2

The great entrepreneur must, in fact, be compared in life
with the male *Apis mellifera*. He accomplishes his act of
conception at the price of his own extinction. The older entrepreneurs combined firms that were not yet technologically
complex. As in the case of steel at the turn of the century
when U.S. Steel was formed, a small corps of managers and
supervisors directed a large and comparatively untrained and
homogeneous working mass. With consolidation came control
of markets—the forerunner of modern planning. But this—
the setting of prices for petroleum, steel, tobacco and other
products—called for very little subtlety. The feelings of customers were not consulted. Competitors were told in idio-
matic English to conform to the prices set by the dominant
firm or be put out of business. None of this required specialized talent.

But the act of combination added new plants and products
and therewith the need for specialization by function and
knowledge. Sooner or later came more complex tasks of planning and control. Technology, with its own dynamic, later
added its demands for capital and for specialized talent with

[1] This was not necessarily exercised directly. As in the case of J. P.
Morgan through Elbert Gary, it could be exercised through agents.

need for yet more comprehensive planning.[2] Thus what the entrepreneur created passed inexorably beyond the scope of his authority. He could build. And he could exert influence for a time. But his creation, were it to serve the purposes for which it was brought into being, required his replacement. What the entrepreneur created, only a group of men sharing specialized information could ultimately operate.[3]

On occasion, entrepreneurs dramatized the point by resisting their loss of authority and thus taking issue with the inevitable. Through the twenties, thirties and into the forties Henry Ford, aging and autocratic, became increasingly resentful of the organization without which his company could not be run. He reacted by shunning employees of specialized technical knowledge—for many years college graduates were not hired at River Rouge. And he systematically fired all who, by rising in the hierarchy, seemed to be arrogating the responsibility he deemed to be his. Many of the most illustrious names in the automobile industry—Couzens, Wills, Hawkins, Rockelman, Knudsen (who helped to build General Motors), the Lelands (who founded Cadillac and Lincoln), Klingensmith and Kanzler—were extruded or axed. For a long time the executioner was Charles E. Sorenson; then Ford executed Sorenson. In the early forties he was left with only one significant senior executive, Harry Bennett, who with assorted pugilists, baccalaureates of the Michigan penal

[2]Before the end of the century the Standard Oil Company of New Jersey—the original Standard Oil—already owed much of the excellence of its technical performance not to its principal founder but to what would now be called a management team consisting of H. M. Flagler, John D. Archbold, H. H. Rogers, Charles Pratt, Oliver H. Payne and others. Cf. Allan Nevins, *Study in Power: John D. Rockefeller*. Vol. 2 (New York: Scribner, 1953), Chapter 22. As early as 1882, John D. Rockefeller had the following report from a subordinate recently at headquarters. "While in New York I was brought in contact a good deal with the Manufacturing Committee [this already was a committee subordinate to the Executive Committee], and privately discussed a good many questions now before them and coming up in the near future. There is some clashing of opinion and a great deal of individuality in the committee . . . that may be detrimental to correct conclusions . . ." Nevins, Vol. 2, p. 21.

[3]The late Professor Ben B. Seligman, an astute observer of these matters, made this point in more general terms. ". . . finance capitalism was surprisingly short-lived, for the new managerial class discovered that with an adequate supply of funds stemming from accumulated profits they could get along quite well without Wall Street tutelage . . . Today, it is the paid professional who governs the corporation." "The American Corporation: Ideology and Reality," *Dissent*, Vol. XI, No. 3, Summer 1964, p. 323.

system, an unfrocked football coach and other colleagues of similar caliber, spent much of his time ensuring that no one threatened the authority that Ford was determined to monopolize.[4]

The result for the company was near disaster. Cars were either obsolescent or technically eccentric. Planning, particularly market control, was highly exiguous. Thus Ford once prohibited advertising for several years and, in the classic manifestation of his attitude toward modern merchandising, said that the customer could have any color of car provided it was black. In the thirties the company lost money in large amounts. In the war years its performance was so deficient that its seizure by the government was discussed, as also the uniquely insulting proposal that it be managed by the Studebaker Company.[5] Withal it is doubtful if Ford replaced group decision. Rather he pressed it down to ever more obscure participants and thus merely impaired it.[6] He was defeated despite his complete ownership of the company. On his death, the technostructure was reconstituted by Ernest Breech. The company promptly retrieved lost ground.

At Montgomery Ward in the thirties and forties Sewell Avery waged a similar struggle. Though he had only a minority stock interest, his legal control was not challenged for many years. ". . . [E]xecutives who reached the top levels at Montgomery Ward knew that their chances of surviving long were meager . . ."[7] On seeming to assume power that Avery believed to belong to him, they were turned out and others turned in as through a revolving door. Some fifty senior officers were fired during his tenure. The company which once had parity of position with Sears, Roebuck fell far behind. And in the end Avery, like Ford, was defeated. The costs of the effort could no longer be sustained; the stockholders fi-

---

[4] I have dealt with the Ford history in "Was Ford a Fraud?" in *The Liberal Hour* (Boston: Houghton Mifflin, 1960), p. 141 et seq. Peter Drucker has come to similar conclusions in his *The Practice of Management* (New York: Harper, 1954). pp. 111–120.

[5] Drucker, pp. 113–114.

[6] Ford executives of secondary rank came, in effect surreptitiously, to Washington during the war to discuss prices with my office or associates. Ford did not concede the right of the government to fix prices. So it was necessary to participate in these negotiations without his knowledge or, at least, without his being fully aware of what was transpiring.

[7] *The Executive Life*, by the Editors of *Fortune* (Garden City, New York: Doubleday, 1956), p. 192.

nally coalesced and ousted him, by now an old and senile man. Power was then lodged firmly with the technostructure.

It will be suggested that Henry Ford and Sewell Avery were men of marked eccentricity in whom the desire for power increased with age. Accordingly, they were singularly unqualified for one-man rule of a great corporation. This is true. But men of lesser eccentricity and greater judgment would not have tried. In most cases control passes smoothly from the entrepreneur to the technostructure. The exceptions show only that the transition must be accomplished.[8]

In the pages that follow, it will be necessary to distinguish between corporations in which age, size and simplicity of operation still accord power to an individual who has control of capital and those where the technostructure has taken over. I will refer to the first as the Entrepreneurial Corporation and to the second, in terms already found convenient, as the Mature Corporation.

3

Until recent times, senior officials of the mature corporation found much personal pleasure in the public mantle of the entrepreneur. Their picture of themselves was of self-reliant men, individualistic, with a trace of justifiable arrogance, fiercely competitive and with a desire to live dangerously. Individualism is the note that "sounds through the business creed like the pitch in a Byzantine Choir."[9] "They're bred to race. It's the same with people. It's something that's born into you."[10] "Business is tough—it's no kissing game."[11] These

[8]The airlines, growing rapidly in size and technical complexity, have provided two more examples of the transition, neither a completely peaceful passage. Howard Hughes, operating from a strong ownership position, long resisted the passage of control of TWA to the technostructure. And Eddie Rickenbacker fought a similar devolution of power at Eastern Airlines. Both companies suffered during this period. Both recovered promptly when the technostructure took over. The most recent period of consolidation, the conglomerate movement of the late sixties, brought a number of entrepreneurs into prominence—James Ling of LTV, the aforementioned Eli Black of United Brands—who proved inadequate or disastrous for serious administration.

[9]Francis X. Sutton, Seymour E. Harris, Carl Kaysen and James Tobin, *The American Business Creed* (Cambridge: Harvard University Press, 1956), p. 251.

[10]Charles "Tex" Thornton, President (later Chairman of the Board) of Litton Industries, describing the qualities of a senior executive. Osborn Elliott, *Men at the Top* (New York: Harper, 1959), p. 21.

[11]J. Peter Grace, President of W. R. Grace and Co. Ibid., p. 69.

characteristics are not readily reconciled with the requirements of the technostructure. Not indifference but sensitivity to others, not individualism but accommodation to organization, not competition but intimate and continuing cooperation are the prime requirements for group action.

This assertion of competitive individualism by the corporate executive, to the extent that it is still encountered, is ceremonial, traditional or a manifestation of personal vanity and capacity for self-delusion. It is not unusual. In World War II, commanders of armored units, functioning from well to the rear and worrying about gasoline, spare parts, reinforcements and their influence with Eisenhower, identified themselves, similarly, with Lord Cardigan and the Light Brigade.

In romance the past always greatly improves on the present. In the history of almost every industry there has been a famous and sometimees flamboyant entrepreneur. Like the tank commander, the head of the modern enterprise, in which all important actions are studiously considered by committees, all contingencies carefully anticipated and all adverse ones either prevented or negated, seeks to see himself in an earlier and more heroic image. It does something for his self-esteem and possibly for his domestic life. Additionally his function is to lend presence and an aspect of power to stockholders' and directors' meetings and other business ceremonials; to salute customers and clients of equal or greater dignity; to give the equivalent of the royal assent to agreements, contracts and indentures; to represent the enterprise in its more honorific relations with government; to act as an emissary to liberal learning; and to affirm on appropriate public occasions faith in free enterprise, the social responsibility of business and the continuing relevance of ancestral virtues. For all these rites the mantle of Carnegie, Rockefeller or Henry Ford is richly rewarding.[12]

And this reaching for the mantle of the classical entrepreneur is, almost certainly, a passing phase. A younger generation of executives accepts the fact of organization and its bearing on behavior. "To a surprising degree, American

---

[12]We have here one reason generals, admirals, and diplomats, after a lifetime in public service, frequently spend their last years as heads of business corporations and serve with success in a role for which they are manifestly unqualified. It is because they are, in fact, well qualified for ceremonial functions, and this (including honorific appearances in Washington) is what the position almost exclusively requires.

businessmen and writers about business have [stopped] interpreting our cooperative society as individualistic [and have stopped] concealing our quest for security in phrases like competition . . ."[13] ". . . [J]ust about *everybody* is a salaried administrator. . . . It is a rare . . . chief executive . . . [of the 500 largest U. S. corporations] who would consider himself an entrepreneur or capitalist."[14] Interdependence is recognized. As in all organization, there is protective compassion for the man who, because of misfortune, temperament, personal inadequacy or alcohol, falls by the wayside.[15] Executive life, so far from being competitive and dangerous, is highly secure. Of some eight hundred senior executives—the recipients of the highest salaries in each of approximately three hundred industrial, railroad and utility corporations—who were in office in 1952, three-quarters had been with their particular company for more than twenty years.[16] In a 1955 study the subsequent careers of 308 senior executives—board chairmen and presidents of the largest corporations—who were in office in 1925 were traced to their end. Of these 265 continued with the same firm until death or retirement. Only 13 resigned before retirement, and this included those who resigned to take better jobs. Sixteen lost their jobs because of changes in the control of the company but this included some who left because they had sold their own interest. Only five lost their jobs because the company failed or because they were fired. These men enjoyed a marked increase in their security of tenure as compared with 313 business executives in 1900 of whom only 157 eventually achieved death in office or an honorable retirement.[17] In 1970, a study of the chief executives of 250 among the 500 largest business firms showed that nearly two-thirds had joined their present company before 1950 and another 9 percent before 1956. Of the executives of the very largest industrial and retail firms—those with sales of over a billion dollars—three out of four had been with their companies for

---

[13]Earl F. Cheit in *The Business Establishment*, Earl F. Cheit, ed. (New York: Wiley, 1964), p. 155.

[14]Charles G. Burck, "A Group Profile of the *Fortune* 500 Chief Executive," *Fortune*, May 1976, p. 308.

[15]Cf. "The Alcoholic Executive," *Fortune*, January 1960, p. 99 et seq.

[16]*The Executive Life*, p. 30. The responses being not quite complete, the number works out to fewer than three to a company.

[17]Mabel Newcomer, *The Big Business Executive* (New York: Columbia University Press, 1955), p. 93 et seq.

more than twenty years.[18] In the recession of 1974–1975, numerous executives, presumably those of lesser competence, did lose their jobs. The impression has also been gaining ground that the senior executive is increasingly likely to move in response to present dissatisfaction or greater prospect. The figures still suggest a marked stability of tenure. A 1976 study showed that the chief executives of the hundred largest industrial firms had been with their companies an *average* of twenty-one years when they assumed the top job.[19]

4

It is noteworthy that the financial markets have long since accepted the reality of the technostructure as distinct from the entrepreneur. Were an entrepreneur decisively in command of the large corporation, anything affecting his tenure in office would have an important effect on its prospective earnings, growth and capital gains. The stock market would then be vitally concerned. Were he taken ill, financial reporters would seek hard news at the hospital. The ticker would carry electrocardiograms. Holders of stock on margin would have doctors' bulletins relayed to them in Nassau. The market would rise and fall with his temperature, blood pressure and cholesterol count.

Similarly, the months preceding his scheduled retirement would be a nervous time. News would be sought on whether a successor had been trained or a replacement found. The new man would be handicapped like a horse—his special talents would be appraised and his experience, temperament, family situation, working hours and drinking habits assessed. Stock in firms headed by an able man who was a heavy cigarette smoker would sell at a slight discount.

None of this happens, for it is known that retirement, death and replacement, however important for the individual involved, have no perceptible effect on the performance of General Motors or IBM.[20] Power, it is implicitly recognized, has passed to the technostructure. So its exercise is unaffected by the age or morbidity of any man. Though men accord the head of the great corporation the deference his position calls for, no one allows this to affect his financial judgment.

[18]*Fortune,* May 1970.
[19]*Fortune,* May 1976.
[20]The stock of a smaller or newer company dominated by one man, in contrast, does move on news of personnel changes.

5

Because individuals have more standing in the culture than organizations, they regularly get credit for achievement that belongs, in fact, to organization. It is not Procter and Gamble that has been winning new worlds in detergents; it is Procter and Gamble under the inspired leadership of its current chief executive. To this myth the principals are not reluctant to contribute. "At every turn the chief executive must be prepared to persuade people that his point of view must prevail."[21]

Clearly some individuals do add luster to organization. The accomplishments of the great physician are his own, not those of the hospital where he serves. The achievements of the poet are his own, not those of the institution where he is currently the poet in residence. Similarly the opera singer or actor and, though not always, the great scientist.

Men are, in fact, either sustained by organization or they sustain organization. They are either esteemed because of organization or the organization is esteemed because of them. The individual is himself rarely a sound judge of these matters. Those who are sustained by organization almost invariably attribute their acclaim to their own personality.

But there is an infallible test. That is to observe what happens to the individual when he leaves the organization or retires. The great physician is not greatly diminished by being separated from his hospital. Nor, except as regards regular salary, is the poet when he leaves the university. Nor is the competent newspaperman when he moves on. Nor the great scientist nor the entertainer. They sustained, and were not sustained by, the organization to which they belonged.

By contrast, the politician when he is defeated, the ambassador when he retires, the university president when he becomes emeritus and the peacetime general who does not become a corporation president face total obscurity. They were sustained by organization; on losing its support, they pass permanently into the shadows. To some who have naturally assumed that their eminence was their own the shock is very severe. Others sense their situation. Nothing so explains the primordial vigor with which politicians fight for

[21]John T. Connor, then President of Merck & Company, in Elliott, *Men at the Top*, p. 10.

office and seek to retain it to senility and beyond. Between being in and being out of political office the difference is not slight. It is total.

But for none is the transition more drastic than for the great business executive. Even the dismally inadequate governor or the tediously time-serving senator can count, after well-merited retirement, on some of the graces of public position. He will be a delegate to national conventions, be introduced at fund-raising dinners as "that great statesman" and always be addressed by his former title. For the corporation president, by contrast, there is only Stygian darkness. Following the final flight in the company jet, there will be only an honorific association with the board of directors and sometimes not that. His memoirs will not be in demand; the United Fund will want a man more affirmatively identified with affairs; his only continuing public responsibilities will be in his own church; his name will not again appear in the papers until the day following his death. The great entrepreneur lived out his last days disposing of his wealth or resisting those who sought to have him do so. The modern executive does not usually have enough money so to occupy himself. Such is his recessional. The conclusion requires no undue emphasis: pre-eminently the organization man is sustained by organization.

A Digression on the Firm
under Socialism

"From the standpoint of the employee, it is coming to make less and less practical difference to him what his country's official ideology is and whether he happens to be employed by a government or commercial corporation . . ."

—Arnold J. Toynbee

IN THE ENTREPRENEURIAL ENTERPRISE power rests with those who make decisions. In the mature enterprise this power has passed, inevitably and irrevocably, from the individual to the group. That is because only the group has the information that decision requires. Though the constitution of the corporation places power in the hands of the owners, the imperatives of technology and planning remove it to the technostructure.

Since technology and planning are what accord power to the technostructure, the latter will have power wherever these are a feature of the productive process. Its power will not be peculiar to what, in the cadenzas of ideology, is called the free enterprise or capitalist system. If the intervention of private authority, in the form of owners, must be prevented in the private firm, so must the intervention of public authority in the public firm. Otherwise it will be damaging, as the intervention of Ford and Avery was damaging.

As a further consequence, the puzzle of capitalism without control by the capitalist will be matched by the puzzle of socialism without control by the society. A final consequence is a drastic revision of the prospects for socialism in the form, at least, in which most socialists think it worth having. Three cases of the technostructure under socialism throw light on these matters.

2

Following World War II, Great Britain committed herself to limited socialism under parliamentary auspices. The British, who have a superior instinct for public administration, much recent argument to the contrary notwithstanding, recognized the need for autonomy for the nationalized industries. A key issue, seemingly small but in fact decisive, was that of parliamentary questions. Were these allowed on the decisions of the technostructure, ministers would have to be informed of such decisions in advance. Otherwise they would confess neglect of duty. But the decisions, or the important ones, which Parliament would be most likely to question would depend on complex and technical information. If the minister were to exercise informed judgment, he would need the help of a staff. Responsibility would thus be removed from the firm to the ministry. The cost in time would also be high. Only if such parliamentary intervention were excluded could the firm, and therein the technostructure, act responsibly and promptly on decisions requiring specialized information. Coal, electricity, gas, transport, the airlines and other publicly owned industries were, in consequence, all accorded such autonomy.

This autonomy is necessary both for small decisions and for what appear to be large questions of policy. Whether to rely on atomic energy for power is, assuredly, a question of policy. But the comparative advantages of atomic and molecular reactions for the generation of electricity are decided only by a variety of scientific, technical, economic and planning judgments. Only a committee, or more precisely a complex of committees, can combine the knowledge, training and experience that must be brought to bear. So also with the question of the kind and national provenance of the aircraft that should fly the North Atlantic. (Nothing, as later experience was to show, could be more discomforting to revenues than political intervention on behalf of supersonic aircraft.) Autonomy was also needed in the management and nationalization of the railways. In each case the group had the monopoly of competent knowledge. In later years a distinguished British economist and socialist observed that, in consequence, in Britain ". . . the public corporation has not up to the present been in any real sense accountable to Parliament whose function has been limited to fitful, fragmentary, and largely ineffective *ex post facto* criticism."[1]

For most socialists the purpose of socialism is the control of productive enterprises by the society. For democratic socialists this means the legislature. None, or not many, seek socialism so that power can be exercised by an autonomous authority. Yet this is where power must reside. And, to repeat, this is true not only of small decisions where delegation might be expected but of great ones where the legislature might reasonably be expected to have a voice. It does not matter that the capitalist, the ancient enemy of the socialist, himself suffers from the same exclusion. Most socialists set store by traditional belief as distinct from reality. Capitalism is still capitalism even though the capitalist is similarly the casualty of organization. But there is considerable distress over how little difference nationalization of an industry means. "If an intelligent observer from Mars or Venus could come and examine all large contemporary industrial concerns—public or private—as *working enterprises* he would notice, I suspect, only their overwhelming sameness."[2] The technostructure in the cases of both public and private ownership assumes similar powers and uses the same group methods for arriving at decisions. That it looks very much alike in both cases is not surprising.

Aneurin Bevan, one of the most intelligent and articulate of British socialists, reacted, not long before his death, to the gravitational descent of power into the technostructure of the public enterprise by asking for much stronger parliamentary control. This, of course, would have collided with the vulnerability of the technostructure to outside interference. Control would then be at the expense of competence, as in cases to be examined in a moment. A much larger number of socialists in the advanced industrial countries have come to feel that public corporations are, by their nature, "remote, irresponsible bodies, immune from public scrutiny or democratic control."[3] They have given up the fight for public ownership or accord it only lip service. Socialism in many countries has come to mean government by socialists who have learned that socialism as anciently understood is impractical.

[1] C. A. R. Crosland, "The Private and Public Corporation in Great Britain" in *The Corporation in Modern Society,* Edward S. Mason, ed. (Cambridge: Harvard University Press, 1959), p. 268.
[2] A. M. F. Palmer, "On Public Accountability," *Socialist Commentary,* January 1960, p. 13.
[3] Crosland, p. 268.

3

In a number of new countries the effort to exercise social control, forsworn in the British experiment, has been tried. It has been perhaps the most uniformly dismal experiment of countries seeking economic development.

At Oxford, the London School of Economics and the Sorbonne the British and French trained the élites of their erstwhile empires to a deep faith in socialism. To this was later added a practical case. Much of the capital for development in new countries comes from abroad as publicly organized aid. Or it is raised locally not from voluntary savings of individuals and corporations but from domestic taxation or other public sources.[4] It has seemed plausible that the state should invest publicly raised funds in publicly owned firms. And private entrepreneurs of requisite competence and responsibility have not always been abundant.

In India and Ceylon, as also in some of the African countries, public enterprises were not, as in Britain, accorded autonomy. Here the socialist faith was thought to require parliamentary control—the right to examine budgets and expenditures, review policies and, in particular, to question management through the responsible minister on any and all actions of the corporation. Here, as elsewhere, if the minister were to be questioned, he had to have knowledge. He could not plead that he was uninformed without admitting to being a nonentity—a condition, common enough in politics, that cannot however be confessed.

Technical personnel was also, and remains, less experienced than in the older countries. Organization is less mature. These lead to error and suggest to parliamentarians and civil servants the need for careful review of decisions by higher and presumably more competent authority.[5] Poverty makes nepotism and favoritism in letting contracts both more tempting and more culpable than in the rich country where jobs are plentiful and business is easier to come by.[6] This calls for

[4]Notably by buying resources away from private individuals and firms and thus imposing a form of saving on the private sector of the economy by inflation.

[5]India, in particular, as a legacy of its colonial past has an illusion of official omnipotence which extends to highly technical decisions.

[6]"Employment policies are especially likely to be subject to external pressure; decisions on how many people are hired, or—more important—fired, and who they are, invite political intervention where unem-

further review. And rigid personnel and civil service rules, the established British answer to limited administrative capacity, extend into the public firm and prevent the easy constitution and reconstitution of groups, with information relevant to changing problems. This, we have seen, is the essence of effective action by the technostructure.[7]

The effect of this denial of autonomy and the resulting inability of the technostructure to accommodate itself to changing tasks has been visibly deficient operations. Delay occasioned by checking decisions has added its special dimensions of cost. In business operations a wrong decision can often be reversed at little cost when the error becomes evident. But the cost of a delayed decision—of the men and capital that stand idle awaiting the decision—can never be retrieved.

As a further consequence of this interference, social control bears most strongly on the two decisions which are of the greatest popular interest—on the prices charged the public and the wages paid to workers. This has the effect of keeping prices lower and wages higher than the more autocratic technostructure would permit. It reduces or eliminates net earnings and therewith this source of savings. The poor country which most needs capital is thus denied the source on which the rich countries most rely.

In India for the first twenty years or so after independence nearly all public enterprises operated at a loss. In very recent times the record has considerably improved, with indication that the essential lessons of effective management, whether public or private, are there being learned.[8]

---

ployment is rife and highly particularistic loyalties persist." Elliott J. Berg, "Socialism and Economic Development in Tropical Africa," *Quarterly Journal of Economics,* Vol. LXXVIII, No. 4 (November 1964), p. 570.

[7]I have discussed these matters, in the context of India, in *Economic Development* (Boston: Houghton Mifflin, 1964), Chapter 8. Also *Economic Planning in India: Five Comments* (Calcutta: Indian Statistical Institute, 1956), and with regard to Ceylon in *Papers by Visiting Economists* (Colombo: Planning Secretariat, 1959).

[8]The exceptions in India in earlier years were Air India and Hindustan Machine Tool Company, both of which had a substantial measure of autonomy and thus affirm the point, and the railroads, which had an ancient tradition of substantial independence. It is interesting that governments which are reluctant to grant autonomy to other enterprises regularly accord it to their airlines, and often with very good results. It seems possible that public officials, who are among the important patrons, sense the unique dangers of denying autonomy in this industry.

4

When the case of democratic socialism began to emerge in the closing decades of the last century, the capitalist entrepreneur was still in authority. The firm was small enough and the state of technology simple enough so that he could wield a substantial power of decision. The belief that his power could be exercised instead by a parliament or by its directly responsible agent was not an idle dream. Certainly a public body could supersede the capitalist's power to set prices and wages and therewith his power to exploit the consumer and the wage-earner.

The misfortune of democratic socialism has been the misfortune of the capitalist. When the latter could no longer control, democratic socialism was no longer an alternative. The technical complexity, planning and associated scale of operations that took power from the capitalist entrepreneur and lodged it with the technostructure removed it also from the reach of social control.

In nearly all the non-Communist world, socialism, like promises to enforce the antitrust laws in the United States, is now less a political program than an overture to nostalgia. The choice being between success without social control and social control without success, democratic socialism no longer seems worth the struggle. There have been few more important consequences of the takeover by the technostructure.

There is, in fact, more to the case for the autonomous public corporation than the modern socialist now sees. Public ownership increases the amenability of the firm to social goals. It is increasingly inescapable in those industries such as housing, health care, mass transporation where an effective technostructure and associated planning do not develop and performance under private auspices is, in consequence, uncomfortably deficient. I shall come back to this in later chapters.

5

If autonomy is necessary for effective performance by the technostructure, it should also be needed by the firm in the Soviet-type economies. The requirement begins with the need to combine the specialized information of different men. There is nothing about this requirement that is peculiar to any economic system or which can be dispensed with by any ideology.[9]

The need for autonomy in the Soviet firm could, however, be somewhat less, for its functions are far fewer than those of an American enterprise of comparable size in a similar industry. That is because much planning that is done by the American or Western European firm is, in the Soviet-type economy, done by the state. The large American corporation sets its minimum prices, organizes the demand for its products, establishes or negotiates prices for its raw materials and components and takes steps to ensure supply. It also establishes or negotiates rates for various categories of trained and specialized talent, as well as of labor, and here again takes steps to ensure supply. In the U.S.S.R. these functions are all performed, well or less well, by the state planning apparatus.[10] Production and investment targets, which are established by the American firm for itself, are given to the Soviet firm, though with some flexibility in application, by the state. The firm is the basic planning unit in the Western economies. In the Soviet system it is still the state.

In consequence, the organization of the Soviet firm is far simpler than that of its American counterpart. There are no comparable sales, merchandising, dealer relations, product planning, procurement or like departments. Most of the top positions in the Soviet firm are held by engineers. This is in keeping with its much greater preoccupation with technical and managerial as distinct from planning functions.[11]

---

[9] "The Soviet industrial enterprise is some hybrid of an American corporation and an American factory. It operates as an autonomous financial entity with its own bank account(s). It also operates on a profit-and-loss basis, although the earning of profits is not a requisite for survival. In essence and law, the Soviet enterprise is the key unit for the administration of state property and productive resources." Barry M. Richman, *Management Development and Education in the Soviet Union* (East Lansing, Michigan: M.S.U. International Business Studies, 1967), pp. 80-81.

[10] Although the public supply of materials and components is far from reliable, the Soviet firm is prohibited, under penalty of law, from hiring "expediters" or otherwise intervening in the procurement process.

[11] "In the United States and other Western countries the problems of management include planning and innovation . . . These decisions are taken in the U.S.S.R. above the level of the enterprise manager." Report of the IIE Seminar on Industrial Technology in the Soviet Union, March 24-25, 1960, Institute of International Education, New York.

It would appear, nonetheless, that considerable and increasing store is set by the autonomy of this, by American standards, very simple organization. There are two[12] major sources of outside interference—the state planning apparatus and the Communist Party.[13] Soviet economic literature recurrently warns against bureaucratic interference by either with the operations of the firm. "The Russians have learnt by experience that you cannot have responsible and efficient action at the level of the firm with continuous intervention and instruction from numerous outside authorities. Conflicting instructions from outside give the manager innumerable excuses for failure, and waste and inefficiency may result from a serious attempt to run the firm from a distance. Every argument for delegation, decentralization, and devolution used in discussions about business administration in the West is echoed, although in a different jargon, in Russia. And the case for such devolution has been pressed with increasing emphasis as Russian industry has grown and become more complex."[14] "In the process of drafting and implementing a plan, decisive importance should be attached to the proper distribution of functions, rights and duties between the planning bodies and executive economic links. No superior agency can have as good a knowledge of internal resources and conditions of production as the enterprise itself. Under centralised planning, therefore, it is especially important to observe the necessary measure of decentralisation, so as to be able to ensure adequate scope for local planning and initiative."[15]

Plant managers do not hesitate to stress to visitors both their need for autonomy and their past difficulties. On occasion they defend the need to ignore or violate orders from

---

[12]A third, the trade union, is clearly of less importance. I advert to it in Chapter XXIV.

[13]I draw here not only on the literature of Soviet planning but on fairly extensive first-hand observation in the spring of 1959 and more briefly in the summer of 1964. I am extensively grateful to Soviet economists and plant managers for help and hospitality.

[14]Ely Devons, "The Enigma of the Russian Economic System," *The Listener*, Vol. LVIII, No. 1483 (August 29, 1957), p. 299.

[15]V. S. Nemchinov, "Socialist Economic Management and Production Planning," *Kommunist*, 1964, No. 5, translated and presented in *Planning, Profit and Incentives in the USSR*, Volume I, Myron E. Sharpe, ed. (White Plains, New York: International Arts and Sciences Press, Inc., 1966), pp. 173-174.

outside.[16] On the other side, managements, especially those of large firms, are frequently condemned for breaking off diplomatic relations with higher authority and behaving as "feudal lords" above the law. In the Soviet Union the most important medium of social comment, poetry apart, has long been the novel; one of the most interesting novels in the years following World War II was Dudintsev's defense of the small and independent inventor and his condemnation of the mindless bureaucracy of the great metal *combinat*.[17]

The position of the Party secretary is also predictably difficult. He enters the plant hierarchy horizontally as a member of the staff or working force and is subject to the external authority of the Party. If he participates as a member of the decision-making group, he naturally becomes responsible for the decisions. He is no longer an independent agent of the Party. If he does not participate, he no longer knows what is going on. If he is too good a source of information, ". . . he may be raised in [Party] rank but . . . [t]hen he will not be able to find out what is going on in the plant. Nobody will have any confidence in him . . ."[18] Professor Granick concludes that the relationship is "an uneasy compromise."[19] Given the

[16]On this see David Granick's *The Red Executive* (Garden City, New York: Doubleday, 1960), p. 162 et seq. And his earlier volume, *Management of the Industrial Firm in the USSR* (New York: Columbia University Press, 1954), especially p. 127 et seq. The reference in the text to feudal lords is from p. 128 of the latter.

[17]Vladimir Dudintsev, *Not by Bread Alone* (New York: Dutton, 1957). The author's affections are in close harmony with the American who, in the tradition of Brandeis, argues for the genius of the small entrepreneur as against the stolid, unimaginative behavior of the great corporation. Both have more support from humane instinct than reality. Neither sees that modern technology makes essential the machinery for mobilizing specialized knowledge. Dudintsev's inventor, however attractive, could have made no useful contribution as a lone individual to getting the cosmonauts into space.

[18]Joseph S. Berliner, *Factory and Manager in the USSR* (Cambridge: Harvard University Press, 1957), p. 265. This study is based on information from individuals familiar with Soviet industrial life who have come to the West. The speaker was an engineer and a former high official of a large machine-building plant. The obsolescence rate of such observations must be kept in mind—along with the danger of attaching undue importance to any single view.

[19]David Granick, *The Red Executive*, p. 205. Soviet critics of the first edition of this book (which was published in the U.S.S.R.) took exception to the discussion of the role of the Party, noting its reliance on the professional Sovietologists who are viewed as biased. However, the objections were not specific and did not clearly indicate the needed change.

imperatives of group decision and the need of the group to protect itself from outside intervention, this would seem to be the only possible result.

In sum, it seems likely that the Soviet resolution of the problem of authority in the industrial enterprise is not unlike that in the West—although no one can be precisely sure. Full social authority over the large enterprise is proclaimed. Like that of the stockholder and the board of directors in the United States, this social control is celebrated in all public ritual. The people and Party are paramount. But in practice large and increasing autonomy is accorded to the enterprise.

This is further suggested by the trend to decentralization, so-called, in the Soviet and other Eastern European countries. This has accorded greater authority to the firm over prices, individual wage rates, production targets, investment and other employment of earnings. In the West, especially among professional ideologists and volunteer propagandists, this has been widely hailed as a step toward control by the market. It isn't. There is no tendency for the large Soviet firm to become subordinate and subject to uncontrolled markets for its products, production needs or labor supply, and thus for its production decisions. Given the level of technology and related commitment of time and capital, and the effect of technology on the functioning of markets, this would no more be possible in the U.S.S.R. than in the United States.

Decentralization in the Soviet-type economies involves not a return to the market but a shift of some planning functions from the state to the firm. This reflects, in turn, the need of the technostructure of the Soviet firm to have more of the instruments for successful operation under its own authority. It thus contributes to its own autonomy. There is no tendency for the Soviet and the Western systems to convergence by the return of the former to the market. Both have outgrown that. There is measurable convergence to the same form of planning.

The next question, important for both socialist and nonsocialist societies, is what the technostructure seeks to do with the autonomy it requires. What are its goals? Do these accord with those of society?[20] What is the interaction between the

[20]Granick, in a more recent work, makes this a central problem of Soviet economic performance. The Soviet plant management has numerous incentives to do less than its best—to engage in what he calls, rather formidably, suboptimizing. "The suboptimizing problem takes a wide variety of forms: misleading data and opinion transmitted to

two? To these questions, after a preparatory look at existing belief, I now turn.

---

higher authorities in the effort to obtain a lower enterprise plan than would otherwise be forthcoming; the slighting of quality in order to reach a higher measured output; the production of undesired proportions of different types of products so as to achieve output and profit targets under conditions of fixed prices that are only weakly related to demand. Investment funds are demanded by all organizations, and many projects are begun with what turns out to be inadequate funding in the justified expectation that more funds will later be added by the state in order to avoid scrapping the project; as a result, investment programs have taken unconscionable periods to complete. Managers have strongly and successfully resisted the starting up of new products in their plans, with the effect that Soviet industry has consistently been slow in adopting product innovations." David Granick, *Managerial Comparisons of Four Developed Countries: France, Britain, United States, and Russia* (Cambridge: M.I.T. Press, 1972), p. 51.

X

The Approved Contradiction

"The beauty of the economic man was that we knew exactly what he was after."

—Alfred North Whitehead

THE MARKET has only one message for the business firm. That is the promise of more money. If the firm has no influence on its prices, as the Wisconsin dairy farm acting alone has no influence on the price of milk, it has no options as to the goals that it pursues. It must try to make money, and, as a practical matter, it must try to make as much as possible. Others do. To fail to conform is to invite loss, failure and extrusion from the business. A decision to subordinate interest in earnings to an interest in a more contented life for workers, cows or consumers would, in the absence of exceptional supplementary income, mean financial disaster. Given this need to maximize revenue, the firm is thus fully subject to the authority of the market.

When the firm has influence on market prices—when it has the power commonly associated with monopoly—it has also long been assumed that it will seek as large a profit as possible. It could settle for less than the maximum but it is assumed that it seeks monopoly power in order to be free of the limitations set by competition on its return. Why should it seek monopoly power and then settle for less than its full advantages? When demand is strong, the monopolistic firm can extract more revenue from the market; when demand slackens, it can get less. But so long as it tries to get as much as possible, it will still be subject to control by the market and ultimately, as sustained by the compulsions of avarice, by the preferences of consumers as expressed by their purchases. Were the monopolist regularly to settle for something less than a maximum return, the causes of this restraint would have to be explained by forces apart from the market. Along with the state of demand these forces would be a factor determining prices, production and profit. Belief in the market as the transcendent regulator of economic behavior requires, therefore, a parallel belief that participating firms will always seek to maximize their earnings. If this is assumed, there is, by exclusion, no need to search for other motives.

When planning replaces the market, this admirably simple explanation of economic behavior collapses. Technology and the companion commitments of capital and time have forced the firm to emancipate itself from the uncertainties of the market. And specialized technology has rendered the market increasingly unreliable. So the firm controls the prices at which it buys materials, components and talent and takes steps to ensure the necessary supply at these prices. And it controls the prices at which it sells and takes steps to ensure that the public, other producers or the state will take the planned quantities at these prices. So far from being controlled by the market, the firm, to the best of its ability, has made the market subordinate to the goals of its planning. Prices, costs, production and resulting revenues are established not by the market but, within broad limits later to be examined, by the planning decisions of the firm.

The goal of these planning decisions could still be the greatest possible profit. We have already seen that a high and reliable flow of earnings is important for the success of the technostructure. But the market is no longer specifying and enforcing that goal. Accordingly, profit maximization—the only goal that is consistent with the rule of the market—is no longer necessary. The competitive firm had no choice of goals. The monopoly could take less than the maximum but this would be inconsistent with its purpose in being a monopoly. But planning is the result not of the desire to exploit market opportunity but the result, among other factors, of the unreliability of markets. Subordination to the market, and to the instruction that it conveys, has disappeared. So there is no longer, *a priori*, reason to believe that profit maximization will be the goal of the technostructure. It could be but this must be shown. And it will be difficult to show if other things are more important than profit for the success of the technostructure—if other goals better serve its interest. Profit maximization will also be difficult to prove, *a priori*, if the technostructure which makes the decisions, has the authority and does not get the profit.

If the technostructure has goals other than profit maximization, this is a matter of considerable interest and importance. At any given time the public aims, professed, unrevealed or concealed, of the President of the United States and of cabinet officials, legislators, jurists and generals nourish a large volume of scholarship, punditry, reportorial enterprise and fantasy. Similarly, in lesser measure, the governments of states, cities and school districts. But much of our life, and nearly all of it that involves the procurement and use of income, is subject to the decisions of the technostructure. It sets our prices, persuades us on our purchases and distributes the resulting income to those who participate in production. The planning of the technostructure also extends, we have seen, to the management of the demand for those products that are purchased by the state. Thus to know how and to what ends we are governed it is necessary to know the goals of the technostructure. These are no longer confined to profit maximization; there is a choice. Depending on this choice prices, production and income will be different. In none of these matters does the corporation have plenary power; but neither do politicians have absolute power, and interest in their intentions does not for that reason diminish. The easily satisfied will seek only to know how they are governed from Washington, Albany, Sacramento and City Hall. Others will ask also for an understanding of the goals of industrial planning.

However, these issues, it will be evident, only come up for consideration when it is agreed that the market is not in full control. And this point is still contested with some vigor. The nature of this resistance must now be examined.

2

That numerous of the firms that comprise the planning system have extensive power over their prices is common ground among economists. Supporters of the market take up their position on a second line of defense: the control of these firms by the market is not the total subservence of the dairy farmer but that to which, in a general way, the classical monopoly is subject.

This defense has two parts. Such firms are not assumed to exercise any significant influence over purchases by the consumer or the state. That these remain sovereign is not argued; it is an article of faith. And it is further assumed that, although it could do otherwise, the firm compulsively maximizes profits. Therefore, as consumer choice varies or the requirements of the state change, the prices and levels of output at which profits are maximized also change. To these changes the firm responds. Thus its behavior remains subject to control by the market and, ultimately, by the consumer. This will be so, however large and powerful the firm may be, as long as it subordinates all discretionary power to the desire to make as much money as possible.

It follows that conservatives should be expected to insist on the assumption of profit maximization. The power of the market, which is the fulcrum of traditional attitudes, depends on the validity of this assumption. It is a far, far better thing to admit to monopoly profits, even at exploitive levels, than to concede that the market is impotent. And devout conservatives perform their priestly office. Profit maximization is held to be "the strongest, the most universal, and the most persistent of the forces governing entrepreneurial behavior."[1] "Few trends could so thoroughly undermine the very foundations of our free society as the acceptance by corporate officials of a social responsibility other than to make as much money for their stockholders as possible."[2]

But profit maximization is also defended by liberals. One branch of the liberal faith for which monopoly is the ancient *bête noire* rejects as special pleading any suggestion that the great corporation does not exact its pound of flesh. To suggest this is to apologize for monopoly. And another smaller convocation, while agreeing that the firm may not maximize its revenues, argues that it should, for this is the only legitimate exercise of business power. If it takes less than the maximum—if it pursues any goal other than profit—it is assuming public responsibilities which are no part of its task. "The function of business is to produce sustained high-level profits. The essence of free enterprise is to go after profit in any way that is consistent with its own survival. . . . It

---

[1]George J. Stigler, *The Theory of Price*, rev. ed. (New York: Macmillan, 1952), p. 149. However, even the most devout are not immune to doubt; later editions of his book are somewhat less dogmatic. Profit maximization is defended partly because no other assumption has been shown to be valid. Cf. 3rd ed. (New York: Macmillan, 1966), p. 177.

[2]Milton Friedman, *Capitalism and Freedom* (Chicago: University of Chicago Press, 1962), p. 133. Also quoted by Earl F. Cheit in *The Business Establishment*, Earl F. Cheit, ed. (New York: Wiley, 1964), p. 163. Professors Stigler and Friedman are, by general agreement, two of the more relentless exponents of the traditional economic attitudes in the United States.

should let government take care of the general welfare. . . ."[3] If business pursues welfare goals, it becomes a governing force. "If we are to have rulers . . . let us join in choosing our rulers—and in ruling them."[4] A more restrained view holds ". . . that business will make no serious contributions to the good of the public—unless there is recognition that, first, business is equipped to do only certain jobs very well and, second, business must make a profit . . . the fundamental charter of every business is to make a profit for the stockholders."[5]

That the consumer and the state are not sovereign in their demand—that they are subject to the management of the firms that supply them with goods and services—is sufficiently argued elsewhere in this book. And the methods used in this management, most notably advertising in managing the behavior of the consumer, are not of a kind that can be practiced in secret. The reader is not without resources for personal verification. The case for (and against) maximization of revenue must, however, be examined in detail. This is necessary even though the self-contradictions involved will seem rather evident to most readers. For the instinct of traditionalists in defending it is strategically sound. Once the assumption of profit maximization is abandoned, the way is open for a flood of new, inconvenient and even disturbing ideas. It is then clear how shrewd is the instinct of traditionalists, those who stand guard against disturbing new truth, in holding to the formula that keeps them out.

Nor is exposure of the contradiction in the case for profit maximization, although it requires a measure of patience, without its further rewards. In our culture few things give more pleasure than the sight of men caught in embarrassments of their own manufacture. Such is the pleasure when a liberal explains why his house deed has a restrictive covenant. Such in past times was the joy when a segregationist mayor was found in a Negro brothel. Such has always been the joy when an advocate of fiscal rectitude is caught with his hand in the cash register. In 1938, Mr. Richard Whitney, recently the President of the New York Stock Exchange, was

---

[3]Theodore Levitt, "The Dangers of Social Responsibility," *Harvard Business Review*, Vol. 36, No. 5 (September-October 1958), pp. 41–50.
[4]Ben W. Lewis, "Economics by Admonition," *American Economic Review*, Supplement, Vol. XLIX, No. 2 (May 1959), p. 395.
[5]David B. McCall, "Profit: Spur for Solving Social Ills," *Harvard Business Review*, Vol. 51, No. 3 (May-June 1973), p. 52.

convicted of stealing some millions of dollars held by him in
trust for others. There was, regrettably, much public pleasure.
This was not because people are cruel or relish seeing a fellow citizen or even a Harvard man enter Sing Sing. It was
because Mr. Whitney had previously been famous for his insistence that both he and all other members of the money
market were touched by a fiscal divinity which excluded any
possible wrongdoing. Spiro Agnew, John Mitchell, Richard
Nixon himself would have been spared much joyous public
assault if they had earlier spared the public their homilies on
law, order and old-fashioned American virtue and morality.
Economists have long been uncompromising in their insistence that no human motive can rival in power the pursuit of
personal profit. There is charm in discovering that their case
for profit maximization must be combined with the assumption that the men who are said to maximize profits do not
and must not maximize their profits.

3

The assumption that men seek to maximize their own return
has an attractively unsentimental quality. It is the behavior
that capitalists have always felt obliged to defend and which
socialists have always thought deplorable but also insistently
human. It would be good were man so constituted that he
would labor on behalf of others. Taking him as he is, this is
not really to be expected, and certainly not in modern
business.

Yet it is also now agreed that the modern large corporation
is, quite typically, controlled by its management. The managerial revolution[6]—the assumption of power by top management—is conceded. So long as earnings are above a certain
minimum, it would also be widely agreed that such management has little to fear from the stockholders. Yet it is for
these stockholders, remote, powerless and unknown, that
management seeks to maximize profits. Management does not
go out ruthlessly to reward itself—a sound management is

[6] The phrase brought into the language by James Burnham in *The
Managerial Revolution* (New York: John Day, 1941). This was an important book which helped change people's minds on the nature of the
modern corporation. Partly, perhaps, because he was a strong and on
occasion eccentric conservative, and change in economics is usually led
by liberals, Burnham's contribution has not always had the recognition
it merited. In the first edition of this book I was negligent in this respect.

expected to exercise restraint. Already at this stage, in the accepted view of the corporation, profit maximization involves a substantial contradiction. Those in charge forgo personal reward to enhance it for others.

The contradiction becomes much sharper as one recognizes the role of the technostructure. If power is regarded as resting with a few senior officers, then their pecuniary interest could be imagined to be at least parallel to that of the owners. The higher the earnings, the higher the salaries they can justify, the greater the return on any stock they may themselves hold, and the better the prospect for any stock options they may have issued to themselves. Even these contentions stand only limited examination. There are few corporations in which it would be suggested that executive salaries are at a maximum. As a not uncritical observer of corporate practice has noted ". . . [the] average level of salaries of managers even in leading corporations is not exceptionally high."[7] Astronomical figures are usually confined to the very top. Stock holdings by management are small and often almost nonexistent.[8] Stock options, the right to buy stock at predetermined prices if it goes up in value, though common, are by no means universal. They are as much affected by broad speculative movements in the stock market as by management effort. And they are more widely valued as a tax dodge than as an incentive.[9] So even the case for maximization of personal return by top management is not strong.

But with the rise of the technostructure, the notion, however tenuous, that a few managers might maximize their own return by maximizing that of the stockholders, dissolves entirely. Power passes down into the organization. Even the small stock interest of the top officers is no longer the rule.

[7]Wilbert E. Moore, *The Conduct of the Corporation* (New York: Random House, 1962), p. 13.

[8]As noted in Chapter VII, in 176 of the largest corporations studied by R. A. Gordon in 1939, the median ownership of officers and directors was 2.1 percent. That of officers was very much less, and it was much lower among older railroad than younger industrial corporations. Gordon's list included some firms, such as Ford, which were still wholly owned by the controlling interest. In the next decades there was a further large decline in management holdings. R. A. Gordon, *Business Leadership in the Large Corporation* (Washington: Brookings Institution, 1945) and Mabel Newcomer, *The Big Business Executive* (New York: Columbia University Press, 1955).

[9]"They are, of course, really tax-avoiding schemes . . . as the profit from sales of stocks is taxed as capital gains at a maximum of 25 percent . . ." Moore, pp. 13–14.

Salaries, whether modest or generous, are according to scale; they do not vary, or not closely, with profits. And with the power of decision goes the opportunity for making money, which all good employees are expected to eschew. Members of the technostructure have advance knowledge of products and processes, price changes, impending government contracts and, in the jargon of our time, technical breakthroughs. Advantage could be taken of this information. Were everyone to seek to do so—by operations in the stock of the company, in that of suppliers or in commodity markets, by taking themselves and their knowledge into the employ of another firm for a price—the corporation would be a chaos of competitive avarice. But these are not the sorts of thing that a good company man does; a generally effective code bans such behavior. Group decision-making ensures, moreover, that almost everyone's actions and even thoughts are known to others. This acts to enforce the code and, more than incidentally, a high standard of personal honesty as well. The technostructure does not permit of the privacy that misfeasance and malfeasance require.

So the technostructure, as a matter of necessity, bans personal profit-making. And, as a practical matter, what is banned for the ordinary scientist, engineer, contract negotiator or sales executive must also be banned for senior officers. Resistance to pecuniary temptation cannot be enforced at the lower levels if it is known that the opportunity to turn a personal penny remains the prerogative of the high brass.

The members of the technostructure do not get the profits that they maximize. They must eschew personal profit-making. Accordingly, if the traditional commitment to profit maximization is to be upheld, they must be willing to do for others, specifically the stockholders, what they are forbidden to do for themselves. It is on such grounds that the doctrine of maximization in the mature corporation now rests. It holds that the will to make profits is, like that to sexual intercourse, a fundamental urge. But it holds that this urge operates not in the first person but in the third. It is detached from self and manifested on behalf of unknown, anonymous and powerless persons who do not have the slightest notion of whether their profits are, in fact, being maximized. In further sexist analogy, one must imagine that a man of vigorous, lusty and reassuringly heterosexual inclination eschews the lovely and available women by whom he is intimately surrounded in order to maximize the opportunities of other men whose existence he knows of only by hearsay. Such are the foundations of the maximization doctrine when there is full separation of power from reward.

4

In earlier stages of the development of the corporation, and notably in the decade of the thirties, it was feared that those in control would make their firm an instrument of their own personal enrichment. And this would, it was also feared, destroy corporate enterprise as a whole.

The portents seemed grave. When the great utility empires of the Insulls and Associated Gas and Electric collapsed in the Great Depression, it became evident that the pecuniary interests of the individual stockholder had been callously subordinated to the wealth and ambition of those in command. Similarly with other great power, transportation and industrial enterprises that fell during this period. In all of them the financial interest of those in control was small or negligible in relation to total assets—O.P. and M. J. Van Sweringen, the eccentric Cleveland railroad collectors, controlled their two-billion-dollar railroad system on an investment on their own behalf of some twenty million dollars. Albert H. Wiggin of the Chase National Bank was heavily short in the stock of the bank he headed at the time of the stock market crash in 1929. As a result, he made a small fortune on the decline of the stock, and, a resourceful man in debate, he later argued that not owning stock, which is the nature of a short position, gave an officer an enhanced interest in the enterprise. After Ivar Kreuger had said farewell to his trusting financial friends in Paris on March 12, 1932, and had short himself to death with a newly purchased pistol, it was learned that he had used his control of corporations in a dozen countries to separate their owners from hundreds of millions of dollars. This was personal profit maximization on a truly massive scale. Scholars concluded that those in control of the great corporations, as they became able to do so, would combine such maximization with personal aggrandizement. The result would be larceny of unprecedented magnitude. Professor William Z. Ripley of Harvard, the leading authority on the corporation in the twenties, warned President Coolidge that "prestidigitation, double-shuffling, honey-fugling, hornswoggling and skulduggery"[10] were threatening the entire economic system. Adolph A. Berle, Jr., Ripley's successor as the prime authority on the corporation, concluded that the mature corporation accorded no effective rights to the owners of the enterprise. There could, in consequence, be only one of two results. Managers would become trustees, properly supervised, on behalf of the "inactive and irresponsible"[11] owners, which would have an unhappy effect on initiative. Or they would "operate it in their own interests, and . . . divert a portion of the asset fund to their own uses."[12] There would develop "a corporate oligarchy coupled with the probability of an era of corporate plundering."[13] Neither of these results being agreeable, Professor Berle concluded that the state would have to take over from the managers.[14]

The danger did not develop. This, without doubt, was partly because some of the more promising avenues of enrichment were closed by law. The Federal Securities Act of 1933 and its subsequent amendments required management to disclose its own compensation and pension rights. It also required disclosure of the value of any property or services sold to the corporation—for these, when overvalued, serve admirably to siphon corporate funds into a privy purse. And it required disclosure of trading, and prohibited short selling, by the insiders. The Public Utility Holding Company Act of 1935 limited pyramiding through the use of holding companies as a device for excluding owners from control. And the Securities and Exchange Commission was created to administer this legislation. The authofs of this legislation believed firmly that profit maximization by those in control of corporations, as distinct from the owners, was deeply inimical to the profit system. It may be added that their efforts to restrict it and thus protect the system earned them the usual reputation for radicalism.

But the legislation principally affected those who, like mur-

---

[10]Quoted in William Allen White, *A Puritan in Babylon* (New York: Macmillan, 1938), pp. 337–338.

[11]Adolf A. Berle, Jr., and Gardiner C. Means, *The Modern Corporation and Private Property* (New York: Macmillan, 1948), p. 354.

[12]Ibid.

[13]Ibid., p. 355.

[14]This formidable conclusion, which was expressed in guarded terms, came toward the end of a long book. It seems to have been overlooked. Had his numerous critics been more diligent, Professor Berle's early commitment to socialism would, one imagines, have been more celebrated during his long and greatly distinguished public career.

derers and thieves in less exalted areas, find it difficult to live
in accordance with the accepted canons of behavior. In most
corporations, even in the twenties, there was no abuse, as personal profit maximization by insiders was even then called.
And the legislation closed only a few of the avenues for enrichment. The management of every mature and profitable
corporation has numerous lawful and unexploited opportunities for increasing its personal revenue at the expense of the
stockholder. Most of the devices—more pay, more deferred
compensation or pension rights, more stock options or stock
purchase plans, more profit-sharing—would require only the
routine blessing of counsel or *pro forma* ratification by the
annual meeting.

The danger of damage, through personal profit maximization, disappeared as power passed into the technostructure. In all of the corporations where personal profit
maximization aroused alarm in the nineteen-twenties and thirties, there was still a dominant entrepreneurial figure. His investment was often small but his control rested on financial
position and not on managerial or technical competence.
With the rise of the technostructure with its new professional
attitudes and its widely diffused power acting as a safeguard
against individual avarice or larceny (each member is his
brother's auditor and watchdog), the danger receded. Although in the twenties and thirties there was widespread
doubt that the corporation could survive the personal profit-
maximizing tendencies of those who might seize financial
control, in the next half century the issue became largely academic.[15]

Some will already have sensed a relation between this discussion and the earlier examination of the changing association of power and the factors of production. When capital
was decisive and the capitalist was in control of the corporation, he maximized that which he provided, namely money.

[15]Isolated cases do appear. In the early nineteen-sixties it became
known that senior officers of the Chrysler Corporation were providing
themselves with notable rewards by virtue of their interest in enterprises selling products or services to the company. But the great attention that this case aroused, together with the prompt correction, is an
indication of its exceptional character. It is also significant that it coin-
cided with generally poor managerial performance. Personal profit
maximization at the top had led to a predictably poor performance by
the technostructure. In 1977, the SEC looked into cases of excessive
management salaries in a number of large corporations—a highly obvious form of profit maximization.

He specifically did so when his investment was small, when in consequence he had little to gain from improved earnings but when he could enrich himself greatly by looting the assets of the firm. The technostructure does not supply capital but specialized talent and organization. There is, *a priori*, no reason to believe that it will maximize the return to capital. More plausibly, it will maximize its success as an organization. Before pursuing this lead, however, it is necessary to say some final words to the defenders of maximization.

5

Quite a few economists avoid reflection on the conflict between profit maximization and what is universally considered sound management behavior by the convenient, although not wholly reassuring, device of simply ignoring the contemporary reality. In teaching and theoretical model-building, the modern large corporation is ignored. An entrepreneur is assumed. To "most economists, even today, the 'entrepreneur' still means only the owner-manager, usually, by implication, of a small manufacturing business."[16]

The caste structure of university departments of economics, an interesting matter, supports this simplification. Economic theory is the most prestigious subject of instruction and study. Agricultural economics, labor economics and marketing are lower-caste fields of study. So are industrial (i.e., corporate) organization and corporate finance. For students of the corporation the divorce of ownership from control in the large enterprise is an old story. But coming from an inferior intellectual tradition, this separation can be ignored by the theorist.

[16] Gordon, p. 11. This was written nearly thirty-five years ago but few sciences have ever shown such stability, at least in error. Almost exactly the same observation was made in 1964 by Robin Marris in his important *The Economic Theory of "Managerial" Capitalism* (New York: Free Press of Glencoe, 1964), p. 5. Professor Gordon added (p. 8) that "Developments in mathematical economics and general equilibrium theory have reinforced the mechanistic approach to entrepreneurial activity." The assumption that ownership is united with management is convenient, even necessary, for such theoretical and mathematical exercise. To accommodate assumptions not to reality but to the requirements of technique will be thought a rather dubious scientific procedure. It is one of the curiosities of economics that it is often employed by the men who most pride themselves on their scientific and technical virtuosity and who even volunteer on occasion to serve as censors of scientific morality.

His higher caste allows him to make such assumptions as he prefers. Accordingly, he assumes that the direction of the enterprise continues to involve extensive participation in revenues. The firm is run by an owner-entrepreneur. This being so, there is no reason to question the assumption that revenues will be maximized.[17] And there is, further, no reason to consider other goals. This will not, to everyone, seem an ideal arrangement; many will react uneasily to the exclusion of General Motors, General Electric and Exxon and their companions in scale and organization from modern economic theory. But to an astonishing degree, this is accomplished and serves in turn to exclude goals other than profit maximization and thus to preserve the authority of the market.

However, and increasingly, modern theorists do accept General Motors. They agree that the modern corporation is run by the managers. They accept its market power. And they cautiously agree that it does not maximize its return. "As soon as the firm becomes of any considerable size and begins to enjoy some control over price, *it can often afford to relax a little* in its maximizing activities."[18]

"Large corporations do certainly have the elbow room for unilateral action denied to a small farmer or conventional family enterprise. They can give money to slum clearance. They can relax in their pursuit of profit. They can pursue growth even when it is more that of cancerous than of healthy cells. They can tempt consumers to buy the goods that the corporation would like to sell."[19]

---

[17]Many theorists are, in fact, more circumspect. My very distinguished colleague, Professor Robert Dorfman, made the following more cautious assumption: "On balance, the maximization hypothesis is not as firmly grounded in the facts of life as a fundamental scientific hypothesis should be. But substantial and prolonged divergences from the behavior it implies are rare, particularly in industries with many participants. It therefore *can still be entertained* as a sound working hypothesis." *The Price System* (Englewood Cliffs, New Jersey: Prentice-Hall, 1964), p. 42. Italics added. In his later *Prices and Markets* (2nd ed. [Englewood Cliffs, New Jersey: Prentice-Hall, 1972], p. 9), Professor Dorfman is slightly less careful. ". . . the 'profit motive' . . . determines how businessmen respond to different circumstances, and thereby how the whole system operates."

[18]Paul A. Samuelson, *Economics*, 10th ed. (New York: McGraw-Hill, 1976), p. 508. The italics in the first quotation are in the original. The second quotation (see below) is part of a characteristically handsome concession to the argument advanced in the early editions of *The New Industrial State.*

[19]Ibid., p. 512.

". . . [W]here significant distortion [i.e., failure to maximize returns] . . . *is present, the fault lies in market power.*"[20] ". . . [T]he profit-maximizing hypothesis works better when applied to industries composed of a large number of firms than when applied to monopolies or to industries with only a few members."[21]

And on closer scrutiny these statements turn out to make no minor concession. They exclude large firms or those with market power from maximization. To say that large firms do not maximize returns or to suggest that there is room for other goals whenever there is market power is to agree that maximization does not occur in the part of the economy with which we are here concerned. It does not occur in automobiles, aluminum, rubber, synthetic fabrics, transportation, turbines, tin cans, chewing gum, glass, breakfast foods, cigarettes, most electrical goods, aircraft, computers, typewriters, most chemicals, all communications and a host of other industries where firms are large in relation to the market and their power over the market is not only considerable but very great.[22] The defenders of maximization are seen to be giving away a great deal while seeming to give little. Profit maximization may be assumed. But, as a concession to reality, the planning system—the largest, most typical and most modern part of the economy—is excluded. The captious would be critical of any description of the social geography of the United States which, by assuming away New York, Chicago, Los Angeles and all other communities larger than Cedar Rapids, was then able to describe the country as essentially a small-town, front-porch community. Only an assumption very important to economics, as it is conventionally taught, would justify such a questionable defense.

In other contexts economists have more explicitly abandoned the commitment to maximization. Thus price increases in the planning system characteristically follow the negotia-

---

[20]Shorey Peterson, "Corporate Control and Capitalism," *Quarterly Journal of Economics,* Vol. LXXIX, No. 1 (February 1965), p. 14. This article by Professor Peterson is a lucid and skillful defense of the orthodox case here under scrutiny.

[21]Dorfman, *The Price System,* p. 42.

[22]The foregoing list, apart from transportation and communications, is selected at random from almost ninety industries in which the eight largest firms were estimated to account for 75 percent of all shipments by value in 1972. United States Department of Commerce, Bureau of the Census, *1972 Census of Manufactures, Special Report: Concentration Ratios in Manufacturing* (1975).

tion of a collective bargaining contract. But if revenues can be increased by raising prices after a wage increase, they could have been increased before. Some consideration other than the goal of maximized return must have been involved in this price setting.

One line of modern economic policy assumes this restraint. It has sought to hold wage increases to what can be afforded from gains in productivity and, costs thus not having increased, to hold prices more or less stable. It is a policy that, in general, has been confined to, or is urged for, the planning system. No one doubts that firms so restrained could make higher returns by raising prices; the policy rests firmly on the fact that they do not need or really expect to maximize returns. Accordingly, economists who urge this policy have abandoned, however tacitly, their commitment to maximization. I later argue that some such policy is an indispensable feature of economic management of the planning system.

Finally, a small group of scholars, Robin Marris now of the University of Maryland, William Baumol of Princeton, Jack Downie of London and, somewhat more circumspectly, my brilliant former colleague, Carl Kaysen of the Massachusetts Institute of Technology, has accepted the separation of ownership from control in the mature corporation and its implications for profit maximization. They have gone on to devise explanations of managerial behavior that are, or seem to be, consistent with this separation. These efforts are still subject to the mystique of the market; were they to accept the full significance of the abandonment of profit maximization, they would go on, as here, to examine the modern corporation as an instrument of planning that transcends the market. Yet, nonetheless, they light a part of the way, and I make full use of them in what follows.[23,24,25,26]

[23]Robin Marris, *The Economic Theory of "Managerial" Capitalism.* See also his review of the first edition of the present volume, *American Economic Review,* Vol. 58, No. 1 (March 1968), p. 240 et seq.

[24]William J. Baumol, *Business Behavior, Value and Growth* (New York: Macmillan, 1959).

[25]Jack Downie, *The Competitive Process* (London: Duckworth, 1958).

[26]Among other papers, Carl Kaysen, "The Social Significance of the Modern Corporation," *American Economic Review,* Vol. 47, No. 2 (May 1957), p. 311 et seq. (also in *The Corporation in Modern Society,* Edward S. Mason, ed. [Cambridge: Harvard University Press, 1959]) and "Another View of Corporate Capitalism," *Quarterly Journal of Economics,* Vol. LXXIX, No. 1 (February 1965), p. 41 et seq.

6

As now sufficiently emphasized, profit maximization excludes other goals. That is why its affirmation is so necessary for holding discussion of corporate behavior within the ambit of the economist. That is why it is so urgently defended.

In recent years, in addition to the few economists who have defected, quite a number of business leaders and spokesmen have abandoned the commitment to maximization. Not all of this is to be taken seriously: in the past, the notably avaricious have often thought it well to protest their fealty to a higher morality than making money. Only the excessively gullible have believed them. Faith in profit maximization is still sustained by the fear of seeming gullible again. But some have quite honestly sensed that the mature corporation exercises plenary power apart from profit-making. This has an effect on the community. They have sought, in accordance with their own lights and preferences, to specify the rules for its use.

The result has been a cacophony of voices proclaiming the purposes of the corporation. These have ranged from the suggestion of Mr. Frank Abrams, former Board Chairman of the Standard Oil Company of New Jersey, that the primary goal is a just distribution of income, i.e., "to maintain an equitable and working balance among the claims of various directly interested groups—stockholders, employees, customers, and the public at large"[27]—to pronouncements of a primary concern for improving higher education, increasing economic literacy, resisting Communist subversion, supporting American foreign policy, building the community, strengthening the two-party system, upholding the Constitution, amending the Constitution to preserve its original intent, defending freedom and free enterprise and rehabilitating the environment. Many years ago Bruce Barton, an advertising man and later a member of Congress, concluded that Jesus, were he alive today, would be a businessman rather than in the building trades. On occasion, so fulsome have been the professions of higher corporate purpose that observers have been led to wonder if the Barton dream has come to pass. "Today pronouncements about social responsibility issue forth so abundantly from the

[27]Quoted by Eugene V. Rostow in "To Whom and for What Ends are Corporate Managements Responsible?" in *The Corporation in Modern Society*, p. 60.

corporations that it is hard for one to get a decent play in the press. Everybody is in on the act, and nearly all of them actually mean what they say! Dedication reverberates throughout the upper reaches of corporate officialdom."[28]

It would be wrong to dismiss these assertions of social purpose by corporate spokesmen exclusively as an exercise in competitive banality. They also reflect an underlying reality, which is that the modern corporation has power to select its goals. And this power does not disappear when its spokesmen, following the advice of economic traditionalists, proclaim that their only purpose is profits. Power can be used to pursue profits. It can also be used to pursue other goals.

However, the real purpose of this power is not proclaimed in the corporate press releases and speeches. What is dispensed, as many have rightly suspected, is mostly hot air. Power is used, as might be expected, to serve the deeper interests or goals of the technostructure. These goals are not proclaimed. Rather, like most human aspirations, they are taken profoundly for granted. Our task now is to identify these goals and the means by which society is accommodated to their service.

[28]Levitt, p. 42.

XI

The General Theory of Motivation

OUR NEED is to know the real goals of the technostructure and how they are pursued. Then we will know to what purposes and by what means we are governed in that large part of our life which is influenced by the planning system. Men have long thought it important to know how governments determine their taxes. It is rather more important to know the governing processes by which their incomes are determined, their prices set and their purchasing habits shaped.

The problem of goals begins with the relation of the individual to organization, in this case to the technostructure. What an organization will seek from society will be a reflection of what its members seek from the organization. If soldiers serve only for pay, the army is not likely to concern itself deeply in politics—at least so long as the pay is forthcoming. But if, as with Cromwell's men, they serve for the salvation of their souls, they are unlikely long to be politically neutral, at least in a wicked country. Parliaments will do well to keep their doors locked. If, as in Latin America, men join the army less from an excess of martial valor than from an element of political ambition, the danger will be even greater. If men principally want money from a corporation, the corporation will be primarily concerned with extracting money from the society. If they are interested in economic security or personal prestige, the corporation can hardly fail to reflect this in the kind of business it conducts.

What the society can ask from organization will depend, similarly, on the relation of the organization to the individual. When soldiers serve for pay, the state must pay the army that it summons to its call. The southern planter could be summoned by the impressment and made to bring his slaves, for slaves had no choice but to come. A laboratory run by the California Institute of Technology can be asked to work long hours to follow a space probe. That is because those who man it are united with the organization by scientific interest.

A textile mill or an auto plant would not be capable of a similar response; its operatives or employees work only for pay.

These matters have not been much studied by economists. Men, it is assumed, act in economic matters soley in response to pecuniary compensation or, as the only alternative, to force. Force in the modern society is largely, although by no means completely, obsolete. So only pecuniary compensation remains of importance. The more of this, broadly speaking, the individual receives, the better and more sustained his effort. Only as to the very poor and those in menial occupations such as domestic service is there occasional concern that excessive pay may prove damaging to character and thus to effort.

Pecuniary compensation as a motivation, in its turn, supports profit maximization as the preclusive goal of the firm. Profit maximization gets the greatest return from the market; this enables the firm to buy the optimum effort from its members.

Though all this notably simplifies the economist's life, it is, unfortunately, at odds with the reality. In addition to pecuniary compensation, two other forces powerfully relate the individual to modern corporate organization. These further motives are inconsistent with the commitment by the firm to profit maximization. This is in keeping. Profit maximization, we have also just seen, is inconsistent with the behavior of the technostructure in the mature corporation. The other motives repair this inconsistency. What is more, they are essential to a satisfactory explanation of the behavior of the technostructure. As always, reality is in harmony within itself.

2

The most famous definition of an organization holds it to be a "system of consciously coordinated activities or forces of two or more persons."[1] The most important word here is coordinated. It means that the participating individuals are persuaded to set aside their individual purposes or goals and pursue those of the organization. All having done so, all work to the common goals. They are coordinated. Motivation is the means or inducement by which such coordination is effect-

[1]Chester I. Barnard, *The Functions of the Executive* (Cambridge: Harvard University Press, 1956), p. 73.

ed—the means or inducement by which individuals are led to abandon their own goals and, with greater or less vigor, to pursue those of the organization.

The essentials of the matter are evident when a group of men dig a ditch. Ditch-digging is unlikely as an original passion for the average person. A useful completed excavation is a plausible goal of a group or organization. The problem is how to win the surrender of individual preference in favor of the disciplined wielding of a spade. This can be brought about in the following ways:

1. The group may compel the acceptance of its goals. Behind the man with the spade is another with a club. Failure to accept the goals of the group brings the negative reward of punishment. Without extravagant novelty, this motivation may be called *compulsion*.

2. The acceptance of the common goal may be purchased—at the end of the trench is a man with money. Acceptance of the goals of the organization brings not a negative but an affirmative reward. In return for this inducement, the individual "offers the organization . . . undifferentiated time and effort."[2] Such is *pecuniary motivation*.

3. The individual, on becoming associated with the group, may conclude that its goals are superior to his own. In the case of ditch-digging the likelihood is less than in a chamber music group, a political conspiracy or the Marine Corps. Yet it exists. If the ditch drains a particularly nauseous and malarial swamp, the individual, on associating himself with the excavators, may then become aware of the utility of their common enterprise. This is to say that he finds the goals of the group superior to his own previous purposes and so he joins. "Humans, in contrast to machines, evaluate their own positions in relation to the value of others and come to accept others' goals as their own."[3] Such an exchange is not compelled. Neither is it purchased, although it is not inconsistent with compensation. Following Professor Herbert Simon, this motivating influence may be called *identification*.[4]

[2]Herbert A. Simon, *Administrative Behavior*, 2nd ed. (New York: Macmillan, 1957), p. 115.

[3]James G. March and Herbert A. Simon, *Organizations* (New York: Wiley, 1958), p. 65.

[4]This term, which has overtones of suburban psychology, is not entirely satisfactory. When first working out these ideas, I used the word *conformance*—and this must appear in the long-forgotten lecture notes of my students. Its tone implies, however, that the individual is somehow pressed or forced to conform, and this is not the meaning sought.

4. Finally, the individual may serve the organization not because he considers its goals superior to his own but because he hopes to make them accord more closely with his own. By being a member of the ditch-digging organization, he can hope for a ditch that, in capacity, depth or direction, conforms more closely to his ideal.

But once again the ditch-digger is not the most powerful example. The cabinet officer or high official who serves and on occasion concurs in action that he finds repugnant in order to advance measures of which he approves is a better case. He came to be part of something approaching a majority of American officialdom as those involved in the Vietnam war came to explain why they went along. Similarly motivated is the politician who would rather influence modestly the policies of a great party than be in full command of a one-man movement. And so is the corporation executive who strings along with much that he thinks unenterprising in the hope of winning support for a few new ideas of his own.

The pursuit of the goals of organization because of the prospect or in the hope of accommodating these goals more closely to the participant's preference is an important motivation. But unlike compulsion, pecuniary compensation or even identification, it has also much less standing in the theory of organization. The name for it must be coined, and I propose to call it *adaptation*. Adaptation, it will be evident, has much to do with the urge for power in a world of organization.

Compulsion, pecuniary compensation, identification and adaptation can motivate an individual either separately or in combination. Their collective influence I shall refer to as the *Motivating System*. The strength of any given motivation or of the motivating system will be measured by the effectiveness with which it aligns the individual with the goals of the organization. The motivating system varies greatly in power depending on the motivations that are combined. Some motivations clash and so neutralize each other. Some combine passively. Some strongly reinforce each other. What is called an effective organization is one which, in substantial measure,

---

Identification has no connotation of compulsion and has the claim of prior use. I should like to acknowledge my debt to Professor Simon and his associates. The literature dealing with organization and organization theory is of singular aridity. By far the most distinguished of the exceptions is the work of Herbert A. Simon and his colleagues. The two key volumes are *Administrative Behavior* and *Organizations*. Everyone professionally concerned with organization must know these difficult but rewarding books.

has a motivational system that is internally reinforcing. The goals of the organization are thus pursued with the greatest possible effect. I turn now to the relation between the several motivating forces.

3

Compulsion and pecuniary compensation exist in varying degrees of association with each other. Those who are compelled to accept the goals of organization by fear of punishment—of negative reward—always have some affirmative compensation for such acceptance. The slave got the whip when he did not work; he got food and shelter of a sort when he did. The controversy as to which of these motivating forces was strongest in the antebellum South is still intense.[5] As we shall see presently, varying amounts of compulsion are associated with pecuniary compensation.

Compulsion is inconsistent with either identification or adaptation. If a person is compelled to accept the goals of an organization, he is unlikely, at least so long as he is under the sense of compulsion, to find them superior to his own. The conflict is not quite absolute. Household slaves—in contrast with field hands—were believed to accept the goals of their masters. In consequence, they were thought unreliable material for insurrections. The reluctant draftee may come, in time, to relish the barracks and parade ground. But the broad rule holds: what is compelled cannot be a matter of choice. Alienation, not identification, will be the normal result. Bondsmen and serfs have regularly been thought to love their masters—in other words, to have identified themselves deeply with their masters' goals. This has not always prevented them, when the opportunity arose, from asserting their own very different goals, frequently after burning the master's house and its occupants or showing some similar manifestation of distaste.

Nor is compulsion consistent with adaptation. If the individual is obliged to accept the goals of organization, he will not embrace them in the hope of accommodating them more closely to his own. When his acceptance is forced, he will understand that he has no power over the goals to which he is compelled. The serf, slave or prison occupant takes the goals of the organization with which he is associated as given and,

[5]In the aftermath of Robert William Fogel's and Stanley L. Engerman's *Time on the Cross* (Boston: Little, Brown, 1974).

eccentric cases apart, is alienated from them all. He does only what avoids punishment. Similarly, the oldest rule of the reluctant soldier is to take life as it comes and never volunteer.

Pecuniary motivation may be associated in greater or less measure with compulsion. This will depend on the level of the compensation and the nature of the individual's alternatives. If the element of compulsion is high, it follows that pecuniary motivation will then be inconsistent with identification and adaptation. If it is low, they are readily reconciled. The difference here is of great importance for understanding modern economic behavior.

The worker in a Calcutta jute mill who loses his job—like his American counterpart during the Great Depression—has no high prospect of ever finding another. He has no savings. Nor does he have unemployment insurance. The alternative to his present employment, accordingly, is slow but definitive starvation. So, though nominally a free worker, he is compelled. The fate of a defecting southern slave before the Civil War or a serf before Alexander II was not appreciably more painful. The choice between hunger and flogging may well be a matter of personal taste. The aversion to the organization that compels the acceptance of its goals will be much the same in each instance. This aversion excludes identification. To repeat, the fact that the worker serves because he is compelled sufficiently reveals to him his powerlessness vis-à-vis the organization and its goals. Adaptation is thus also excluded.

The modern industrial employee who loses or abandons his job has, by contrast, every expectation of finding another. In the meantime he has unemployment compensation and perhaps some personal resources, and, if the worst comes to the worst, he can go on welfare. The danger of physical discomfort has been much reduced and therewith, in general, the element of compulsion. In higher income brackets it will be yet lower. As the aspect of compulsion in pecuniary compensation diminishes or disappears, so do the barriers to identification and adaptation.

4

The diminishing role of compulsion in pecuniary compensation has been a force of no small historical importance. Among other things it goes far to explain the disappearance of slavery itself. Until two centuries ago the motivation of the wage laborer in most parts of the world was not radically different from that of the bondsman. Both got little; both toiled in fear of the alternative.

The slave, accordingly, had no reason to regard the free wage-worker with much envy. He did not press aggressively to change his position. Nor did society on his behalf. But as the wage-worker improved his material position, the element of compulsion to which he was subject diminished. Then the contrast between free man and slave deepened and slavery became untenable. In the absence of the Civil War, slavery in the United States could have lasted only a few more years. For, in a relatively short time, industrialization and rising living standards in the North together with improving communications would have made it increasingly difficult to keep the slaves in the fields. And the cost of patrols and the machinery for redeeming fugitives, together with the capital loss from those who made good their escape into northern employments, would have been intolerable. Planters would have been forced to pay inducements, i.e., wages, to hold their men. As in other countries at a roughly similar stage in economic development, slavery would have been given up. The reform would have been attributed to the innate humanity of man to man. By 1880 or 1890 at the latest, the more respected philosophers would have been congratulating the nation on having accomplished peacefully what men once feared could only have been done by war.

As it is wrong to deny the role of conscience in human affairs, it is also an error to minimize that of economics. Speaking to the same subject, when bondsmen were still valuable property, Adam Smith observed: "The late resolution of the Quakers in Pennsylvania to set at liberty their negro slaves, may satisfy us that their number cannot be very great."[6]

5

As compulsion and pecuniary compensation are associated in varying mix, so also are identification and adaptation. The two are highly complementary. An individual, on becoming associated with an organization, will be more likely to adopt its goals in place of his own if he has hope of changing those

[6]Adam Smith, *Wealth of Nations*, Book 3 (New York: Modern Library, 1937), Chapter 2, p. 366.

he finds unsatisfactory or repugnant. And if he is strongly identified with the goals of an organization, he will be moved all the more strongly to try to improve it—to alter (i.e., adapt) any unsatisfactory goals so that they accord with his own. A member will identify himself more enthusiastically with a political party if he feels that he has some power to influence its platform. This is why effective political leaders seek to give their rank and file the impression, if not the reality, of participation in the making of the party program.

The relation of identification to adaptation is partly a matter of temperament; the disposition of some on associating themselves with an organization is to accept its goals and of others to improve them. Some college presidents and diplomats, by disposition, accept the goals of their respective institutions; others seek to advance the purposes of education or peace. Adaptation is also partly a matter of position in the hierarchy of the organization. It more strongly motivates a President of the United States than a postman making his rounds, more strongly the general manager than the receptionist, the pastor than the sexton.

6

Pecuniary motivation cannot be combined with identification and adaptation when the element of compulsion is large— when there is no tolerable alternative to the toil that gets the income. It can be when the element of compulsion is small. This means that the motivational system will be different in the poor country as compared with the rich, and different for the poor man as compared with the well-to-do. And what begins as a difference in degree widens, ultimately, into a difference in kind.

In the poor country, and among the poorly paid, labor relations will, in general, be harsh and angry. The compulsion associated with low compensation alienates the worker from the employer. This being so, the employer does not seek to cultivate his employee's loyalty—to encourage his identification with the firm—for this he knows to be impossible. There being nothing to lose, nothing is lost by arrogant or offensive behavior. The worker, not being identified with the employer, will be receptive to the goals of the union. He will also be vulnerable to threats from the employer that he will be fired if he joins, for this is precisely the hardship he fears and which compels his effort. The stage is thus set for disagreeable behavior on both sides. Those concerned have rarely failed to conform to expectation.

In the richer country and among the well-to-do, everything is more benign. Compulsion has receded. In consequence, there is little or no alienation; the way is open for the worker to accept the goals of the organization. The worker will have less inducement to join a union but much less to fear in doing so. The employer will seek to encourage the identification of the worker with the firm; the worker having less to fear, the employer will find it less useful to play on his fears. The worker being more identified with the firm, the union has less enmity to arouse. On both sides the motivational system both allows and rewards more agreeable behavior. This mellowing of industrial relations, the result of wealth, will be attributed to humane instincts, greater employer enlightenment, more responsible unions and the spread of industrial statesmanship.[7]

Here is the paradox of pecuniary motivation. In general, the higher the amount the less its importance in relation to other motivations. With higher income there is, under most circumstances, a lessened dependence on a particular employment. So there is a lessened element of compulsion, and this paves the way for identification and adaptation. These supplement and may transcend pecuniary compensation in their importance in the motivational system.

It will be clear that we have here a solution, or in any case a clue, to the contradiction encountered in the last chapter. Pecuniary compensation need not be the sole or even the main motivation of members of the technostructure. Identification and adaptation may be driving forces. Above a certain level these may operate independently of income. Maximization of income by members of the technostructure is not an imperative. The question of what goals members of the technostructure identify themselves with, and to what personal goals they seek adaptation, remains. But it will be clear that there is no absolute conflict with the stockholders as there would be if both were seeking to maximize pecuniary return—if, in short, the conventional economic motivation were accepted.

[7] I return to these matters in Chapters XXIII and XXIV.

7

One test of sound social analysis is that it explains small matters as well as great. One of the most puzzling pleas of the American business executive, regularly echoed in public rituals, is for lower taxes to encourage initiative and effort. The puzzle lies in the fact that few executives would ever admit to putting forth less than their best effort for their present income after taxes. To suggest such malingering would be considered a gross insult.[8]

An explanation is now at hand. The reference to incentives is traditional, a hangover from a more primitive association of income and effort. It accords seeming respectability and social utility to the desire for lower taxes or the natural wish to shift more of the existing burden to the poor. But the reality is that the executive's present level of income allows for identification and adaptation. These are the operative motivations. They are also the only personally reputable ones: the executive cannot afford to have it thought that his commitment to the goals of the corporation is less than complete or that he is at all indifferent to his opportunity to shape these goals. To suggest that he subordinates these latter motives to his response to pay would be to confess that he is an inferior executive.

[8]See Robin Barlow, Harvey E. Brazer and James N. Morgan, *Economic Behavior of the Affluent* (Washington: Brookings Institution, 1966), which strongly affirms the point. "A Group Profile of the *Fortune* 500 Chief Executive" (*Fortune*, May 1976) shows that the median work week of the chief executives of the 500 largest industrial firms in the United States is 55.7 hours, the median vacation a modest three weeks. To increase this work week and year by reducing taxes would have elements of inhumanity or social abuse.

XII

Motivation in Perspective

POWER in economic life has, over time, passed from its ancient association with land to association with capital and then on, in recent times, to the composite of knowledge and skills which comprises the technostructure. Reflecting the symmetry that characterizes reality, there have been associated shifts in the motivations to which men respond. Compulsion had an ancient association with land. Pecuniary motivation had a similar association with capital. Identification and adaptation are associated with the technostructure.

Land, as the strategic factor of production, made highly advantageous the use of compulsion. Agriculture, by its nature, scattered men over a wide space. Thus they required protection. The feudal lord who commanded their effort as cultivators also organized them into elementary military units for their mutual defense. As a further manifestation of the consistency that characterizes these matters, the relation of the lord to his temporal ruler was similar. As the price of peaceful possession of his land, he provided his ruler with armed men for the common defense or aggression. Dispersion also protected serfs and helots from the heresies and discontents which association of large numbers of people brews in the towns and cities. It also minimized the chance that they would come together for the ceremonial immolation of their masters.

Urbanization and compulsion go poorly together; the city, all but inevitably, has accorded the individual opportunities to escape his bond. And it has nurtured the ideas that give this escape moral sanction. Nor has slavery been easily adapted to the factory. In the early stages of the factory system, wage labor compelled by the fear of hunger was also, almost certainly, cheaper than slave labor compelled by the fear of physical violence. So with the emergence of capital as the strategic factor of production, pecuniary compensation became the primary motivation. Ownership of capital accorded power in the industrial enterprise. Nothing could seem more natural than that money—the physical manifestation of capital—should buy effort. As the feudal lord had access to force and used force to align others with his goals, so the capitalist had capital and used capital to align others with his goals. No one celebrated the change so vividly as Marx. Capital, through the agency of the bourgeoisie, has "pitilessly torn asunder the motley feudal ties which bound man to his 'natural superiors,' and has left remaining no other nexus between man and man than naked self-interest, than callous 'cash payments.'"[1] So cash payments, callous and otherwise, came, in time, to be considered the only motivation worthy of serious attention in the economic system.

Specialized knowledge and its coordination have now, as we have seen, become the decisive factor in economic success. This requires that men work in groups. And power passes to these groups. The participants are well-compensated; few regard their compensation with disinterest. But on associating with the group the individual finds himself attracted or compelled by its goals. He substitutes these goals for his own. He sees also the advantage—the access of power and influence—from exchanging a major pursuit of his own goals to a much smaller influence on the much greater power of the organization. Thus, from organization, comes a further system of motivation. As with pecuniary compensation and capital and land and compulsion, it is appropriate to its context. Pecuniary compensation, as an explanation of effort, has now a relatively much diminished role.

This is not a conclusion which will come easily to economists or perhaps even to others. There is again the muscular vigor of the assumption that people are primarily motivated by money and the reassurance that resides in the knowledge that one is relying on the seemingly crude manifestations of human nature. That one need never look beyond the love of money for an explanation of human behavior is one of the most jealously guarded simplifications of our anthropology.

It is worth recalling, however, that the commitment to force was once equally strong. The classical economists, writing in the late eighteenth and early nineteenth centuries, felt it necessary to enlarge at length on the advantages of free over slave labor. It was not what the sound and practical cit-

---

[1]Karl Marx, *The Communist Manifesto*.

izen could yet be expected to believe or what the colonial plantation owner could even contemplate.[2] There was long an atavistic conviction that superior social attitudes were associated with land ownership. More remarkably, there is still an atavistic conviction that force has a unique motivational value. In consequence, those who, because of deficient conscience or lack of respect for civilized behavior, are able to employ it are believed to have great advantage. Where its use is still allowed to civilized communities, it is, for the same reason, greatly admired. The point is worth a moment's notice.

2

During World War II, it was widely believed that the ruthlessly exercised power of the German dictatorship was a major source of strength, and one manifestation was its ability to command more than seven million foreign workers[3] from all the races of Europe. Here was the awesome power with which the opposition had to contend. Closer examination revealed no advantage. The slaves were brought, not in preference to wage workers, but as an expedient to replace them. And it is not evident that it was the best expedient. The most responsible and intelligent German leaders felt that more production could have been obtained by leaving French and other Western European workers to work for wages in their own factories than by bringing them as slaves to Germany. Or they favored greater reliance on voluntary recruiting of wage-workers.[4] Or they urged greater employment of women

---

[2] Adam Smith resorted to egregious exaggeration in making the point. "The experience of all ages and nations, I believe, demonstrates that the work done by slaves, though it appears to cost only their maintenance, is in the end the dearest of any." *Wealth of Nations,* Book 3 (New York: Modern Library, 1937), Chapter 2, p. 365. This is wholly untrue. In their time and for their mainly agricultural tasks they were more economical than any alternative supply of free labor.

[3] Of which 1.8 million were prisoners of war and of which some portion came voluntarily. *The Effects of Strategic Bombing on the German War Economy,* United States Strategic Bombing Survey, 1945, p. 34.

[4] This was a major point of controversy between Fritz Sauckel, minister in charge of labor recruitment, and Albert Speer, the highly intelligent arms minister. At one time during the war Speer arranged that designated industrial establishments in France would be given orders for munitions and their workers would be exempt from recruitment for forced labor in Germany. Sauckel's men promptly descended on these

and domestic workers as in Great Britain and the United States. A careful postwar study of the German experience concludes that the slave workers in Germany were an indifferent substitute for the women and domestic workers whom Britain brought into her labor force. ". . . [C]ivilian employment was maintained in Britain by internal mobilization, in Germany, by the importation of labor."[5] But the atavism which dominated so many of the attitudes of, as well as toward, the Third Reich set high store by compulsion. Compulsion was believed by Nazis and foreigners alike to be a manifestation of strength.

Similarly it was widely assumed that the Soviet Union, in the past, gained great advantages from its power to compel effort. "Thus, in the West by free consent, and in the Soviet Union largely by compulsion, two different conceptions of the ends and means of social life have [been devised] . . . for the economic development of their societies . . . The liberal Western way of development is economically more difficult and morally more demanding than the totalitarian or authoritarian way. But its material and spiritual rewards are correspondingly greater."[6] But again, on closer examination, the gains from compulsion dissolve. Presumably these were at their greatest in the labor camps of the Stalinist era. The dissolution of these by Khrushchev was widely thought to be a concession to more civilized procedures rather than efficiency. Yet few if any of these camps seem ever to have provided la-

---

factories and carried off the workers to forced employment in the Reich. Since there was no chance that others would expose themselves to the dangers of recruitment by making themselves so conveniently available, he effectively put an end to the experiment. The quarrel between Sauckel and Speer was still raging when they fell into Allied custody—I was one of the custodians—at the end of the war. Each intimated that hanging would not be inadvisable for the other. Sauckel was hanged. Speer, to Sauckel's presumptive distress, received twenty years from the Nuremberg Tribunal, from which he emerged to become one of the most widely read memoirists of World War II.

[5]Burton H. Klein, *Germany's Economic Preparations for War* (Cambridge: Harvard University Press, 1959), p. 144.

[6]*The Political Economy of American Foreign Policy,* Report of a Study Group Sponsored by the Woodrow Wilson Foundation and the National Planning Association (New York: Holt, 1955), p. 179. The ten authors of the book, including William Y. Elliott, Harry D. Gideonse, H. van B. Cleveland, were all undeviating exponents of the establishment view of American foreign policy in the postwar years.

bor for modern industry. They were in remote areas and devoted to land clearing, forestry, mining or construction, where labor productivity was almost certainly low. The closing of the camps made possible the employment of the inhabitants, together with their guards and keepers, in more productive enterprises. The gains must have been appreciable.

In the normal case in the Soviet Union men work for wages and are at liberty to change their places of employment. Much store is set in Soviet industry by both identification and adaptation. The bulletin boards of the factories are papered with the pictures of the more committed proletarians. The latter are heavily decorated with medals and conspicuously featured in public ceremonials. All are given the impression that their suggestions for improved performance are gratefully received and closely considered. A sense of compulsion would be inconsistent with this emphasis on identification and adaptation; it would weaken, not strengthen, the motivational system. It is characteristic of many who speak most of individual freedom in such matters that they do not think well enough of it to imagine that it might also be efficient.

A similar commitment to compulsion long survived in the United States in the case of military service. This too was atavistic. Once military service was uniformly painful and hazardous. By modern standards nations were poor and their tax systems weak; their predominantly rural populations were not easily attracted to other employments. Men might not have responded in sufficient numbers to a promise of higher pay. Had they done so, it would have been prohibitively expensive. Taxes would have been insufferable and war itself economically unsound.

With time, and reluctantly, there was accommodation to the modern reality. In the United States the Navy, Air Force and Marine Corps had long recognized that compulsion was destructive of identification and the use of volunteers, in a comprehensive sense, more efficient. Eventually, and influenced by the spectacular lack of identification on the part of Vietnam draftees, the Army came to agree. The abandonment of compulsion—of the draft—continues to be regarded by many as a moral retreat. Compulsion is deemed to be morally beneficial for those it strikes. It also, of course, is thought to transfer some of the cost of military service from the well-to-do taxpayer to the draftee who serves at less than market rates.

3

The strength of the surviving commitment to compulsion measures our task as we move on from pecuniary motivation to win even a supplementary role for identification and adaptation in the mature corporation. There is a unique sanctity about what has long been believed. Moreover identification and adaptation do not lend themselves to quantification and comparison, as does the amount paid to different men. And for this reason they are not easily adapted to the simplifications of mathematics and symbolic logic. Scientific truth in economics is not always what exists; often it is what can be handled by seemingly scientific methods. There is a further problem concerning what is taught. This depends on the textbook, and here truth must be tempered by what is marketable. What is marketable in a textbook is what is commonly believed or what is commonly believed to be believed. This, needless to say, is that pecuniary compensation is the only "hard" motivating force of analytical importance. Those who, for any reason, find the present ideas unpalatable should not be unduly disturbed. They will not have an easy passage. I venture to refer the reader to the addendum to this volume on the nature of social argument and its resistance to change.

Yet these ideas are consistent with everyday attitudes. A President of the United States is measured, as a matter of course, by the extent to which he is motivated by identification and adaptation—by the depth of his commitment to the goals, commonly called the welfare, of the nation, and by his willingness to use his office to advance the goals which he thinks desirable. This, in the common phrase, is to exercise leadership. A candidate for President who was thought too subject to pecuniary motivation—whose career had been too palpably devoted to making money out of oil, real estate, lumber, television or the stock market—would be under serious handicap. Once in office, a President must, of course, eschew all pecuniary interests.[7]

---

[7]Such was the argument in the early editions of this book. Since then the validity of the point has been amply demonstrated by the experience of Richard Nixon. His commitment to personal enrichment by tax avoidance and real estate prestidigitation contributed appreciably to his demise.

The same is true, in deteriorated form, for other politicians. Identification with the goals of the nation, state or community and adaptation expressed as a desire "to make something of the office" are the only acceptable motives. To suggest to a candidate that he is running for Congress or similar office because of the pay is to invite indignant denial.

The motivation of lawyers, physicians, artists or scientists is assumed to be similar. A good man is committed to the common professional, artistic and scientific goals; he seeks to alter these in accordance with his instinct, taste or knowledge. These alone are respectable motives. To be preoccupied with pecuniary return is to be substandard. Even the economist, who most takes for granted the primacy of pecuniary motivation, looks askance at the colleague who is too avid for consulting fees from corporations or textbook revenues or travel at the expense of the Ford Foundation. Academic courtesy may require that he refrain from first-person comment but duty dictates that he be vigorously critical of the transgressor when the latter is absent.

To reject adaptation and identification is to commit oneself to some difficult distinctions. In recent years, leadership in the exploration of distant space has been assumed by the Jet Propulsion Laboratory. This is operated on behalf of NASA by the California Institute of Technology. It is a nonprofit enterprise. It is taken for granted that the scientists, engineers and technicians associated with it are strongly identified with its goals and deeply proud of their contribution (i.e., their adaptive role) in the enterprise. It would seem silly, as well as insulting, to suggest that pecuniary compensation is the sole or even the dominant motive. A few miles away, similar scientists, engineers and technicians are employed on tasks of similar character and complexity at Lockheed and Hughes Aircraft. These are private corporations. Their men, it is assumed, are more or less exclusively motivated by the money they earn. Obviously such distinctions make no sense.

A decent respect for reality requires that we recognize that men serve organizations in response to a complex system of motivations. The mixture will be different in different cases. In the entrepreneurial corporation, in which those in charge have a primary concern for income, pecuniary motivation may be strong throughout the enterprise. In the mature corporation, identification and adaptation may be much more important, and this is especially probable if the firm has a strong scientific and technical orientation. And in the mature corporation the motivation will be very different for different levels or kinds of participants. To these differences I now turn.

XIII

Motivation and the Technostructure

THE MATURE CORPORATION is a large and complex organization, and individuals align themselves with its goals in response to different and varying combinations of the basic motives. This motivational system can best be understood if we abandon the conventional image of the corporate structure. This image is of a geometric hierarchy. Authority passes down from the top. At the summit, in a rectangular box, are the stockholders, the repository of ultimate power. Next come their representatives, the board of directors; then the executive officers or top management. Off to the sides are counsel, auditors, public relations experts, government relations men and other staff. From the top executives, the line of authority continues down through departments, divisions, plants, units and other subdivisions. It ends, untactfully, at the bottom with the proletarians.

In the mature corporation, however, the stockholders are without power; the board of directors is normally the passive instrument of the management; decisions, since complexity is usually associated with importance, are effectively the work of groups. These decisions move up through the organization more characteristically than down. It follows that the conventional image of organization—the customary organization chart—is aggressively misleading. So, accordingly, will be any analysis which uses it as a guide in relating individuals and groups to the corporation. The notion of a formal structure of command must be abandoned.

It is more useful to think of the mature corporation as a series of concentric circles. The band within each pair of circles represents a group of participants with a different motivational system. In the more spacious bands at the outer reaches are the most numerous groups. Such, in general, is their motivational system that they are the most loosely attached. At the center is what is now called the top management. Theirs is the firmest attachment. Between are the others. With this image in mind the motivational system of the various participants in the corporation can be much more intelligently considered.

2

In the outermost circle in the mature corporation are the ordinary stockholders. This, for all practical purposes, is a purely pecuniary association. The typical stockholder does not identify himself with the goals of the enterprise; he does not expect to influence these goals. He has a share in the ownership; normally his only concern is that it return him as much money as possible. If he can get more income or capital gain with equal security elsewhere, he sells and invests there. No sense of loyalty—no identification with the goals of the enterprise—normally prevents his doing so.

This is the general case. That of the sizable stockholder who sits or is represented on the board is different. So is that of the owner who, in the past manner of the Du Pont family, participates in management. But these cases diminish in significance as the corporation matures. At the time of his death the largest stockholder in American Telephone and Telegraph was, reputedly, the late Billy Rose, a noted songwriter and theatrical entrepreneur in his time. It seems unlikely that he identified himself closely with the telecommunications industry or regarded himself as a force therein. The relation to the corporation of the largest stockholders of Exxon, General Motors, United States Steel and like enterprises, with few exceptions, is equally impersonal. Certainly it is so of the ordinary stockholders.

As earlier noted, corporate folk rites seek to have the stockholders think possessively of their company. Few are fooled. The relation of the ordinary stockholder to the corporation is the purest case of pecuniary motivation.

3

The next inward circle is occupied by the production workers. Here, already, motivation becomes mixed. Clearly, pecuniary compensation is important; one test is the effect of a reduction in pay at the margin—say, a cut from double to straight time for overtime work. In most enterprises it would bring a prompt reduction in hours worked and effort expended. Some part of this effort is tedious or monotonous. Whatever the goals it serves, they are not those of the worker. These he would expect to pursue with a fishing rod, a television screen or a blend of whiskey and grain neutral spirits. He has no illusion that he can adapt the goals of the organization to his own.

Yet, in fact, motives are more complex. The worker, unlike the stockholder, lives in immediate daily association with the organization. This is itself an inducement to identification; an individual comes to think of himself as an IBM man, a Corning Glass man or a Sears man. The element of compulsion in the association has receded and, therewith, this barrier to identification. The entrepreneurial corporation sought to maximize the returns to the owners. The maximization of the pecuniary return of distant and manifestly well-to-do persons of carefully different social pretense was not a goal with which the ordinary worker, human nature what it is, would be likely to identify himself. The more ambiguous and less visibly egotistical goals of the technostructure[1] are less sharply in conflict with identification by the worker. Comparative security of tenure and the physically untaxing and, in occasion, interesting character of modern technological processes also lower the barriers to identification.

In fact, the motivation of the production worker is a mixture of pecuniary compensation and identification. The particular combination will vary greatly with the circumstances of the industry and firm. If the pay is high, the work interesting and the security of tenure great and the firm seems plausibly concerned with some goal other than making the most money for stockholders or management, identification will be significant. Given the routine and tedious assembly-line work that is subject to recurrent lay-offs and a seeming commitment to simple money-making, the likelihood of identification will be less. One indication is the smaller number of second-generation workers who follow their fathers onto the assembly line.

These differences bear strongly on the strategy of the firm in its labor policy. If identification is strong and can be strengthened, it will narrow the opportunities for the union. The latter has a chance only when commitment to the goals of the corporation is sufficiently slight so that it can win commitment to its own. (In everyday language, loyalty to the

[1]Chapter XV.

company must not conflict unduly with loyalty to the union.)
And identification can be increased by substituting automated
for manual processes. This, at one step, reduces the number
of workers susceptible to union goals and, by adding to the
pay, interest and physical ease of those remaining, increases
the tendency to identification.[2] With such identification and
the associated elimination of union power, industrial planning
becomes more secure. Wage costs are predictable; there is no
danger of the withdrawal of the labor force in a strike. It follows that even though automated processes are more expensive, the resulting identification and support to planning may
make them worthwhile. These, obviously, are matters of first
importance for judging the prospects for labor relations in the
planning system. I return to them in later chapters.[3]

4

Next, as one moves inward, are foremen and supervisory personnel and the clerical, sales and other routine white-collar
personnel. These merge at their inner perimeter with technicians, engineers, sales executives, scientists, designers and
other specialists who comprise the technostructure. Beyond
these at the center are the executives or management. As one
moves through these inner circles, identification and adaptation become increasingly important.

The barriers to identification disappear. There is no sense
of compulsion and thus no bar to voluntary adoption of the
goals of the employing organization. In the entrepreneurial
corporation men at all levels work, in principle at least, for
the enrichment of someone else. This, as noted, is not an easy
goal for men of average meanness to adopt. In the mature
corporation, in contrast, power has passed to the technostructure. Whatever its goals they cannot be, and as we shall see
are not, hostile to those of its own members. Identification is
thus facilitated. That the technostructure has power assures
that, within limits, it has power to adapt the goals of the enterprise to its own. Adaptation is thus further facilitated. As
one moves to the center of the technostructure, identification
and adaptation become increasingly powerful motivations.

[2]IBM is an interesting case in point. It has largely avoided union organization.
[3]Chapters XXIII and XXIV.

Regarding identification, Professors Simon and March suggest that it will be strong if members see, or sense, that the goals of the organization are shared by its participants. This restates the tendency just described. They list, in addition, four other circumstances inducing identification, as follows:

1. If the prestige of the group or organization attracting identification is high and widely perceived.
2. If there is frequent interaction between the individuals who comprise the organization.
3. If a large number of the needs of the individual are satisfied within the organization.
4. If competition between members of the organization is minimized.[4]

All of these requirements are met in the mature corporation, and increasingly so in the inner circles of the technostructure. Although, as later chapters will suggest, the prestige of business organization may well be declining, the large corporation continues to be a symbol of success and achievement in the culture.[5] It endows its members with this prestige; it is obviously better to be a General Motors or Western Electric man than an ordinary, unattached citizen. The question automatically asked when two men meet on a plane or in Florida is, "Who are you with?" Until this is known, the individual is a cipher. He cannot be placed in the scheme of things; no one knows how much attention, let alone respect, he deserved or whether he is worthy of any notice at all. If, however, he is with a large, well-known corporation—a good outfit—he immediately counts. The organization man has been a subject of much sorrow. But all who weep should recall that he surrenders to organization because organization does more for him than he can do for himself. For the moment it is sufficient that the mature corporation has the prestige which induces and encourages the individual to accept its goals in place of his own.

The requirement of frequent interaction between participants is also met. The technostructure, we have seen, is a mechanism for group decision-making. Such decisions are the

[4]James G. March and Herbert A. Simon, *Organizations* (New York: Wiley, 1958), pp. 65–66. The foregoing is a paraphrase of their specifications.

[5]Ibid., p. 67.

result of intense interaction between individuals.[6] So, by its very nature, the technostructure provides this inducement to identification.

The technostructure, and especially in the inner circles, also meets a large share of the needs of the individual. In very recent times, it has become fashionable, although not yet obligatory, for the corporation executive to have some non-business interests apart from therapeutic recreation and community service. The collection of abstract art, Indian pottery, old campaign posters or antique harmonicas; or patronage of the ballet or birth control; or cultivation of eccentric office designs are all manifestations of this trend. But it is still normally a matter of pride that the corporation absorbs nearly all his waking energy. All else, including family, politics, sex, even alcohol, is secondary. "To the executive there is between work and other aspects of one's life a unity he can never fully explain . . . How can you overwork, executives ask, if your work is your life?"[7] "The corporation, the job has dominated my whole life. Everything else has been secondary, and I know I've paid a price for it. I've had some fun and some successes, but I've paid a price—there's no question about that, but I'd probably pay that price again. For instance, I lost two wives to my job and I've reached a conclusion that there's no way to be happily married and successful in business at the same time. I believe that today."[8] None can doubt that for men who so testify the organization satisfies all needs with marked repleteness—that this inducement to identification is also fully satisfied.

Finally, although there is rivalry within the technostruc-

[6]On the basis of interviews supplemented by questionnaires with 221 executives and managers of various rank, William H. Whyte, Jr., concluded that ". . . the average executive spends roughly six of his eight office hours talking with other executives in meetings and conferences, and he would be considered an odd bird indeed if he went out to lunch by himself." *The Executive Life*, by the *Editors of Fortune* (Garden City, New York: Doubleday, 1956), p. 69.

[7]Ibid. Whyte quotes a steel executive in this further idyll of business and family life:

"Instead of relaxing at night with a mystery story, you keep at it until eleven o'clock and finally you say to yourself, 'The devil with it, I'm going to have a highball or two and go to bed.' But I sit there stewing until twelve-thirty or one. As a result I'm very uncompanionable at breakfast. My wife says I just sit there and dream, and maybe she's right. But I get a kick out of keeping informed about business."

[8]An executive vice president quoted in George de Mare, *Corporate Lives* (New York: Van Nostrand Reinhold, 1976), p. 123.

ture, the competition is not that of a zero sum game. Even though only one man gets promoted to the top job, all can get promoted. This also is consistent with identification. The small-town automobile dealer pursuing a customer or a small-city contractor pursuing a particular paving contract is, by contrast, in a zero sum game. (Significantly the participants themselves call it a cutthroat game). When he wins a sale or contract, his competitor loses it and vice versa. The inducement is to individually asserted goals and not to cooperative acceptance of common ones.

Within the technostructure, we may concede, the factors making for identification as specified by Simon and March have a clear run.

5

The technostructure, to repeat once more, lodges the power of decision with groups. And these involve the participation of a large number of individuals of widely varying rank and position. Thus a large number of people have access, or the illusion of access, to power. The goals of the entrepreneurial corporation were rigidly identified with the pecuniary interest of the entrepreneur. As these goals discouraged identification, so the rigidity of the commitment discouraged adaptation. In the mature corporation there is already indication that the goals are less rigidly prescribed. And they are within the ambit of the technostructure. The scope for adaptation is thus markedly enhanced.

Adaptation, as a motive, will be stronger as one approaches the inner circles of the technostructure. Here both the illusion and the fact of power are greatest. The individual will have increasing reason to feel that, by serving the organization, he can align it more closely with his own goals. The decisions of the groups in which he participates will be wider in scope. And his higher position in the hierarchy will contribute to his impression of power.[9]

[9] The modern management text emphasizes the effect of participation, and therewith of adaptation, on the quality of decision and on the quality of performance of the participants. "The best planning is done when managers are given an opportunity to contribute to plans affecting the areas over which they have authority. A good way of assuring adequate knowledge of plans, with the extra dividend of loyalty to them, is to have as many managers as possible participate in planning." Harold Koontz and Cyril O'Donnell, *Essentials of Management* (New York: McGraw-Hill, 1974), p. 122.

Adaptation, in the mature corporation, is also reinforced by the nearly invariable tendency for individuals to narrow the universe so that it is coterminous with their own horizons. This is most important. The schoolteacher's world is the school. The world of the preacher is bounded by the spiritually more marginal members of his congregation; the souls of those beyond are housed, not in theory but in practical attitude, in second-class citizens. The world of the bureaucrat is his unit, section, branch or bureau; for the prerogatives and performance of this he feels an intense responsibility and for the rest of the government a certain indifference, resentment or even contempt. Nothing is so important for the university professor as the department in which he serves. The university is a more impersonal world beyond. Only the exceptionally ambitious seek influence in the distant world of the Modern Language Association. It is in these circumscribed worlds, not the world at large, that each man observes the struggle, chicanery, duplicity, favoritism and political alliances which, as he sees them, really count. And it is this sub-universe that he seeks to accommodate to his own goals. To the desire of the individual to mold the world to his goals, a thoughtful Providence has added the illusion of a great ability to do so. This is accomplished by reducing each individual's world to manageable size. Adaptation, as a motive, is much strengthened as a result.[10, 11]

[10] The ancient and well-recognized pleasure in talking shop stems from this preoccupation with one's immediate community. Those who belong share the feeling that theirs is the only world that counts. Only to outsiders does their conversation seem parochial or uninteresting.

[11] This tendency is of great importance in government where small administrative subdivisions regularly acquire a larger-than-life reality to those associated with them and thus enlist diligent, devoted and ingenious service as well as fierce bureaucratic loyalties. After World War II, when Ph.D. thesis requirements in economics at Harvard were being extensively satisfied by war memoirs, I received a document of several hundred pages on the operation of the unit of the Office of Price Administration which had been concerned with price control for leather and synthetic shoe soles and heels. Price control for these products, I learned from this account, had been administered with energy, intelligence and ingenuity—heels were even tested on the shoes of Washington mail carriers and priced according to the mileage so survived. The thesis came close to associating success or failure in wartime administration with the success or failure of this unit of the price control organization. Though in charge of price control, I had not previously known of the unit or of its accomplishments. Nor did the thesis mention my office except as a distant and generally obtuse point of clearance.

These sub-universes in the mature corporation are numerous and come, for their members, to be similarly large in life. For those concerned with hiring, nothing is so important as personnel policy; for those concerned with information, data control and the computer, all other activities are secondary; for those teamed for the development of a new product, nothing is so central. For the lawyers, the general counsel's office is the brain of the enterprise. For the accountants, it is accounting. For the sales staff, it is sales. All this enhances the role of adaptation.

6

So it can reasonably be concluded that identification—the voluntary exchange of one's goals for the preferable ones of organization—and adaptation—the association with organization in the hope of influencing its goals to accord more closely with one's own—are strong motivating forces in the technostructure and become increasingly so in the inner circles. This is obscured because, as one moves to the innermost circle—to what is called top management—pecuniary compensation becomes generous. For the senior executives of the large corporation it is, on occasion, spectacular. Those who respond simplistically to the visible, associate motivation with this high compensation.

But, as we have previously seen, few things are so certain as the absence of any close relationship between compensation and effort in the inner circles of the mature corporation.[12] At the center of the corporation compensation is only a part of a larger motivational system which allows also for the full manifestation of identification and adaptation. To the specific goals these serve, after a word of summary, we now proceed.

[12]Cf. R. A. Gordon, *Business Leadership in the Large Corporation* (Washington: Brookings Institution, 1945), p. 312 et seq., and Mabel Newcomer, *The Big Business Executive* (New York: Columbia University Press, 1955), p. 121 et seq. Both authors conclude, in effect, that above a given level of compensation and subject to inevitable exceptions, pecuniary motivation is of secondary importance. As earlier indicated, this is to say that increases or decreases in compensation would not affect effort. In the course of interviews with executives W. H. Whyte, Jr., found that while complaints of high taxes were common, most conceded that such taxes had no effect on their effort. This was at a maximum in any case. *The Executive Life*, p. 66. See also Robin Barlow, Harvey E. Brazer and James N. Morgan, *Economic Behavior of the Affluent* (Washington: Brookings Institution, 1966).

XIV

The Principle of Consistency

IT IS NOW necessary to summarize and to reaffirm a rule. The relationship between society at large and an organization must be consistent with the relationship of the organization to the individual. There must be consistency in the goals of the society, the organization and the individual. And there must be consistency in the motives which induce organizations and individuals to pursue these goals.

As always, in social matters, we have here a deeply interconnected matrix. And it follows that if we know the goals of the society, we will have guidance to the goals of the organizations that serve it and the individuals who comprise these organizations. And the reverse will also hold. Similarly, if we know how individuals are motivated, we will know how organizations are motivated and also the reverse.

Unfortunately, to lay down a principle is neither to win understanding nor establish proof. Some elaboration is necessary.

2

In simple cases, consistency in the motivation of organization and individuals, and in the goals they pursue, is taken for granted. When, to recur to a previous illustration, the feudal lord was summoned to his military duty, he summoned, in turn, the liege men who were bound to accompany him. Compulsion, disguised or reinforced by tradition, motivated both. And compulsion, by its nature, required lord and subject to accept the same goals. Were the lord required to make a maximum display of martial ardor, this objective would have also to be imposed upon his followers. Otherwise his goal would be defeated, as has not infrequently happened in history, by a jarring contrast between the sanguinary courage of a leader and the extreme prudence of the led.

The lord could not be called to duty with his men unless

the power by which he was commanded was available to him, in turn, to command his followers. Since he was unpaid, it would have been impossible, or in any case fiscally unattractive, for him long to induce service by hiring men at going rates. And if he were himself rewarded for his service, he would have had, sooner or later, to negotiate some mercenary arrangement with his men, most likely a profit-sharing arrangement on plunder.[1] No one would be likely to supply him with power to enforce service for which they had already paid, and not many would be likely to serve well without pay for the profit of another. Thus do circumstances compel symmetry in the motivation and goals or organizations and the individuals comprising them.

These rules hold equally in the market economy. The accepted goal of such a society was to maximize its wealth and income. This measured its success. It is consistent with this social goal that business firms should seek to maximize their income. And it is consistent with this goal of the firm that individuals should seek to maximize their personal return. The society frowned on those who settled for less than the best they might earn or on firms which did not maximize their income (those which were poorly run) or which maximized return in such fashion—as by monopoly or fraud—as to prevent the society from doing so. As force motivated both the lord and his liege, so pecuniary return motivated both the business firm and its members.

The mature corporation, as we have seen, is not compelled to maximize its profits and does not do so. This, in principle, allows it to pursue other goals, and this accords similar alternatives to the members of the technostructure. The need for consistency, nonetheless, still holds. The goals of the corporation, though so freed, must be consistent with those of the society and consistent, in turn, with those of the individuals who comprise it. So also must be the motivations.

3

More specifically, the goals of the mature corporation will be a reflection of the goals of the members of the technostructure. And the goals of economic society, since the large corporations have a dominant position therein, will tend to be those of the corporation. If, as we have seen to be the case,

[1] As was established naval practice until well along in the last century.

the members of the technostructure set high store by autonomy and the assured minimum level of earnings by which
this is secured, this will be one objective of the corporation.
The need for such autonomy and the income that sustains it
will, in turn, be conceded or stressed by the society. If growth
of the corporation is good for the technostructure, economic
growth will surely be a social good.

So with other goals, and so matters work also in reverse. If
the society sets high store by technological virtuosity and
measures its success by its capacity for rapid technical advance, this will become a goal of the corporation and therewith of those who comprise it. It may, of course, be
subordinate, as a goal, to the need to maintain a minimum
level of income—the fact that the goals of the mature corporation are plural rather than singular does not mean that
all have the same priority. Rather a hierarchy of goals is
quite plausible. And given the requisite consistency between
social, corporate and individual goals, there is no *a priori* reason for assuming that the priorities will be exactly the same
for any two corporations.

The same consistency characterizes motivation—the stimuli
that set individuals and organizations in pursuit of goals.
Pecuniary compensation is an extremely important stimulus
to individual members of the technostructure up to a point. If
they are not paid an acceptable and expected salary, they will
not work. But once this requirement is met, the offer of more
money to an engineer, scientist or executive may bring little
or no more effort. Other motivation will take over. Similarly,
until the minimum requirements of the corporation for earnings are reached, pecuniary motivation will be strong. Above
a certain level, other goals can become more important.

Consistency is equally necessary in the case of identification. The individual will identify himself with the goals of the
corporation only if the corporation is identified with, as the
individual sees it, some significant social goal. The corporation that is engaged in developing a line of useful drugs wins
loyalty and effort from the social purpose its products serve
or are held to serve. Those engaged in the design or manufacture of a vehicle for a space probe identify themselves with
the goals of their organization because it, in turn, is identified
with scientific purpose or the more compelling hope of out-
distancing the Russians. The manufacturer of an exotic missile
or a better trigger for a nuclear warhead attracts the loyalty
of its members because their organization will be believed to

be serving the cause of freedom. It may also be held that human beings, whose elimination these weapons promise, have an inherent tendency to abuse freedom.

There is no similar identification if the firm is simply engaged in making money for an entrepreneur and has no other claimed social purpose. It is noteworthy that when a corporation is having its assets looted by those in control, it simultaneously suffers a very sharp reduction in executive and employee morale. All concerned recognize that the corporation is no longer serving any social purpose of any kind.

4

Consistency in the identification of individuals and organizations with social goals is possible because running as a parallel thread from individual through organization to social attitudes is the presence of adaptation as a motivating force. The individual serves organization, we have seen, because of the possibility of accommodating its goals more closely to his own. If his goals reflect a particular social attitude or vision, he will seek to have the corporation serve that attitude or vision. More important, he will normally think that the goals he seeks have social purpose. (Individuals have a well-remarked capacity to attach high social purpose to whatever—more scientific research, racially restrictive zoning laws, manufacture of the lethal weapons just mentioned—serves their personal interest.) If he succeeds, the corporation in turn will advance or defend these goals as socially important. The corporation becomes, thus, an instrument for attributing social purpose to the goals of those who comprise it. Social purpose becomes by this process of adaptation what serves the goals of members of the technostructure.

This process is highly successful in our time. Much of what is believed to be socially important is, in fact, the adaptation of social attitudes to the goal system of the technostructure. What counts here is what is believed. These social goals, though in fact derived from the goals of the technostructure, are believed to have original social purpose. Accordingly, members of the corporation in general, and of the technostructure in particular, are able to identify themselves with the corporation on the assumption that it is serving social goals when, in fact, it is serving their own. Even the most acute social conscience is no inconvenience if it originates in one's own conscience and is identical therewith.

5

The process by which social goals become adapted to the goals of the corporation and ultimately the technostructure is not analytical or cerebral. Rather it reflects a triumph of unexamined but constantly reiterated assumption over thought. The technostructure is principally concerned with the manufacture of goods and with the companion management and development of the demand for these goods. It is obviously important that this be accorded high social purpose and that the greater the production of goods, the greater be the purpose served. This allows the largest possible number of people to identify themselves with social function.

From a detached point of view, expansion in the output of many goods is not easily accorded a social purpose. More cigarettes cause more cancer. More alcohol causes more cirrhosis. More automobiles cause more accidents, maiming and death; also more pre-emption of space for highways and parking; also more pollution of the air and the roadsides. What is called a high standard of living consists, in considerable measure, in arrangements for avoiding muscular energy, increasing sensual pleasure and for enhancing caloric intake above any nutritional requirement. Nonetheless, the belief that increased production is a worthy social goal is very nearly absolute. It is imposed by assumption, and this assumption the ordinary individual encounters, in the ordinary course of business, a thousand times a year. Things are better because production, Gross National Product, is up. There is exceptional improvement because it is up more than ever before. That social progress is identical with a rising standard of living has the aspect of a faith. No society has ever before provided such a high standard of living as ours, hence none is as good. Sanction of an essentially priestly sort is supplied by the economists of the accepted neoclassical faith. They concede that an increase in Gross National Product is not a perfect measure of human progress. But they accord canonical blessing to no other view. Those who question have standing in these matters only for manifesting an interesting eccentricity.

There are other examples. Successful planning in areas of expensive and sophisticated technology requires that the state underwrite costs, including the costs of research and development, and that it ensure a market for the resulting products. It is important to the technostructure, therefore, that technological change of whatever kind be accorded a high social value. This too is agreed. In consequence, the underwriting of sophisticated technology by the state has become an approved social function. The burden of proof is on those who oppose state intervention for improved applications of nuclear power for peaceful purposes, even more on those who resist innovation for military purposes.[2] Social purpose is again the result of adaptation. This is a matter of obvious importance, and again one to which I will return.

None of this is to suggest that all social attitudes originate with the technostructure and its needs. Society also has goals stemming from needs which are unassociated with its major economic institutions and which it imposes on the mature corporation. As elsewhere, I argue only for a two-way process. The mature corporation imposes social attitudes, as it also responds to social attitudes. Truth is never strengthened by exaggeration. Nor is it less the truth by being more complex than the established propositions that assert the simple eminence of pecuniary goals and pecuniary motivation.

Happily, this complexity diminishes appreciably as these general rules are put to practical use.

[2] Although the tendency to such questioning has increased since the first edition of this book. I then cited public investment in supersonic travel as something above social criticism.

XV

The Goals of the Planning System

THE INDIVIDUAL member of the technostructure identifies himself with the goals of the mature corporation as, and because, the corporation identifies itself with goals which have, or appear to him to have, acceptable social purpose. And members seek to adapt the goals of the corporation to accord with their own, with the further result that the corporation seeks to accommodate social attitudes to its needs. What is deemed to be sound social purpose is thus, in part, a reflection of the goals of the corporation and the members of the technostructure. What remains now is to give concrete form to these relationships. We need to specify the social goals with which the corporation and the members of its technostructure identify themselves. And we need to specify the goals to which, in accordance with their needs, they ascribe social purpose.

These are, we may remind ourselves once more, problems of some novelty. As economic life is ordinarily regarded, they do not arise. The sovereign consumer has wants and desires original to himself or herself, or which, at most, arise by imitation from the consumption of fellow consumers. These wants and desires or the lack of them he or she manifests by his purchases or nonpurchases in the market. This, with the like action of others, is the social edict. To it the corporation, and all other producers, respond and, because of their commitment to maximize return, they do so without latitude or choice. The firm is wholly subordinate to the social edict as so prescribed. So, accordingly, are the people who comprise the firm. They do not impose their imprint on the goals of society.

This is a reassuring formula. The social will to which the business firm is subordinate is exercised in simple fashion from public master to corporate servant. The influence or power of the latter can cause no concern. If the reader senses that this may understate the social role of such evidently influential and conceivably omnipotent organizations as General Motors or Exxon, General Electric or General Dynamics, he will have correctly guessed the thrust of this book, and he will be receptive to its argument. If he suspects that economics, as it is conventionally taught, is, in part, a system of belief designed less to reveal truth than to reassure students and other communicants as to the benign tendency of established social arrangements, he will also be right.

For it is so. Modern economic belief is the servant, in substantial measure, of the society which nurtures it. And not the least of its services to that society is to render instruction to the young which, rather systematically, excludes speculation on the way the large economic organizations shape social attitudes to their ends. Nor is the service less important for being rendered, in the main, in innocence and in the name of scientific truth. On the contrary, were it arranged and paid for, it would cease to be of much effect. The wiles of the prostitute can be far more professional and superficially compelling than those of her artless competition but many more men succumb to the latter.

2

For any organization, as for any organism, the goal or objective that has a natural assumption of pre-eminence is the organization's own survival. This, plausibly, is true of the technostructure.

The first requisite for survival by the technostructure is that it preserve the autonomy on which its decision-making power depends. This means, we have seen,[1] that it must have a secure minimum of earnings. Power passes to the technostructure when technology and planning require specialized knowledge and group decision. The power remains securely with the technostructure as long as earnings are large enough to make accustomed payments to the stockholders and provide a supply of savings for reinvestment. If earnings are less than this level, it will be necessary to appeal to outside suppliers of capital. These, in turn, can ask questions and impose conditions and thus abridge the autonomy of the technostructure. And if the accustomed dividends are not covered, stockholders cannot wholly be counted upon to remain quiescent; as we have seen, struggles for control in

[1]Chapter VI.

large corporations occur all but exclusively in those that are suffering losses or which have meager and irregular earnings.[2]

The effects of low and high earnings on the technostructure are not symmetrical. With low earnings or losses it becomes vulnerable to outside influence and loses its autonomy. But above a certain level more earnings add little or nothing to its security therein. This autonomy, especially for the very large corporation, has become nearly absolute. This casts light, in turn, on the assumption that the mature corporation will seek to maximize its profits. By the most elementary calculation of self-interest, the technostructure is compelled to put prevention of loss ahead of maximum return. Loss can destroy the technostructure; high revenues accrue to others.[3] If, as will often happen, the maximization of revenues invites increased risk of loss, then the technostructure, as a matter of elementary interest, should forgo it.[4]

The need of protecting a minimum level of return will have, in turn, an important effect on industrial planning. While it will be desirable to achieve planned results, it will be

[2]There is a further and poignant reason for wanting to protect a minimum rate of return. While suppliers of capital tend to recognize, at least implicitly, that decision-making in the modern corporation requires autonomy—that they must not "interfere" with management decision—investigation and study are legitimate and are invited by inadequate return. And the management consulting industry, which exists in response to this opportunity, is highly available for such tasks. It, in turn, brings the pay, position and performance of members of the technostructure under a scrutiny that most executives would wish to avoid.

[3]"They [executives of the large corporation] do not receive the profits which may result from taking a chance, while their position in the firm may be jeopardized in the event of serious loss." R. A. Gordon, *Business Leadership in the Large Corporation* (Washington: Brookings Institution, 1945), p. 324.

[4]The importance of a minimum level of return is stressed, although not as strongly as here, by William J. Baumol, in *Business Behavior, Value and Growth* (New York: Macmillan, 1959), especially pp. 48–53, and by Robin Marris in *The Economic Theory of "Managerial" Capitalism* (New York: Free Press of Glencoe, 1964). Professor Carl Kaysen states the same conclusion as follows: "While the firm in the highly competitive market is constrained to seek after maximum profits, because the alternative is insufficient profit to insure survival, the firm in the less competitive market can choose whether to seek maximum profit or to be satisfied with some 'acceptable' return and to seek other goals." In "The Corporation: How Much Power? What Scope?" in *The Corporation in Modern Society*, Edward S. Mason, ed (Cambridge: Harvard University Press, 1959), p. 90.

even more important to avoid unplanned disasters. The first is pleasing; the second can be mortal. Even more important than a good price is protection against a price collapse. Even more important than a strong demand for the product is protection against a wholesale rejection. I return to the effect of these needs on the management of prices and demand in the next three chapters. And we shall see, thereafter, that the relation of the mature corporation to the state—its support of steps to regulate aggregate demand and its strong encouragement of public underwriting of expensive technology—arises from the same effort to exclude any threat to minimum levels of earnings. Similar considerations will be seen to underlie modern labor policy.

3

If the principle of consistency holds, the autonomy of the technostructure should be a goal of social policy. And, as a moment's thought will suggest, it is.

The doctrine of the planning system stresses powerfully its inherently and functionally independent character. It is the *private* enterprise system. A great gulf is deemed to divide the state from the business firm. Only in the rarest instances does the accepted theology approve any constraining action across this chasm. On nothing is the burden of proof so strong as on a measure—to provide standards of automobile safety, of drug advertising, of weights of packages, of health claims on behalf of cigarettes—which involves regulation, i.e., public interference with the autonomy of the industrial enterprise.

The grounds on which this autonomy is defended are palpably bogus. It is held that nothing must interfere with the independent operation of the market mechanism to which the firm is subject. The reality in the case of the mature corporation, as we have sufficiently seen, is that prices are substantially controlled by the firm, and the latter goes on to exercise influence on the amounts that are purchased and sold at these prices. The imperatives of technology and capital use do not allow the firm to be subordinate to the market, and the mature corporation, so far from being separated organically from the state, exists, as we shall presently see, only in intimate association with it.

The real reasons why autonomy is needed not being clearly seen, the power of the market and the allegedly deep and inherent separation between private enterprise and government are advanced in their place. Both, as noted, are articles of faith. It is a tribute to the power of adaptation that it can win social attitudes favorable to the autonomy of the technostructure that have such negligible relation to reality.

And, none can doubt, the requisite social attitudes have been secured. The right of the technostructure to autonomy, and more than incidentally to the earnings that assure it, is wholly accepted. Until very recent times no serious aspirant for public office ran on a platform of tighter regulation of business. Only as the fraudulent basis of the claim to autonomy has come to be understood have any begun to do so, and the number is still limited. A demand that government get off the back of business, the reference being to those public measures unlike the procurement of arms, the regulation of the airlines or the provision of roads that do not serve the planning system, has a resonant appeal to most politicians. Almost no one questions the need for an adequate level of profits, this being, generally speaking, whatever the firm is making.

The fear of public regulation is much misunderstood. To the entrepreneurial corporation the state was a threat to its income. It resisted public regulation for the purpose of protecting its profits. The modern observer, noticing that the mature corporation is making a good return and has an ample legal and clerical establishment to take care of the procedural details occasioned by public regulation, is surprised to find its executives alarmed about government intrusion or asking for comfort that none is intended. "Why are they so worried?" he asks. "Surely they are making plenty of money." He fails to see that the technostructure is protecting something more important than its profits—something, indeed, which profits themselves protect. That is its autonomy.[5]

4

Once the safety of the technostructure is ensured by a minimum level of earnings, there is then a measure of choice as to goals. There is little doubt as to what goal is emphasized. It is the greatest possible rate of corporate growth as measured in sales.

[5] I have discussed somewhat related considerations in *American Capitalism: The Concept of Countervailing Power*, rev. ed. (Boston: Houghton Mifflin, 1956), Chapter VI.

This is the goal that commends itself most strongly to the self-interest of the technostructure. Expansion of output means expansion of the technostructure itself. Such expansion, in turn, means more jobs with more responsibility and hence more promotion and more compensation. "When a man takes decisions leading to successful expansion, he not only creates new openings but also recommends himself and his colleagues as particularly suitable candidates to fill them."[6] "Simply, expansion of the individual corporation means increase in the height of the pyramidal hierarchy of managerial posts, and inflation of the rewards of money and power available at the top."[7] The paradox of modern economic motivation is that profit maximization as a goal requires that the individual member of the technostructure subordinate his personal pecuniary interest to that of the remote and unknown stockholder. By contrast, growth as a goal is wholly consistent with the personal and pecuniary interest of those who participate in decisions and direct the enterprise. The reader will sense once more how important profit maximization must be for the defense of traditional economic theory and specifically the rule of the market. Its use survives in competition with goals which reflect the self-interest of those immediately involved.[8] Empirical evidence is consistent with the hypothesis here offered. Monsen, Chiu and Cooley for the twelve years 1952 through 1963 have compared the earnings of large firms in which there is full management (i.e., technostructure) control with those in which there is substantial ownership interest. The return on invested capital for the

[6]Marris, p. 102. Although reached by highly theoretical techniques, Mr. Marris's conclusions as to the goals of the mature corporation are consistent with mine. So are Professor Baumol's, which are based partly on theoretical argument and partly on empirical observation.

[7]Tom Burns, "On the Rationale of the Corporate System" in *The Corporate Society*, Robin Marris, ed. (New York: Wiley, 1974), p. 131.

[8]Professor Shorey Peterson has argued ("Corporate Control and Capitalism," *Quarterly Journal of Economics*, Vol. LXXIX, No. 1 [February 1965], p. 11) that the need for profits to finance growth means that there is little practical difference between growth as a goal and profit maximization as a goal. Growth may be the best long-run strategy for maximizing profits. This is not so. While, if one waits long enough, one may sooner or later find one strategy miscarrying and another serving its ends better, the proper test is *ex ante* not *ex post* behavior. Price, sales, cost and other policies to maximize growth will differ within any given time horizon from those to maximize profits. Nor will profits be maximized if, as in the case of the technostructure, there is special reason to minimize risk.

management-controlled firms was substantially and consistently lower.[9]

The growth of the firm serves another important purpose for the technostructure. It is the best protection against contraction. For the firm with a small contingent of managers and supervisors and a large undifferentiated mass of blue-collar workers, a moderate shrinkage in production presents no great difficulties. A notice is posted and the men go; when needed they are called back. Those who post the notice are not personally involved.

With the rise of the technostructure, any contraction of output becomes much more painful and damaging. Costs can no longer be reduced simply by laying off blue-collar workers. A substantial share of total costs are now accounted for by the technostructure. If this remains intact, the firm will have a burdensome overhead in the form of a partially employed organization. In the technostructure men work in groups. Whole groups cannot be discharged. The discharge of individuals—or their voluntary withdrawal in response to their easily perceived unemployment—can impair the working efficiency of those who remain. Moreover, decisions for curtailment are made within the technostructure itself. They involve its own members. They do not have the agreeable impersonality which is associated with firing someone at a greater distance or of a different social class.

All of these unpleasant contingencies are avoided by expansion. Their avoidance may even justify comparatively unremunerative expansion. This is the meaning of the frequently heard statement that business is being taken, not for its profit, but "to hold the organization together." It can be a highly rational course.[10]

[9] R. Joseph Monsen, John S. Chiu and David E. Cooley, "The Effect of Separation of Ownership and Control on the Performance of the Large Firm," *Quarterly Journal of Economics*, Vol. LXXXII, No. 3 (August 1968), p. 435 et seq.

[10] In another view, as the technostructure grows, the proportion of the working force that must be treated as an overhead cost grows. But it is a special type of overhead. Unlike machinery or plant it disintegrates if not fully employed.

5

The growth of the firm as a goal of the technostructure is strongly supported by the principle of consistency. No other social goal is more strongly avowed than economic growth. No other test of social success has such nearly unanimous acceptance as the annual increase in the Gross National Product. And this is true of all countries, developed or undeveloped; Communist, socialist or capitalist. Japan has been deemed a successful society since World War II because of its very high rate of increase in Gross National Product. So also Germany and, for most of the period, France. Britain, with a much smaller increase, has been perilously close to being a failure. The Communist countries have been greater or less rivals of the non-Communist states in accordance with their greater or less increase in output. There are differences of opinion between Communist and non-Communist scholars on the validity of the statistics and concepts which are employed in the two worlds to measure economic growth. But there is no disagreement on the validity of the goal itself. Similarly it is now agreed that ancient cultures—India, China and Persia (the modern Iran)—should measure their progress toward civilization by their percentage increase in G.N.P. Their own scholars are the most insistent of all.

Given the agreement on economic growth as a social goal, the goal of the technostructure has a strong social purpose. Members can identify themselves with it in the secure knowledge that they are serving a larger purpose than their own. They seek to further the growth of their firm. This furthers the growth of the economy. Identification, as a motivation, reinforces the self-interest that is associated with such expansion.

The question inevitably arises to what extent economic growth, as a greatly agreed and advertised social goal, reflects adaptation. Does it reflect original social need? Has it been imposed on society by the technostructure? This question cannot be answered categorically. No doubt, the emphasis on economic growth is partly grounded in man's ancient and seemingly always inadequate supply of goods. And in modern times growth has been a principal remedy for unemploy-

ment.[11] Also economic growth eases many problems of allocation in the economy—it is much easier to find resources for
education or the poor by taking these from increased output
than by subtracting them from the existing standard of living.
But, as always, we must be alert to a two-way influence. The
acceptance of economic growth as a social goal coincides
closely with the rise to power of the mature corporation and
the technostructure. And the latter has had every reason to
value it as a social goal. It does not argue the merits of this
goal. As always it proceeds by massive assumption. What
other goal *could* be socially so urgent?[12]

6

Associated with growth as a goal of the technostructure is
technological virtuosity. This also serves the needs of its members. Progressive technology means jobs and promotion for
technologists. Capacity for expansion likewise depends very
largely on capacity for innovation. It is by technical innovation, real or simulated, that the firm holds and recruits customers for its existing products and expands to produce new
ones. Such capacity for innovation is obviously important for
keeping or expanding the firm's share of weapons, space and
other businesses with a high technological dynamic. But such
innovation tends also to have standing in its own right. As in
the scientific work of a university, prestige adheres to successful practitioners; it is a goal with which men readily identify
themselves. Here again the principle of consistency leads us
to look at social attitudes. And here again we find technological *advance*, as significantly it is called, solidly enshrined as a
social good. It is progress. It is synonymous with social
achievement. One would encounter less dispute, on the whole,
by questioning the sanctity of the family or religion than the
absolute merit of technical progress.

Technological virtuosity can be a goal of the technostructure only if it does not prejudice a minimum level of earn-

[11]Not infrequently in Western countries the amount of unemployment
is cited as a measure of the success or nonsuccess of the system. But
this, for nearly all scholars, is merely an indication of an insufficient
output. Given a greater rate of increase in Gross National Product—a
more successful economy by this standard—unemployment or most of
it would disappear.

[12]The reader in search of verification has an easy way of satisfying
himself on this point. He need only examine the dominant tone of the
orthodox reviews of the earlier editions of this volume.

ings. Given the costs and uncertainties associated with research and development, such a threat to earnings can easily happen. Then this goal must be abandoned or the cost and attendant risk must be transferred to the state; that is to say, government support for the particular development or the underlying research must be sought. Given the high social purpose attributed to technological change, this socialization of development is strongly approved. Adaptation—the acceptance of technological advance as a social goal—has paved the way. Nor need attention be paid to whether this investment of resources in technological and underlying scientific development is important in relation to alternatives. There is no need to measure the advantages of space achievements against help to the poor. In the nature of successful adaptation, the absolute virtue of technological advance is again assumed.

7

Now a concession must be made to seeming orthodoxy. A rate of earnings that allows, over and above investment needs, for a progressive rise in the dividend rate will also regularly be a goal of the technostructure. This return must not be achieved by prices which would prejudice growth. Nothing better suggests the primacy of growth as a goal than the vehemence with which the sacrifice of growth to profit would be condemned as unsound business practice. The risks taken for higher return, it is axiomatic, must not jeopardize the basic level of earnings. But tradition inherited from the entrepreneurial firm associates success with a rising level of realized earnings. And social attitudes, on the whole, take such an improvement in earnings over time as an indication of sound service to the community. Further, although the threat does not arise for the largest corporations of the planning system, for the somewhat less large a rising level of earnings helps secure the management against the danger of a takeover bid. Dissatisfied holders of low-priced stock can be persuaded to sell. Improving earnings and improving values are a defense against this possibility.

A secure level of earnings and a maximum rate of growth consistent with the provision of revenues for the requisite investment are the prime goals of the technostructure. Technological virtuosity and a rising dividend rate are secondary in the sense that they must not interfere with the two first-mentioned objectives. After these ends are achieved, there is further opportunity for a variety of other and lesser goals. These are subject only to the limitation that they must not interfere with the two primary objectives. They are in no sense rational or legitimate. But since these further goals will sometimes threaten minimum earnings and will not always contribute to the growth of the firm, their role will be closely circumscribed.

Building a better community; improved education; better understanding of the free enterprise system; an effective attack on heart ailments, emphysema, alcoholism, hard chancre or other crippling disease; participation in the political party of choice; and renewed emphasis on regular religious observances are all examples of such further goals. Some may also serve the primary and secondary goals—they contribute to what is called a sound corporate image and thus help recruiting and worker morale, avoid unwelcome taxes or cultivate a better public attitude toward products. But this is not necessary to justify the activity. It is sufficient that it serve goals that the technostructure (and the society) think good and that it not be in conflict with higher goals.

Nearly all economists, and a great many others, dismiss pursuit of such goals as irrelevant window-dressing. This is, in fact, an error. So long as their wholly subordinate role is clearly recognized, including the limitations imposed by cost, they are a perfectly plausible expression of the goals of the individual members of the technostructure and, thus, collectively of the mature corporation. What has been called the "social corporation" is a logical manifestation of the mature corporation and the motivation of its members. However, the role of window-dressing and rhetoric in the assertion of social goals is not negligible.

8

At any given time the symbols of business success will faithfully reflect success in pursuit of the currently accepted goals. In the latter half of the last century, the greatest folk hero of the economic system was the elder Rockefeller. This was the era of the entrepreneurial corporation; by its goals he was the greatest success, for he had made more money than anyone else.

In our time no man of wealth enjoys comparable distinction. Nor is esteem associated with individuals; by the nature of the technostructure they are submerged in the group. Esteem is associated with corporations. And among these, the first requirement is a secure earnings record. Any firm that fails this requirement is a dog. Its management is regarded with condescension. Sooner or later even subordinate employees will sense their loss of public respect and match it with a loss of self-respect. In the manner of the latter-day railway employee, they will conduct themselves in a slovenly and offensive manner indicating their feeling that the world in general and their customers in particular are their enemy. Or they will go elsewhere.

Given a secure level of earnings, the esteemed firms are those which are large—which have a record of achieved growth—or which are growing with particular speed. Increasingly, esteem is associated with the latter. And if a firm has a reputation for technological innovation, it is additionally known as a smart outfit. Thereafter the dividend record will be mentioned. One knows little of life unless he has a theoretical system by which to interpret it. But there is little in theory that cannot be tested in life.

XVI

Prices in the Planning System

IT WILL BE EVIDENT that the need to keep the modern corporation subordinate to the market causes grave problems for the once estimable subject of economics. But nowhere are the contradictions so evident and the problems of illogic so melancholy as in the theory of price behavior. And nowhere are the clarifying rewards of reality so great.

The way prices are set—what economists have always called value theory—was until very recent times the heart of the subject. For thousands of reluctant scholars, a few distantly remembered curves depicting the interaction of supply and demand to establish prices have for long been the only permanent return on an investment in economic education. Let me now state in more detail an argument earlier introduced.

There has long been agreement on how, in an ideal world, prices should be set. The process would be impersonal. No individual or firm by its presence or absence in the market would have power durably to affect that market. If it could do so, it would influence prices in its own favor. Such power would be least when all participants are small in relation to the market in which they participate. It would be greatest where there are few sellers or buyers or only one. The latter situation, that of the monopolists, is the apogee of improper influence. In the English language only a few words—fraud, subversion and sodomy—have a greater connotation of non-violent wickedness.

Yet in the characteristic market of the planning system there are only a handful of sellers. The domestic automobile market is shared by four firms and dominated by three. Markets for primary aluminum, copper, rubber, cigarettes, soap and detergents, explosives, glass, refrigerators, cellulose fibers, photographic equipment, cans, calculating machines, chocolates and numerous other items are dominated by four firms.[1] Nearly all are examples of the mature corporation with which we are here concerned. Such is the planning system.

This market situation is recognized in all modern microeconomic theory. Under the cognomen of oligopoly it is assumed to have, in its price-making, some of the powers of a monopoly and some of the restraints of competition. A variety of arrangements and conventions facilitate its approach to the monopoly goal. There may be, though perhaps rarely, some clandestine negotiation on prices to establish the one that is best for all. Or one firm acts as a price leader. It calculates the price that will best serve the interest of all, presumably with some special attention to its own needs. Others unfailingly follow. Or, on the basis of a common knowledge of costs and demand, each firm calculates and proclaims the price that will serve the interests of the industry. Minor differences in the resulting published schedules are then composed. The uncertainty of these procedures may keep the oligopoly price from being as precisely optimal to the participants as that of a monopoly. There is a tendency, also, to leave it unchanged for appreciable periods of time since any substantial movement invites some risk that others will not follow.

Although price competition is inconsistent with the common concern to achieve the closest possible approach to a monopoly price and profit and, indeed, is a source of grave alternative dangers, this does not mean, in the conventional view, that competition is exorcised. Competition is held to be inherent in the animal spirits of the entrepreneur. In response thereto he advertises and merchandises his product with even greater energy and aggressiveness for not being allowed to cut prices. And for the same reasons he remodels, repackages and, on occasion, seeks to improve his product in order to entice customers from his rivals.[2]

---

[1] In the case of all mentioned, the largest four firms in 1972 had 60 percent or more of the market. United States Department of Commerce, Bureau of the Census, *1972 Census of Manufacturers, Special Report: Concentration Ratios in Manufacturing,* (1975). Walter Adams, in *The Structure of American Industry,* 4th ed. (New York: Macmillan, 1971), shows how this control is further reinforced by the extension of the control by large firms to different markets, related as well as unrelated.

[2] "An oligopolist's primary concern is with his sales strategy. His firm stands or falls with his success in attracting sales without changing price, a situation that is quite alien to all other market forms. His situ-

Although the theory of price-making under oligopoly is subject to some further refinements, it is not an especially complicated area of economics. Dubious as the reader may be of anything so simple, the foregoing is the essence of what is now taught.

2

In this analysis the oligopolistic firm, however large, remains safely subject to control by the market. It wishes, in general, to maximize its profits. It does the best it can, and though it fails, and though the failure makes its performance more tolerable than that of a monopoly, it does not make it less subject to the control of the market. So the genie of independent pursuit of alternative goals—of exercise of plenary power unrelated to market motivation—is kept safely in the bottle. Oligopoly is in safe descent from its competitive antecedents. But the price of this accomplishment is rather appalling. It is that oligopoly, the prevailing form of industrial market organization, is inefficient and shouldn't exist.

That is the ancient conclusion concerning monopoly. It extracts prices higher in relation to costs than does a competitive firm. It gets wealth which, otherwise, would remain with the buyer in the form of lower prices. And the counterpart of the higher prices is a smaller volume of sales and a smaller output of goods than if prices were those that a competitive firm would have to set. The labor and capital that are not employed because of these higher prices and the consequent smaller production for smaller sales must find less advantageous employment elsewhere. An oligopoly is not as iniquitous as a monopoly. But that is not because of aspiration but ability. Oligopoly is an imperfect monopoly. Like the despotism of the Dual Monarchy, it is saved only by its incompetence.

These somber implications are not evaded in contemporary economic discourse and instruction. It is accepted that oligopoly—and therewith the corporations that comprise the planning system—are economically inefficient. This being agreed the matter is then resolved by a further, usually tacit agree-

---

ation is complicated by the fact that his competitors will not stand idly by while he does his best: they will ape his innovations, make some of their own, and match his advertising campaigns with theirs." Robert Dorfman, *Prices and Markets,* 2nd ed. (Englewood Cliffs, New Jersey: Prentice-Hall, 1972), p. 159.

ment that nothing of importance should be done about it. It is conceded, finally, that what is inefficient in each part is efficient in the aggregate. This will not seem very satisfactory on purely logical grounds but difficulty must always be expected in reconciling an erroneous view of how things work with reality. The standard literature readily reveals the contradiction.

The Department of Commerce in one of its forays against economic illiteracy, it will be recalled, established the requirements for efficient pricing as follows: "To the extent that a price is reached by means that are *not* impersonal—to the extent that either the buyer or the seller can dictate or influence the setting of the price—to that extent our system of controlling the efficient use of resources is not working properly."[3] Since all large firms can dictate or influence prices, this means that wherever they are present, the economy will not work properly. Without being conscious of its action, the Department came up with a massive indictment of the American economy, and had the implications of its assertion been fully understood, its Secretary would have needed impeachment. The most distinguished textbooks come to the same subversive conclusion. "Oligopolies suffer from being peculiarly rigid and unresponsive to market conditions. They also are practically compelled to dissipate economic resources in advertising and in meretricious variations in product characteristics. . . . The prevalence of monopoly and oligopoly is a serious defect in the free-market system of organizing economic activity."[4] "The economic evils of [oligopoly and other market imperfections] transcend the mere matter of monopolistic profits. . . . monopolistic and oligopolistic pricing . . . brings distortion of resource allocation (inefficiency and non-responsiveness) even if the firms involved have their excess-profits taxed or competed away."[5] "To reduce imperfections of competition, a nation must maintain perpetual vigilance."[6]

The main point may again be stressed. Most industrial production comes from large firms which have extensive power in the market. They are oligopolies. So the finding in the

[3] *Do You Know Your Economic ABC's? Profits and the American Economy*, United States Department of Commerce, 1965, p. 13.
[4] Dorfman, p. 168. Professor Dorfman, with characteristic honesty, concedes that what is very bad in principle has a "surprisingly small" adverse effect.
[5] Paul A. Samuelson, *Economics*, 10th ed. (New York: McGraw-Hill, 1976), p. 532.
[6] Ibid., p. 531.

textbooks is that the modern economy is mainly exploitive in the prices that it charges, wasteful and inefficient in the way it employs resources and challenging in its need for reform. Then from the same books comes the conclusion that the modern economy is generally satisfactory. Theoretical performance is bad but aggregate performance is good.[7] To the person who insists on asking how this contradiction is resolved, the answer is that it is not. The theory of price-making under oligopoly leads to conclusions that cannot be reconciled with the results (i.e., the productivity gains) on which the theorists themselves agree.[8,9]

3

The public policy which derives from the present view of pricemaking in the planning system involves the same contradictions as the theory and a roughly similar resolution. Monopoly is illegal. The market power associated with oligopoly or small numbers is not in principle presumed to yield dif-

[7]In recent writings both Professors Dorfman and Samuelson have become more restrained in their view of economic performance. Samuelson, who in earlier editions of his textbook foresaw a steady 4 percent rate of growth "even if we do not rouse ourselves" (*Economics*, 8th ed. [New York: McGraw-Hill, 1970], p. 816), now concludes that ". . . there is some indication of a slowing down, but not nearly to a halt." (10th ed., p. 370).

[8]In much contemporary economic instruction the conflict is again concealed by the division of labor. Market theory belongs to what is called microeconomics. Here oligopoly prevails and the problem of efficiency and performance is very grave. The growth of the economy as a whole is treated under the rubric of macroeconomics, which has to do with aggregate movements in income and output. Here the problems of market behavior are not examined, oligopoly is not considered and productivity gains are very high.

[9]As a purely technical safeguard, I must point out that the contradiction cannot be resolved by claiming that while market behavior and consequent resource distribution under oligopoly are very inferior, this is offset by the high capital investment, effective organization and technological virtuosity of the oligopolist. For apart from the fact that it is the usual claim against the oligopolist that he keeps prices too high and has an undercommitment of capital and labor, it is evident that he makes effective use of capital, organization and technology because he is big and because he is big, he is also an oligopolist. No one can ask him to be an oligopolist for the purposes of capital investment, organization and technology and to be small and competitive for the purposes of prices and allocative efficiency. There is a unity in social phenomena which must be respected.

ferent results. So it is under similar suspicion. But since it is pervasive and in practice seems to serve quite well, nothing is done about it. This evasion is then disguised by a great deal of peripheral litigation and by the well-understood tendency for any learned discussion, if sufficiently voluminous, to obscure the issue.

Since 1890, in the United States, the wickedness of monopoly, anciently asserted in English common law, has been affirmed by statute. In that year the Sherman Act prohibited combinations in restraint of trade and made it a misdemeanor to "monopolize or attempt to monopolize" any interstate or foreign commerce. The Clayton and Federal Trade Commission Acts of the early Wilson Administration extended the prohibition to particular steps—price discrimination, exclusive contracts, acquisition of stock in a competing corporation, undefined unfairness—which might lessen competition. And legislation following World War II—the Celler-Kefauver Antimerger Act—proscribed mergers between firms which might promote monopoly. This made effective an earlier ban on purchase by one firm of the stock of a competitor, a ban which, conveniently, had not prevented forthright purchase of its assets.

Everyone concerned with the enforcement of the antitrust laws agrees, in principle, that oligopoly is an imperfect form of monopoly. This has also a measure of acceptance in the court decisions. In 1946, the large cigarette companies were successfully prosecuted for tightly parallel action in setting cigarette prices, a commonplace aspect of oligopoly pricing.[10] And there is an increasing measure of agreement that oligopoly is not a special but a general case—it is the market structure of the planning system. An antitrust policy that would go "to the problems of the existence and significance of market power" would not be "aimed at merely marginal or special phenomena, but at phenomena spread widely through the economy."[11]

The solution has been nonetheless, to ignore oligopoly. Monopoly is illegal. Oligopoly, which is agreed to have the same consequences but with diminished force, is not. In the parallel case in criminal law, a man who hits his neighbor heavily

---

[10]*American Tobacco Company vs. United States.* 328 U.S. 781 (1946).
[11]Carl Kaysen and Donald F. Turner, *Antitrust Policy: An Economic and Legal Analysis* (Cambridge: Harvard University Press, 1959), p. 41. Mr. Turner subsequently became Assistant Attorney General in charge of the Antitrust Division, United States Department of Justice.

over the head with a sledge hammer is guilty of assault. A man who uses a slightly blunter instrument, or has a poorer aim, is innocent. The reason in the case of oligopoly is that, the theory notwithstanding, it is impracticable to indict and prosecute—if possession of market power be the test—the whole planning sector of the economy. It is also, on occasion, conceded that performance under oligopoly does not, in fact, accord with what the theory leads one to expect. "We can . . . [not] predict market performance from market structure."[12] It may not be bad at all.

The conflict between the legal condemnation of monopoly and its *de facto* acceptance in slightly imperfect form as oligopoly is stark. In real life it is blurred, as noted, by the very exhaustiveness of the discussion surrounding the subject and also by a good deal of enforcement activity which deals not with the fact of oligopoly and market power but with actions which might promote it. This leads to further contradictions.

The law is very severe on any overt collusion in the setting of prices. Such collusion simplifies the task of the oligopolists in seeking to arrive at the most advantageous price for all. And the government closely scrutinizes mergers which might have the effect of increasing the market power of the individual oligopolist. The most important effect may thus be to deny market power to those who do not have it or have difficulty in exercising it while according immunity to those who already have such power.

Thus the three majors in the automobile industry, as the result of long and intimate study of each other's behavior within the confines of one city, are able to establish prices which reflect the common interest. And they can do so with precision. No consultation is required. The procedure is legally secure. Not much would be changed were the companies allowed, in fact, to consult and agree on prices.

A group of smaller suppliers of parts or sub-assemblies to the automobile industry will not have the same capacity for estimating each other's needs and intentions. They may also be more numerous—that is to say, they will have less market power. Should it become known that in response to their

[12]Ibid., p. 61. The authors elsewhere (pp. 44–45) go even farther to suggest that "the primary goal of antitrust policy be the limitation of undue market power to the extent consistent with maintaining desirable levels of economic performance." This, of course, implies that higher levels of market power are associated with higher levels of economic performance. Market power, in other words, can be socially efficient. The imprecision, economic and legal, becomes total.

weaker (and more competitive) position they have come together to discuss prices, and thus to win some of the ability to control prices that the automobile majors possess as a matter of course, the law would be upon them like a tiger. It exempts the market power of the strong. And it partly disguises this exemption by attacking efforts by the weak to acquire like power.

Similarly, if a large and puissant corporation has forty or fifty percent of the market for some steel, chemical, drug, vehicle or other product and is expanding its share vigorously, it is regarded by the law with a benign eye. But if two smaller competitors unite and the resulting union has more than a mere fifteen percent of the market, there is every likelihood that the law will be invoked. Again the law exempts those who possess the market power and concentrates on those who would try to possess it. The form is prosecuted; the substance is exempt. We discriminate against those who, as a result of numbers and weakness, must use crude or overt methods to control their markets and in favor of those who, because of achieved size and power, are under no such compulsion.

This, to be sure, is not the whole story of the antitrust laws. They also prevent unfair aggression, as the community regards it, by large firms against the small. And they curb, on occasion, the rapacity of individuals and firms who survive in the entrepreneurial mold and who unite to enrich themselves at the popular expense. But in their bearing on the planning system and their need to exempt in practice the market power that they condemn in principle, the antitrust laws are sadly at odds with reality.

They have also an obscurantist role. In some rather special circumstances, when the price behavior of another firm in the industry cannot easily be foretold and illegal communication becomes necessary, members of the technostructure risk running afoul of the antitrust laws. They are then, if caught, made to suffer considerable personal indignity. Otherwise the antitrust laws are harmless to the large firm. And meanwhile these laws add to the illusion of control by the market. What the theory asserts as to the paramountcy of the market, the law affirms. Enforcement is announced or promised or demanded. The susceptible, and those who love the market as a mistress, can persuade themselves that it is being restored or could be restored. The fig leaf by which power is kept out of sight is held in place not only by economists but by the statutes of the United States and the decisions of its courts.

The antitrust laws still claim the full affection of lawyers; this, no one should doubt, is partly because of the handsomely rewarded litigation that they nourish. In the last ten years or so, their place in the economists' decalogue has diminished. Most men of flexible mind would agree that they have little real bearing on the major sources of market power. And there would be a measure of agreement that present enforcement attacks the symbols of market power and leaves the substance.[13] But the question as to why market power does not have the inimical tendencies anciently associated with monopoly remains largely unanswered and ignored in modern economic theory. It will remain thus until prices are seen in their modern role as instruments of industrial planning in the service of the goals of that planning.

[13] For an interesting and important account of the declining faith in the antitrust laws and the reasons, which parallels much of the present argument, see Richard Hofstadter, "What Happened to the Antitrust Movement?" in *The Business Establishment*, Earl F. Cheit, ed. (New York: Wiley, 1964), p. 113 et seq.

XVII

Prices in the Planning System
(Continued)

THE CONTRADICTION between a price theory that condemns the inefficiency of the system and a result that is applauded for its efficiency is, or should be, troublesome. This is the consequence of the orthodox view. The contradiction disappears when prices are viewed in the full context of industrial planning and in full service to the goals of the technostructure.

Specifically, industrial planning requires that prices be under control. Modern technology, we have seen, reduces the reliability of the market. And it increases the commitment of time and capital that are required in production. For this reason prices cannot be left to the vagaries of the unmanaged market.

But this control, naturally enough, is so exercised that it serves the goals of the technostructure. These, we have seen, are first, to minimize the risk of loss and therewith of damage to the autonomy of the technostructure, and secondly, to maximize the growth of the firm with concomitant attention to rising profits. Prices are so managed as to serve these goals. Price competition with its attendant dangers must be prevented. Prices must be low enough to facilitate the recruitment of customers and the expansion of sales and at the same time high enough to provide earnings to finance growth and keep the stockholders content. These prices are readily reconciled with accepted social goals or what society has been persuaded to accept as goals. There is no barrier to identification with these goals by members of the technostructure, as there would be were the goal the unmitigated pursuit of monopoly profit for the benefit of unknown, nonparticipant stockholders.

This is why price control by the mature corporation is combined not with inefficient performance as the traditional theory prescribes but with the generally favorable performance that its exponents concede. And it is also why this con-

trol enjoys immunity under law. However socially inimical
the control of prices is in principle, the results are not so
viewed. The law is helpless in applying penalties to what is,
on balance, socially acceptable.

We may look first at the way price control is effected, and
how protection against disastrous price failure is ensured, and
then at the level that is set.

2

The planning system provides the price control that it requires as an effortless consequence of its own development.
Modern industrial planning requires and rewards great size.
This means that a comparatively small number of large firms
will share the typical market. Each will act with full consideration of its own needs and of the common need. Each must
have control of its own prices and will recognize this to be
the common requirement. Each will forswear any action, and
notably any sanguinary price-cutting, which would be preju-
dicial to the common interest in price control. This control is
not something that must be contrived. Nor, except in a few
peculiarly complex cases, is it very difficult to sustain.

We are all conditioned by the theology of the market. Con-
sequently nothing seems good or normal that does not accord
with the requirements of the market. A price that is fixed by
the seller to a singular degree does not seem right. Accordingly, it requires a major act of will to think of price-fixing as both normal and having economic function. In fact, it
is normal in all advanced industrial societies.[1] The nonsocial-

---

[1]Even modern agriculture, although generally subject to the market,
cannot accommodate itself effectively to radical price changes, and all
countries with highly developed agriculture have moved toward planning in this industry to the extent of establishing systems of price control in the form of minimum price guarantees. This has been the direct
result of advancing technology and increasingly heavy capital requirements. And the consequence (and most notably in the United States)
of price security and the associated ability to plan has been much increased investment by farmers in new capital and technology. The further result has been gains in productivity in recent years that have
been considerably greater in agriculture than in industry. It should be
noted that, farmers being numerous, there is no chance for the nongov-
ernmental regulation of prices that, as a matter of course, characterizes
the planning system. It has had to be done by the government. And so
deep is the commitment to the illusion of control of the enterprise by
the market that this price regulation—which cannot be concealed—is
still not wholly accepted by economists, including those who otherwise

ist economies of countries other than the United States employ it, usually in a less embarrassed and more overt fashion. Formal price-fixing by cartel or other agreements covering the members of the industry are commonplace. So is a good deal of straightforward communication between firms in setting prices. But even where tradition frowns on such agreements or communications, as in Canada and to some extent in Britain, there is the same tacit control as that of oligopoly in the United States. Were there something peculiarly efficient about the market and inefficient about formal price-fixing, the countries eschewing the first and using the second would have suffered drastically in their development. There is no indication that they have. The reason is that theirs is merely a more formal variant on American industrial price control.

Socialist industry also works, as a matter of course, within a framework of controlled prices. In recent times the Soviet Union and some of the other Eastern European countries, following the earlier Yugoslav practice, have been according to firms and industries some of the flexibility in adjusting prices that the more informal evolution has accorded to the American system.[2] This has been widely hailed as a return, by these countries, to the market. That is a mirage. It does not mean, any more than in the American system, that the large socialist firm is subject to control by market prices over which it exercises no influence. It means only that its control can be more flexibly exercised in response to change.

3

The first concern of the technostructure, as we have seen, is to protect the minimum level of return which secures its autonomy and hence its survival. For this reason it must minimize the risk of any development that might threaten minimum return and thus its survival. A breakdown in prices, a possibility that is inherent in an uncontrolled market or which might result from an outbreak of competitive price-cutting, is preeminently such a danger. This danger the technostructure

---

applaud agricultural efficiency. The fixed prices, by distorting resource use, are thought to be a source of inefficiency. It is not observed that the same fixed prices make possible the advanced technology and higher capital inputs which greatly enchance productivity.

[2] Most often it has been in that part of the economy—service industries, handicrafts, agriculture—that is characterized by small units.

is at great pains to exclude. And, with rare exceptions, it is successful.

This is accomplished, in all ordinary circumstances, by a common response to a clearly recognized and common danger. Any large firm in a modern industry of few firms which used prices as a weapon of competitive aggression would force the others to respond in kind. All would suffer. Accordingly, no matter how great the rivalry between firms or how carefully cultivated the institutional feuds and dislikes, such action is exorcised by the strongest rules governing acceptable corporate behavior. It is a tribute to the social capacity of man that such mutually destructive tendency is so successfully banned.

It does occur, however, in exceptional circumstances where there are technical difficulties in arriving at equal prices. This requires resort to illegal collusion and explains the occasional brush of the mature corporation with the antitrust laws.

Thus, in the early nineteen-sixties, General Electric, Westinghouse, Allis-Chalmers, Ingersoll-Rand and other manufacturers of electrical equipment were prosecuted for conspiring to fix the prices of heavy electrical apparatus. A number of senior executives in several of these companies were lodged very briefly in the common jail, a fate from which, quite correctly in light of all experience, such executives, whatever their breach of law, are believed to be immune. It was then a matter of some wonder as to what sacrificial avarice could cause paid executives to risk such infamy on behalf of stockholders they would never know. The explanation, however, is clear. The price-fixing was for transformers and switch-gear which are built to individual specification and sold, in part, by sealed bids. Unlike standard electric motors, washing machines or refrigerators, these have no common price. There being no such price, taut adherence to a given price or price schedule was impossible. And the low bidder took all of the business. In the past, in consequence, there had been severe price-cutting; there was, at the time, a prospect of heavy losses.

It was this—the technical difficulty of tacit control and the prospect of losses—that caused the executives to come together. It is most unlikely that a simple desire to enhance profits would have led to the conspiracy. The error of the executives was not in fixing prices but in being engaged in a branch of the business where price-fixing involved such exceptional difficulty. Prices were equally regulated for electric motors or household appliances, but there it could be done without collusion.

Subsequent suits against the steel companies charged collusion in setting the prices for specialized steel products. These, evidently, involve a similar problem in setting prices. This collusion was singled out for prosecution, although not even the most devoted friend of the antitrust laws would argue that prices of ordinary steel are governed other than by a well-recognized industry-wide schedule to which all firms adhere as a matter of course.

4

Once established, industrial prices tend to remain fixed for considerable periods of time. None supposes that prices of basic steel, aluminum, automobiles, machinery, chemicals, petroleum products, containers or like products of the planning system will be sensitive to the changes in cost or demand which cause constant price readjustments for commodities, such as lesser agricultural products, where producers are still subject to control by the market. This stability of prices, in face of changing costs and demand, is a further indication, it may be noted, that in the short run the mature corporation pursues goals other than profit maximization.

Stable prices reflect, in part, the need for security against price competition. Under modern industrial conditions a seller has rarely a single price. More often the firm has an infinitely complicated schedule for all of the models, grades, styles and specifications that comprise its offering. For several firms to change prices more or less simultaneously and without according some price advantages to part of the product line of any one firm and without discussion of the matter is a delicate procedure. And there is always a chance that a firm will be thought to be seeking a competitive advantage on some part of its product line. This, in turn, could invite the retributive price-cutting that so contravenes the canons of corporate behavior with the danger that the whole price schedule would be broken down. Convenience as well as the security of the earnings of the firm thus counsel keeping prices unchanged for relatively long periods.

But price stability also serves the purposes of industrial planning. Prices being fixed, they are predictable over a substantial period of time. And since one firm's prices are another's costs, so costs are also predictable. Thus stable prices facilitate control and minimize the risk of a price collapse that could jeopardize earnings and the autonomy of the technostructure. In this they serve a prime goal of the technostructure. At the same time they facilitate planning by the firm in question and by those to which it sells.

This structure of control is far more important than the precise price level at which it exists. Profits of the major automobile companies vary sharply as between firms and from year to year. On occasion Chrysler has posted losses. But all (including Chrysler) are or have been protected against anything approaching a collapse of prices and earnings at both extremes of profit. Planning was possible at the higher as well as the lower level of profit. All could function. But none could have operated successfully had the prices of a standard model fluctuated, depending on whim and reaction to the current novelties, from $3000 to $10,000 with steel, glass, plastics, paint, tires, sub-assemblies and labor moving over a similar range.

5

However, the level of prices is not unimportant. And in response to major changes in cost—often when the renegotiation of a wage contract provides a common signal to all firms in the industry—prices must be changed.

The prices so established will reflect the commitment of the technostructure to the goal of expansion or growth. They will involve a compromise between two conflicting requirements for such growth. The need to expand sales, which are the *sine qua non* of growth, will argue, generally, for low prices. At the same time, depending on the nature of cost behavior, demand and the problems of demand management, the need for earnings to finance the growth will argue for higher prices. No rule can be laid down as to the result. It seems likely that prices will most often be set by an industry at a level that provides for an established payment to stockholders and covers the investment requirements (with some margin of safety) of the expansion that is possible at that price.[3] But

[3]And there is danger in assigning one-way causation. Prices have anciently been assumed to be an adjustable instrument of economic policy as wages, for example, are not. But as control and stability become objects in themselves, then prices are not adjusted and other magnitudes adjust themselves to the level of prices. Prices may not be set at the level that produces the maximum growth that can be financed from in-

this is at best only a probability. There is no *a priori* reason why the policy pursued by any two mature corporations will be the same, for there is no reason to assume that the goals—the commitment to growth as modified by the need for earnings—will be the same in any two cases. Further, where firms are large, they will deal, increasingly, with other firms that are large. And size and associated power in one place make it necessary elsewhere. Prices, under such circumstances, will reflect not an independent judgment as to what is required but an accommodation between firms.[4] And, although the policy does not yet enjoy formal acceptance—we encounter here another radical departure of practice from principle—price-making in the planning system is also modified by the social pressures for price stability and stable price-wage relationships.[5]

6

When price control is seen to be directed toward ensuring the security of the technostructure, as serving also the goal of growth and, more than incidentally, as providing, as well, a stable numerator for planning decisions, there is no longer anything startling in its *de facto* exemption from the antitrust laws. It would be more startling were it attacked. There is considerable injustice in the immunity enjoyed by those who have achieved a strong market position as compared with those who, being much weaker, seek, by merger or collusion, to win a stronger position. No doubt in a just society such anomalies in law enforcement should not exist. But when revision comes, it must be in light of full recognition that the antitrust laws were placed on the statute books to preserve the power of the market against those who might subordinate it to the purpose of monopoly. Meanwhile something very different has happened. The mature corporation has taken control of the market—not alone the price but also what is purchased—to serve not the goal of monopoly but the goals

---

vestment. Rather, after satisfying stockholders, the volume of investment may be determined, at least in the short run, by the earnings yielded by the current level of prices. Cf. John R. Meyer and Edwin Kuh, *The Investment Decision* (Cambridge: Harvard University Press, 1957).

[4] I have dealt with this phenomenon in detail in *American Capitalism: The Concept of Countervailing Power*, rev. ed. (Boston: Houghton Mifflin, 1956).

[5] See Chapter XXII.

of its planning. Controlled prices are necessary for this planning. And the planning, itself, is inherent in the planning system. It follows that the antitrust laws, in seeking to preserve the market, are an anachronism in the larger world of industrial planning. They do not preserve the market. They preserve rather the illusion of the market. In the past the man who argued against the antitrust laws was often suspected, sometimes rightly, of ulterior interest. He wished to violate the laws or was the paid or unpaid theorist for those who did. Now it is the friend of the antitrust laws who serves, almost always unwittingly, ulterior purpose. He defends and gives legitimacy to a charade—an act that helps to conceal the reality of industrial planning and associated price control by the great corporation.

XVIII

The Management of Specific Demand

"Bristol-Myers does not, in general, develop products in its labs and then determine how they might be marketed. It ordinarily *begins* with extensive consumer testing and other market research, proceeds from there to develop some concept of a marketing opportunity, including even some notions about advertising campaigns; and only then does it turn to the labs for products that might meet these specifications."

—*Fortune*, February 1967

"On the question of the determinants of consumer wants, he is in fact astoundingly naive. He seems to believe that it is the affluence of America that has made wants susceptible to manipulation . . ."

—From a review of orthodox tendency of the first edition of this book by Professor Scott Gordon

FOR ALL INDUSTRIAL PLANNING, that of the United States as well as of other industrial societies, the control of prices is strategic. These must be subject to the authority of the planning unit; otherwise there is risk of loss from uncontrolled price movements, and there is no reliable number by which units of product and input can be multiplied to get projected income and outlay. If these estimates are not available in reliable form, there is a large random element in decisions as to what to produce, and with what and by what means, and there is total uncertainty as to the outcome—whether there will be profit or loss and in what dimension. Such error is the antithesis of effective planning. A moment's thought will suggest not only how nearly impossible it would make modern industrial performance but how remote, in practice, such uncontrolled prices are from real life.

The control of prices in the planning system is not perfect, and the fact of this imperfection is important not only in itself but also for economic polemics. It is a well-established, though perhaps somewhat transparent, technique of argument, on encountering something which cannot easily be reconciled with preferred belief, to point to the exceptions. What does not invariably exist is then held not to exist. Economics is committed by ancient faith to the control of the firm by the market. Some, accordingly, are tempted to argue that since the control of prices by the mature corporation is not complete, it can be dismissed. This mode of argument need not detain us; once recognized as a polemical device, it becomes unpersuasive. It is worth noting that, until comparatively recently, trade unions were held by those who found them analytically inconvenient to be relatively unimportant in wage-setting because their sway was incomplete or their powers circumscribed.[1] And even the large corporation was ignored because it had not completely replaced the proprietary firm. Though imperfect, control of prices in the planning system is organic—it serves its most fundamental goals. And the fact of such control, fortunately for anyone who urges the reality, is admirably visible.

Control of prices is for a purpose—for the security of the technostructure and to allow planned pursuit of its further goals. But price control does little to advance these goals unless there is also control over the amounts that are bought or sold at these prices. Security, growth and effective planning to achieve these would be jeopardized by erratic or unpredictable price behavior. But these would equally be frustrated by a decision by the public not to buy at the controlled prices. It would be quixotic for the mature corporation to seek control over its prices and then leave purchases at these prices to the random fate of taste and accident. Such fluctuations in the amounts taken would be no less damaging to planning and the goals that it serves than fluctuations in prices. Moreover, the fluctuations in amounts taken are accentuated by price control; a fall in prices (through elasticity of demand) no longer acts to arrest a fall in purchases and vice versa. So, intimately intertwined with the need to control prices is the need to control what is sold at those prices.

[1] "[The] weak unions are probably more numerous than the strong . . . statistical studies find little relationship between unionization and long-term wage movements." George J. Stigler, *The Theory of Price*, rev. ed. (New York: Macmillan, 1952), pp. 256–257. Cf. also "Addendum on Economic Method and the Nature of Social Argument" in this volume. In later editions Professor Stigler, who has long commanded admiration for his ingenuity in subordinating fact to belief, does seem to concede a somewhat greater effect.

The control or management of demand is, in fact, a vast and rapidly growing industry in itself. It embraces a huge network of communications, a great array of merchandising and selling organizations, nearly the entire advertising industry, numerous ancillary research, training and other related services and much more. In everyday parlance, this great machine and the demanding and varied talents that it employs are said to be engaged in selling goods. In less ambiguous language, it means that it is engaged in the management of those who buy goods.

The key to the management of demand is effective management of the purchases of final consumers—of individuals and the state. If these are under effective control, there will then be a comparatively reliable demand for raw materials, parts, machinery and other items going into the ultimate product. If the demand for its automobiles is reliable, General Motors can accord its suppliers the security of long-term contracts. And, in the absence of such contracts, there will still be a reliable and predictable flow of orders which allows of planning. Although the techniques for managing government purchases are different from those employed for consumer demand, they make the same contribution to planning by prime- and sub-contractors.

The effective management of consumer behavior does not embrace the whole task of controlling demand. An automobile company must ensure that consumers devote a dependable share of their outlays to automobiles in general and to its cars in particular. But its sales will still be highly irregular if, though they spend a constant share of their income on its vehicles, there is a radical fluctuation from year to year in what they have to spend. It follows that effective control of consumer demand requires management not only of how income is spent but also of the amount of income that is available for spending. There must be management of demand both for the specific product and for products in general. Measures to maintain a desired level of aggregate demand are part and parcel of the task of industrial planning.[2] We are

[2] A circumstance, as previously noted, which greatly diminishes the significance of one of the common distinctions in economics—that between microeconomics or the theory of prices and the market, and macroeconomics or the theory which concerns itself with national aggregates. Both prices and aggregate demand are ultimately accommodated to the planning needs of the technostructure. I return to this problem in Chapter XX. Chapters XXVI and XXVII take up the special problems of managing the state as a consumer.

here concerned with the management of demand for the specific product.

2

As so often, change in the planning system has made possible what change requires. The need to control consumer behavior is a requirement of planning. Planning, in turn, is made necessary by extensive use of advanced technology and capital and by the related scale and complexity of organization. These produce goods efficiently; the result is a very large volume of production. As a further consequence, goods that are related only to elementary physical sensation—that merely prevent hunger, protect against cold, provide shelter, suppress pain—have come to comprise a small and diminishing part of all production. Most goods serve needs that are discovered to the individual not by the palpable discomfort that accompanies deprivation but by some psychic response to their possession. They give him a sense of personal achievement, accord him a feeling of equality with his neighbors, divert his mind from thought, serve sexual aspiration, promise social acceptability, enhance his subjective feeling of health, well-being or orderly peristalsis, contribute by conventional canons to personal beauty, or are otherwise psychologically rewarding.

Thus it comes about that, as the planning system develops to the point where it has need for the management of the consumer that planning requires, it is also serving wants which are psychological in origin and hence admirably subject to management by appeal to the psyche.

Hunger and other physical pain have an objective and compelling quality. As noted, no one whose stomach is totally empty can be persuaded that his need is not for food but for entertainment. A man who is very cold will have a strong, absolute preference for what makes him warm. But psychic reactions have no such internal anchor; since they exist in the mind, they are subject to what influences the mind. Though a hungry man cannot be persuaded as between bread and a circus, a well-nourished man can. And he can be persuaded as between different circuses and different foods. The further a man is removed from physical need the more open he is to persuasion—or management—as to what he buys. This is, perhaps, the most important consequence for the economics of increasing affluence.[3]

3

Along with the opportunity for managing consumer demand, there must also be a mechanism for managing it. Authority is not well regarded here. By giving him a ration card or distributing to him the specific commodities he is to use, the individual can be required to consume in accordance with plan. But this is an onerous form of control, ill-adapted to differences in personality. Save under conditions of great stress as during war or by way of food stamps for the very poor, it is not thought acceptable in advanced industrial societies. (Even the formally planned economies—the Soviet Union and the Eastern European states—regard rationing as a manifestation of failure.) It is easier and, if less precise, still sufficient to manage demand in the planning system by persuasion rather than by fiat.

Although advertising will be thought the central feature of this management and is certainly important, much more is involved. Included among the managers are those who sell goods and design the strategies by which they are sold. And so are many who are thought of as engaged in the production of goods. The management of demand consists in devising a sales strategy for a particular product. It also consists in devising a product or features of a product around which a sales strategy can be built. Product design, model change,

[3] I have dealt with this tendency on two earlier occasions (*American Capitalism: The Concept of Countervailing Power*, rev. ed. [Boston: Houghton Mifflin, 1956], Chapter VIII; and *The Affluent Society*, 3rd. ed., rev. [Boston: Houghton Mifflin, 1976], Chapter XI). Accordingly, I am confining myself here to the barest essentials. These notions, particularly the distinction between physical and psychologically based wants, together with a declining marginal utility of income, though they will seem eminently sensible to the reader, are only gradually being accepted by economists. (See Professor Scott Gordon's resistant comment at the beginning of this chapter.) There are certain methodological excuses for this resistance but the reason has, alas, more to do with the instinct for professional self-preservation than with science. As elsewhere noted, a central problem of economics, and long *the* central problem, was the allocation of resources between uses, that is to say, between products. If this choice is not terribly important and becomes increasingly less important with increasing income, the economic problem in its accustomed form also diminishes in importance and so, more poignantly, do the scholars who dwell on it without intellectual alternative.

packaging and even performance reflect the need to provide what are called strong selling points. They are thus as much a part of the process of demand management as an advertising campaign.[4]

4

The purpose of demand management is to ensure that people buy what is produced—that plans as to the amounts to be sold at the controlled prices are fulfilled in practice. Not all advertising and selling activity is directed to this end. This fact has the polemical importance hitherto observed, for it is readily possible to cite forms of advertising or sales effort which are unrelated to the purposes of demand management and industrial planning.

Thus a certan amount of advertising, that of the classified ads and the department store displays, has no great purpose beyond that of conveying information—of advising the public that a particular person or enterprise has a particular item for sale and at what price. Such advertising is seized upon to show that the function of advertising in general is merely to convey information, although, as I have noted on other occasions, only a gravely retarded citizen can need to be told that the American Tobacco Company has cigarettes for sale.

Economic theory, under the cachet of monopolistic competition, has also long featured the case of the seller, one among many, who seeks by advertising to associate particular qualities with his product and thus reduce the chances for substitution by another. He then has liberty to charge a higher price and, at least in the short run, reward himself with monopoly profits. This too is a possible case, although its requirements as imposed by the textbooks—*numerous* sellers who have comparative ease of entry into the industry— make it of small practical importance. The accounts of the monopolistically competitive sellers are not those that are cherished by J. Walter Thompson, McCann-Erickson or Ogilvy and Mather.

[4]In a culture which places high value on technological change, there will be a natural presumption that any "new" product is inherently superior to an old one. This attitude will be exploited by those who devise sales strategies, with the result that a great many changes in product and packaging will be merely for the sake of having something that can be called new. We have here the explanation of the repetitious claims in virtually all advertising that the item is new. No other word is so much used.

Finally, conventional economic theory associates advertising and related arts with oligopoly. Here the characteristic firm of the planning system eschews price competition as too dangerous and channels its rivalry into ever-changing strategies for winning customers away from another. "Oligopolies ... are practically compelled to dissipate economic resources in advertising and in meretricious variations in product characteristics."[5]

If it be assumed that the consumer is sovereign, save that he is in doubt as to whose product he will buy, this conclusion—that advertising and, by implication, many other expenditures, including that for model and design changes, are without function[6]—is inescapable. Firms spend money to take business away from each other; all cannot succeed so the result is a standoff. The only consequence is that resources are wasted and prices are higher and profits are lower than if, by some act of government or industrial statesmanship, the struggle were curbed.[7]

But such a notion of a functionless, wasteful deadlock is nonsense. If advertising affects the distribution of demand be-

[5]Robert Dorfman, *Prices and Markets,* 2nd ed. (Englewood Cliffs, New Jersey: Prentice-Hall, 1972), p. 168.

[6]Franklin M. Fisher, Zvi Griliches and Carl Kaysen, "The Costs of Automobile Model Changes Since 1949," *Journal of Political Economy,* Vol. 70, No. 5 (October 1962), p. 433 et seq.

[7]A study ("Advertising Market Structure and Performance" by William S. Comanor and Thomas A. Wilson, *Review of Economics and Statistics,* Vol. XLIX, No. 4 [November 1967], p. 423 et. seq.) shows substantially higher profit rates among industries that advertise heavily. The authors of this study attribute this in orthodox fashion to the monopoly gains made possible by the resulting product differentiation. These conclusions are re-emphasized in their book, *Advertising and Market Power* (Cambridge: Harvard University Press, 1974). There is a logical flaw in their attribution of higher profits to monopoly gains. It is not at all evident how *all* members of an oligopoly can so gain from differentiation. But all are beneficiaries of the planning of which effective demand management is a part.

It should be noted that a finding of higher rate of return in industries that advertise is not essential to the present argument. Planning has other and superior goals, including, notably, the growth of the firm. And yet other factors influence profits as between industries. A further reason for not wishing to be tied to an association between advertising and rate of return as an index of successful planning is the differing assessments of that relationship. See Robert Ayanian, "Advertising and Rate of Return," *Journal of Law and Economics,* Vol. XVIII (2) (October 1975), p. 479 et seq., and Stanley I. Ornstein, "The Advertising-Concentration Controversy," *Southern Economic Journal,* Vol. 43, No. 1 (July 1976), p. 892 et seq.

tween sellers of a particular product and forces defensive counteraction, it must also be supposed that it affects distribution as between products. This will not be functionless; rather it must increase the flow of revenue to all who advertise. And in the context of planning, in fact, advertising does much more. For, along with the other arts of demand management, it allows the firm a decisive influence over the revenue it receives. What seems to the traditional market economists a sense-deadening struggle between the detergent makers leading only to stalemate serves a deeper and highly important purpose.

There will be comfort of a kind in this conclusion. The present disposition of conventional economic theory to write off annual outlays of many billions of dollars of advertising and similar sales costs by the planning system as without purpose or consequence is, to say the least, peculiar. No other legal economic activity is subject to similar rejection. The discovery that sales and advertising expenditures have an organic role in the system will not, accordingly, seem wholly implausible.

The general effect of sales effort, defined in the broadest terms, is to shift the locus of decision in the purchase of goods from the consumer where it is beyond control to the firm where it is subject to control. This transfer, like the control of prices, is by no means complete. But again what is imperfect is not unimportant. The "general rule, with fewer exceptions than we would like to think, is that if they make it we will buy it."[8]

The specific strategy, though it varies somewhat between industries and over time, consists first in recruiting a loyal or automatic corps of customers. This is variously known as building customer loyalty or brand recognition. To the extent that it is successful, it means that the firm has a stable body of custom which is secure against the mass defection which might follow from freely exercised consumer choice. This is the initial contribution to the firm's planning.

A purely defensive strategy will not, however, suffice. Given the goals of the technostructure, all firms will seek to expand sales. Each, accordingly, must seek to do so if it is not to lose out to others. Out of this effort, from firms that are fully able to play the game, comes a crude equilibrating

[8]Andrew Hacker, "A Country Called Corporate America," *The New York Times Magazine,* July 3, 1966.

process which accords to each participant a reasonably reliable share of the market. It works, very roughly, as follows.

When a firm is enjoying patronage by its existing customers and recruiting new ones, the existing sales strategy, broadly defined, will usually be considered satisfactory. The firm will not quarrel with success. If sales are stationary or slipping, a change in selling methods, advertising strategy, product design or even in the product itself is called for. Testing and experiment are possible. Sooner or later, a new formula that wins a suitable response is obtained. This brings a countering action by the firms that are then failing to make gains.

This process of action and response, which belongs to the field of knowledge known as game theory, leads to a rough equilibrium between the participating firms. Each may win for a time or lose for a time but the game is played within a narrow range of such gain or loss. As in the case of Packard or Studebaker (as a producer of cars), firms that do not have the resources to play—particularly to stand the very large costs of product design and redesign—will lose out and disappear. And the firms that can play the game will, on occasion, find customers adamant in their resistance to a particular product; no response can be obtained at tolerable cost by any strategy that can be devised.[9] The size and product diversification of the mature corporation allow the firm to accept an occasional such failure without undue hazard. But it is the everyday assumption of the planning system that, if sales are slipping, a new selling formula can be found that will correct the situation. By and large, this assumption is justified, which is to say that means can almost always be found to keep exercise of consumer discretion within workable limits.

Were there but one manufacturer of automobiles in the United States and no imports, it would still be essential that it enter extensively on the management of its demand. Otherwise consumers, exercising the sovereignty that would be inconsistent with the company's planning, might resort to other forms of transportation and other ways of spending their income. (This is the answer to the orthodox contention that ad-

---

[9]As in the case of the Edsel. I mention this again, for, to a quite remarkable extent, this disaster is cited by those who are made uncomfortable and perhaps obsolete by these ideas to prove that planning of demand does not work. It proves what I unhesitatingly concede, which is that it doesn't work perfectly. All but the truly resistant now realize that the Edsel owes its deathless notoriety to its being so exceptional.

vertising is principally induced by market oligopoly.) And under present circumstances a slippage in automobile sales as a whole sets in motion by all the firms the sales strategies (including always the product redesign) by which it is offset. This, in turn, stabilizes the expenditures accruing to the industry.

5

Persuasion on the scale just outlined requires that there be comprehensive repetitive and compelling communication by the managers of demand with the managed. It should be capable of holding the attention of the consumer for considerable periods of time and in a comparatively effortless manner. It should reach people in all spectrums of intelligence. None should be barred by illiteracy or unwillingness to read. Such a means of mass communication was not necessary when the wants of the masses were anchored primarily in physical need. The masses could not then be persuaded as to their spending—this went for basic foods and shelter. The wants of a well-to-do minority could be managed. But since this minority was generally literate or sought to seem so, it could be reached selectively by newspapers and magazines, the circulation of which was confined to the literate community. With mass affluence, and therewith the possibility of mass management of demand, these media no longer served.

Technology, once again, solved the problem that it created. Coincidentally with rising mass incomes came first radio and then television. These, in their capacity to hold effortless interest, their accessibility over the entire cultural spectrum and their independence of any educational qualification, were admirably suited to mass persuasion. Radio and more especially television have, in consequence, become the prime instruments for the management of consumer demand. There is an insistent tendency among solemn social scientists to think of any institution which features rhymed and singing commercials; provides intense and lachrymose voices urging highly improbable enjoyments; offers caricatures of the human esophagus in normal or impaired operation; and which hints implausibly at means for enhancing the opportunity for effortless and hygienic seduction, as inherently trivial. This is a great mistake. The planning system is profoundly dependent on commercial television and could not exist in its present form without it. Economists who eschew discussion of its economic significance or dismiss it as a wicked waste are protecting their reputation and that of their subject for Calvinist austerity. But they are not adding to their reputation for relevance.

6

The management of demand, as here to be seen, is in all respects an admirably subtle arrangement in social design. It works not on the individual but on the mass. Any individual of will and determination can contract out from its influence. This being so, no case for individual compulsion in the purchase of any product can be established. To all who object there is a natural answer: You are at liberty to leave! Yet there is slight danger that enough people will ever assert their individuality to impair the management of mass behavior.

The management of demand is a make-or-break matter for presently accepted economics. If the consumer can be reached and influenced by the producer, then much is changed and much that happens is at the behest of the producer, not the consumer. If the consumer cannot be so reached, all is well, all remains as before. The importance of a solid stand at this point has been amply sensed by critics of these ideas. And a number have dug in on the line that the critic himself being immune to persuasion—having contracted out—so, *pro tanto*, have all others. "I know it is not true of me, and I do not fancy myself cleverer than the next man in this regard." That one's personal reactions signify the public reaction is not, scientifically, a defensible proposition but where the preservation of precious intellectual capital is involved, scientific method is readily sacrificed.[10]

[10]See Robert Solow, "The New Industrial State or Son of Affluence," *The Public Interest*, No. 9 (Fall 1967), p. 100 et seq.
Professor Solow, a skilled and intelligent defender of the established view, assumed a major role in the orthodox attack on these ideas when they were first published. The hope, as always, was that they might be aborted before having damaging effect. Such effort, it might be noted, is a thankless and generally futile task which those undertaking and those reviewed rarely understand. Only limited space is available to the motivated critic and often also only limited time. In consequence, assertion, undocumented and frequently inaccurate, regularly replaces careful argument. Also very few such reviewers know how to avoid the graceless literary posture of seeming to assert a superior scholarly wisdom. In the end, most are reduced to the cliché assertion that there is

This management performs yet another service. For, along with bringing demand under substantial control, it provides, in the aggregate, a relentless propaganda on behalf of goods in general. From early morning until late at night, people are informed of the services rendered by goods—of their profound indispensability. Every feature and facet of every product having been studied for selling points, these are then described with talent, gravity and an aspect of profound concern as the source of health, happiness, social achievement or improved community standing. Even minor qualities of unimportant commodities are enlarged upon with a solemnity which would not be unbecoming in an announcement of the combined return of Christ and all the apostles. Most important services, such as the advantages of whiter laundry, are treated with proportionately greater gravity.

The consequence is that while goods become ever more abundant, they do not seem to be any less important. On the contrary, it requires an act of will to imagine that anything else is so important. Morally we agree that the supply of goods is not a measure of human achievement; in fact, we take for granted that it will be so regarded.

Yet it might not have been. In the absence of the massive and artful persuasion that accompanies the management of demand, increasing abundance might well have reduced the interest of people in acquiring more goods. They would not have felt the need for multiplying the artifacts—autos, appliances, detergents, cosmetics—by which they were surrounded. No one would have pressed upon them the advantages of new packages, new forms of processed foods, newly devised dentifrices, new pain-killers or other new variants on older products. Not being pressed by the need for these things, they would have spent less reliably of their income and worked less reliably to get more. The consequence—a lower and less reliable propensity to consume—would have been awkward for the planning system. That system requires that people will work without any limiting horizon to procure more goods. Were they to cease to work after acquiring a certain sufficiency, there would be limits on the expansion of the system.

---

nothing new and what is new isn't proven. For what could be an extreme example of these misfortunes, see Harold Demsetz, "The Technostructure, Forty-Six Years Later," *The Yale Law Journal*, Vol. 77, No. 4 (March 1968), p. 802 et seq. It is my impression that no person of competence need fear the motivated critic. But the motivated critic should greatly fear the wounds he inflicts upon himself.

Growth could not then remain a goal. Advertising and its related arts thus help develop the kind of man the goals of the planning system require—one who reliably spends his income and works reliably because he is always in need of more.

This effort has the further effect of sustaining the prestige of the planning system. Goods are what the planning system supplies. Advertising, by making goods important, makes the planning system important. And therewith it helps to sustain the social importance and prestige that attach to the technostructure. As the landowner and the capitalist lost prestige when land and capital ceased to be socially decisive, so the technostructure would soon sink into the background were the supply of industrial products to become routine, in the manner of water from a waterworks in a year of adequate rainfall. This would have happened long since had not advertising, with its unremitting emphasis on the importance of goods, kept people persuaded to the contrary.

When viewed not in the context of absolute virtue but in the narrower context of industrial planning, it will be evident that advertising and its related arts have a large social function. This extends on from the management of demand, the necessary counterpart of the control of prices, to the shaping of attitudes necessary for the performance and prestige of the planning system. For advertising men it has long been a sore point that economists dismissed them as so much social waste. They have not quite known how to answer. Some have doubtless sensed that, in a society where wants are psychologically grounded, the instruments of access to the mind cannot be unimportant. They were right. The functions here identified may well be less exalted than the more demanding philosophers of the advertising industry might wish. But none can doubt their importance for the planning system, given always the standards by which that system measures achievement and success.

IXX

The Revised Sequence

"The consumer is, so to speak, the king . . . each is a voter who uses his votes to get things done that he wants done."

—Paul Samuelson

THE TIME HAS COME for yet another word of summary. In virtually all economic analysis and instruction, the initiative is assumed to lie with the consumer. In response to wants that originate within himself or which are given to him by his environment, he buys goods and services in the market. The opportunities that result for making more or less money are the message of the market to producing firms. They respond to this message of the market and thus, ultimately, to the instruction of the consumer. The flow of instruction is in one direction—from the individual to the market to the producer. All this is affirmed, not inappropriately, by terminology that implies that all power lies with the consumer. This is called consumer sovereignty. There "is always a presumption of consumer sovereignty in the market economy."[1] The unidirectional flow of instruction from consumer to market to producer may be denoted as the *Accepted Sequence*.

We have seen that this sequence does not hold. And we have now isolated a formidable apparatus of method and motivation causing its reversal. The mature corporation has readily at hand the means for controlling the prices at which it sells as well as those at which it buys. Similarly it has means for managing what the consumer buys at the prices which it controls. This control and management is required by its plan-

---

[1]Franklin M. Fisher, Zvi Griliches and Carl Kaysen, "The Costs of Automobile Model Changes Since 1949," *Journal of Political Economy*, Vol. LXX, No. 5 (October 1962), p. 434. These three men are highly regarded among economic theorists. Their statement is noteworthy, for they are unwilling to give full acceptance to the notion of consumer sovereignty. It is merely the frame in which they work.

ning. The planning proceeds from the use of technology and capital, the commitment of time that these require and the diminished effectiveness of the market for specialized technical products and skills.

Supporting this changed sequence is the motivation of the technostructure. Its members seek to adapt the goals of the corporation more closely to their own; by extension the corporation seeks to adapt social attitudes and goals to those of the members of its technostructure. So social belief originates, at least in part, with the producer. Thus the accommodation of the market behavior of the individual, as well as of social attitudes in general, to the needs of producers and the goals of the technostructure is an inherent feature of the system. It becomes increasingly important with the growth of the planning system.

It follows that the accepted sequence is no longer a description of the reality and is becoming ever less so. Instead the producing firm reaches forward to control its markets and on beyond to manage the market behavior and shape the social attitudes of those whom it, ostensibly, serves. For this we also need a name, and it may appropriately be called the *Revised Sequence*.

2

Those who yearn for the defeat of their enemy are said to wish that he might write a book. Far better that he should resort to overstatement. I do not suggest that the revised sequence has replaced the accepted sequence. Outside the planning system—beyond the limits of the large corporations in what remains the market system—the accepted sequence still rules. Within the planning system the consumer can still reject persuasion. And, in consequence, through the market he and his fellows can force accommodation by the producer. But consumers, and the prices at which they buy, can also be managed. And they are. The accepted and revised sequences exist side by side in the manner of a reversible chemical reaction. Doubtless it would be neater were it one way or the other. But, again, the reality is plausible but untidy.

In the form just presented, the revised sequence will not, I think, be challenged by many economists. There is a certain difficulty in escaping from the inescapable. There is more danger that the point will be conceded and its significance then ignored. To ensure against this—to provide text for all who ally themselves in the preventive therapy—it is well that the consequences of the revised sequence be briefly adumbrated.

3

The revised sequence sends to the museum of obsolete ideas the notion of an equilibrium in consumer outlays which reflects the maximum of consumer satisfaction. According to this doctrine, beloved in economic instruction and still honored in the economics textbooks, the individual or household arranges his or its purchases so that there is approximately equal satisfaction from the last dollar spent for each of the several opportunities for consumption or use of goods.[2] Were it otherwise—were it so that a dollar spent on cosmetics returned more satisfaction than a dollar spent on gasoline—then spending on cosmetics would have been increased and that on gasoline diminished. And the reverse being true of comparative satisfaction from cosmetics and gasoline, the reverse would have occurred. In other words, when the return to a small added outlay for different purposes is unequal, satisfaction can always be increased by diminishing the expenditure where the satisfaction is less and enlarging it where the satisfaction is greater. So it follows that satisfaction is at a maximum when the return to a small increment of expenditure is the same for all objects of expenditure.

But it is also true that, since an individual's satisfaction from his various opportunities for expenditure is his own there must be no interference with this equalizing process. Instruction from any second person on how to distribute income however meritorious, will not reflect the peculiar enjoymen

---

[2] "Each good—such as sugar—is demanded up to the point where the marginal utility per dollar (or penny) spent on it is exactly the same as the marginal utility of a dollar (or penny) spent on any other good—such as salt. Why must this law hold? If any one good gave more marginal utility per dollar, the consumer would gain by taking money away from other goods and spending more on that good. . . . If any good gave less marginal utility per dollar than the common level, the consumer would buy less of it until the marginal utility of the last dollar spent on it had risen back to the common level." Paul A. Samuelson, *Economics*, 10th ed. (New York McGraw-Hill, 1976), pp. 435–436.

pattern of the person in question. It will reflect the preferences, value system, enjoyments or needs of the instructor.

Such is the established doctrine. And if the individual's wants are subject to management by the producer, this is interference. The distribution of his income between objects of expenditure will reflect this management. There will be a different distribution of income—a different equilibrium—in accordance with the changing effectiveness of management by different producers.[3] It is to the nature and purposes of this management, not simply to the effort of the individual to maximize his satisfactions, that the scholar must look if he is to have any adequate view of consumer behavior.

It is true that the consumer may still imagine that his actions respond to his own view of his satisfactions. But this is superficial and proximate, the results of illusions created in connection with the management of his wants. Only those wishing to evade the reality will be satisfied with such a simplistic explanation. All others will notice that if an individual's satisfaction is less from an additional expenditure on automobiles than from one on housing, this can as well be corrected by a change in the selling strategy of General Motors as by an increased expenditure on his house.[4] Similarly a perfect state of equilibrium with marginal utilities everywhere equal can be upset not by a change in the individual's income or by a change in the goods available but by a change in the persuasion to which he is subject.

The problem of economics here, once again, is not one of original error but of obsolescence. The notion of the consumer so distributing his income as to maximize satisfactions that originate with himself and his environment was not inappropriate to an earlier stage of economic development. When goods were less abundant, when they served urgent physical need and their acquisition received close thought and attention, purchases were much less subject to management. And, on the other side, producers in that simpler and less technical world were not under compulsion to plan. Accordingly, they

---

[3] What the reader will recognize to be the ordinary and expected result of the changing effectiveness of advertising campaigns.

[4] As a related technical point, indifference curves do not survive the revised sequence. The indifference map reflects, at any given time, the comparative effectiveness of the sales strategies behind the products in question. It will change as these change. The logic of the indifference curve requires that it be original with the individual whose preferences it describes.

did not need to persuade—to manage demand. The model of consumer behavior devised for these conditions was not wrong. The error was in taking it over without change into the age of the planning system. There, not surprisingly, it did not fit.[5]

4

To jettison the accepted sequence has more than pedagogical consequences. Even the most jejune and precious social theory is likely to support some structure of social attitude and action. The accepted sequence, with the resulting doctrine of consumer maximization of satisfactions, sustains a great deal.

Specifically, it supports the conclusion that the individual is the ultimate source of power in the economic system. And it assures us that this exercise of power grows out of his own unaided tendency and ability to make the most out of his situation. It is highly reassuring that the individual should have, or be imagined to have, such power in association with such capacity to use it. It is, perhaps, especially reassuring in a culture which sets a high and even mystical store by the individual and which may suspect that, somehow, he is being threatened by organization. Thus, and understandably, do the custodians of orthodox values rally to the defense of the accepted sequence.

The accepted sequence also raises barriers against a wide range of social action. Such action, though in fact inconvenient or objectionable to organization and specifically to the technostructure, is held by the theory to be in conflict with the maximization of satisfaction by the individual. We have seen how jealously the technostructure seeks to safeguard its autonomy of decision. The management of demand requires, also, that it have the greatest possible freedom in the exercise of persuasion. Anything that limits or circumscribes the claims that it can make for a product interferes in some measure with the management of demand. The accepted sequence holds that the individual guides the economy while obtaining for himself the highest level of satisfaction from the

[5]Economists, all but invariably, have used a simple but revealing device to improve the fit. That is to illustrate the theory of consumer behavior with commodities—bread, tea, oranges, salt, sugar—which are produced outside the planning system or for which the management of demand is peculiarly difficult. Cf. Samuelson, footnote 2 of this chapter.

income he receives. Any interference with his exercise of choice leads to a less satisfactory result—a lower level of satisfaction—for the individual. In a society composed of, and guided by, individuals it will be socially less good. Accordingly, government objection to lethal automobile design, disabling drugs, disfiguring beauty aids or high-calorie reducing compounds is interference with the individual's choice and thus with his design for maximizing his satisfaction and the resulting economic response. The accepted sequence thus outlaws a wide variety of public regulations and does so in the name of the individual. This accords powerful protection to the autonomy of the technostructure and great immunity to its techniques for managing demand. A doctrine that celebrates individuality provides the cloak for organization. And this depends wholly on the accepted sequence. Once it is agreed that the individual is subject to management in any case—once the revised sequence is allowed—the case for leaving him free from, say, government interference evaporates. It is not the individual's right to buy that is being protected. Rather it is the seller's right to manage the individual.

The accepted sequence, with its emphasis on the assumed power of the individual, serves in other ways to sanction organization. Men accept the disciplines of the great industrial enterprise in order to serve the ultimate interests of the individual consumer. By bowing to rules, subordinating their personality to organization, being good members of the team, they help to enlarge the range of choice of individual consumers. It is proper that they subordinate their lesser liberty to that greater one. Or such is the justification from conventional economics.

Much more is so justified. Industrial squalor, air and stream pollution, sacrifice of aesthetic values—even the rhymed commercials and billboards which are part of the process of consumer management—expand the quantity and variety of product. So they increase the scope for exercise of the sovereign power of the consumer. Again, it is held, lesser values are subordinated to the greater liberty that is allied with the ultimate and controlling power of the individual in an economic system with a maximum range of choice. Again economics renders service to industrial purpose.

None of these contentions survives the revised sequence. There is no case for subordinating the lesser liberty of the organization man to the greater liberty of the consumer unless that latter liberty exists. If that has already been subordinated to organization, the argument lapses. Industrial squalor serves not the larger liberty of the consumer. It serves industrial convenience.

The authority that is exercised in industrial production by the industrial firm also acquires legitimacy from the larger freedom that it accords the consumer. This, under the accepted sequence, is power only to serve; in the last analysis the greatest corporation is but the humble servant of the consumer. "One way of shedding awkward responsibility is to believe that the consumer is the real boss, that the businessman merely carries out his . . . orders. . . . It is not by chance that consumer sovereignty is generally described in terms suggesting the processes [i.e., balloting in the marketplace] of political democracy."[6] If the consumer is not sovereign—if the ballots are cast partially at the behest of the producer—this argument does not merely disappear. Rather it could come to react against the person who employs it, for it draws attention to power that embraces also the management of the consumer.

5

It is possible that people need to believe that they are unmanaged if they are to be managed effectively. We have been taught to set store by our freedom of economic choice; were it recognized that this is subject to management, we might be at pains to assert our independence. Thus we would become less manageable. Were instruction in economics, supported by the formidable wisdom of the economics textbooks, to proclaim that people are partly in the service of those who supply them, this might cause those so educated to desert that service.

Whether this be so or not, it will be clearly evident that attitudes of the highest importance flow from the accepted sequence—attitudes that are highly protective of the planning system. Such is the very considerable service of myth.

It would be optimistic to imagine that so serviceable a myth will be easily abandoned or even to expect universal gratitude for those who dispel it. Yet even here there is change—as most will recognize. When the first editions of this book appeared, much regulatory activity—of advertising

---

[6]Francis X. Sutton, Seymour E. Harris, Carl Kaysen and James Tobin, *The American Business Creed* (Cambridge: Harvard University Press, 1956), p. 361.

of drugs, cigarettes, beauty aids, obesity control; all were prominent examples—was being resisted on the grounds that such regulation was an undue restraint on free market choice. This argument would now be dismissed by most as special pleading. The pertinent regulation is now recognized to be a restraint on the management of the consumer, and, except in the textbooks, such management is considered a fact of life. The movement of ideas toward truth may be glacial but, like a glacier, it is hard to stop.

XX

The Regulation of Aggregate Demand

THE PLANNING SYSTEM requires that prices be under effective control. And it seeks the greatest possible influence over what buyers take at the established prices. And it seeks certainty in the supply and prices of the important requisites of production—as we shall see presently, it is adding steadily to the certainty of its manpower supply. All of this gives precision to its planning. And it serves admirably the goals, those of security and growth in particular, of the technostructure. But another exceedingly important risk remains uncovered. That is of severe fluctuation in the total demand available for all the products of the planning system. We must look now at the larger dimensions of this problem and its solution.

From the viewpoint of the industrial firm, the regulation of total or aggregate demand is a matter of the highest urgency. Not only is it necessary that the public be persuaded to buy its automobiles, packaged cereals or household appliances in roughly predetermined volume but it is also necessary that people be able to do so. The best management of consumer behavior will come to nothing if there is a sharp reduction in employment and therewith in incomes and if consumers, in consequence, are no longer able (or disposed) to buy as before. A man in imminent danger of being hanged is little worried about catching cold. There is no point in eliminating a minor source of uncertainty if a major one remains. Purchasing power must be reliably available in sufficient volume to absorb the current production of the planning system at the established prices.

By nature of its own development, the planning system has made the regulation of purchasing power or demand ever more urgent. An economy pays out in the course of production the wages, salaries, interest and profits that comprise the wherewithal for buying what it produces. In a poor and simple society what is paid and spent tends to match in value what is produced. People of small income do not have the option of suddenly not spending that income, i.e., of suddenly increasing their savings. Spending is in the straitjacket of physical need. The consumption function is stable.

Also in such a society, since savings are small, investment will be small. Most production will be for current consumption. Production for such current use is more stable than production in response to investment decisions, with their changing estimate of an unknown future.

We have seen also that in an earlier and simpler stage of society in which savings are small, capital is scarce and of decisive importance for production. That is to say that, ordinarily, there are many claimants for the savings that are available. What the community spends for consumption is, quite obviously, spent. But under these more primitive circumstances what it saves from consumption is subject to the insistent need for investment and thus is also spent. So all income made in production goes for production. One of the familiar antiquities of economics is Say's Law of Markets. This holds that an economy always provides demand sufficient to buy its own output. A deficiency of purchasing power or demand is thus impossible. Say's Law no longer commands belief. But in the world of its author, nearly two centuries ago, it had much merit.

2

In the planning system, by contrast, personal savings are no longer made at the cost of physical hardship. Most personal saving is by persons in the upper half of the income brackets; for many it is automatic. And far more important than such savings by individuals—which in 1976 amounted to $77.8 billion—are the retained earnings of business firms which were $198.6 billion in that same year. This saving is by decision of the technostructure. Consumers do not press to spend these funds. They are not accorded the option of doing so.

In general, the technostructure will increase its investment as its retained earnings increase. Having taken care of its stockholders and creditors and therewith assured its own security, it then devotes funds to the next highest priority among its goals, which is growth. And if the funds so available are inadequate, the technostructure will increase its earnings or withhold more from the stockholders.[1]

[1] ". . . [The] investment outlay on fixed and working capital seems, in the short run . . . a residual . . . between the total net flow of

Thus within the planning system savings and outlay for investment will tend to rise and fall together. But this does not mean that they will be equal—that investment will offset savings. Nor is there any mechanism in the organized economy by which savings decisions and investment decisions are made to equal each other.[2]

If the various decisions to increase savings are not offset by decisions to invest a like amount or if decisions to reduce capital outlays and other investments are not matched by a reduction in savings, then some of the current production of the planning system will be without purchasing power and buyers. Output and employment will fall. In the world of Jean Baptiste Say the prices of goods will fall; the increased savings would then be offset by the increased purchases of other people at the lower prices. But in the planning system prices, we have seen, are controlled, so the initial effect will be on output and therewith on employment. This could, in turn, lead on to a further curtailment of investment, a further curtailment of production and employment, and thence to a self-generating downward spiral.

In summary, the planning system has built into itself very comprehensively the need to regulate aggregate demand. Its advanced technology and high use of capital require planning. From this planned use of resources comes an ample production that allows of a high level of savings. The technostructure has strong inducements to keep these savings at a high level. These savings, if not offset, can lead to a serious and cumulative reduction in aggregate demand. The same advanced technology and high capital use which force the industrial firm to plan make it vulnerable to a fall in aggregate demand. The technostructure is similarly vulnerable. So, effective regulation of such demand is imperative.

Nor is this quite all. As earlier noted, effective regulation of aggregate demand adds paradoxically to the need for such regulation. Such regulation prevents a cumulative downward

---

funds realized from current operations less the established or conventional dividend payments." John R. Meyer and Edwin Kuh, *The Investment Decision* (Cambridge: Harvard University Press, 1957), p. 204.

[2] Interest rates, the classical equilibrating mechanism, have for many years been thought by economists to perform this function. While changes in interest rates are assumed to have an effect on investment, there is no agreement as to their effect, if any, on the total volume of savings.

spiral in income and saving. This, in the past, has borne the same relation to saving and capital accumulation as famines to the population of India. The Great Depression reduced personal savings from $4.2 billion in 1929 to a net dissaving of $900 million in 1933 and gross business savings from $11.2 billion to $3.2 billion.[3] In the third quarter of 1974, in consequence of the 1974–1975 recession, personal and business savings were, at an annual rate, $34 billion below the prerecessionary peak in the fourth quarter of 1973.[4] In the absence of recessions, savings continue high; so does capital investment and so does the purchasing power generated by such investment. And so, therefore, does the dependence of the economy on the measures by which savings are offset.

If savings are not offset, output and employment fall. If savings are more than offset when the economy is at or near full employment, output and employment cannot rise or cannot rise appreciably. Instead prices rise, and, in the planning system, while there is elaborate protection against price reduction, price increases, which are without similar danger to the technostructure, occur far more easily. This, as we shall see presently, leads to the need for yet further government intervention. It requires also that the regulation of aggregate demand be reversible. There must be means for correcting both a shortage and an excess of demand.

The regulation of aggregate demand, it will be evident, is an organic requirement of the planning system. In its absence there would be unpredictable and almost certainly large fluctuations in demand and therewith in sales and production. Planning would be gravely impaired; capital and technology would have to be used much more cautiously and far less effectively than now. And the position of the technostructure, since it is endangered by the failure of earnings, would be far less secure. The need for regulation of aggregate demand is now fully accepted. However, its integral relationship to modern economic development has never been fully appreciated. There is an impression, growing partly out of some curiosities in the history of this regulation and partly out of a continuing failure to look at the process of regulation as a whole, that

[3] *Economic Report of the President, 1970*, p. 198. It is this reduction in savings that eventually brings them back into equilibrium with a smaller but less drastically reduced level of investment.
[4] *Economic Report of the President, 1976*, p. 192. Private saving in constant dollars did not reach prerecession levels until the beginning of the recovery in the second quarter of 1975.

the business firms that comprise the planning system have
been hostile to it. This, on closer examination, turns out to
have been far from the case.

3

The regulation of demand became a recognized public policy
during the thirties. The policy was decisively advocated by
John Maynard (later Lord) Keynes[5] and was propagated in
the United States by a comparatively small number of liberal
economists—members of a community generally considered
at the time to be antipathetic to large-scale business enterprises.[6] It was put into effect by the Roosevelt Administration, which also had its quarrels with business. The policy
was seen primarily (although not exclusively) as a remedy
for unemployment—a coloration which it still retains—and
thus appeared to be an action on behalf of the labor movement. Additionally it had the support of labor, and at a time
of bitter labor-management disputes. Not remarkably, in consequence, it was regarded by the public at large, as well as by
businessmen, as a dubiously experimental welfare measure
which could be expected to prove costly or damaging to
business in some unspecified way.

[5]In particular in *The General Theory of Employment Interest and
Money* (New York: Harcourt, 1936), although it had been fore-
shadowed in numerous earlier proposals of Keynes, as also of others.

[6]Conservatives have long contended that the Keynesian Revolution in
the United States was the work of a handful of Keynes's disciples, advocates and interpreters, centering mostly on Harvard University and
led principally by Professor Alvin Hansen with Professor Seymour
Harris as the most articulate spokesman and Professor Paul Samuelson
of M.I.T. as the author of the first great Keynesian textbook. These
men are held to have applied Keynes's ideas to the American scene
and, directly or through students, sold Keynes's ideas to Washington
and the public. The charge has been protested, and even denied, and it
is somewhat difficult to see why, for it is essentially true. The Keynesian Revolution was also an epochal contribution to the development
of the planning system and the preservation of what is commonly
called capitalism. Architects of such a useful revolution should have
pride in their work. I have dealt at some length with the history of the
Keynesian Revolution in an article in *The New York Times Review*,
May 16, 1965, celebrating the publication of a paperback edition of
Keynes's *General Theory*—the original did not get reviewed—and
reprinted in *Economics, Peace and Laughter* (Boston: Houghton Mifflin, 1971). A shorter version of the history is in *The Age of Uncertainty* (Boston: Houghton Mifflin, 1977).

More important, the regulation of aggregate demand has a very different impact on the entrepreneurial and the mature corporations. In the thirties, reflecting a common and indeed invariable cultural lag, business spokesmen were still giving voice to the interests of the entrepreneurial corporation under the impression that this reflected the common interest of all business.

The entrepreneurial corporation has much less need than the mature corporation for the regulation of aggregate demand. The mature corporation is an accommodation to advanced technology and heavy capital use. Planning is part of this accommodation. So is the technostructure. Regulation of aggregate demand is necessary to give certainty to this planning and to protect the technostructure. The entrepreneurial corporation with simpler technology and a smaller commitment of capital has less need to plan. And it has no (or a much smaller) technostructure. This means, in practical terms, that if demand falls, it can adjust to it by laying off workers. The mature corporation, by contrast, cannot lay off its capital. The technostructure is large and costly, and to curtail it is to disintegrate the brain of the enterprise.

The autonomy of the technostructure, we have also seen, is vulnerable to a failure of earnings, and this is most likely to result from a curtailment of demand and accompanying depression. Control of the entrepreneurial corporation rests firmly on ownership. If it is not burdened by debt, it can ride out a temporary failure in earnings.

Further, it is possible that a few farsighted entrepreneurs in the thirties may have seen or sensed that the regulation of demand would require a drastic enlargement of the role of the state in the economy and that it would change the tax system from an instrument for raising revenue to one for regulating demand. This too would have a very different effect on the entrepreneurial as compared with the mature corporation.

The actual burden of both corporate and personal income taxes is, in substantial measure, on the entrepreneur. The corporation income tax does not directly affect the member of the technostructure. And the impact of the personal income tax, the size of the income considered, will often be lighter than on the entrepreneur. As between paying greater or smaller income taxes oneself, there is a difference.

Finally, a close look at the particular form of regulation that eventually came into use discloses the interesting fact that it did, indeed, have the very strong support of the mature corporations and their technostructures.

4

In the thirties, in the first years of the Keynesian Revolution, it was generally believed that aggregate demand could be regulated by increasing or decreasing government spending, the level of taxation remaining the same. The policy was not regarded as altering in any basic way the relation of the state to the economy. The government would increase its outlays at some periods, reduce them at others, but, on the average, remain on about the same scale in relation to the economy as a whole.

This view of the policy was chimerical. Public expenditures can be increased, although this requires time. Once increased, however, they are not readily reduced. Spending, all agree, must be for useful or seemingly useful purposes. Like private consumption, any new public service quickly becomes a part of the accustomed standard of living. Once given, support to schools or hospitals or parks or public transportation cannot be readily withdrawn. Nonrecurrent expenditures, notably for public works, can be curtailed by the device of not starting new ones. But this takes time, and such expenditures are also rather slow to take effect.[7] Demand, by contrast, can fall rather rapidly and with cumulative effect.

The alternative is to have a permanently high level of public expenditures. From this large base increases are readily possible when needed. These expenditures, in turn, are supported by taxes that increase as incomes increase, thus curtailing demand, and fall as incomes fall, thus releasing spending to support demand. This alternative has been adopted. Since World War II, government spending has been high and has been increased substantially in periods of recession or stagnation. And these outlays have been supported by a self-adjusting level of taxation.[8]

[7] Cf. J. K. Galbraith and G. G. Johnson, *The Economic Effects of the Federal Public Works Expenditures, 1933–1938.* National Resources Planning Board, Washington, 1940. Some expenditures, most notably for unemployment, increase automatically when demand falls and unemployment increases.

[8] Between 1973, a comparatively good year, and 1974, which was one of incipient recession, the Nixon/Ford Administration increased the government contribution to spending in the economy by 4.8 billion. This resulted from the difference between a $34.7 billion increase in expendi-

The taxes that render this service are the personal and corporate income taxes. Both are admirably designed to regulate demand: and since both antedate this function and were, in fact, originally designed to raise revenue and induce a greater measure of equality in income distribution, much good luck must be assumed to manifest itself on occasion in the affairs of modern states. With higher income in the economy, individuals, inevitably, have higher income. They thus become subject to the personal income tax or, if already subject to it, to a higher surtax rate. Thus the personal income tax takes an increasing proportion of increased income and so acts progressively to curtail demand as income rises. In the opposite case of declining income, the yield of the tax reduces itself more than proportionately as people move off the tax rolls or to lower brackets. It thus releases an increasing share of income for spending. Although the corporation income tax is levied at approximately fixed percentage rates, its effect is similar, for, with rising income, corporation earnings rise very rapidly—much more rapidly than any other class of income.[9] These earnings being subject to the corporation tax, an increased share of all income is subject to this tax. The reverse is again true when national income falters or falls.

But this regulation, however admirable, will work only if the magnitudes are great enough to count. Taxes must be appreciable in relation to income if they are to affect incomes and therewith demand. They will be large enough, it follows, only if the operations of the state are sufficiently large in relation to the economy as a whole. Government must also be large if changes in its expenditures are to be used with effect. A $20 billion increase in public outlays can be easily and promptly made if it increases government outlays by only 10 percent. It will be very time-consuming if it involves a doubling of public expenditures. So an adequate scale of government expenditure—a sufficient public sector—is the fulcrum for the regulation of aggregate demand.

---

tures and a $29.9 billion increase in receipts. The next year, during which the economic decline reached bottom, the same (avowedly conservative) administration added $59.8 billion to income. Receipts fell by $1.7 billion; spending was increased by $58.1 billion. *Economic Report of the President, 1977*, p. 270.

[9]*Cf. Economic Report of the President, 1977*, pp. 277–279.

5

In 1929, federal expenditures for all goods and services amounted to $6.9 billion; by 1939, they were $22.6 billion; in 1976, they were $97 billion.[10] In relation to Gross National Product they increased from 2 percent in 1929 to 8 percent in 1976.

Although there is a widespread supposition to the contrary, this increase, on balance, has the strong approval of the businessmen of the planning system. The contrary belief notices only the ritual objection to expenditure for civilian services, much of which, more than incidentally, comes from the small entrepreneurs of the market system. It does not notice the strong approval which the planning system accords to military expenditures, space exploration, support to industrial research and development, highways or directly to individual firms of the planning system when, in the manner of the eastern railroads or the Lockheed Corporation, they experience financial difficulty.[11] Military expenditures, although their share in total outlays has declined in the seventies, are still the fulcrum on which public support to the planning system rests. They provide underwriting for advanced technology and, therewith, security for the planning of the planning system in areas that would otherwise be excluded by cost and risk. And they constitute a large bloc of outlays which is assured of business approval. The executive of the great corporation routinely opposes prodigality in government expenditure. But from his pleas for public economy defense expenditures are meticulously excluded. Thus these expenditures have a justification that transcends ordinary questions of economic policy or everyday fears of socialism and the state. Legislators who most conscientiously reflect the views of the business community regularly warn that insufficient funds are being spent on particular weapons. No more than any other social institution does the planning system disapprove of what is important for its success. Those who have thought its ex-

[10]Ibid, p. 189. Figures are in 1972 prices.

[11]When a large firm in the planning system has difficulty in meeting its obligations, an infrequent but not wholly exceptional occurrence, resort to the state is now commonplace in all of the industrial countries, including the United States. Previous oratory warning of the risk of socialism quickly converted to approval of constructive government action.

ecutives suspicious of Keynesian fiscal policy have failed to
see how precisely they have identified and supported what is
of highest importance for that policy.

6

In much social comment, including that of numerous
economists, there has been a tendency to minimize or ignore
the role of military expenditures in the regulation of demand.
There is much that is unsettling about dependence on such
outlays. That weaponry in the higher megaton ranges of
destructive power has an organic relation to the performance
of the economic system leads to unpleasant introspection. It
seems also a poor advertisement for the system and lends
comfort to a frequent allegation of Marxists. So scholarly and
textbook discussion slights the role of military spending in the
regulation of demand and concentrates, instead, on refinements of tax policy or other more appetizing issues. The
subject of military spending is dismissed by saying that were
it not required by higher national policy, then the same effect
could easily be obtained by shifting the outlays to civilian
purposes or returning them to private use.[12]

This, it will be evident, is too simple. Income released to or
taken from private expenditure will only serve effectively to
regulate demand if the public sector is large and the resources
released or absorbed are large enough to count. Military
expenditures help make the public sector large, and, as noted,
they help to win it vital business support. And in addition to
contributing to the requisite volume of expenditures (and taxation), the military spending also underwrites the technological risks of the planning system. Spending for schools, parks
and the poor would not do this. Substitute spending would
have neither the same direct appeal nor the same relation to
technology as the military spending it replaces. To this, in
much greater detail, I presently return.

7

The revised sequence, we have seen, accommodates the consumer to the goals of the technostructure and provides a climate of social belief that is favorable to this result. It would

[12]Cf. Paul A. Samuelson, *Economics*, 10th ed. (New York: McGraw-
Hill, 1976), pp. 820–821. I once, I must note, held the same view.

be odd, indeed, were this tendency to operate only in relation to the consumer—were the state and the climate of belief in which it functions to be wholly uninfluenced by those who sell it goods. But if the revised sequence operates in relation to public procurement, then defense expenditures in their present magnitude are, in part, an accommodation to the needs of the planning system and the technostructure.

That military expenditures serve the needs of the planning system—and that the underlying climate of belief on national policy is favorable to their doing so—will seem reasonable to many, and perhaps most, readers. This does not mean that it will be readily accepted. Our practice in these matters is to be guided less by truth than by formulas. To this end we also place public responsibility with those who are untroubled by the use of such conventional formulas—who, as the need arises, can react with moral fervor in support of the absurd. That defense requirements are set purely by national interest, that they are independent of any needs of the planning system, is a useful formula. It sanctifies expenditures that could not be defended if they were specifically for support to the planning system. It likewise lends credence to the belief, important for the autonomy of the technostructure, that a deep chasm separates state and private business. The first decides and commands; the second responds. Were the function of the state admitted to be an accommodation to the needs of the planning system, it would no longer be possible to regard the latter as an independent entity.

But formulas are not the best guide for the concerned and intelligent in these matters. Important questions are involved, including human safety, even survival. We should not risk less than the truth. Modern military and related procurement and policy are, in fact, extensively adapted to the needs of the planning system. (It seems very probable that this is a tendency of all planning, Communist, socialist or nonsocialist, however denoted.) The reversible or two-way reactions of the revised sequence operate here as elsewhere. And the line dividing the state from what is called private enterprise, or at least from the highly organized part of it, is a traditional fiction. However, this problem must be allowed to rest at this point until the further regulation of prices and wages and the role of labor and unions in the planning system are examined.

XXI

The Nature of Employment
and Unemployment

"There is no rate of pay at which a United States pick-and-shovel laborer can live which is low enough to compete with the work of a steam shovel as an excavator."

—Norbert Wiener

ON FEW MATTERS is the image of industrial civilization so sharp as on that of its labor force. This is a great mass—the word itself is ubiquitous—which streams in at the beginning of the shift and out at the end. It consists of comparatively unskilled operatives who guide or attend the machines and do the factory housekeeping, and a smaller aristocracy which has skills beyond the scope of the machine. When the system is functioning well, all or nearly all are at work. When it is not, the notices appear on the board, the men remain at home or in the bars and the rising percentage of unemployed in the labor force as a whole measures the extent of failure of the economic system. Similarly, when labor relations are tranquil, men pass peacefully through the gates. When they are not, a picket line appears, and the plant either shuts down or functions in face of the threats of the milling crowd outside. There are others in the enterprise—managers, engineers, designers, clerks, auditors and salesmen—but they are part of a shadowed background. The labor force, that which counts, is the great homogeneous blue-collar proletariat.

The image is not yet at odds with the reality of the planning system. But it is strongly at odds with its trend. Within the system the blue-collar proletarian is sharply in decline, both in relative numbers and in influence. And the notion of unemployment, as traditionally held, is coming year by year to have less meaning. More and more, the figures on unemployment enumerate those who are effectively unemployable given the needs of the modern economy in general and the planning system in particular. This incapacity may coexist with acute shortages of more highly qualified talent. The view of the system in the preceding chapters makes these tendencies predictable; and the statistics, which in this case are good, affirm the expectation or are consistent with it.

2

The planning system, we have seen, has a strong technological orientation; indeed, one of the subordinate goals of the technostructure is a showing of technical virtuosity. And the technostructure itself, among other things, is an apparatus that brings into conjunction the various branches of specialized scientific, engineering and other knowledge which bear on the solution of particular problems.

We have seen, also, that advanced technology, in combination with high capital requirements, makes planning imperative. All planning seeks, so far as may be possible, to ensure that what it assumes as regards the future will be what the future brings. This accords, too, with the concern of the technostructure for its own security, for such control minimizes the likelihood of developments which might jeopardize its earnings and thus its tenure.

These considerations tell with considerable precision the manpower requirements and labor policies of the planning system and forecast virtually all of its principal tendencies.

That it will have a large and growing requirement for qualified talent is evident. Technology, planning and the co-ordination of the resulting organization all demand such talent. This requirement, it is perhaps unnecessary to notice, is for *educationally* qualified, as distinct from skilled, manpower. Engineers, salesmen and sales managers, managers and management engineers and the near infinity of other such specialists, though they are trained in their particular task, can usually only be so trained if they have prior preparatory schooling. This is not necessarily the case of the tool-and-die maker, carpenter, plasterer or other skilled craftsman. The engineer, sales manager or personnel director applies specialized mental qualifications to a particular task. He must have, before learning his particular specialty, the requisite intellectual or mental preparation. The skilled journeyman brings manual dexterity and experience to bear. For this there is no minimum educational level.

At the same time the planning system reduces relatively, and for long periods absolutely, its requirement for blue-collar workers, both skilled and unskilled.

This situation arises partly from the nature of technology. Machines do easily and well what is done by repetitive physical effort unguided by significant intelligence. Accordingly, they compete most effectively with physical labor, including that of no slight dexterity and skill.[1]

But to see mechanization and automation purely as a problem in comparative cost is greatly to minimize their role—and to pay further for the error of confining economic goals, and economic calculation, to profit maximization.[2] The technostructure, as noted, seeks technical progressiveness for its own sake when this is not in conflict with other goals. More important, it seeks certainty in the supply and price of all the prime requisites of production. Labor is a prime requisite. And a large blue-collar labor force, especially if subject to the external authority of a union, introduces an element of uncertainty and danger. Its cost is not under the control of the technostructure, although in the planning system there is, of course, the power to offset labor cost changes with price changes. There remain the risk and consequences of a strike.

In contrast, mechanization adds to certainty. Machines do not yet go on strike. Their prices are subject to the considerable certainty which, we have seen, is inherent in the contractual relationships between large firms. The capital by which the machinery is provided comes in large proportion from the internal savings of the firm. Both its supply and cost are thus largely under the control of the firm. More white-collar work-

[1]This is a generalization. There are numerous operations—the sensory-manipulative operations that are involved in handling a power shovel for example—which have no appreciable educational requirements but which do not lend themselves to automatic processes.

[2]For such an argument see Charles E. Silberman, "The Real News About Automation, *Fortune*, January 1965. For an opposing and, I believe, more persuasive case see Ben B. Seligman, "Automation and the Unions in *Dissent*, Vol. XII, No. 1, Winter 1965. The word "automation," narrowly construed, refers to an industrial process which provides data from its own operations and feeds this back, usually through a computer, to controls which fully govern the process. It thus dispenses with all direct manpower. But automatic machinery dispensing with much but not all human guidance is, of course, very important. And this too is called automation. Because of this ambiguity I have used the word automation sparingly, and mostly where paraphrasing popular argument.

ers and more members of the technostructure will be required with mechanization. But white-collar workers tend to identify themselves with the goals of the technostructure with which they are fused. Such is the result of replacing twenty blue-collar workers with two men or women knowledgeable in computers.

Thus the technostructure has strong incentives, going far beyond considerations of cost (which may themselves be important), to replace blue-collar workers.

In the eighteen years from 1958 to 1976, the employed civilian labor force grew by about 24 million—from 63 million to over 87 million. From 1958 to 1963, however, the blue-collar labor force remained roughly constant. Thereafter it increased by only about five million. White-collar employment increased from 42.6 percent of the employed labor force in 1958 to 50.0 percent in 1976; the proportion of blue-collar workers dropped from 37.0 percent to 33.1 percent in the same period.[3]

The foregoing figures are for the economy as a whole, excluding only agriculture and the service industries. Thus they include blue-collar workers outside the planning system and where, it can be assumed, the decline in relative numbers was much less. Thus, from 1964 to 1976, blue-collar employment was constant or declining in steel and petroleum production—characteristic industries of the planning system. In automobile production there was a modest increase but from 1951 to 1976, although the total output of the automobile industry doubled, the number of production workers declined by almost twenty thousand.[4]

A recent study of manpower requirements concludes that between 1974 and 1985, there will be an increase in white-collar employment of some 28 percent. The increase in blue-collar employment is put at only 13 percent. Much of this latter increase, it should again be stressed, will be outside the planning system.[5]

[3]*Employment and Training Report of the President, 1977.* United States Departments of Labor and of Health, Education and Welfare pp. 135, 162–163.

[4]*Ibid.,* pp. 223–226 and *Economic Report of the President, 1977,* pp 231–232.

[5]*Employment and Training Report of the President, 1976.* United States Departments of Labor and of Health, Education and Welfare, p 336.

3

As the relative demand for blue-collar workers declines, the requirement for those with higher educational qualifications increases. These are needed by the technostructure. And, though with more modest educational qualifications, they are required for the white-collar tasks.

It follows, further, that if the educational system does not keep abreast of these requirements, both quantitatively and qualitatively, there will be shortages in particular areas of higher education qualification and a surplus in areas of lesser or no requirement. This is the present situation.

It is the vanity of educators that they shape the educational system to their preferred image. They may not be without influence but the decisive force is the economic system. What the educator believes is latitude is usually latitude to respond to economic need.

In the early stages of industrialization, the educational requirement for industrial manpower was in the shape of a very squat pyramid. A few lawyers, engineers, bookkeepers, timekeepers, clerks and the like were needed in or by the office. The wide base reflected the large requirement for repetitive labor power for which even literacy was something of a luxury. To this pyramid the educational system conformed. Elementary education was provided for the masses at minimum cost. Those who wanted more had to pay for it or to forgo income while getting it. This ensured that it would be sought only by a minority. To this day the school systems of the older industrial communities in West Virginia, central and western Pennsylvania, northern New Jersey and upstate New York still manifest their ancient inferiority. It is assumed that an old mill town will have bad schools.[6]

By contrast, the manpower requirements of the planning system are in the shape of a tall urn. It widens out below the top to reflect the need of the technostructure for administrative, coordinating and planning talent, for scientists and en-

---

[6] The same for long was true outside the planning system, for example in the rural areas of the South. Here, too, the need was for crude, illiterate labor power, and provision, accordingly, was made for nothing more. Northern agriculture was more demanding and the rural schools better. However, differences in income were a cause as well as a result of the difference.

gineers, for sales executives, salesmen, those learned in the other arts of persuasion and for those who program and command the computers. It widens further to reflect the need for white-collar talent. And it curves in sharply toward the base to reflect the more limited demand for those who are qualified only for muscular and repetitive tasks and who are readily replaced by machines.

This revision of educational requirements is progressive. The top of the urn continues to expand while the bottom remains the same or contracts. To this change the educational system responds. It does so with a lag, which is partly in the nature of any social response. But also the newly demanded education has required a sharp break with the earlier social attitudes of the entrepreneurs. These, as noted, held the state to be an incubus; accordingly, they sought to confine it to the provision of law and order, the protection of property and the common defense. Now the technostructure of the mature corporation must acknowledge dependence on the state for a factor of production more critical for its success than capital. Such a revision of attitudes takes time, and so, accordingly, does the public response to it.

4

The effect of this delayed response is that when employment is comparatively high, there will be numerous vacancies for those of higher qualification, particularly of a specialized character, and most of the unemployed will be without educational qualifications or without compensating work-experience or seniority. The recruitment efforts of the planning system in the universities and colleges and, even more, its newspaper advertising attest to the fact.[7] At the same time, since these vacancies are not yet fully recognized as the normal counterpart of unemployment, statistics thereon are meager.

The figures on the educational qualifications of the unemployed are better. In the spring of 1975, when the official unemployment rate was 9.2 percent of the labor force, it was 12.4 percent for those with less than eight years of elementary school, 11.3 percent for those with eight years, 15.2 percent for those with three years or fewer of high school. For

[7]A Boston newspaper editor noted, some years ago, that his revenues from advertising of job opportunities had come to exceed those from department stores, with much less interference with editorial policy.

college graduates it was 2.9 percent.[8] Of all who were officially counted as unemployed at that time, 44 percent, not much short of half, had fewer than four years of high school education. Additionally, it should be remembered that the individual with only a few years of schooling will usually have had poorer schools and schooling than the individual who has had more.

The unemployment situation for young persons with the combined handicaps of limited work experience, limited schooling and the wrong color is even more grim. For whites of 16 to 24 years of age with eight years of schooling the unemployment rate in the spring of 1975 was 28.9 percent. For young nonwhites the comparable rate was 43.2 percent.[9,10]

5

The position of the minorities calls for a special word. It has anciently been observed that the black worker is the last to be hired when employment is expanding and the first to be fired when it is contracting. Blacks do suffer a special handicap. But a great deal must be attributed to the low level of educational qualification, reflecting not discrimination, *per se,* by the planning system but prior disadvantage in schools and environment. A well-educated black is not so necessarily the first fired or the last hired.[11]

[8]Bob Whitmore, "Educational Attainment of Workers, March 1975," United States Department of Labor, Bureau of Labor Statistics, *Monthly Labor Review,* Vol. 99, No. 2 (February 1976), pp. 46–48.

[9]Ibid. By way of comparison, national unemployment was estimated at 25 percent of the civilian labor force in 1933, the worst year of the Great Depression.

[10]It must be kept in mind that the educational requirements and disqualifications discussed here are those of the planning system while the educational characteristics of the unemployed are those of the labor force as a whole. And, without doubt, the opportunities for employment of those with minimal educational qualifications are better outside the planning system. The service industries, construction and agriculture all have a substantial continuing requirement for common labor. In the case of migrant agricultural labor, one sees again how responsive the educational system is to context. No education is required for harvesting crops. And by more or less effectively denying education to the children of those who participate, further generations of such labor are assured.

[11]Although earnings of educated blacks remain below those of white citizens of comparable qualifications. In 1969, the median earnings of black men with four years of college, aged 25 to 34, were 78 percent of the earnings of whites of the same age and formal qualifications.

Some unemployment is also associated with industrial change—with the decline of anthracite coal-mining in central Pennsylvania, the mechanization and consolidation of mining in the bituminous region, the loss of industry by mill towns in New York, New England or elsewhere. Here again, however, much must be attributed to the exiguous educational system which served the industries of these regions where, characteristically, a boy went into the mine or mill at the earliest age at which he was capable of manual labor. A well-educated population would not have remained stranded or it would have drawn industry to itself. An aeronautical engineer, with the decline in demand for manned military aircraft, may have trouble finding employment in his specialty. But with a little training and some slight loss of dignity he becomes an excellent appliance salesman.

The point is of much importance. Unemployment in the planning system includes those who cannot find work in their particular craft or skill. It also includes qualified workers who are in the wrong place and who are reluctant to move. The number who fall in these catagories will increase as demand presses less strongly on the capacity of the labor force and unemployment rises in consequence. But the increasing educational requirements of the planning system add to the mobility of the working force both as between occupations and regions. The skilled craftsman of modest education does not easily learn a new skill. And the risks of movement are his own. So if he establishes himself as a tool-and-die maker in Detroit, there is a fair chance that he will remain there. The engineer or sales executive, though he is strongly specialized as to task, can acquire another, perhaps less demanding, qualification if he must. He is but little tied to his surroundings. If there is greater need for his specialty on the other side of the country, he moves in response to a promise of employment or is moved by his new employer as a matter of routine.

Economists have recurrently debated whether unemployment in the modern economy is primarily structural, which is to say the result of a poor adaptation of the worker's qualifications and skills to need, or whether it is the result of a general shortage of demand. Professional blood of a replaceable

"The Social and Economic Status of the Black Population in the United States, 1972." United States Bureau of the Census, *Current Population Reports*, Series P-23, No. 46, p. 25.

sort is regularly spilled, for the argument has an important bearing on remedy. If unemployment is structural, the remedy is to retrain those who are out of work. But if the problem is merely a shortage of demand, then general action to increase spending or reduce taxes is in order, always assuming that inflation can be prevented or is not more feared than unemployment. The use of tax reduction as a remedy for insufficient demand adds a point to the debate, for advocates of structural causes and remedies naturally fear that this may limit spending on education, training and retraining, which is the remedy for unemployment.

We now see the answer. Unemployment, as most now indeed concede, can be both structural and the result of inadequate demand, but also something more. It will appear with slackening of aggregate demand, and it will be among those who are most inflexibly tied to particular occupations and locations. At the same time there will be vacancies in positions requiring high and specialized qualifications. Employment would be higher both with stronger demand and with a better accommodation of preparation to need.

But unemployment can also reflect the cultural development of the system. It will be smaller at any given level of demand, the better the *cultural* accommodation to the needs of the planning system. If this accommodation is good, there will be a smaller core of functional illiterates who cannot be used at all. And there will be a larger number of people not only to fill the vacancies calling for higher qualifications but also with the added mobility between occupations and regions that goes with education.[12] Modern unemployment reflects not only a shortage in aggregate demand and a poor adjustment of skills to need but a lag in cultural development.

In consequence of the foregoing, unemployment, as a simple statistical concept, now has little relevance in the plan-

---

[12]In recent years, in much of Western Europe the unemployed have been consistently a smaller proportion of the labor force than in the United States. Something, perhaps, is to be attributed to a more reliable pressure of demand and to relatively larger employment opportunities outside the planning system. But national educational standards and, in consequence, a more homogeneously qualified labor force have certainly been contributing factors. Also, of course, Germany, France, Switzerland and other countries have taken foreign workers of lower qualification roughly in the numbers needed and left the unemployment associated with such lower qualification behind in Spain, Turkey, Yugoslavia or southern Italy where it does not get counted.

ning system. This system requires a progressive accommodation of educated manpower to its needs. If this accommodation is imperfect, there will be a shortage of workers for specialized tasks. And there will, at the same time, be unemployment. Both measure the failure in accommodation. Depending on the qualitative nature of the failure, the unemployed will consist of those who are unemployable because of insufficient education, or those who are occupationally or geographically immobile because of absence of education, or those who have a skill or specialty for which there is no demand and which, for reasons unrelated to education, they cannot exchange for one that is wanted. Or unemployment may have a quite different cause. It may be the result of an insufficiency of aggregate demand, which reflects yet another needed accommodation of society to the requirements of the planning system. Simple statistics of unemployment reveal, it will be evident, almost nothing about the nature of the failure of accommodation at any given time. The crude steel capacity of a country was once a rather good indication of its ability to build railroads and meet its other needs for steel, and the statistics on the finishing capacity told where, with expansion, idle capacity would persist or bottlenecks would occur. Technology has made such figures far less meaningful. One must now know how well the industry can accommodate to the more refined, more specialized and constantly changing requirements for the metal. A surplus of steel can now be combined with a shortage. So it is with labor. Here too one must look beyond the totals to the accommodation to educationally more refined, more specialized and constantly changing requirements. Here also totals have slight meaning. And here, as with steel, technology is one of the things that have made it so.

6

Much may be learned of the character of any society from its social conflicts and passions. When capital was the key to economic success, social conflict was between the rich and the poor. Money made the difference; possession or nonpossession justified contempt for, or resentment of, those oppositely situated. Sociology, economics, political science and fiction celebrated the war between the two sides of the tracks and the relation of the mansion on the hill to the tenement below.

In recent times education has become the difference that divides. All who have educational advantage, as with the moneyed of an earlier day, are reminded of their *noblesse oblige* and also of the advantages of reticence. They should help those who are less fortunate; they must avoid reflecting aloud on their advantage in knowledge. But this doesn't serve to paper over the conflict. It is visible in almost every community.

Thus a part of the country with a high rate of accommodation to the requirements of the planning system, i.e., a good educational system and a well-qualified working force, will attract industry and have a strong aspect of well-being. It will be the natural Canaan of the more energetic among those who were born in less favored communities. This for long explained the migration from the South, Southwest and border states to California, the upper Middle West and the eastern seaboard.[13] Many of these migrants were unqualified for the employment in the planning system. They thus contributed heavily to welfare and unemployment rolls in the communities to which they moved. The nature of the opprobrium to which they were subject is indicated by the appellations that sometimes still are applied to them—hillbillies, Okies, jungle-bunnies. It is not that they were and are poorer but that they were and are culturally deprived. It is such groups, not the working proletariat, that now react in resentment and violence to their subordination.

Politics also reflects the new division. In the United States suspicion or resentment is no longer directed at the capitalists or the merely rich. It is the intellectuals—the effete snobs—who are eyed with misgiving and alarm. This should surprise no one. Nor should it be a matter for surprise when semiliterate millionaires turn up leading or financing the ignorant in struggle against the intellectually privileged and content. This further reflects the relevant class distinction in our time.

A further consequence of the new pattern of employment and unemployment is that full employment, though it remains an important test of the successful performance of the economic system, can be approached only against increasing resistance. For, as noted, while the unemployed are reduced in number, they come to consist more and more of those, pri-

---

[13]As education and the supply of technically qualified people have improved, this movement has, predictably, declined and even reversed itself.

marily the uneducated, who are unemployable in the planning system. The counterpart of this resistant core is a growing number of vacancies for highly qualified workers and a strong bargaining position for those who are employed. This leads to the final source of instability in the planning system and to yet a further resort to the state. This we now examine.

XXII

The Control
of the Wage-Price Spiral

MEN OF CONSERVATIVE TEMPERAMENT have long suspected that one thing leads to another. The effect of the regulation of aggregate demand on public wage and price policy admirably validates their suspicion.

The state seeks to regulate aggregate demand by providing a volume of purchasing power sufficient to employ the available labor force. A low level of unemployment is a recognized test of the success of the economy and of the proficiency of those who guide it. And this, as the last chapter has shown, is not easily achieved. The notion of employment and unemployment has only imprecise meaning in the planning system. What is involved is a complex fitting of highly diverse qualifications to highly diverse needs. For those with the least educational qualification, there is comparatively little need. Only a very high level of aggregate demand will bring them into employment, if they can be employed at all, and by that time there will be great shortages of manpower in the higher levels of qualification.

At any reasonably high level of demand, prices and wages in the planning system are inherently unstable. This is certainly so when demand is strong enough to begin enrolling the hard core of more or less unemployable unemployed. Then wages and prices press each other up in a continuing spiral. It is convenient, in describing this spiral, to break into it at the point where wages act on prices. But it is a continuous process, and no causal significance should be attached to wage increases merely because they are the starting point.

2

When unemployment is small, the bargaining position of unions is, in general, strong. Members can face a strike with the assurance that they cannot be replaced. As a more practical matter, they know that they will be inflicting the maximum loss of business on the employer and that after the strike is over, they will promptly be recalled to work.

Employers, on their side, will deem it wise under such circumstances to grant increases in wages. The strong demand ensures that the added costs of the higher wages can be passed along to the consumer or other buyer. By the time unemployment is reduced to the hard-core categories, there will invariably be a shortage of some classes of production workers.[1] Higher wages will seem to be a way of holding or recruiting manpower. Collective bargaining ordinarily embraces a substantial part of the industry. This means that all or most firms are affected by the wage increase at the same time. All will thus be led to increase prices at the same time. This, together with the strong demand, eases or erases the fear that the control over prices so essential for planning will be jeopardized because some firm will not go along.

The rise of the mature corporation has added significantly to the likelihood of the spiral. The entrepreneurial corporation was presumed to maximize the profits that were allowed to it by the current state of demand. And this, we may agree, was its tendency. If the profits had previously been at a maximum and prices were then at the level that yielded this maximum, wage increases could not be passed on in the form of higher prices. One cannot improve on the most. If wage increases could not be passed on, they would have to be paid for out of earnings. And in the nature of the entrepreneurial enterprise these earnings accrued in substantial measure to the entrepreneur. Again there is the special poignancy in paying when the individual himself has to pay. The entrepreneur had reason to resist. If he did yield, the wage increase did not necessarily increase prices since, to repeat, these were already set to yield the maximum profit.

In the mature corporation the technostructure sets prices not where they maximize profits but where they best contribute to the security of the technostructure and to the growth of the firm. This means, with rare exceptions, that it has latitude to increase revenues by increasing prices. Accordingly, it can pass wage increases along. It will be led to do so because a strike, implying contingencies and uncertainties beyond the control of the technostructure, is always a

[1] To be distinguished from the unfilled positions in the higher levels of qualification in the technostructure.

threat to its security. More important, perhaps, labor conflict cultivates attitudes that are hostile to identification and thus damaging to the motivational system. This is evident when motivation is seen in modern and comprehensive terms. And, finally, the technostructure, with which the decision on wages resides, does not, itself, have to pay.

The circle can now be completed. Price increases become cost increases for customers—either other industries or ultimate consumers. In either case, eventually or immediately, they raise living costs and thus become an inducement to another round of wage demands. Given regulation of demand with the goal of providing full employment, and in the absence of other steps, this spiral of wage and price increases is an organic feature of the planning system.[2,3]

It also accords solidly with experience. That the modern

[2] For many years there was debate among economists as to whether demand pulls up prices or wages push them up. Considerable polemical blood was spilled on the issue. Again something more than scientific verity was involved. If demand is the activating factor, then unemployment could be minimized and inflation could be controlled by precise regulation of demand—by a competent and perhaps lucky management of monetary and fiscal policy. No questions of price and wage control arose. But if wages shove up prices and the higher prices lead to new wage demands, the plausible course is to control one or both. The cost-push thesis is also inconsistent with the doctrine of maximization, for, as noted, if a firm can respond to a wage increase by raising prices and increasing its net revenues (some fairly refined responses to changes in marginal costs apart), it could have done so before the wage increase. It did not, so it was not maximizing its revenues prior to the wage increase.

In fact, within the planning system, as just indicated, both strong demand and the push of costs are factors in the instability of prices at or near full employment. And those most reluctant to believe that wages act on prices and prices on wages have been succumbing to the visible reality. For a further and competent discussion of these relationships, see William G. Bowen, "Wage Behavior and the Cost-Inflation Problem" in *Labor and the National Economy*, edited by the same author (New York: Norton, 1965). An important study, affirming the cost-push thesis, to which I am much indebted is Sidney Weintraub's *Some Aspects of Wage Theory and Policy* (New York: Chilton Books, 1963). See also Abba P. Lerner, *Flation* (New York: Quadrangle, 1972).

[3] It is not necessarily characteristic of the economy outside the planning system. In agriculture, professional and other services, imported products and some raw materials, the push of wages is likely to be unimportant. Prices rise primarily in response to strong demand. Some of the past debate among economists over the comparative importance of cost-push and demand-pull inflation has been the result of different men looking at different parts of the economy.

large firm has the option of passing on wage increases is taken for granted. If demand and employment are high, no one ever asks whether the steel, automobile or aluminum industry can raise their prices following the conclusion of a new collective bargaining contract but only whether they will need or choose to do so.[4]

3

The seemingly obvious remedy for the wage-price spiral is to regulate prices and wages by public authority. In World War II and the Korean War in the United States, demand strongly pressed the capacity of the labor force as well as that of the industrial plant. Apart from the exceptional strength of this pressure, especially in World War II, there was nothing unique about the wartime situation. Economic institutions and behavior are not drastically altered either by declared or undeclared war. During both conflicts the wage-price spiral was successfully contained by controls. In the two years of 1941 and 1942 in the United States, the wholesale price index of industrial products rose a little more than 7 points. In the following three years, with greatly increased demand and virtual full employment, but with controls in effect, the index increased only 2.4 points. Price increases for machinery, chemicals and metal products, all closely identified with the planning system, were even less. Between 1950 and 1951, after the outbreak of the Korean War, the wholesale index of capital goods showed prices rising by 7 points; that of consumer durables rose by 5 points. The following year, after wage and price controls were imposed, each index rose by only about one point.

This experience was not, however, greatly influential. It was assumed that war had somehow established new conditions as well as new imperatives. These made the experience irrelevant for peacetime. All groups influentially concerned also had a tradition that was hostile to controls.

The entrepreneurial firm resisted price control because it could only be for the purpose of reducing profits. This attitude still influenced the technostructure, which also feared that public interference with prices could impair its auton-

---

[4]This is a choice which nearly all economists concede but which cannot be reconciled in any practical way with the doctrine of profit maximization.

omy. A theology that associated free prices with freedom, though without intellectual content, was also influential.

Unions, as well, had long reacted adversely. This was a legacy of their experience with the entrepreneurial firm. That firm had a strong interest in resisting union demands. It had privileged access to newspapers, public opinion and the state. Any wage regulation, other than that establishing minimum wages, would be, it was felt, for the purpose of keeping wages down. To be dependent even on a friendly government was to lose capacity for independent action to press rightful demands.

For economists, as will be sufficiently evident, a massive intellectual vested interest was involved. As noted, nearly all teaching and technical discourse assumed markets in which producers sought to maximize their return. To admit of the need for price or wage control was to admit of the inadequacy of this system and the associated theoretical apparatus. Goals other than profit maximization governed the setting of prices. Instead of revealing to students by precise and rational diagrams the prices that would maximize profits for a producer, it would be necessary to consider what price a bureaucrat might believe consistent with wage and price stability. Economics would be reduced to the level of political science. Truth has its obligations to dignity.

Besides, it was argued, it would not work. Here we encounter again the commitment to avarice. Only the soft-minded could suppose that government, by regulation, could thwart the primal instinct for self-enrichment.

In consequence, professional economists accepted the inevitability of inflation at full employment or simply evaded the issue with whatever grace they could command. "It would be nice if we could insist upon having complete price stability and maximal employment and growth. . . . it may be that citizens of a modern mixed economy can find no shelters within which they can live with full security and without compromise."[5] Professor Carl Kaysen has stated the position with succinct accuracy: "Some businessmen and bureaucrats call for wage and price controls and most economists oppose them. Yet it is a brave economist who is ready to assert that

[5]Paul A. Samuelson, *Economics*, 8th ed. (New York: McGraw-Hill, 1970), p. 816. In later editions Professor Samuelson appears to have concluded that an economist could not so apologize for imperfection. He has abandoned this compromise.

enough competition is achievable in the present institutional framework to place confident reliance on market forces to counter inflation. Only a minority of economists are that brave."[6]

4

Yet, paradoxically, all associated with the planning system also benefit substantially from restraints on prices and wages. What is opposed in principle is useful in practice. Uncontrolled price and cost increases are much less dangerous to the security of the technostructure than uncontrolled price reductions such as might result from price competition or be forced by a severe shrinkage of aggregate demand. Given the strong demand that induces the price and cost increases in the first place, it is possible to offset cost increases by raising prices. It is not easy to offset falling prices by reducing wages or other costs. Nevertheless, planning is greatly facilitated if prices and costs are stable. Inflationary price and cost increases, moving unpredictably through the system, make long-term contracts impossible and everywhere introduce an unwelcome element of randomness and error. Price stability also facilitates the management of demand. Prices being given, the way is open to persuade the customer on other points. If prices are changing, he may respond in his purchases to these. This response is unpredictable, which is to say it interferes with effective management.

If wages are rising, increases in compensation for white-collar employees and in the technostructure will also be required. This will be at a time when there are unfilled positions. There will be some resulting danger of unsettling the salary structure and inducing competition for scarce talent. Another random element thus enters and interferes with planning. The mature corporation and its technostructure therefore have good reasons for wishing to avoid the wage-price spiral. And to accept restraint, since it applies to both costs and wages, is not necessarily to sacrifice earnings. Should there be sacrifice, as always in the mature corporation, it is not suffered by those who agree to it.

Thus once again economic development shows a remark-

---

[6]Carl Kaysen, "Government and Business in the United States: A 225 Year Perspective" in *Business and The American Economy*, Jules Backman, ed. (New York: New York University Press, 1976), p. 79.

able degree of internal consistency. The planning system must, by its nature, be subject to external restraint on its prices. As the mature corporation evolves, it can accept and possibly even welcome such restraint.

Restraint can even be useful in practice to the unions. The spiral requires that they invest much of their energies in keeping abreast of price increases. Only a small and unpredictable portion of a pay rise brings higher real income. The rest compensates for price increases. Thus, with uncontrolled wages and prices, the union has a large and essentially unproductive task of merely keeping even. For the rank and file the effect is even worse. Gains are won as the result of lengthy and elaborate collective bargaining. If only for demonstration purposes there will be an occasional strike. And then these gains evaporate as prices rise. The whole process has an unpleasant aspect of legerdemain. "It makes no sense to have the boss put a nickel in wages in your pocket with one hand and take out a dime in prices with the other."[7]

Outside the planning system, the spiral also has adverse effects. And this sector of the economy is important in forming public attitudes. Here are farmers, civil servants, the self-employed and the employees of small enterprises. Within the planning system, as wages force up prices and prices force up wages, those who receive these payments remain automatically abreast. A passenger in even a very fast automobile is reasonably certain of keeping up with it. A man running alongside is not so well situated. The insiders are protected against loss of real income; the outsiders are not. More generally, the individual who gets added income as a result of a general inflationary movement attributes it not to larger economic causes but to his own virtue and diligence. The higher prices that take it away he attributes to bad public policy. Finally, there are many categories of income recipients—municipal employees, hospital and library and like workers, pensioners of all kinds—whose incomes do not reliably keep pace with prices. Their complaint, even if sometimes unvoiced, is yet more acute.

In fact, the wage-price spiral is functionally associated in the economy with unemployment. Unemployment occurs when there is insufficient demand; the spiral operates when

[7] A. H. Raskin, "The Squeeze on the Unions, *The Atlantic Monthly*, April 1961. Reprinted in Bowen, p. 8. He was commenting on a common attitude of steel workers.

there is too much demand and also, something which orthodox economists have the greatest difficulty in believing, when
there is just enough. Both unemployment and inflation are
taken by the public to be indications of economic failure.
Here the economists reenter. Whatever their predilections,
they cannot escape public attitudes. These will no more allow
excuses for inflation than for unemployment. And since the
system is unstable at full employment, there is no alternative
to control. However regretted, it is inescapable. This even the
most ardent defenders of the market have discovered when
they have arrived in Washington to take a position with the
Council of Economic Advisers or otherwise experience the
chilling realities of responsibility. For the duration of their
service, the notion of maintaining full employment without
interference with markets has to be put aside. Only when
they are safely back in the universities again, with the
freedom that teaching accords to error, can it be gratefully
exhumed.

5

Since all the relevant groups affirm the importance of free
markets in principle, while needing control in practice, the recurrent solution has been to impose control in practice while
affirming the commitment to free markets in principle. This
semantic triumph has been aided by long-standing recognition
that what is not permissible in principle is often necessary in
practice.

It has also been aided by the technological dynamic of the
planning system. This, with its associated use of capital, ensures a progressive increase in output per worker, although in
varying amounts from industry to industry. These productivity gains allow, in turn, for annual wage increases without either higher prices or reduced earnings. Given a reasonably
affluent wage level—an exemption from the pressures of
physical need—workers may be more content to accept a moderate wage increase with stable prices than a larger one with
the prospect of partial loss from rising living costs. Since the
corporation is not experiencing rising costs, it can accept
stable prices as its part of the bargain. All that remains is for
the state to give a clear initiative in this regulation.

This initiative was the most important innovation in

economic policy of the administration of President John F. Kennedy. In the earliest days of the administration, it was agreed among those concerned with economic policy that some special mechanism for restraint would be required were there to be a close approach to full employment. Generalized pleas to unions and employers for restraint had been sufficiently tried; in the absence of definition, all parties identified restraint with their normal behavior. Accordingly, in September of 1961, the United Steelworkers, then engaged in contract negotiations with the steel companies, were asked by President Kennedy to hold their demands within what could be granted from productivity gains. And the steel companies were asked to keep their prices stable. The policy and the standards for its application were then detailed the following January in the annual Economic Report. "The general guide for noninflationary wage behavior is that the rate of increase in wage rates (including fringe benefits) in each industry be equal to the trend rate of over-all productivity increase."[8] In April 1962, after negotiating a wage contract generally consistent with these standards, the steel companies, led by the United States Steel Corporation, announced an increase in steel prices averaging six dollars a ton. Strong government pressure, strongly adverse public and business opinion and some historic presidential invective brought a recision of the increase. Thereafter for several years the wage guideposts, as they came to be called, and the counterpart price behavior were a reasonably accepted feature of government policy. Wage negotiations were closely consistent with the guidelines. Prices of manufactured goods were stable.

Nevertheless, of the various adaptations of government policy to the planning of the planning system, the control of wages and prices remained on the least secure footing. Partly this was because the divorce of ideology from action excluded any deliberate effort to devise a fully effective system of control. On occasions of public ceremony, businessmen and numerous union leaders still proclaim their commitment to the free market. And so did economists. It was hard to turn from these liturgical exercises to a consideration of practical measures for ensuring that the guideposts would be observed. In the thirties, although the commitment of

[8]*Economic Report of the President, 1962,* 189.

economists to the canons of sound finance was still strong, a minority accepted the implications of the Keynesian system and proceeded to work out its application to practical fiscal policy. Though radical, this was not wholly disreputable. To work on methods of wage and price control was not reputable.

This absence of both ideological sanction and effective design left the mechanism of wage and price restraint subject to both misuse and nonuse. In one sense controls do not prevent inflation. Rather they keep the wage and price spiral from producing inflation—from causing increases in prices over a wide range that are not associated with expansion in output—when demand is at levels sufficient to provide full or nearly full employment. But demand must not be too greatly in excess of this level. If it is, there will be inflation outside the planning system, i.e., where the wage-price spiral is not a factor. And the pressure of demand within the planning system will be too strong for the controls. There will be shortages; premiums will be paid for preferential deliveries; jobs and wages will be upgraded, and inflation will proceed here as well. The absence of ideological sanction left the danger that someone would appear in a position of responsibility for whom the liturgy of the free market was a guide to action.

In the latter sixties, the administration of President Johnson, seeking to prosecute an unpopular war in Vietnam and unwilling to have higher taxes add to that unpopularity, allowed demand to become excessive. The guideposts, still imperfect and voluntary, broke down. Then with the advent of the Republican administration in 1969, their ideological weakness became for a time decisive. The Nixon economists were strongly committed to the antique market beliefs; they affirmed strongly their conviction that they could combine stable prices with high employment without any direct intervention on wages and prices. Controls, voluntary or otherwise, were specifically eschewed. As frequently before, reality showed its power in opposition to ideological preference. While demand was curtailed and unemployment rose, prices continued to rise. Instead of combining high employment with stable prices, insufficient employment was predictably combined with wage-price inflation. After a year and a half—in the summer of 1970—Mr. Nixon's economic advisers were compelled to concede the role of the wage-price spiral and to plead for restraint. The Congress, meanwhile, had taken steps toward authorizing controls with the force of law. In 1971, after stating that he was "unalterably opposed" to such action,[9] Richard Nixon imposed price and wage controls. Inflation in 1972 was at a rate of approximately 4 percent; unemployment was 5.6 percent of the civilian labor force and went down to 4.9 percent the following year.[10] Then, the election having been won, the controls were abandoned. The Secretary of the Treasury, Mr. George Schultz, said that, although the controls were working well, when the economy expanded strongly (and they were more needed), they would not work so well.

6

The history of controls, in some form or other and by some nomenclature, is still incomplete. As noted, neither inflation nor unemployment is an acceptable alternative.[11] No other advanced industrial community, socialist or nonsocialist, has found it possible to dispense durably with such regulation or some equivalent moral restraint on prices and union demands. The United States, the most developed of the industrial communities, will not be an exception.

The necessity for control arises in the apparatus of industrial planning. This planning, we have seen, replaces prices that are established by the market with prices that are established by the firm. The firm, in tacit collaboration with the other firms in the industry, has wholly sufficient power to set and maintain minimum prices. And the firm goes on to exercise control over what is purchased at these prices. Given this management of demand for the individual product together with an effective regulation of aggregate demand, the minimum prices so set are secure.

This price control accords protection, however, only against price reduction. It does not embrace the unions and hence does not provide any protection against concessions to

[9] Which he referred to, rather pejoratively, as "the Galbraith scheme." *The New York Times*, August 5, 1971.

[10] *Economic Report of the President, 1977*, pp. 221, 241.

[11] I once considered it possible that, by adequate compensation, a volume of unemployment consistent with stable prices could be made socially and politically tolerable. Cf. *The Affluent Society* (Boston: Houghton Mifflin, 1958), pp. 298–307. This view I no longer hold.

them and concurrent price increases. And the remedy is beyond the scope of the individual firm. It knows that others will forswear price reductions that are disastrous for all. But it cannot count on others to resist wage increases and to forgo resultant price increases, for these, however inconvenient for planning and the economy at large, are not disastrous. The market having been abandoned in favor of planning of prices and demand, there is no hope that it will supply this last missing element of restraint. All that remains is the state. So, in the end, there is no alternative to having the state complete the structure of planning.

With minimum prices established by the firms, demand that is managed by them for specific products, demand that is managed in the aggregate by the state and maximum levels established by the state for wages and prices, the planning structure of the planning system is effectively complete. All that remains is to ensure that everyone, at all times, refer to it as an unplanned or market system. This will, no doubt, prove possible.

In this connection, it is worth noting that the machinery for enforcing maximum prices in the planning system does not need to be especially powerful. The entrepreneurial firm, since it was under the dominance of the market, had substantial independence from the state. Were an attempt made to control its prices, it could bring to bear formidable powers of obstruction and resistance. The mature corporation, as part of a comprehensive structure of planning in which the state plays an important part, has no similar independence. It identifies itself with social goals and adapts these to its needs. It cannot easily fight that with which it is so associated. More specifically, if the state is effectively to manage demand, the public sector of the economy, as we have seen, must be relatively large. That means that the state is an important customer, and it is especially needed in developing advanced technology which would otherwise be beyond the scope of industrial planning. So the mature corporation is deeply dependent on the state—its opportunity for independent or obstructive action is closely circumscribed. It does not, accordingly, have the luxury of defiance. It may go far in adapting the goals of the state to its needs. But it cannot, any more than a department of government itself, pursue objectives sharply at odds with those of the state. And since other large firms are also identified with social goals which reflect adaptation, they will tend to consider resistance antisocial and the sanctions justified.[12] There is no chance, on this issue, of a solid front by mature corporations against the state.

---

[12]Efforts by the steel industry—U.S. Steel in 1962 and Bethlehem in 1966—to break through current price restraints are a case in point. These efforts were a reflection of older entrepreneurial attitudes. The government on both occasions threatened use of its power as a customer—though it is less in the case of steel than in many industries. Both public and a good deal of business opinion condemned the actions as antisocial or, at a minimum, showing a poor sense of public relations. On the latter, see Richard Austin Smith, *Corporations in Crisis* (New York: Doubleday, 1963), p. 157 et seq.

XXIII

The Planning System and the Union I

". . . [T]he public still thinks of trade unions as Goliaths of power."

—Solomon Barkin*

FOR MOST of their brief history in the United States, trade unions have been embattled. Employers have usually wished they did not exist. The wish has often been strengthened by belief. These desires and convictions have led regularly to resistance suitably supported by scholarly argument. The later has always been available. One of the small but rewarding vocations of a free society is the provision of needed conclusions, properly supported by statistics and moral indignation, for those in a position to pay for them.

Quite commonly, arguments of this genre have led to the conclusion that, with industrial progress and enlightenment, unions have lost their function. Class conflict is the nostalgia of the antique revolutionary. Unions exist only because they have fastened themselves on the back of the worker and, like the Old Man of the Sea, cannot be dismounted. Impressionable employers, captivated by such arguments, have on occasion held out the hand of friendship to their men only to have it enthusiastically bitten.

Against this background, a conclusion that unions have a drastically reduced function in the planning system will be received by many with skepticism. Another man has fallen victim to nonsense. The measure of a scholar is not how he reacts to evidence but how well he resists tendentious propaganda.

Yet, as this is written, union growth within the planning system has long since tapered off. In almost any view the unions are less militant in attitude and less powerful in poli-

*A long-time and highly regarded trade union official.

tics than in earlier times. Industrial relations have become markedly more peaceful as collective bargaining has come to be accepted by the modern large industrial enterprise. Union members and their leaders appear in support of conservative causes—or in militant opposition to radical ones. All this suggests some change.

The present analysis foretells further such change and leads to the conclusion that it has durable significance. The increasingly conciliatory character of modern industrial relations, especially in the larger corporation, has come about not because labor leaders and vice presidents in charge of labor relations have entered upon an era of pacific enlightenment, the operative agent being the rise of industrial statesmanship and the somewhat delayed triumph of Judeo-Christian ethics and the golden rule. It has come about because interests that were once radically opposed are now much more nearly in harmony. Behavior is not better; it is merely that interests are concordant. Were interests still opposed, labor relations would still be characterized by argument and invective, accented on occasion by clubs, stones and low-yield explosives. The unquestioned expertise of the modern industrial relations man would not appreciably ease the passion.

2

All of the changes here examined—the shift in power from ownership and the entrepreneur to the technostructure, technological advance, the regulation of markets and aggregate demand and the imperatives of price and wage regulation—have had an effect on the position of the union. In every case they have subtracted from its role.

The employee was linked to the entrepreneurial firm by pecuniary motivation. There was an unquestioned conflict in pecuniary interest between the employee and employer. As indicated in the last chapter, an increase in labor costs, when the firm was already maximizing profits, could (practically speaking) only reduce profits.[1] These profits, or a substantial

---

[1]That is to say, if wages go up independently of any increase in productivity. As a concession to technical precision, it should perhaps be noted that with certain market structures and demand and cost functions, longer-run adjustments may occur which pass along the costs. These do not impair the present case, which is that there is an immediate conflict of pecuniary interest.

share of them, accrued to the entrepreneur. And his interest in pecuniary return, since, among other things, it rewarded the capital he supplied or commanded, was also strong.

The union, in these circumstances, had the power, unavailable to the individual worker, of forcing the employer to accept the higher costs and reduced profits by threatening the even greater cost and profit reduction of a strike. It follows that the employer had every reason to resist the union and regret its existence. And the worker had equal reason for wanting it. The resistance of the employer might keep the union from gaining a foothold. But its importance to the worker was equally a factor in giving it strength. Additionally, the man who sided with the employer was abetting the income of another man instead of his own. If he was rewarded, he was a fink and if not, he was a fool. In either case, any tendency he might have to identify himself with the goals of the employer could be regarded with contempt and be, by the union, so characterized.

In the United States the classic last-ditch battles against the unions—those of Ford, Ernest Weir, Thomas Girdler and Sewell Avery—were all waged by entrepreneurs or, as in the more recent case of J. P. Stevens, by a firm in an industry—textile manufacture—that approaches the market system in general structure. In the original battle over union organization it was the mature corporations that led the way in surrender.

The first goal of the technostructure is its own security. Profits, provided that they are above the minimum necessary for security, are frequently secondary to growth. Labor relations, naturally enough, are conducted in accordance with the goals of the technostructure.

This means that the technostructure may readily trade profits for protection against such an undirected event with such an unpredictable outcome as a strike and its accompanying effect on identification and motivation. Once again there is the important fact that those who make the decisions during union negotiations do not themselves have to pay.

But no reduction in profits may be required from yielding to the union. Since the mature firm does not maximize profits, it can often maintain income by increasing its prices. The wage settlement, since it affects all or most firms in the industry, provides all with a common signal to consider such action.

In fact, no absolute rule can be laid down on the reaction of the technostructure to a union demand. It will depend on the existing level of prices and earnings, the effectiveness of the management of demand for the products or product, the importance of wage costs and other factors. But it can be said that the mature corporation, in the pursuit of its own goals, will accede far more readily than the entrepreneurial enterprise to the demands of the union and, accordingly, is much less averse to its existence. It will even pay something for what is called a good employer image, for this, in turn, will help attract talent at all levels. These tendencies, far more than Christian revelation, explain the harmony that increasingly characterizes the labor relations of the mature corporation, to the pride of all concerned.

But while the task of the union is much easier, the union is also much less essential for the worker. What the technostructure gives to the union, it can also give without a union or to avoid having a union. At a minimum the union shrinks in stature. A fighting lawyer is a figure of great majesty before a hanging judge.

3

It has long been a minor tenet of trade union doctrine that all employers are essentially alike. All seek their own best gain. All, accordingly, are inimical to the interest of the worker. Thus any worker who identifies his interest with that of his boss is making a mistake. The vehemence with which this doctrine has been enunciated in modern times may indicate uneasiness as to the truth of the proposition in the case of the mature corporation. Such teaching was not so necessary in the age of the Homestead massacre and the Pullman strike. In any case, it is not true.

As compared with the entrepreneurial firm, not only is there a much less flat opposition of interest between workers in the mature corporation and those who have the power of decision on matters relating to wages and other conditions of employment but identification is part of the established and accepted system of motivation. And, although identification is most important in the technostructure, its existence there serves to make it a more general tendency. Loyalty to the firm will often be part of the general mood. This is adverse to the union. Additionally, in the earlier stages of industrial technology—in the early steel mills or on the early automobile assembly lines—hard, repetitive and tedious work acted as a barrier to identification. Among machinists, toolmakers, steamfitters and other skilled workers there was the sense of common interest arising from a shared skill. As machinery replaces both repetitive and drudging work and eliminates skilled occupations, it lowers these barriers to identification. This increases the difficulties of organization and thus adds to the problems of the union.

But much more important, modern technology opens the way for a massive shift from workers who are within reach of unions to those who are not. Both the capital resources and the goals of the technostructure of the mature corporation strongly facilitate and encourage such a shift.

This tendency has already been observed.[2] In its planning, the technostructure seeks to minimize the number of contingencies that are beyond its control. Labor costs and supply are significantly of this character, and more so when there is a union. To substitute capital in the form of machinery, the supply and cost of which are wholly or largely under control, for labor which is not and which can strike, is an admirable bargain. It is worth the sacrifice of some earnings. It is also adverse to the union, for that is the purpose.[3]

The substitution, as earlier noticed, has been proceeding rapidly. Its visible manifestation is the decline in the relative number of blue-collar workers employed in industry. In the eighteen years from 1958 to 1976, to remind, white-collar workers in the United States—professional, managerial, office and sales workers—increased by 17 million. In the same years blue-collar workers—craftsmen, operators and laborers, excluding farmers and miners—increased by only 5½ million.

[2]Chapter XXI.

[3]We have here another example of the way the planning system accommodates belief to its convenience. It has been the lurking conviction of quite a few unions that technical change is an instrument adverse to their interests and thus to be resisted. This attitude has been uniformly deplored as wrong and regressive and no more fitting of civilized advocacy than sodomy, self-flagellation and the refusal to use soap. All right-thinking people should accept machines and participate in the general fruits of progress. In fact, the instinct of the unions was sound. And, from the point of view of those immediately involved, the tactic of resistance may also have been sound. Over a longer period, of course, the resisting unions have been outflanked by competitive change—as the anthracite miners were outflanked by oil and the railroad brotherhood by automobiles, trucks and planes.

By 1976, there were about 15 million more white-collar than blue-collar workers—43.7 million as compared with 28.9 million. During the same years the number of professional and technical workers, the category most characteristic of the technostructure, increased by about 83 percent—a greater rate of increase than for any other category. No other group increased so rapidly.[4] In industries strongly typical of the planning system the change has been much more dramatic. Between 1947 and 1975, the number of nonproduction workers increased from 16 to 29 percent of employed workers in durable goods manufacturing industries. In the primary metal industries, the increase was from 12.9 to 21.6 percent; in fabricated metal products, from 16.5 to 24.6 percent; in transportation (automotive) equipment, it was from 18.5 to 22.2 percent; in electrical equipment, it was from 21.7 to 33.9 percent. In the manufacture of military ordnance, the increase was especially dramatic—from 18.5 to 54.8 percent.[5]

White-collar workers in the private sector have not been readily susceptible to organization in the United States, and, with the rise of the technostructure, they are almost certainly less so. In the entrepreneurial corporation a visible line divided the bosses—those whose position depended on ownership or their ability to produce profits for the owners—from clerks, bookkeepers, timekeepers, secretaries, salesmen and others who were purely employees. In the mature corporation this line disappears. Decision is divorced from ownership; the location of decision moves in the direction of the body of white-collar workers. Distinctions between those who make decisions and those who carry them out, and between employer and employee, are obscured by the technicians, scientists, market analysts, computer programmers, industrial stylists and other specialists who do, or are, both. A continuum thus exists between the center of the technostructure and

[4]*Employment and Training Report of the President, 1977.* United States Departments of Labor and of Health, Education and Welfare, p. 161.

[5]Ibid., p. 224. The 1976 figures are subject to minor revision. As earlier stated, there is strong indication that these trends will continue. The United States Department of Labor (in *Occupational Outlook Handbook,* 1976–1977 edition, Bulletin No. 1875, p. 16) forecasts through the mid-nineteen-eighties "a continuation of the rapid growth of white-collar and service occupations, a slower-than-average growth of blue-collar occupations, and a further decline of farm workers."

the routine white-collar workers on the fringe. At some point, power or the chance for moving toward the center becomes negligible. But it is no longer possible to recognize that point.

In consequence, white-collar workers identify themselves with the technostructure from which they are not visibly distinct. A survey of such workers in 1957 showed that more than three-quarters regarded themselves as being more closely associated with management than with production workers.[6] As a result, with "a few notable exceptions, white-collar workers have traditionally been cool to unions, especially professional and technical employees."[7] For them, "Persuasion, pressure, and manipulation [and bureaucratic gamesmanship] . . . take the place of the face-to-face combat of an earlier age."[8] One can imagine circumstances that would increase white-collar organization. Women make up a large part of the white-collar force; a continuing increase in their political and social consciousness might have such effect. There is also the effect of continuing inflation which, since the early editions of this book, has had a stimulating effect on organization by public employees. However, the weight of expectation remains strongly against white-collar organization in the planning system.

4

Finally, both relatively secure employment resulting from the regulation of aggregate demand and comparative affluence reduce the dependence of the individual worker on the union. Once again we see the interconnected character of change. If unemployment is endemic and incomes are close to the minimum required for physical survival, men are held to their jobs by the threat of physical suffering. In these circumstances the union greatly enhances the liberty of the worker. The worker cannot walk off the job by himself. But he knows that if things become intolerable, he can walk off with all the others. Shared privation is easier to bear than individual pri-

[6]A. A. Blum, "Prospects for Organization of White Collar Workers." United States Department of Labor, Bureau of Labor Statistics, Monthly Labor Review, Vol. 87, No. 2 (February 1964), p. 125 et seq.

[7]Derek C. Bok and John T. Dunlop, Labor and the American Community (New York: Simon and Schuster, 1970), p. 44.

[8]Clark Kerr, John T. Dunlop, Frederick H. Harbison and Charles A. Myers, Industrialism and Industrial Man (Cambridge: Harvard University Press, 1960), p. 292.

vation. And a union may have strike pay or a soup kitchen to mitigate, however slightly, the hardship involved.

Both high and secure employment and high income are solvents for the sense of compulsion and thus are substitutes for the union. If employment is high, there will be alternative jobs. Accordingly, a man can quit. It is favorable employment conditions, not the union, that rescue him from his slavish dependence on the job he holds. In the United States, as in Britain, Canada and elsewhere, the regulation of aggregate demand to ensure better and more secure employment prospects was strongly pressed by the unions. It was the accommodation of the state to the needs of the planning system that the labor movement most sought. It was the thing most designed to make unions less needed.[9]

High income also lessens the danger of fear of physical privation. Thus it accords the worker liberty that he once obtained from the union. And, therefore, it too weakens dependence on the union. However, the relation of income to the need and willingness to work in the planning system is a complex and much misunderstood matter. A digression is necessary here to explain it.

5

The natural tendency of man, as manifested in primitive societies, is almost certainly to work until a given consumption is achieved. Then he relaxes, engages in sport, hunting, orgiastic or propitiating ceremonies or other forms of physical enjoy-

[9]The role of unemployment in according a firm control by employers over the labor force was strongly stressed by Marx. "The industrial reserve army [i.e., the unemployed], during the periods of stagnation and average prosperity, weighs down the active labour-army; during the periods of over-production and paroxysm, it holds its pretensions in check. Relative surplus-population is therefore the pivot upon which the law of demand and supply of labour works. It confines the field of action of this law within the limits absolutely convenient . . . to the domination of capital." Marx was equally insistent on the intolerable effects (from the viewpoint of the capitalist) of full employment. (*Capital*, [New York: Modern Library, 1936], Chapter 25, p. 701.) One imagines that Marx would have regarded a full employment policy, if successfully pursued over any length of time, as having radical implications for his system, the class struggle and the laws of capitalist accumulation. His followers, until comparatively recently, were unwilling to attach such significance to the policy. Keynesian economics was long dismissed as a superficial effort to prop up capitalism which did not affect the fundamental position of the worker.

ment or spiritual betterment. This tendency for primitive man to achieve contentment has been the despair of those who regard themselves as agents of civilization and remains so to this day. What is called economic development consists in no small part in divising strategies to overcome the tendency of men to place limits on their objectives as regards income and thus on their efforts. Commodities involving physical and progressive addiction were long considered especially useful in this regard; this explains the great esteem that attached, in the early stages of modern civilization, to tobacco, alcohol, coca and opium as trade goods for more primitive peoples so-called, a value that they have not entirely lost in the present day. However, goods which by their novelty appeal to vanity or to emulative or competitive adornment or display are now considered more legitimate. Also, though need for food and shelter, especially in benign climates, is rather readily satisfied, the pressures of emulation and competition in adornment and display have no clear terminal point. California farmers and labor contractors once, as a matter of established policy, encouraged their Filipino workers to invest heavily in clothing. The pressure of debt and the pressure on each to emulate the most extravagant quickly converted these happy and easygoing people into a modern and reliable work force. In all underdeveloped countries, the acquisitive desires and resulting physical effort inspired by the introduction of modern consumer goods—cosmetics, motor scooters, transistor radios, canned food, bicycles, phonograph records, movies, American cigarettes—are recognized to be of the highest importance in the strategy of economic development.

In the advanced industrial countries, the creation of wants, and therewith the need to work, is a matter of considerable sophistication but the principles are the same. It is also a task of great importance. In 1939, the real income of employed workers in the United States was very nearly the highest on record, and it was then the highest of any country in the world. In the next quarter century it doubled. Had the 1939 income been a terminal objective, work effort would have been cut in half in the ensuing twenty-five years. In fact, there was a slight increase in weekly hours actually worked. This was a remarkable achievement.

It was accomplished partly by the now well-understood ability of the planning system to adapt belief to its needs. To increase income and consumption is held to be socially and morally sound. Leisure is something to be regarded with misgiving, especially in lower income brackets. Accordingly, a reduction in the standard work week must always be considered dubious social policy, inducing moral or spiritual weakness.

Economists, performing one of their now well-recognized functions, have accorded important canonical reinforcement to these beliefs. They have made the rate of increase in the production of goods the prime test of social achievement. To substitute leisure for work is, thus, to be antisocial. Economic theory has long insisted on the homogeneity and insatiability of wants. There is no proof that an expensive woman obtains the same satisfaction from yet another gown as does a hungry man from a hamburger. But there is no proof that she does not. Since it cannot be proven that she does not, her desire, it is held, must be accorded equal standing with that of a poor man for meat. Doctoral aspirants in economics still risk failure and, at a minimum, get a warning rebuke if they assert otherwise. If all wants are of equally good standing, it follows that the moral and social obligation to work to fill them remains undiminished in power no matter how much is produced.[10] Corporate executives with an overly acute sense of persecution have sometimes supposed that economists, in the ideas they advance, are their enemies. In fact, the economics profession is strongly in the service of the beliefs they most need. It would, *prima facie*, be plausible to set a limit on the national product that a nation requires. The test of economic achievement would then be how rapidly it could reduce the number of hours of toil that are needed to meet this requirement. Were economists to advocate this goal, with the revolutionary effects that it would have on the planning system, there would be grounds for complaint. None has been so uncooperative.

However, the more immediate device for ensuring that there is no terminal objective as regards income is advertising and the related arts of salesmanship. Here we have yet another of the interlocking developments which so admirably serve the planning system. Advertising and salesmanship—the management of consumer demand—are vital for planning in the planning system. At the same time, the wants so created ensure the services of the worker. Ideally, his wants are kept

[10] I have dealt with the underlying theory in *The Affluent Society*, 3rd ed., rev. (Boston: Houghton Mifflin, 1976), Chapters X, XI.

slightly in excess of his income. Compelling inducements are then provided for him to go into debt. The pressure of the resulting debt adds to his reliability as a worker.

It is held, of course, that wants are not contrived. They are deeply organic in the human situation. Their satisfaction is not only a source of rich reward to those served but the highest secular function of the society. Even to hold this process up for examination is to invite the suggestion that one is ascetic, unworldly, determinedly impractical and disposed to substitute one's own odd and esoteric values for the lustier instincts of the masses. Yet one cannot have it both ways. If wants are inherent, they need not be contrived. But few producers of consumer goods would care to leave the purchases of their products to the spontaneous and hence unmanaged responses of the public. Nor, on reflection, would they have much confidence in the reliability of their labor force in the absence of pressure to purchase the next car or to meet the payments on the last.[11]

It is now time to return to the union.

---

[11]Professional advertising men, who, as earlier noted, have wished for a substantial social justification for their services, have frequently argued that, without their efforts to stimulate wants, men would not work and the economy would falter. Economists, almost without exception, have dismissed this as the special pleading of an economically unlearned and conscience-ridden community. In fact, the advertising men have a good case. It has been rejected by economists because to admit that advertising promotes wants is, not surprisingly, to concede that the goods would be unwanted in the absence of such persuasion. This casts doubt on the pivotal contentions that wants are homogeneous and insatiable and that the volume of production measures the success of the society. One cannot give equal status with bread to what must be contrived by advertising, and one cannot measure the success of an economy by its ability to keep up with Madison Avenue. Again these are matters which I have dealt with at more length in *The Affluent Society.*

The Planning System and the Union II: The Ministerial Union

THE PLANNING SYSTEM, it seems clear, is unfavorable to the union. Power passes to the technostructure, and this lessens the conflict of interest between employer and employee which gave the union much of its reason for existence. Capital and technology allow the firm to substitute white-collar workers and machines that cannot be organized for blue-collar workers who can. The regulation of aggregate demand, the resulting high level of employment together with the general increase in well-being, all, on balance, make the union less necessary or less powerful or both. The conclusion seems inevitable. The union belongs to a particular stage in the development of the planning system. When that stage passes, so does the union in anything like its original position of power. And, as an added touch of paradox, things for which the unions fought vigorously—the regulation of aggregate demand to ensure full employment and higher real income for members—have contributed to their decline.

Yet it would be premature to write the union off. Numerous organizations—the Fishmongers and the Cordwainers in the City of London, the board of directors of the great corporation, the Board of Overseers of Harvard University—regularly survive their function. Once a union is in being, there is nothing in continuing its existence—the collection or deduction of dues, the enrollment of newly hired members, the holding of conventions and the designation of officers—that is nearly so difficult as bringing it to an end. And while the planning system undermines old functions, it does not eliminate them entirely, and it does add some new ones. Finally, not all unions are within the planning system, and those outside have a better prospect. The overall effect of the rise of the planning system is greatly to reduce the union as a social force. But it will not disappear or become entirely unimportant.

2

The trend in union strength is clearly adverse. After 1956, total union membership in the United States began to fall, and
in the next seven years, although the number of workers in
nonagricultural employment increased by more than four million, the number enrolled in unions fell by about one million.
(Unions had an estimated 17.5 million members in 1956 and
16.5 million members in 1963.)[1] The decline was especially
severe in manufacturing,[2] and within manufacturing the
unions suffering the most severe losses were the Automobile
Workers and the Steelworkers. Both are in industries strongly
characteristic of the planning system.[3] Between 1956 and
1972, the proportion of the nonagricultural labor force belonging to unions fell from 33.4 percent to 26.7 percent.[4] In the
years following 1963, large gains in employment brought a
substantial rise in union membership but the proportion of all
nonfarm workers belonging to unions continued to decline.[5]

As observed in the last chapter, white-collar workers, including technical and professional workers, are a rapidly expanding proportion of the labor force—17.7 percent of the
labor force in 1900 and 50.0 percent in 1976.[6] Only about
10 percent of all white-collar workers belong to unions, and

[1]*Handbook of Labor Statistics, 1969,* United States Department of
Labor, Bureau of Labor Statistics, Bulletin No. 1630, p. 351.

[2]*Directory of National and International Labor Unions in the United
States, 1967,* United States Department of Labor, Bureau of Labor Statistics, Bulletin No. 1596, p. 61.

[3]Ibid., p. 58. A third union which suffered a major decline in membership was the United Mine Workers. These were years of rapid consolidation and mechanization of bituminous coal production—in brief,
of movement toward the planning system. I do not suggest, of course,
that all changes in union membership are explained by this one factor.

[4]*Directory of National Unions and Employee Associations, 1973,*
United States Department of Labor, Bureau of Labor Statistics. Supplement 3, January 1976, p. 70.

[5]*Handbook of Labor Statistics, 1969* and *Handbook of Labor Statistics, 1976* (United States Department of Labor, Bureau of Labor Statistics), Bulletins Nos. 1630 and 1905, pp. 351 and 297 respectively.

[6]U.S. Bureau of the Census, *Historical Statistics of the United States,
Colonial Times to 1970,* Bicentennial Edition, part 2, p. 140. The distribution in 1976 was white-collar workers 50.0 percent; blue-collar
workers 33.1 percent; service workers 13.7 percent; and farm workers
3.2 percent. *Employment and Training Report of the President, 1977,*
United States Departments of Labor and of Health, Education and
Welfare, p. 162.

two thirds of these are in nonmanufacturing industries. In the decade 1962-1972, union membership among government employees increased by about 1.2 million, and this accounted for over one third of the increase in total union membership during this period. About 40 percent of white-collar employees of federal, state and local governments belong to unions as compared with only 20 percent in private nonmanufacturing employment and fewer than 5 percent of white-collar employees in manufacturing.[7]

Nor is the white-collar worker the only problem. Production workers in areas of advanced technology—computer and data-processing industries, instrumentation, telemetry, specified electronics and the like—are not easily organized. If the number of production workers is large and the firm has closely related branches that have unions, the new workers are often added to the existing unions without difficulty. In isolated branches or otherwise unorganized firms, or where the proportion of engineers and technicians is high, the unions do not as easily make headway.[8] The workers, in effect, become an extension of the technostructure and evidently so see themselves.

---

[7] *Handbook of Labor Statistics, 1971* and *Handbook of Labor Statistics, 1976*, United States Department of Labor, Bureau of Labor Statistics, Bulletins Nos. 1705 and 1905, pp. 304 and 295 respectively. The comparative percentages of union members among white-collar employees in government, private nonmanufacturing and manufacturing are for 1966. In contrast with the mature corporation, among government employees there has been no shift in the locus of control over wages and working conditions toward the worker. This remains with legislative bodies. Accordingly, the white-collar public employee feels himself more removed from his employer, in sharper pecuniary conflict with him as a taxpayer and, in consequence, less inclined to identify himself with his goals than does the white-collar worker in the planning system. This has contributed to union organization in this field. A more relaxed attitude, legal and otherwise, to union membership by public employees has also contributed. Most important of all have been inflation and the example of steel workers, coal miners, other industrial workers, whose annual income now frequently exceeds that of policemen, firemen, teachers or other civil servants.

[8] I am indebted to my colleague, the former Secretary of Labor, Professor John T. Dunlop for guidance here. For a confirming view, see Solomon Barkin, "The Decline of the Labor Movement" in *The Corporation Take-Over*, Andrew Hacker, ed. (New York: Harper, 1964), pp. 223–245.

3

However, there are opposing trends. In the early stages of industrialization the working force was, as previously noted, a homogeneous mass. Members could be paid and treated alike or, at most, they fell into a few simple classifications. The modern working force, by contrast, is highly differentiated. The rules that regulate pay, other benefits, seniority and conditions of promotion and retirement for the various classes of workers are voluminous. Any unilateral application of such rules would, however meticulous, seem arbitrary or unjust to some. By helping to frame the rules and by participating in their administration through the grievance machinery, the union serves invaluably to mitigate the feeling that such systems or their administration are arbitrary or unjust. It is a measure of the importance of this function that, where the union does not exist, good management practice calls for the development of some substitute. In helping to prevent discontent and, therewith, a sense of alienation, the union also removes barriers to identification—barriers which once contributed to its own power.

Also, while some unions have resisted technological change, others have greatly helped it by aiding the accommodation to change. They have helped to arrange a trade of higher pay, a shorter week, severance pay or other provisions for those sacrificed for smaller employment. And they have persuaded their members to accept the bargain. The planning system attaches great importance to such help. The union leader who provides it is accorded its highest encomium, that of labor statesman.[9]

In the Soviet-type economies the union has long had an ambiguous and somewhat unsettled role. As the historic voice of the worker in the class struggle, it had to exist and be nurtured. But unions could not be accorded any role which was inconsistent with the full identification of their members with the goals of the firm by which they were employed. In the end, their functions have been much the same as those just

---

[9] John L. Lewis is the classical case. In early years, when fighting for wage and welfare improvement, he was a highly inimical figure in American industrial relations. He was awarded the title of labor statesman for his later undeviating support of the mechanization of coal-mining.

mentioned. Along with educational and welfare activities, which are also of some importance in some American and Western European unions, the Soviet unions serve as a channel of communications between the firm and its workers and a way of according the latter a voice in the framing of rules and in their administration.[10]

4

However, in the non-Soviet systems the union renders a further service; it is an important factor in planning and, therewith, in the relations of the planning system with the state.

We have already noticed that the unions assumed the principal role in winning approval of the policy of regulating aggregate demand. Though commonly billed as having the objective of providing full employment, this policy is also essential for the planning of the planning system. Unions, furthermore, have a potentially important role in stabilizing demand for particular products procured by the state. Such procurement, that for defense needs in particular, cannot be claimed as something that serves the purposes of the firm. A plea for more defense spending to help business is considered unduly crude. It must be justified strictly as a requirement of broad national policy. So, in seeking contracts, the technostructure cannot publicly plead the pressure of its own convenience, necessity or earnings. But it can with more decency plead the adverse effect of contract termination, or failure to win renewal, or denial of a new contract, on its legal working force or the community. And here the union can be a valuable seconding voice. On spending for highly technical weapons the relevant union leaders, in recent years, have, on balance, been less inhibited than management. Still, cooperation between unions and technostructure is by no means complete; in all legislative matters there is a residue of traditional hostility to overcome.

The much more important service of the union to planning is to standardize wage costs between different industrial firms and to ensure that changes in wages will occur at approx-

[10]David Granick, *The Red Executive* (Garden City, New York: Doubleday, 1960), p. 219 et seq. Also Emily Clark Brown, "The Local Union in Soviet Industry: Its Relations with Members, Party, and Management," *Industrial and Labor Relations Review*, Vol. 13, No. 2 (January 1960), p. 209 et seq.

imately the same time. This greatly assists price control by the industry. And it also greatly facilitates the public regulation of prices and wages. Both services are far more important than is commonly recognized.

Specifically, if there is an industry-wide union, one of its tasks will be to ensure that rates of pay will be more or less the same for the same kinds of work. This is done in the name of fairness and equity but it means too that no firm can reduce prices because of lower wage rates and none will be impelled to seek higher prices because its rates of pay are higher. Price-setting and maintenance where there are a number of firms are thus facilitated. So is planning.

Rates will also change when the labor contract for the industry expires. This change will affect all firms at approximately the same time and by approximately the same amount. All, accordingly, have a common signal to adjust their prices; the same change is called for by all. So wage adjustment and related changes, which might otherwise be a threat to minimum price-setting in the industry, cease to be a serious problem.

At the same time the union contract brings wage levels within the purview of the state. The situation here is akin to that of diplomacy. It may be difficult to do business with a strong government such as that of the Soviet Union. But when business is done, something is accomplished. This is not the case where, as was true in Laos or South Vietnam, the writ of the government ran only to the airport. There is no way of enforcing that to which governments agree. Similarly wage control may be difficult with a union. The latter may resist energetically the terms. But it also brings workers within the ambit of control.

The union negotiates a bargain that is binding on all of its members. If this bargain can be influenced by the state, then the level of wages is subject to influence—or control. And since collective bargaining contracts are for some period of time—a period that, in yet another accommodation to the planning system, is tending to become longer—the occasions when the state must intervene are kept down to a practical number. In between, the contract acts as a ceiling on wage payments.[11] Were wage bargains struck by individuals or for a vast number of small categories of workers and were they

---

[11]Rather more in the United States than in Europe, where employers, on occasion, have gone beyond contract levels to attract workers.

of indeterminate duration, control and surveillance would be impossible.

5

The union renders a yet further potential service. The commonplace stragegy of wage and price stabilization, when formally undertaken, is to hold wage increases within the amounts that can be paid from gains in productivity. The amount of the productivity gain—the increase in output per worker—only becomes known over time. And it differs for different firms. The period of the contract allows time for knowledge of the gains in productivity to accumulate and for calculation as to what increase can be afforded without prejudice to price stability. The union, since it bargains for an industry-wide membership, settles not for what the individual firm can afford, which would mean different wage rates for different firms—an impossible complication—but for what all can afford as an average. This is an invaluable simplification for a policy that, in the long run, is inescapable.

The union does not render these services to wage and price stabilization deliberately or even willingly. It has no choice. Should it refuse to conform to a broad strategy of stabilization, the firms with which it has contracts would, in turn, raise their prices. If an appreciable number of unions got wage advances greater than justified by gains in productivity, then all would have to be accorded them. Responding price increases would then be general. And part or all of the gains from wage increases would be lost in price increases. The union would have opposed public authority, and perhaps risked popular displeasure, for gains that its own members would recognize to be transitory. This alternative will recurrently be pressed. But the accompanying acceleration of inflation makes it a less than attractive one.[12]

In summary, the planning system has now largely encompassed the labor movement. It has dissolved some of its most important functions; it has greatly narrowed its area of action; and it has bent its residual operations very largely to its own needs. Since World War II, the acceptance of the union by the industrial firm and the emergence thereafter of an era

[12]As this is written, we are in such a period. Washington leadership finds itself in a delicate balance between fear of inflation and fear of controls.

of comparatively peaceful industrial relations have been hailed as the final triumph of trade unionism. On closer examination, it is seen to reveal many of the features of Jonah's triumph over the whale.

Such then is the present stage in the journey on from the Tolpuddle Martyrs.

XXV

The Educational and Scientific Estate

As THE TRADE UNIONS RETREAT, if gradually, into the shadows, a rapidly growing body of educators and research scientists emerges. This group connects at the edges with scientists and engineers within the technostructure and with civil servants, journalists, writers and artists outside. Most directly nurtured by the planning system are the educators and scientists in the schools, colleges, universities and research institutions. They stand in relation to the planning system much as did the banking and financial community to the earlier stages of industrial development. Then capital was decisive, and a vast network of banks, savings banks, insurance companies, brokerage houses and investment bankers came into existence to mobilize savings and thus to meet the need. In the mature corporation the decisive factor of production, as we have seen, is the supply of qualified talent. A similar complex of educational institutions has similarly come into being to supply this need. And the values and attitudes of the society have been appropriately altered to reinforce the change. When savings and capital were decisive, thrift was the most applauded of social virtues. It mattered not that most of the population lived and died in abysmal illiteracy and ignorance. As qualified manpower has become important, thrift, as a virtue, has acquired overtones of antiquity and even eccentricity. Education, instead, has now the greatest solemnity of social purpose.

The educational and scientific estate,[1] like the financial

[1]There is no good term for this large group which is associated with education and scientific research apart from that undertaken by the technostructure. In political discourse they are grouped with writers and poets and referred to either as intellectuals or eggheads. The first term is too restrictive in its connotation and, if not too restrictive, too pretentious. The second is insufficiently solemn. One should coin a new term only as a last resort; we have a great many words already, and new ones always afflict the ears. Accordingly, I have appropriated and somewhat altered the usage of my friend Professor Don K. Price who

community before it, acquires prestige from the productive
agent that it supplies. Potentially, at least, this is also a source
of power. Likewise, and even more than the financial community, it acquires a position within the apparatus of government. The nature of this educational and scientific estate, the
sources of its influence and its relation to the technostructure
and the state are now the subject for consideration.

2

The parallel between the financial community and the educational and scientific estate cannot be carried too far. Both
owe (or owed) their prestige and influence to their association with the decisive factor of production. But the power of
the financial community was that of the hand that holds the
spigot. It could turn the supply of capital for a user off or on.
Appearances in connection with the use of this power, it
should be noted, are untrustworthy. Power must always be
exercised with appropriate gravity of demeanor. If a man
must be subject to the authority of another, he can at least
ask that it not be an occasion for glee. Financial transactions—a new issue of stock or debentures, the provision of a
new line of credit—are still occasions for solemn ritual even
when the transactions are not greatly more complex than the
purchase of a typewriter and alternatives are readily available. This is a carry-over from the days when power was involved. Much of the ceremony that surrounds the largely
ministerial functions of a central bank is of the same order.[2]
None of this should be allowed to obscure the reality, which
is that the power has passed.[3]

The educational and scientific estate has no control over the

---

speaks of the scientific community (including that part employed by industry and the government) as The Scientific Estate. See his book by
this title (Cambridge: Harvard University Press, 1965).

[2] The insistence in the United States that the central bank should,
though only nominally, be independent of the federal executive reflects
a similar nostalgia, a reminder of the days when the central bank
could facilitate or prevent borrowing by the government and thus control its policies on taxation and expenditure.

[3] Specifically, by way of reminder, the power of the lender depends on
the absence of alternatives for the borrower. When capital is abundant
and the firm has internal sources of savings, there are such alternatives.

supply of talent similar to that of the banker over access to savings. It can, to some slight extent, influence its people on their choice of employment, and this is not an insignificant sanction. But most of its influence follows from its rapidly increasing numbers with the consequent political implication; from its privileged access to scientific innovation; and from is nearly unique role in social innovation. These are the sources of influence to be examined.

Until well along in the present century the educational community in the United States was very small and concerned largely with elementary education. This has changed explosively in recent times. College and university professors, who numbered 24,000 in 1900 and 49,000 in 1920, totaled 381,000 in 1960 and 907,000 in 1972, virtually a forty-fold increase in less than eighty years. Only 238,000 students were enrolled in colleges and universities in 1900 as compared with 3,216,000 in 1959 and 8,519,000 in 1973. Fewer than 700,-000 students were in high school grades in 1900 as compared with 9,600,000 in 1959 and a total of 15,427,000 in 1973.[4] In 1900, 1583 Master's degrees were conferred in the United States and 382 Ph.D.s or their equivalent. In 1974, 277,033 Master's degrees were conferred and 33,816 Ph.D.s.[5] Before the development of the planning system only a modest number of people were needed with advanced technical or other skills. Colleges and universities were principally required to train men for the learned professions—medicine, law, the church, veterinary medicine and the like—or to supply the very exiguous cultural adornment thought appropriate to the offspring of the well-to-do.

Apart from their numerical insignificance, educators in the earlier stages of industrial development—in the United States until well into this century—were also, economically and socially, an inferior caste. Funds for financing higher education in private colleges and universities came from the well-to-do either in the form of charitable gifts or as tuition paid on behalf of their offspring. It was naturally assumed

[4]Figures are from the *Digest of Education Statistics, 1975* (1976,) United States Department of Health, Education and Welfare. Total educational expenditures, which were approximately $3,233,600 in 1929 (3.1 percent of Gross National Product), reached $108,700,000 in 1974 (7.8 percent of G.N.P.). In 1947, 26 percent of the 18-to-21-year-old population was enrolled in college; in 1972, 45 percent was enrolled.
[5]*The Condition of Education,* United States Department of Health, Education and Welfare, Vol. III, Part 1 (1977), p. 187.

that, here as elsewhere, provision of money accorded right of proprietorship. This should be exercised by the men most accustomed to wielding such authority, namely the business entrepreneurs. "The fact remains, the modern civilized community is reluctant to trust its serious interests to others than men of pecuniary substance, who have proved their fitness for the direction of academic affairs by acquiring, or by otherwise being possessed of, considerable wealth."[6] The principle, having been accepted for private institutions, was applied to public colleges and universities as well. These also, since attendance involved both expense and ability to defer earning a living, were seminaries for the education of the offspring of families of much better than average income.

The doctrine of financial paramountcy—of the ultimate power of those who paid the bills—was not fully accepted by the academic community. In principle, and on occasion also in practice, educators asserted their right to speak their minds and even to criticize those who paid their salaries. This tendency was associated with a sharp conflict of goals. The entrepreneur had a straightforward pecuniary measure of success. A man was judged by what he made. But the application of any such measure in the academic community would have either conceded mass failure, given the modest pay, or have been immoderately expensive. So while educators on occasion admitted social inferiority and more often simply assumed it, many also professed the goals they held to be intellectually more demanding or aesthetically more refined than the pecuniary preoccupations of the entrepreneur. This was ill received by businessmen. As a result, suspicion and dislike, leading recurrently to minor conflict between the business and academic communities, was until recent times an established feature of the American academic scene.[7,8]

[6]Thorstein Veblen, *The Higher Learning in America*. A memorandum on the conduct of universities by businessmen (Stanford: Academic Reprints, 1954), pp. 67–68.

[7]The tension created by this relationship extended into the universities and colleges themselves. College presidents and other administrative officials were obliged by financial expediency or conviction to defend the value system of their boards of trustees and the larger business community. In doing so, they frequently aroused the mistrust or contempt of the faculty. An even more interesting case is that of the business school or faculty of business administration. In virtually all universities of academic merit, its professors were, until fairly recent times, accorded a second-class citizenship. The allegedly unsubstantial character of the subject matter was partial cause. But the professor of business administration was also required by his position to accept and even avow

This conflict was aggravated by the role of the colleges and universities as a principal source of social innovation in the United States. While they have great power in carrying or resisting legislation, business firms, unions and those professionally concerned with politics in the United States are not socially inventive. On the contrary, they are, in this respect, comparatively sterile. Some ideas for social change come from unattached reformers and the bureaucracy. But their most important source for many years has been the academic community.

In the early stages of industrialization, most of these suggestions were for the purpose of making industrial development more equitable, humane or just. The need for such reform was always far more evident to the professors than to those who saw themselves as their natural masters. The latter had to look on while proposals for limiting monopoly power, regulating prices or rates of natural monopolies, encouraging and protecting unions, making taxes more progressive, supporting the bargaining position of farmers, limiting the exploitation of natural resources, regulating conditions of employment, and, on occasion, for abolishing private entrepreneurship and substituting socialism emanated from the colleges and universities and were defended as an exercise of academic freedom. Nor did these reforms remain an academic matter. Many had a tendency to be taken up.

Without question, inconvenient views were often muted by discretion or suppressed. Academic expression was accommodated to "the views and the prepossessions prevalent among the respectable, conservative middle class; with a

---

the goals of the business entrepreneur but without receiving his emoluments. Thus he had the worst of all worlds—the comparative indigence of the academic community but without its pretension to superior goals.

⁸The alienation of the artist and unattached intellectual from the business community had similar sources. Business imposed a pecuniary valuation on his work. In a community in which the educational and cultural standards were accommodated to the requirements of the early planning system, the standards of taste were not high. Also, the market for new cultural wares, even of modest sophistication, could be very thin. So the pecuniary value placed on the work of the artist or intellectual was low. They, accordingly, ascribed their own value to their work and dismissed that of the businessman as inherently bogus, vulgar or naïve. These adjectives were synonymous with bourgeois taste. On this, see the discussion by Seymour Martin Lipset in *Political Man* (Garden City, New York: Doubleday, 1960), p. 318 et seq.

more particular regard to that more select body of substantial
citizens who have the disposal of accumulated wealth."[9] But
this is not the whole story. A very large amount of legislation
or policy regarded as highly inimical by the entrepreneurial
enterprise received its initial impetus from the academic community. Laws against monopoly, regulating access to the capital markets, in support of a wide range of welfare measures,
in support of progressive taxation and on behalf of unions,
owed much to such origins.

During the years of burgeoning industrial development, the
academic community—indigent, subordinate and weak—has
invariably been pictured by historians in its relation to
business as the aggrieved party. Its position in society combined much courage with great peril. On the record, none of
this is certain. In consequence of its capacity for social innovation, the academic community may well have given more
punishment than it received. This has been obscured partly
by the fact that members of that community have written the
history, no minor source of power in itself, and also by the
different ways in which influence manifests itself. Pecuniary
power expresses itself in highly unsubtle form; it offers financial reward for conformity or threatens financial damage for
dissent. Proposals for reform, by contrast, begin as seemingly
eccentric and implausible suggestions. Gradually they gain
adherents; in time, they emerge as grave needs; and then they
become human rights. It is not so easy to attribute power to
those who set this process in motion.

The power that is associated with capacity for social innovation is important for what follows. For the moment, it is
sufficient that it once provided a very good reason for conflict
between the entrepreneurial enterprise and the academic community.[10]

[9] Veblen, p. 194.
[10] We have here the explanation of the seemingly neurotic preoccupation of conservative organizations and individuals in the United States
with education, and especially with the ideas held and taught in the
universities. Such groups reflect older entrepreneurial attitudes; these attitudes are strongly applauded by the independent oil man or real estate operator and often disdained by the self-respecting member of the
technostructure. And the plaintiffs are not wrong in believing both that
the colleges and universities are influential and that they have been the
source of the ideas that have brought about a decline in the power that
once went with pecuniary achievement and worth. Accordingly, their
reaction, however discomfiting, is not without cause. Academic people
should be philosophical. They cannot, as on occasion in the past, hope
to combine influence for their ideas with immunity from attack.

3

With the rise of the technostructure, relations between those associated with economic enterprise and the educational and scientific estate have undergone a radical transformation. There is no longer an abrupt conflict in motivation. Like the educational and scientific estate, the technostructure is no longer exclusively responsive to pecuniary motivation. Both see themselves as identified with social goals or with organizations serving social purposes. And both, it may be assumed, seek to adapt social goals to their own. If there is a difference, it is not in the motivational system but in the goals.

At this stage, the educational and scientific estate is no longer small; on the contrary, as we have seen, it is very large. It is no longer dependent on private income and wealth for its support; most of its sustenance is provided by the state. Private influence is weakened in an important further respect. The entrepreneur combined a strong proprietary instinct with owned wealth. The members of the technostructure, though they may be generously rewarded by salary and capital gains, are unlikely to have any similar amount of wealth at their disposal. Owners—those known to the modern academic money-raiser as the old rich—do. And the alternative to the use of such wealth for education is often an only moderately lower loss through taxation. But being divorced from influence in the corporation, these men no longer reflect its attitudes in any reliable way. And they are considerably less likely than the erstwhile entrepreneur to expect to exercise influence as the result of the support they accord. They have learned from their experience with the corporate ownership that wealth does not accord such power of intervention.

Meanwhile the technostructure has become deeply dependent on the educational and scientific estate for its supply of trained manpower. It needs also to maintain a close relation with the scientific sector of this estate to ensure that it is safely abreast of scientific and technological innovation. And, unlike the entrepreneurial corporation, the mature corporation is much less troubled by the social inventiveness of the educational and scientific estate. The costs of reform legislation—improvements in medical care, guaranteed incomes for the poor, protection or salvaging of the environment, regeneration of slums—can be passed forward to customers or back to stockhholders. The burden of interpreting or abiding by regulation is absorbed by lawyers, accountants, industrial relations specialists and other parts of the corporate bureaucracy. By contrast, the entrepreneur paid for—and the smaller one struggled with—the regulation by himself. The burden of regulation, like that of taxation, is appreciably lessened by having it fall on someone else.[11]

Also it must be borne in mind that two important recent measures of social innovation—the regulation of aggregate demand and the more tentative steps toward stabilization of prices and wages—are both important for planning, or at a minimum consistent with it, and thus are important for or consistent with the success of the technostructure. The latter, we have seen, is wholly responsive to its own interest.

Further—and perhaps a lesser matter—what may be called the reputable social science no longer has overtones of revolution. Rather it denies the likelihood, even the possibility. This too is the result of the intricate web of change which we are here unraveling. The revolution, as delineated by Marx, assumed the progressive immiserization of the working class. Instead of the expected impoverishment, there has been increasing affluence. Marxists themselves no longer deny this or convincingly suggest that worker well-being is illusory or transitory. The revolution was to be catalyzed by the capitalist crisis—the apocalyptic depression which would bring an already attenuated structure down in ruins. But the planning system has, as an integral requirement, an arrangement for regulating aggregate demand which, while permitting it to plan, gives promise, with minimal management, of preventing, or at least mitigating, depression. So the danger of an apocalyptic crisis seems more remote. The trade union, militantly expressing the power of the worker, was to be the cutting edge of the revolution. But the planning system, as the last chapters have shown, mellows and even absorbs the union. Finally, the revolution has occurred in some countries. And there the lineaments of industrialization—planning, large producing organizations, the resulting discipline, the measure

[11]The resistance of the doctors to federal measures for improved medical care is at least partly so explained. ". . . the practitioner of medicine is a member of the shrinking body of American entrepreneurs. Most doctors continue to 'run their own business' and are understandably opposed to interference with their economic affairs . . ." Louis Lasagna, "Why Are Doctors Out of Step?" *The New Republic*, Vol. 152, No. 1, January 2, 1965, p. 15.

of success by economic growth—no longer seem as spectacularly different or wonderful as they did in the fears and hopes of a half century or more ago. Everything on which the revolution seemed to depend, and even the revolution itself, have disintegrated.

4

As might be expected, the new dependence of the technostructure on the educational and scientific estate is reflected in the relation between the two. The business executive no longer sits on the college board as a source of worldly knowledge and as a guardian against social heresy. Rather his presence provides him with an opportunity to maintain closer liaison with sources of talent or to keep more closely aware of the world of scientific, technological and social innovation. Apart from this, he is being accorded a traditional obeisance which he recognizes, appreciates and enjoys. While the corporation president has become increasingly a traditional or ceremonial figure in his association with education, the modern scholar of science, mathematics, information systems or communications theory is ever more in demand to guide the mature corporation through its besetting problems of science, technology and computerization. The name of a famous banker on a board of directors once advertised to the world that the corporation had access to the full capital resources of the economy. Now the name of a scientist or, at a minimum, a college president is sought, along with those of former Air Force generals, to show that the corporation is attuned to the very latest in technological advance.

In social matters we customarily attribute to improving intelligence or virtue or better manners what, in fact, is brought by circumstance. In the context of the earlier difference in motivation and goals between the academic community and the entrepreneurial firm, the more articulate and dedicated entrepreneurs recurrently denounced professors for long-haired radicalism, impractical idealism, irrelevant theorizing, suborning attacks on the Constitution and the rights of private property, and for failing to support individual freedom which, in context, meant freedom to make money. This now only rarely happens. The member of the technostructure finds little in university discussion that so arouses him. And if he were to express such sentiments, he would promptly be warned by more circumspect colleagues that he was alienating "an important sector of public opinion," making life otherwise difficult for the public relations department, possibly handicapping those who visit campuses to recruit talent and that he might be risking having his more distinguished academic consultants take their knowledge and their possible secrets to some less vocal leadership.

5

The question remains as to how closely the educational and scientific estate, which owes its modern expansion and eminence to the requirements of the planning system, will identify itself with the goals of the latter. No generalization is possible, for the educational and scientific estate is not homogeneous. We have seen that economics, as a discipline, has extensively and rather subtly accommodated itself to the needs of the planning system. Conclusions which are not serviceable to these needs—which minimize the role of the market and profit maximization, accord importance to the effect of advertising on and cast doubt on consumer sovereignty or the approved sequence, look candidly on the close association of the mature corporation with the state or otherwise pierce the veil of ideas that conceals corporate power—have an aspect of heresy. The same tendencies can doubtless be expected elsewhere. The chemist who devotes a substantial share of his time to Du Pont or Monsanto can be expected to identify himself with the goals of these corporations. (He may also have some adaptive effect on university goals—his department may come to measure its success by the number of its commercial and governmental contracts, the size of its physical plant and the growth in its personnel and payroll.) At the same time numerous other scholarly disciplines—the classics, humanities, some of the social sciences—are largely unaffected by this new relation with the technostructure. They will retain and (observing the prosperity and perquisites of their scientific colleagues) avow with increasing vehemence the older goals of the academy. They will criticize their scientific colleagues for doing excessively purposive research, for no longer having a primary obligation to knowledge and its transmission and, implicitly, for abandoning the vow of academic poverty. The scientists will reply with hurt protestations of the immunity of their virtue to pecuniary corruption and the need for someone to pay the bills. This is a familiar discussion in nearly all universities.

6

But there remain more general sources of conflict between the educational and scientific estate and the technostructure. One is the management of individual behavior.

In the absence of a clear view of the nature of this conflict, much of the dispute centers not on its ultimate causes but on the techniques of management. Management requires extensive access to means of communication—newspapers, billboards, radio and especially television. To ensure attention, these media must be raucous and dissonant. It is also of the utmost importance that this effort convey an impression, however meretricious, of the importance of the goods being sold. The market for soap can only be managed if the attention of consumers is captured for what, otherwise, is a rather incidental artifact. Accordingly, the smell of the soap, the unique texture of its suds, the whiteness of textiles treated thereby and its user's resulting esteem and prestige in the neighborhood are held to be of highest moment. Housewives are imagined to discuss such questions with an intensity otherwise reserved for unwanted pregnancy and nuclear war. Similarly with cigarettes, laxatives, pain-killers, beer, automobiles, dentifrices, packaged foods and all other significant consumer products.

The educational and scientific estate and the larger intellectual community tend to view this effort with disdain. The technostructure, sensing this but aware also of the vital importance of the management of demand, reacts defensively and with earnest protestations of its importance for the health and survival of the economic system. Its case is closer to the truth than is commonly imagined.

Thus the paradox. The economy, for its success, requires organized public bamboozlement. At the same time, it nurtures a growing class which feels itself superior to such bamboozlement and deplores it as intellectually corrupt. The subculture which requires such obfuscation for its existence can only be regarded with disdain. That culture responds with a sense of hurt and guilt and the indignation which comes from the knowledge that its needs sustain and nourish its academic critics.

This conflict, in one form or another, is inevitable with planning. That requires that the needs of the producing mechanism take precedence over the freely expressed will of the individual. This will always invite the disaffection of the individual. In the Soviet-type economies the resentment is expressed against the state and the heavy and visible apparatus by which it exercises control over the individual. Over non-Soviet planning it is expressed against the techniques and instruments—advertising and the mass communications that carry it—by which the individual is managed. Curiously, in neither society does the attack center on the planning which is the deeper cause.

7

Next there is the conflict, highly visible in very recent years, between the individualistic ethic of the academic community and the need in the planning system for a disciplined acceptance of the goals of organization. This may well be the greatest single source of tension in the industrial state and one that (I believe) is sharply illuminated by this analysis. In the universities large numbers of students are brought together by the unprecedented demands of the planning system for qualified manpower. They are given a sense of personality as the older industrial proletariat was not; the older proletariat, indeed, was taught by the unions to submerge personality into a sense of class. And students are also exposed with some sense of righteousness to social doctrine—economic and political theory—which hold that the individual is possessed of ultimate power. And, in contrast, they see a world in which organization exercises large, even seemingly plenary, power and to which they, as citizens, soldiers, consumers or organization men are expected to be subordinate. At a higher level of subtlety an increasing number sense—as here shown—that some part of their education, that in traditional economics in particular, is designed to dull their perception of corporate power. None of the resulting discontent could occur in a society in which the consumer or the citizen is sovereign. The individual cannot be at war with his own exercise of power. It is predictable in a society in which producing organizations are sovereign—in which they have power to pursue purposes of their own that are different from those of the consumer or citizen.

8

Finally, there is potential competition and conflict between the educational and scientific estate and the technostructure growing out of their respective relations to the state. The member of the technostructure is strongly inhibited in his political role. He cannot divest himself of the organization which gives him being. And he cannot carry it with him into political life. On the other hand, he wields great public influence as, in effect, an extended arm of the bureaucracy.

The educational and scientific estate is not inhibited politically by the ties of organization. It is also growing rapidly in numbers. It still lacks a sense of its own identity. It has also sat for many years under the shadow of entrepreneurial power. A seemingly respectable measure of cynicism as well as a residual Marxism join in deprecating any political power not founded firmly on the possession of money. Yet the educational and scientific estate is becoming a decisive instrument of political power. This, in turn, is threatening established associations between the bureaucracy and the technostructure, for they, in a fashion not different from the management of demand for consumer products, require a substantial measure of popular illusion. I now turn to these matters.[12]

---

[12]In the first edition, a somewhat more tentative formulation of the political prospects of the educational and scientific estate provoked sharp dissent, some of it a trifle contemptuous. This came to an end when this community showed itself the decisive influence in opposing the established policy in Vietnam.

The Planning System and the State I

QUALIFIED MANPOWER is decisive for the success of the planning system. The education on which it depends is provided mostly in the public sector of the economy. By contrast, capital, which was once decisive, comes mostly from the private sector. The market for the most advanced technology and that which best allows of planning is also in the public sector. Much scientific and technical innovation comes from, or is sponsored by, the state or by publicly supported universities and research institutions. The state regulates the aggregate demand for the products of the planning system. This is indispensable for its planning. And still discreetly and with infirmity of intent, somewhat in the manner of a conservative cleric viewing an erotic statue, the state provides the wage and price regulation without which prices in the planning system are unstable. Clearly the modern organized economy was designed with a perverse hand. For how, otherwise, could so many needs unite to make a system which rejoices in the name of free enterprise be in truth so dependent on government?

The planning system, in fact, is inextricably associated with the state. In notable respects, the mature corporation is an arm of the state. And the state, in important matters, is an instrument of the planning system. This runs strongly counter to the accepted doctrine. That assumes and affirms a clear line between government and private business enterprise. The position of this line—what is given to the state and what is accorded to private enterprise—tells whether the society is socialist or nonsocialist. Nothing is so important. Any union between public and private organization is held, by liberal and conservative alike, to be deviant sin. To the liberal it means that public power has been captured for private advantage and profit. To the conservative it means that high private prerogative, the right to act without government interference, has been lost to the state. In fact, the line between public and private authority in the planning system is indistinct and in large measure imaginary, and the abhorrent association of public and private organizations is normal. When this is perceived, the central trends in American economic and political life become clear. On few matters is an effort to free the mind from conventional myth more rewarding.

The relationship between the technostructure and the state is very different from that between the state and the entrepreneurial enterprise. This difference is our point of departure.

2

The relationship between the state and the entrepreneurial corporation was, like all of the other relationships of this institution, principally pecuniary. It was also unstable, with a tendency to be a zero sum game. The corporation might be strong. Then it would be independent of public restraint. It would, if it could, use an essentially public power to enhance its own revenues. Or the state might be strong, in which case it curbed the private power, and therewith the profits, of the entrepreneur. If extremely powerful, the state would move to socialize such enterprise. Weakness on one side would be exploited by the other. Constant and reciprocal vigilance would be necessary to prevent domination of the state by business or of business by the state.

Such was the common view of the relationship between the entrepreneurial corporation and the state. The balance in this relationship is assumed to have altered over time. Eighty-five years ago, in the United States, it was believed that the corporation was naturally the paramount power. Business control of the state was the thing to fear. Men of subtle mind agreed with Marx that the state was or would become the executive commitee of capitalist enterprise. With the passage of time, however, fear of business domination receded while fear of state domination increased. The corporation was once the octopus. This became, at least to businessmen, the image of government. Where entrepreneurs had once gathered in the Senate to consider the needs of their class, they now gathered in convention to deplore the intentions of Washington. Golf, once an opportunity for consolidating power over some aspect of the life of the community, became an occasion for collective complaint about bureaucrats. Both the earlier and later fears reflect the circumstances of the entrepreneurial corporation. Though both continue to influence contemporary attitudes, neither reflects the modern reality.

As noted, the relationship of the entrepreneurial corporation to the state, in accordance with the principle of consistency, was primarily a pecuniary one. The state had much to offer that was of pecuniary advantage, and, through taxation and regulation, it could do much to deny revenues to the corporation. The entrepreneurial corporation, in turn, had much with which to pay for what it wanted. And it had few legal or other barriers to doing so.

Thus the state, through the tariff, could accord the entrepreneur protection from foreign competition; it also had railroad, power or other public utility franchises to grant; it possessed land, mineral rights, forests and other natural resources for private exploitation; it could offer exemption or mitigation of taxes; and it could provide moral or armed support in managing refractory workers. As a further and important point, these and other benefits could all be given or withheld in response to relatively simple decision.

The entrepreneurial enterprise had, in turn, the ability to deploy financial resources for political ends that reflected its advantage. The entrepreneur united in his own person the right to receive and dispose of the revenues of the enterprise. So revenues were at his command for purchase of votes, legislators or legislative action. If he were subject to some legal constraint in the expenditure of corporate funds for political purposes, he could transfer them, as dividends, to himself and his associates and spend from a privy purse. The public benefits so purchased accrued to the entrepreneur. This, along with the commitment to pecuniary motivation, meant that the entrepreneurial corporation had opportunity and incentive to spend for political advantage. The financial resources of the corporation could be fully and lawfully released, and by the men who derived personal advantage from doing so.

In a society where economic activity is subject strongly to pecuniary motivation, such motivation will seem normal in the relations between business firms and the state. It will be assumed that public officials will be responsive to opportunity for pecuniary gain. Nor will this seem totally iniquitous. Where the society approves and applauds moneymaking as the highest social purpose, public servants will often think it natural that they should sell themselves or their decisions for what they are worth to the buyers.

In the heyday of the entrepreneurial corporation this occurred. The company town and the company-dominated state—California of the Southern Pacific, Montana of Anaconda, Pennsylvania of the steel and coal companies, Michigan of the automobile companies—were familiar features of the industrial landscape. It was assumed that congressmen and senators would be the spokesmen, paid or otherwise, of the industrial firms of their states or districts. From those so financed or controlled, the entrepreneurial corporation got much of what it wanted. The control was not absolute but it was sufficiently extensive to justify belief in corporate domination of the state as a normal fact of life.

To this day, the independent entrepreneur—the highway contractor, insurance firm, real estate operator, loan shark— is, year in and year out, the most important source of political funds and the principal remaining exponent of purchased influence. Those who have won major distinction in this general area in modern times have all been independent entrepreneurs. Texas oil operators, for example, are able to obtain implicit obedience from their state's congressional delegation. Not so the automobile or steel companies from theirs.

While the entrepreneurial corporation had resources with which to purchase pecuniary opportunity from the state, it was also independent of the state. Its revenues were made in the market. Thence came its instructions. Had it need to fight the state, the battle might cost it money but it would not be mortal.

3

In time, as noted, the fear that the corporation would dominate the state was matched, perhaps partly replaced, by the fear that the state would dominate business. This change occurred especially in the thirties. There were two causes; the rise of the trade union and the response of the state to the new needs of the planning system.

The Great Depression gave a strong impetus to the trade union movement. By destroying his alternatives and thus increasing the element of compulsion in his attachment to his job, the depression arrested any tendency for the worker to identify himself with the goals of his employer. And it made the union more important to the worker. He needed its support against pressures for wage reduction. As his alternatives dwindled, unions compensated for his weakness and countered his sense of compulsion. As they grew in membership in this favorable environment, the unions became a factor in politics; as their role was adversary within the corporation, so it was adversary in their influence on the state. What the unions lacked in financial resources they compensated for in voting power. They found an ally in the emerging educational and scientific[1] estate with its long-standing alienation from the entrepreneurial corporation. This, with some support from the farmers, was the heart of the Roosevelt coalition. It was easy for business enterprise to imagine that it was about to pass under the political authority of a state permanently dominated by the unions and the "intellectuals."

At the same time the entrepreneurial corporation was steadily giving way to the mature corporation and to control by the technostructure. In their study of the 200 largest nonfinancial corporations in 1930 in the United States, Berle and Means reported that, by then, 44 percent of the firms by numbers and 58 percent by wealth were effectively controlled by their management.[2]

For direct political action the technostructure is far more circumscribed than the entrepreneur. This is a matter of prime importance. The members of the technostructure do not themselves receive the revenues of the corporation. An early gesture, designed to limit the political advantage of the business enterprise resulting from its wealth, prohibited the use of corporate funds for political purposes. This did not greatly hurt the entrepreneur; he could, as noted, transfer the funds to his own account as dividends and spend with impunity. But this the technostructure cannot do; it does not get the dividends.

Nor does it have the same incentive to do so. Bribery of public officials, purchase of the electorate or promiscuous use of financial power to influence public decision (e.g., the

---

[1] Still rather more educational in this period than scientific.

[2] That is to say, the board of directors was selected by the management rather than by the stockholders and, in turn, selected the management. Adolf A. Berle, Jr., and Gardiner C. Means, *The Modern Corporation and Private Property* (New York: Macmillan, 1948), p. 94. In effective control of important decisions, as discussed in Chapter VIII, the erosion of the power of the owners had, unquestionably, gone much farther.

threat to discharge workers or close a plant) are not especially prestigious activities. They often result in unpleasant publicity; there is risk in all bribery that the practitioner's hand will slip and that he will be publicly pilloried by all who have not received his subvention and by the more adaptable of those who have. These risks were often worthwhile for the entrepreneur; the mantle of the sanguinary industrial pirate can be worn with some comfort if the wearer receives the loot. But it is not something one does on a salary.

The technostructure is also handicapped in its political activity by its collegial character. Political leadership, persuasion and political corruption are activities of individuals; they are not readily undertaken by men who are accustomed to operating as a group. The mature corporation is run by committees. But the suborning of a legislature or even the persuasion of an electorate is accomplished, on the whole, by men working as individuals.

This point cannot be carried too far. The technostructure has ready access to communications media—press, television, radio—and thus to political influence. In mature corporations which have particular need for favorable political action, executives can pay themselves salaries which provide a margin for political purposes.

In the great afterwash of the Nixon scandals it was discovered that numerous corporations had broken the law prohibiting political contributions.[8] Much minor bribery is still used by mature corporations to buy needed action or inaction from state legislatures. And ample funds are available for persuasive lobbying, as distinct from the older forms of direct purchase of legislatures or votes. Nevertheless the conclusion stands. The technostructure of the mature corporation is far less able to deploy financial resources for political purposes than was the entrepreneurial corporation, has less incentive to do so and, in consequence of its group character, is far less effective in direct political action.

The opposition to the rising power of the state in the decisive years of the thirties, like the opposition to the rising power of the unions, was led not by the mature corporations but by the surviving entrepreneurs. The names of Ernest Weir, Thomas Girdler, Henry Ford, the Du Ponts and Sewell

---

[8]Although the penalties imposed were insignificant, the adverse publicity was probably sufficient to ensure future compliance, at least for some time.

Avery are associated with this resistance. General Motors, General Electric, U.S. Steel and other mature corporations were much more inclined to accept such innovations as NRA, to be more philosophical about Roosevelt and otherwise to accommodate themselves to the New Deal.

In the decades since, this tendency to accommodate has been strongly affirmed. Business ritual still requires the executive of the mature corporation to speak apprehensively of government, to warn in the condescending, admonitory tones that are obligatory for all corporate public expression of the malign tendencies of the state. But the deeper reality is accommodation by the mature corporation, reassurance by government and a distaste for confrontation by both.

4

Nor is this all. We have seen that much government activity has a very different effect on the entrepreneurial corporation as compared with the mature corporation. What is damaging to the first is benign for the second. The striking case is the regulation of aggregate demand. Such regulation, we have sufficiently seen, is essential for effective planning and, accordingly, for the security and success of the technostructure. A large public sector, supported by a progressive tax structure and with such added offsets to declining income as unemployment insurance, is not welcome in itself. But it is the fulcrum of the regulatory apparatus. Members of the technostructure do not themselves have to pay the corporation income tax which is a central part of this machinery. It falls on the stockholders or, given the control of prices, can be passed along to customers. Social security taxes and associated record-keeping are, for the technostructure, merely administrative problems to be solved.

The entrepreneurial corporation, by contrast, had less need for the regulation of aggregate demand, and its owners stood much more of the cost. Being in an earlier stage of development, it did less planning. So it was less troubled by fluctuations in demand. The entrepreneur was answerable to himself for a failure in earnings; however disagreeable, it did not necessarily threaten his survival. He had less organization to protect. Meanwhile since he sought, in principle, to maximize earnings, higher corporation taxes came out of that maximum, and with incidence on himself. Similarly with his share of social security taxes. And similarly with administrative costs and annoyances.

Other accommodation by the state to the needs of the planning system also had a contrasting effect. The entrepreneurial corporation, again as a result of its lower level of development, had less need for the trained personnel that the state provided. Its technology being more primitive, it had less to gain from public underwriting of research and markets. Unions, the subject of state encouragement and support, perform, we have just seen, a ministerial and communications role for the mature corporation; for the entrepreneurial corporation their purpose remained the winning of a larger share of the profits. Restraints on prices, which for the mature corporation helped ensure wage and price stability, could be a way of reducing returns for the entrepreneur.

It would again be a mistake to paint this contrast in unduly sharp tones. The tendency, nonetheless, is unmistakable. What seemed, at first glance, to be a damaging accession of power by the state was damaging principally to the entrepreneurial corporation. For the mature corporation it was not. Rather it reflected the accommodation of the state to its needs.

From the thirties on, the fear of government by business seemed to be a uniform and permanent feature of the American political landscape. ". . . .[O]pposition to government is more than disaffection from the policies of a particular party or administration. The [American business] creed contains a generalized distrust and scorn of politicians and bureaucrats, whatever their party and whatever the policies they advocate and execute."[4]

But appearances are deceiving. Until comparatively recent times the tone and attitude of business in these matters were set by the entrepreneurs. Being without the political inhibition of organization, they were most outspoken. Unlike members of the technostructure they also had grievances. The members of the technostructure said nothing or they echoed the complaints of the entrepreneurs about government, for this was the conventional wisdom of the businessman. Or they reacted only to their need for autonomy on internal decisions. The staffs of the business organizations continued, un-

---

[4]Francis X. Sutton, Seymour E. Harris, Carl Kaysen and James Tobin, *The American Business Creed* (Cambridge: Harvard University Press, 1956), p. 369.

der inertial guidance, to recite the liturgy of entrepreneurial complaint. Entrepreneurs did not see that the accommodation of the state to the needs of the mature corporation was a substantial source of their discomfort. They did not see that they were, in effect, the victims of a passive conspiracy between other businessmen and the state.

5

The threads may now be drawn together. Business in its relations with the state is anything but homogeneous. Once, in the day of the entrepreneur and the entrepreneurial corporation, it was so. And it was also transcendent in its direct political power—its power over votes and legislators. The mature corporation does not exercise similar power. But it has won an accommodation by the state to its needs that is highly favorable. And this accommodation has not been nearly so favorable to the surviving entrepreneurs. Their position in relation to the state has been substantially weakened. While they seemed to have the general support of all business, they, in fact, did not. The mature corporations were all the time seeking many of the things the entrepreneurs most opposed.

It will be evident that at this stage there is a certain puzzle in the political position of the mature corporation. As we have seen, its capacity for, and incentive to, direct political action—management of the electorate, control of legislatures, procurement of legislation—is much less than that of its entrepreneurial antecedents. But, at the same time, the trend of public policy has been highly favorable to its needs. If this is accidental, it reflects, from the point of view of the mature corporation, one of the happiest conjunctions of circumstance in history. But to explain anything of this importance in the closely interlocked system we are here examining as an accident would be odd. And it is nothing of the kind. As the planning system in general, and the mature corporation in particular, have lost direct political power, they have acquired other methods of influencing social action of far, far greater significance. These explain the benign tendencies, from their viewpoint, of the state.

XXVII

The Planning System and the State II

". . . power in the NAM [National Association of Man-
ufacturers] used to center [on the presidents of] . . .
the middle-sized companies. . . . Most of them are gone
now; they have been replaced by representatives of the
major corporations whose biggest customer is government, which, as the biggest customer, has a claim to be
if not always, at least often enough, right."

—Murray Kempton

"The NASA administrator . . . stated that a government
agency could not contract out the entire management of
a new technology such as space systems. It must have
competence to specify the tasks it wants industry to perform."

—Murray L. Weidenbaum

THE ENTREPRENEURIAL FIRM had a pecuniary relationship
with society. The market transmitted to the entrepreneur the
instructions of the consumer in the only language that the
market can employ—namely, the offer of more or less revenue for more or less product. His relationship with his employees was predominantly pecuniary; they served him not
for love or duty but for money. The governing factor in his
relationship to the state was the same; the principle of consistency holds as always. He sought to influence the state in order to enhance his pecuniary return. The state obtained his
services, when needed, by paying for them. It used its tax and
regulatory powers to influence his behavior and regulate his
income. As in relations between entrepreneur and employees,
that between entrepreneur and state regularly involved conflict over the amount of the return. This conflict minimized

or excluded identification by the entrepreneurial corporation with the goals of the state. It especially did so as the balance in this relationship swung from control of the state by the entrepreneur to a substantial fear of the reverse.

We have seen that, as a usual circumstance, the technostructure of the mature corporation neither deploys the resources nor has the incentive for forthright purchase of political power. At the same time it has become much more dependent on the state. The entrepreneurial corporation, from public resources to favorable tariffs to tax concessions, had much to get from the state. And from adverse regulation and higher taxation it had considerable to lose. But, apart from the provision of law and order which, on occasion, it supplied to itself, it was not deeply dependent on the government. The mature corporation, by contrast, depends on the state for trained manpower and the regulation of aggregate demand. These are important for the planning with which it replaces the market. The state, through military and other technical procurement, underwrites the corporation's largest capital commitments in its area of most advanced technology. It provides highways, airways and, though the need is not conceded, much indispensable regulation.[1] When, as occasionally happens, a great corporation runs into financial difficulty, the government, on one pretext or another, comes to the rescue. The mature corporation cannot buy political power. Yet, obviously, it requires it.

Its influence on the state is, in fact, incomparably greater than that of the entrepreneurial corporation. Those who look for it usually look in the wrong place. Given the past pre-eminence of pecuniary relationships, they naturally look for these. They look for legislators who are in the pay of corporations and for public officials who are responsive to financial blandishment. They delve for lobbyists who dispense alcohol, hospitality in Nassau and New York hotel suites and the attentions of far more vivid and adaptable young women than the politician or public servant encounters of a neighborly evening in Falls Church, Virginia. The best dicovery of all is of a traditionalist who carries money in a black bag, has a congressman in his pay or, at a minimum, has requisitioned his office and telephone. Every year, in fact, one or more exponents of one or another of these techniques of bribery or

[1]As this is written, the major airlines, with one or two exceptions, are vigorously opposing proposals to reduce the extent of regulation.

illegal influence is disovered and drummed out of the company of respectable men, often with the help of those who, until recently, had thought well of such resourcefulness. These victims are the archaic survivors of an earlier era and methodology. Their public destruction for minor peculation—it rarely amounts to the price of the most insignificant modern weapon—is a purification rite. Minor sin is washed away in an orgiastic burst of indignation. Iniquitous influence is thus extirpated from government. It may well be to the advantage of the planning system that simple men should continue to suppose that influence is exerted on the state principally by such means.[2]

2

Members of the technostructure, we have seen, identify themselves with its goals because they find these goals superior to their own and because there is a chance of adapting them to their own. The relationship of the technostructure of the mature corporation to the state is the same. The state is strongly concerned with the stability of the economy. And with its expansion or growth. And with education. And with technical and scientific advance. And, most notably, with the national defense. These are *the* national goals; they are sufficiently trite so that one has a reassuring sense of the obvious in articulating them. All have their counterpart in the needs and goals of the technostructure. The technostructure requires stability in demand for its planning. Growth brings promotion and prestige. It requires trained manpower. It needs government underwriting of research and development. Military and other technical procurement support its most developed form of planning. At each point the government has goals with which the technostructure can identify itself. Or, plausibly, these goals reflect adaptation of public goals to the goals of the technostructure. As the individual serves the technostructure in response to a complex system of motivation in which identification and adaptation are extremely important, so the same motivation is reflected in the relations of the mature corporation to the state. Again we find the principle of consistency rendering faithful service. Therein lies the influence of the mature corporation—an influence which makes purely pecuniary relationships pallid by comparison.

[2]This case was first made in 1967. In the aftermath of the Nixon Administration there was an especially powerful purification rite.

Let us now give these abstractions specific form—and put them to test.

3

The practical manifestation of this process is to be seen most clearly in defense procurement. The Department of Defense supports, as noted, the most highly developed planning in the planning system. It provides contracts of long duration, calling for large investment of capital in areas of advanced technology. There is no risk of price fluctuations. There is full protection against any change in requirements, i.e., any change in demand. Should a contract be canceled, the firm is protected on the investment it has made. For no other products can the technostructure plan with such certainty and assurance. Given the inevitability of planning, there is much attraction in circumstances where it can be done so well.

This leads the technostructure to identify itself closely with the goals of the armed services and, not infrequently, with the specific goals of the particular service, Army, Navy or Air Force, which it most intimately serves. Simple association, as in the case of individual and organization, supports this tendency. In consequence, the technostructure comes to see the same urgency in weapons development, the same security in technical pre-eminence, the same requirement for a particular weapons system, the same advantage in an enlarged mission for, say, the Air Force or Navy, as does the particular service itself. Its members develop the same commitment to these goals as do officers of the services.

This relationship accords parallel opportunity for adaptation. The need to combine the work of diverse specialists and technicians means that the development of, say, a new weapons system requires organization. This the technostructure, and frequently it alone, can provide. So the armed services are deeply dependent on their supplying corporations for technical development. And in practice, numerous other tasks requiring the resources of organization—the planning of logistics systems, planning and development of base facilities, even on occasion the definition of the missions of a particular service or one of its branches—are contracted out to supplying corporations. "In its rapid climb during the fifties, the Air Force fostered a growing band of private companies which took over a substantial part of regular military operations, including maintaining aircraft, firing rockets, building and maintaining launching sites, organizing and directing other contractors, and making major public decisions . . . The Air Force's success over her sister services . . . established the magic formula that all federal agencies soon imitated."[3]

A firm that is associated with the development of a new generation of fighter aircraft is in an admirable position to influence the design and equipment of the plane. It can have something to say on the mission for which it is adapted, the number of planes required, their deployment, and, by implication, on the choice of the enemy toward which it is directed. This will reflect the firm's own views, and, *pari passu*, its own needs. If the firm has been accorded a more explicit planning function, it helps to establish assumptions as to the strength and intentions of the probable enemy, in practice the U.S.S.R., the nature of the probable attack and of the resulting hostilities and the other factors on which defense procurement depends. In conjunction with other such planning, including, of course, that of public agencies, it helps to establish the official view of defense requirements and therewith of some part of the foreign policy. These will be a broad reflection of the firm's own goals; it would be eccentric to expect otherwise.

This influence is not absolute. It is greatest in the large, specialized weapons manufacturers and diminishes with the size of the firm or a less specialized commitment to defense production. On occasion, it does not survive poor planning or extreme managerial incompetence by a particular technostructure. (The case of Lockheed in the late sixties and early seventies is an example.) But such failures are exceptional and thus their notoriety.[4]

4

Not only are identification and adaptation important for influencing decisions by the technostructure on weapons procurement, they are very nearly the only source of such influence.

[3]H. L. Nieburg, *In the Name of Science* (Chicago: Quadrangle Books, 1966), pp. 188–189. This study provides admirably detailed documentation on the relation of government and technostructure as here outlined. Cf. particularly Chapters X and XI.

[4]The public rescue of Lockheed was also predictable—an affirmation of the close symbiosis between government and corporations.

We have seen that the head of the modern corporation cannot order up a new civilian product in response to a major exercise of imagination. The toaster will be recalled. It must emerge from the teams of scientists, engineers, designers, production experts, market researchers and sales executives. That is why power has shifted to, and into, the technostructure. For the same reason the modern business firm cannot buy defense decisions favorable to itself. There is, to speak loosely, no decision available for purchase. There is, instead, a process of decision-making in which many people participate over a long period of time. Some are members of the technostructure, some of the public agency. From this process come decisions on the feasibility, need for and design of a new combat aircraft or a new missile of unexampled, evasive and destructive power. By then, familiarity with the design and other requirements, including possession of the requisite technical knowledge and experience, will have gone far to decide who gets the contract. A new contender, entering at this point, would have little chance. Others have, as it is said, bought in. There is influence only if there has been this prior intimate and long-continued participation.

This was not always so. When the Army contracted for mules, blankets, shoes or muskets, an open-handed lobbyist or a determined legislator could have influence on the award. Only a single simple decision was required; to control the decision or the man who made it was to control the outcome. To this day the Congress retains a certain voice on whether army bases, arsenals, ships' repair facilities and other relatively uncomplicated installations of an earlier period are to be used or abandoned. It has at best only a limited voice in the decision to proceed with or abandon a weapons system and even less on who the manufacturer will be. (Most of the speaking is done by committee chairmen who in the past have been rubber stamps for the armed services.) Decisions are taken by teams and committees and then passed for review through a hierarchy of teams and committees. Participation in this process is again the key to power. Even a competent and effective Secretary of Defense is deeply subordinate to this group decision-making, and the usual one is utterly so.

5

In the nature of the market, one organization or enterprise sells to another, and the boundaries between the two are sharp. This same delineation characterizes the private firm selling, say, powdered milk to the Department of Agriculture. But when planning replaces the market and identification and adaptation supplement pecuniary compensation, matters are very different. No sharp line separates government from the private firm; the line becomes very indistinct and even imaginary. Each organization is important to the other; members are intermingled in daily work; each organization comes to accept the other's goals; each adapts the goals of the other to its own. Each organization, accordingly, is an extension of the other. The large aerospace contractor is related to the Air Force by ties that, however different superficially, are in their substance the same as those that relate the Air Force to the United States government. Shared goals are the decisive link in each case.

This notion is rather fiercely resisted. Tradition, derived from the antecedent separation of government and its suppliers by the market, defends a sharp separation of public from private activity. Socialism is not an evocative word in the United States. The myth of separation helps to suppress any suggestion that the mature corporation, in its public business, is, in principle, a part of a larger public bureaucracy. It also helps the technostructure defend its autonomy—and protect itself from a good deal of awkward supervision. Government interference on rates of executive pay, expense accounts, plant location, executive nepotism and patronage and numerous other matters of public or political interest can be minimized (though not wholly resisted) on the grounds that this is a *private* operation. Expenditure of public funds by a public agency is governed by a fairly stern ethic. Attitudes toward nominally private firms, even when spending public funds, are considerably more relaxed. Only those who wish to be fooled will, however, ignore the reality, which is that the modern motivational system blurs the line into irrelevance.

Although the firm is related to the procurement agencies by shared goals, the result of identification and adaptation, these do not, of course, exclude pecuniary compensation and motivation. As we have seen in Chapter XI, a motivational system that combines identification and adaptation with pecuniary reward is internally consistent and self-reinforcing. But as pay fails to explain the relationship of a general or a Pentagon official to his job, so pecuniary motivation fails equally to explain the relationship of the mature corporation to the procurement agencies. To suppose that the modern weaponsmaker offers his wares to the government only for pay and profit, as did the vintage maker of muskets, has an overtone of hardy, muscular intelligence which appeals to the social radical, including the Marxist. But so to believe is to see almost nothing of the modern reality of industrial power.

Nor, of course, is this power exercised only in relation to the Department of Defense. The National Aeronautics and Space Administration, the Nuclear Regulatory Commission, the Federal Aviation Administration and other public bodies all underwrite industrial planning with long-term contracts involving large capital outlays and advanced technology. There are few mature corporations which do not have this relationship with the modern state.

6

Identification and adaptation cannot ordinarily be reconciled with political hostility to the state or any particular party or administration. As noted, the entrepreneurial corporation did not have an intimate and continuing dependence on the state; its fortunes in respect of the state were affected by individual and discreet actions—the award of a contract, sale of public lands, imposition of a tax or tariff, passage of a regulation—which it could influence as such without worrying excessively about the general political environment. But the mature corporation has a continuing and intimate relationship for which doors must always be open and access to public officials always be easy and without tension. Adverse political action or even hostile oratory lessens this ease of access. Men arriving with their briefcases for the day's meetings in Washington cannot have the added burden of explaining the testimony of a company president who has just attacked the current administration and all its minions hip and thigh.

But this is not a mere matter of expediency. Identification is a psychological phenomenon. If it is operative, there can be

no mental or moral barriers to accepting the goals of the
state. Such will be the consequence of political polemics and
conflict. To denounce Democrats as destroyers of business
and liberal Republicans as unwitting agents of Communism is
to proclaim one's alienation from their goals. For the technostructure it means rejecting the identification and therewith
the adaptation which are the source of its power. This, obviously, makes no sense.

We have here a guide to the political tendencies of the
modern large corporation. Its executives will, no doubt, continue their moral affiliation with the Republican Party. But
they will not speak out on partisan issues.[5] To some extent,
their corporation will take on the political coloration of
whichever party is in office. Clearly it will expect to have influence and access whichever party is in office.

All of this is by way of protecting a much stronger and
more vital position of influence which follows from a continuing and intimate association with the bureaucracy. In this
role the corporation can participate in the decisions that
count. It can help shape the highly technical choices which,
in turn, govern the demand for its own military and other
products. It will have access to the decisions on military
strategy which establish the need for such products. And it
will help to shape the current beliefs or assumptions on foreign policy. These, obviously, are far more important powers.
It is the difference between the formal grandeur of the legislative hearing and the shirt-sleeved rooms with blackboards
and tables heavy with data, drawings and tapes where the important decisions, bit by bit, are actually made. The technostructure selects its theater of influence with discrimination
and intelligence.

7

Industrial planning, we have seen, requires the control of
prices and the management of the consumer. As a result, instruction passes not alone from the sovereign consumer to the
producer; it proceeds also from the producer to the consumer
in accordance with the needs of the technostructure. This is

[5]This point, so stated in the first edition, was affirmed by the nature
of the business opposition to the Vietnam war. Smaller businessmen
formed an effective lobby against the war. Executives of the large mature corporations participated virtually not at all.

the revised sequence. The revised sequence operates also in the field of public procurement.[6]

Those who, for purposes of rebuttal, would wish to find that I had argued that all public spending is an accommodation to the needs of the modern corporation will be disappointed. The influence of the industrial firm on military procurement is singularly a matter where those who reach inconvenient conclusions are impelled to make themselves vulnerable by overstatement. They are then destroyed by those who say that, since they do not value exact truth, they do not value truth. I seek to be less obliging. I argue only for a complex two-way flow of influence.

---

[6] Indeed, economists who defend the established view of oligopoly, the market and consumer sovereignty are rarely so bold as to extend their case to weapons firms and the Pentagon. Here most would concede the case for producer sovereignty.

A Further Summary

THE PRINCIPAL TOPOGRAPHY of the planning system is now in view. Most will think it a formidable sight. Few will minimize the complexity of its probable social effect; the only man who must surely be wrong about the planning system is the one who essays a simple judgment upon it.

The system produces goods and renders services in vast and increasing volume. There are many poor people left in the industrial countries, and notably in the United States. The fact that they are not the central theme of this treatise should not be taken as proof either of ignorance of their existence or indifference to their fate. But the poor, by any applicable tests, are outside the planning system. They are those who have not been drawn into its service or who cannot qualify. And not only has the planning system—its boundaries as here defined are to be kept in mind—eliminated poverty for those who have been drawn into its embrace but it has also greatly reduced the burden of manual toil. Only those who have never experienced hard and tedious labor, long continued, can be wholly indifferent to the advantages of its elimination.

Once it was imagined that the economic system provided man with the artifacts by which he has anciently surrounded himself in response to his original and sovereign desires. This source of economic motivation is still celebrated in the formal economic liturgy of the system. But, as we have sufficiently seen, the system, if it accommodates to man's wants, also and increasingly accommodates men to its needs. And it must. This latter accommodation is no trivial exercise in salesmanship. It is deeply organic. High technology and heavy capital use cannot be subordinate to the ebb and flow of market demand. They require planning; it is the essence of planning that public behavior be made predictable—that it be subject to control.

And from this control flow further important consequences.

It ensures that men and increasing numbers of women will work with undiminished effort however great their supply of goods. And it helps ensure that the society will measure its accomplishment by its annual increase in production. Nothing would be more discomforting for economic discipline than were men to establish goals for themselves and on reaching them say, "I've got what I need. That is all for this week." Not by accident is such behavior thought irresponsible and feckless. It would mean that increased output would no longer have high social urgency. Enough would be enough. The achievement of the society could then no longer be measured by the annual increase in Gross National Product. And if increased production ceased to be of prime importance, the needs of the planning system would no longer be accorded automatic priority. The required readjustment in social attitudes would be appalling.

The management to which we are subject is not onerous. It works not on the body but on the mind. It first wins acquiescence or belief; action is in response to this mental conditioning and thus devoid of any sense of compulsion. It is not that we are required to have a newly configured automobile or a novel reverse-action laxative; it is that we believe that we must have them. It is open to anyone who can resist belief to contract out of this control. But we are no less managed because we are not physically compelled. On the contrary, though this is poorly understood, physical compulsion would have a far lower order of efficiency.

2

The planning system has brought its supply of capital, and in substantial measure also its labor supply, within its control, and thus within the ambit of its planning. And it has extended its influence into the state. Those policies of the state that are vital for the planning system—regulation of aggregate demand, maintenance of the large public (if preferably technical) sector on which this regulation depends, underwriting of advanced technology and provision of an increasing volume of trained and educated manpower—are believed to be of the highest social urgency. This belief accords with the needs of the system. And the influence of the technostructure of the mature firm extends to shaping the demand for its particular product or range of products. Individual members of the technostructure identify themselves with the design, development and production of items purchased by the government as the technostructure identifies itself with the social goal, say, of an effective national defense. And the members of the technostructure adapt design, development or need for items procured by the government to what accords with their own goals. These goals reflect, inevitably, the needs of the technostructure and of its planning.

Paralleling these changes, partly as a result and partly as a cause, has been a profound shift in the locus of economic and political power. The financier and the union leader are, relative to others, dwindling influences in the society. They are honored more for their past eminence than for their present power. The technostructure exercises less direct political power than did the antecedent entrepreneur. But that is because it has far more influence as an arm and extension of the public bureaucracy and in its effect on the larger climate of belief. The scientific, technical, organizational and planning needs of the technostructure have brought into being a large educational and scientific estate. And, while the commitment of the culture, under the tutelage of the planning system, to a single-minded preoccupation with the production of goods is strong, it is not complete. Rising income also nurtures a further artistic and intellectual community outside of the planning system.[1]

3

Such in briefest sketch are the principal results of this pilgrimage. Two questions inevitably follow: Where does it take us? How, in consequence, should we be guided?

Neither question is, in fact, as important as those already considered, and, one hopes, resolved. Agreeable as it is to know where one is proceeding, it is far more important to know where one has arrived. And while there will always be resistance to accepting what has come to exist—a resistance nurtured by nostalgia, vested intellectual interest in painfully acquired error which is thus understandably precious, and the omnipresent need to sustain belief in what is convenient as distinct from what is real—one has, where the present is con-

---

[1] An important matter which I take up, along with other aspects of the market system, in *Economics and the Public Purpose* (Boston: Houghton Mifflin, 1973).

cerned, appellate rights in two great courts, namely, the internal consistency of the ideas and their coherence with what can be seen. It will perhaps be agreed that these tests have rendered good service here. I venture to think that most readers will find themselves reassured thereby. When one turns to the future, these guides are lost. There are wise and foolish predictions but the difference between them is not so clear.

There are also difficulties in talking, at the same time, about what will happen and what should happen. Marx must on occasion have wondered why, if revolution was inevitable, as he proclaimed, it required the passionate and unrelenting advocacy which he accorded it.[2] Should baleful tendencies be predicted when one hopes that popular understanding will bring the reaction that reverses them? No one who believes in ideas and their advocacy can ever persuade himself that they are uninfluential. Nor are they. And those who deal in ideas, if they are wise, will welcome attack. Only a peaceful passage should dismay them, for it proves that the ideas do not affect anyone very much. I have hopes that popular understanding will reverse some of the less agreeable tendencies of the economic system and invalidate, therewith, the predictions that proceed from these tendencies. And I am not without hope for the controversy that attests the importance of such change.

4

There is another reason why, whatever the inconvenience, the future must be faced. Although those who presume to loftier, scientific attitudes regularly deplore it, the Anglo-American tradition in economic discourse is strongly normative. The test of whether a diagnostician is to be taken seriously or not is his response to the question: "Well, what would *you* do?" I have been primarily concerned to tell what the planning system is like. But to do this and no more would be to persuade most people that the description was not terribly useful.

Moreover, some problems of no small importance have been suggested by the preceding discussion. There is, for example, the prime role of technology in the planning system and its peculiar association with weapons of unimaginable ferocity and destructiveness. How are we to be saved from

[2] A slightly pedantic speculation, perhaps. Any determined revolutionary would seek to advance the date of the inevitable.

these? There is also the question of the individual in this system—a system that requires, both in production and consumption, that individuality be suppressed. Given our commitment to the sovereignty and sanctity of the person, by what means, if at all, is human personality to be saved? Obviously there are dimensions of life, those of art for example, which the planning system does not serve. One is led to inquire whether education remains education when it is chained too tightly to the wheel of the planning system. And there is the relation of the planning system to intellectual expression and political pluralism. This requires a special word.

5

For most of man's history, as philosophers of such diverse views as Marx and Alfred Marshall have agreed, political interest and conflict have originated in economic interest and economic conflict. And so it has been in the United States. Our politics have been the expression, in clash and coalition, of debtor and creditor interests, domestic and export interests, urban and rural interests, consumer and producer interests and, notably and classically, of the interests of the capitalist entrepreneur and the industrial working class.

To a remarkable extent, as we have seen, the planning system absorbs these class interests. It does so partly by minimizing the reality of conflict and partly by exploiting the resulting malleability of attitude to win control of belief. The goals of the planning system, in this process, become the goals of all who are associated with it and thus, by slight extension, the goals of the society itself.

In the past, criticism and introspection concerning the economic system and its goals have been both allowed and induced by the conflict in economic interest and the resulting political division. The capitalist entrepreneur or the labor leader has rarely been a source of penetrating criticism of himself or his own goals. But much scholarship has flourished in the interstices of the conflict between the two. When conclusions were unfavorable to one side, they had the implicit protection of the other.

The question arises whether the planning system, in absorbing economic conflict, ends all examination of social goals. Do its techniques of control—its management of market behavior and its identification with and adaptation of social goals—serve also to minimize social introspection? In brief, is the planning system monolithic by nature? And also very bland? To what extent does a society draw strength from pluralism of economic interests, which, in turn, sustains pluralism of political discussions and social thought?

An interesting and widely remarked political phenomenon of recent years has been an ill-defined discontent, especially among students and intellectuals, with the accepted and approved modalities of social thought. These, whether espoused by professed liberals or conservatives, have been held to be the views of "the Establishment." Not inappropriately, the rejection has extended at times, and for a greater or lesser number, not only to the economic, social and political views of the Establishment but also to its clothing, conventional housing and even to the soap, depilatory apparatus and other goods, the ample use of which is the sanctioned measure of success. All these are eschewed by the dissidents in a highly visible manner. Is this the natural line of dissent in a society in which the previous lines of conflict have been subsumed? To this range of questions I now turn.

I begin in the next chapter with some of the near-term consequences and needs of the economic system and, in particular, of the planning system. Thereafter I look at more distant horizons. But let me repeat once more that, on the whole, I am less interested, in this volume at least, in telling where we are going or should go than in telling where we have come.

The Planning System and the Arms Race

"Every man, woman, and child lives under a nuclear
sword of Damocles hanging by the slenderest of threads,
capable of being cut at any moment by accident or miscalculation or by madness."
—John F. Kennedy, while President

EVERYONE who wins a positive score in an intelligence test
recognizes that the selling of goods—the management of demand for particular products—requires well-considered men-
dacity. Most goods perform commonplace functions—they
suppress hunger, serve alcohol or nicotine addiction, move
people gradually through heavy traffic, move waste products
more rapidly through the intestinal tract or assist in removing
filth. Little or nothing of importance can truthfully be said
about the way a product performs these routine functions.
Flat lies as to their performance are generally impermissible.
But a surrogate for the truth, in which minor or imagined
qualities confer great benefits, is essential.

It is hard to compromise on the advantages of rigorous
candor but it may be, as a practical matter, that this contrivance does little direct damage. As noted, only in a comparatively affluent country are people open to persuasion on
how they spend their money. Being affluent, it does not matter so much how they spend it. Meretricious argument, if it
influences unimportant decision, is evidently undamaging.
And, more important, the case is recognized, subjectively, as
being meretricious. That is because modern man is exposed
to a large volume of information of varying degrees of unreliability. In response he establishes a system of discounts
which he applies to various sources almost without thought.
Information from a friend or neighbor, in the absence of a
specific reputation for falsehood, is assumed to be reliable.
Similarly that from a teacher or a scientist on his subject, and

that from a physician, prognoses of the effects of overeating, alcohol and tobacco and the assessment of cures for cancer apart. Historians, as distinct from official historians and auto-biographers, are assumed to tell the truth. So are most journalists. For pundits and preachers on the probability of doom there is a very heavy discount, as there is for politicians discussing moral integrity, peace and disarmament. The discount becomes nearly total for all forms of advertising. The merest child watching television dismisses the health and status-giving claims of a breakfast cereal as "a commercial." Conceivably, for nonlethal products, the government should not presume to insist on truth in advertising. People might assume success and then fail to apply the automatic discount which is their present more comprehensive protection.

Failure to win belief does not wholly impair the effectiveness of the management of demand for consumer products. Management involves the creation of a compelling image of the product in the mind of the consumer. To this he responds more or less automatically under circumstances where the purchase does not merit a great deal of thought. For building this image palpable fantasy may be more valuable than circumstantial evidence.

2

Fantasy and image-building also play an important role in the relationship between the planning system and the state. By contriving an appropriate image of the position, prospects, problems or dangers of the state the planning system can ensure a reaction favorable to its needs. If the image is one of country lagging in technological development in a world where that is a prime test of national success, it can ensure investment in scientific research and technological development. If the image is of a nation beset by enemies, there will be responding investment in weapons. If it is one of a state in which liberty is threatened by controls, there will be resistance to regulation of various kinds.

However, the process of building these images is a good deal less obvious than that by which the demands of the consumer are created. In consequence, belief is a good deal deeper. A measure of amiable cynicism is associated with the management of demand for cigarettes or soap; not all involved will imagine that their use provides a formula for long, happy or infinitely inoffensive life. More often, perhaps, there is professional pride in a measure of workmanlike bamboozlement. But the images of the state, in contrast, are taken very seriously. The men who contrive, or in the more frequent case perpetuate, them do so with the utmost gravity. They persuade themselves. They see the result not as the image of reality but as the reality. To suggest that it is imagery is to be irresponsible, eccentric or, conceivably, subversive. As a result, though in public affairs as well as in private affairs and for the same reasons we are subject to the contrivance that serves the planning system, it takes a far greater effort of mind to see imagery as imagery and contrivance as contrivance in the field of public affairs. But since, for that reason, the normal discounts do not operate, it is much more important that they be identified.

3

The planning system requires, we have seen, a large public sector for the stabilization of aggregate demand. And the system's planning, we have seen, reached its highest state of development in conjunction with modern military procurement. The latter is supported by large sums of money. These are easily obtained by a process that is routine; it would require far more effort by a President to reduce military spending by 20 percent than to increase it by a like amount. To hold at a given level or, better, to allow modest increases from year to year, is the easiest of all.[1] It is necessary, however, that there be an image of the world which justifies or rationalizes the military expenditures that the arrangement requires.

The requisite image has long been that of conflict with the Communist world in one or another manifestation. That this image owes its existence only to the needs of the planning system is not suggested for a second. The revolutionary and

[1] ". . . an established tradition . . . holds that a bill to spend billions of dollars for the machinery of war must be rushed through the House and the Senate in a matter of hours, while a treaty to advance the cause of peace, or a program to help the undeveloped nations . . . or . . . guarantee the rights of all our citizens, or . . . to advance the interests of the poor must be scrutinized and debated and amended and thrashed over for weeks and perhaps months." Senator Gaylord Nelson, United States Senate, February 1964. Quoted by Julius Duscha, *Arms, Money, and Politics* (New York: Ives Washburn, 1965), p. 2.

national aspirations of the Soviets, and less reliably of the Chinese, and the compulsive vigor of their assertion, were an undoubted historical source. But history must be separated from result.

In its more simplistic outline, the relation of the arms race to the needs of the planning system has been remarkably close. It is occasioned by a relentless, implacable, permanent, but ultimately benign, struggle with the world Communist movement as led by the Soviet Union. And it is further occasioned by the difference in economic systems, from which, primarily, are derived differences in individual liberty.[2] The latter contrast is stark and unshackled. The highly organized and planned system of the Soviets requires the subordination of the individual to the goals of the state. He is constrained in his expression to a spectrum of acceptable belief. No such constraint by organization or planning is required by the Western system of free enterprise.

Both systems must be evangelistic. Communism, tactical concessions to coexistence or détente notwithstanding, is held to be committed to ultimate and universal dominance. But no man who believes in liberty can accept a world that is forever half slave and half free.

The incompatibility of the systems and the associated evangelism lead directly to military competition. The Soviets would impose their system by force if they could; a strong deterrent prevents this and sustains faith in the ultimate and necessary triumph of liberty. In the main, this competition is technological—its decisive feature is the competitive development of weapons and weapons systems and related defenses.

This competition is not unlimited; it proceeds within generous but real limits of cost. But although it is deemed reckless to say so, the competition is ultimately benign. That is because, if the competition is energetically pursued, it tends to a stalemate—neither side can destroy the other without suffering unacceptable damage itself. And, both being rational, the

[2] "The Soviet leadership is irrevocably committed to the achievement of the ultimate Communist objective, which is annihilation of the capitalist system and establishment of Communist dictatorship over all nations of the world . . . Any pacts and agreements with the Soviets can be expected to be as meaningless and one-sided in the future as they have been in the past. . . . The Soviets endeavor to attain their ends without getting involved in a nuclear war, even if they were certain of winning it." Thomas S. Power, General, USAF Ret., *Design for Survival* (New York: Coward, 1964), pp. 43–44.

showdown is avoided. By agreement, disarmament is held to be a dangerous threat to a balanced prospect for reciprocal destruction. For, since ambitions are unrelenting and good faith lacking, there is danger of being tricked by negotiations into concessions which would allow the other side to destroy with impunity. The competition is held to be safer, so, although it is discussed, few associated with these matters take seriously the possibility of disarmament. Rather the discussion is an act of obeisance. It makes clear that the arms competition is being undertaken in lieu of successful disarmament instead of for its own sake.

All features of this competition are closely congruent with need. Since the aspirations of the Communists are implacable, there is no danger that momentary accommodation or easing of tension will lead to a reduction in outlays. It can only be tactical or a trick. Their ruling passion will always be "how to get on with their world revolution."[3] In an orthodox conflict the arrival of peace abruptly removes the support for further outlays. A war without fighting neatly obviates the danger that fighting will stop. By its nature a technological competition is never resolved. Safety depends on keeping innovations at a high level—although not at the highest possible level, for there are some things that are simply too expensive. Obsolescence in a technological competition is a nearly perfect substitute for battlefield attrition. Formal agreement to arrest the competition is excluded by the belief that it is more dangerous than the competition. Once war involved the conscription of a large mass of low-wage participants on whom the dangers and discomforts of the battlefield fell with particular weight. In consequence, it encountered, although by no means universally, the opposition of the working masses. The arms competition arouses no such antipathy. Nor has the modern union energy to spare for what would seem to be a purely intellectual reaction against immediate interest. So the unions, too, find the image of continuing competition agreeable.

Even a calculation that the competition may, at some point, lead to total destruction of all life is not a definitive objection. Liberty, not material well-being, is involved. This is an ultimate value that cannot be compromised in the face of any threat. "I am confident that the vast majority of the

[3] Dean Rusk in an address before the American Political Science Association, Washington, D.C., September 1965.

American people would passionately reject . . . ignominious defeatism and, instead, proclaim: 'Rather dead than Red!' "[4] Thus the competition is protected from even the most adverse estimates of its outcome.

In the decade of the fifties the image of conflict, then called by all the Cold War, reached something of a zenith. The then Secretary of State, John Foster Dulles, saw its acceptance not only as an exercise in social belief but as a test of religious ardor and moral stamina. Nor was acceptance entirely voluntary. Congressional committees, other public investigatory bodies, personnel security boards and private magistrates in the motion picture and communications industries reasoned that if the struggle for liberty were so important, it should be obligatory. Dissent or even insufficient zeal could lead to loss of employment, other economic sanction or social ostracism. These circumstances were highly favorable to the weapons competition. It proceeded with vigor and even abandon. Numerous weapons systems, some emerging from the services and some from firms individually identified with a service, were put into simultaneous and overlapping development. To the competition with the Soviets was added the further zest of competition between the sponsoring services. Identification and adaptation were facilitated by drawing officials of the Defense Department for short terms of duty—the average during much of the decade was less than a year—from the industrial technostructure. Secretaries of Defense, during this period, refrained from interfering with subordinate decision-making and, indeed, were principally functional in their public relations. That the weapons competition, and the image of international relations on which it depended, originated partly in the planning system was recognized with remarkable explicitness by President Eisenhower. He noted just before leaving office that the "conjunction of an immense military establishment and a large arms industry" was something new in the American experience and urged that the nation "guard against the acquisition of unwarranted influence, whether sought or unsought, by the military industrial complex. The potential for the disastrous rise of misplaced power exists and will persist . . . We should take nothing for granted."[5]

[4]Power, p. 69. This language, as presently noted, would now seem unduly brave.

[5]Dwight D. Eisenhower, 1890–1969, Robert I. Vexler, ed. (Dobbs Ferry, New York: Oceana Publications, 1970), p. 143.

4

The problem is what not to take for granted—and how. The planning system helps to win belief for the image of implacable conflict (with associated features) that justifies its need. Belief being won, the arms competition seems normal, natural and inevitable, as do the actions based upon it. Dissent seems eccentric and irresponsible. Herein is the power of a system that depends on persuasion rather than on compelled support.

Yet, on examination, much of what is believed turns out to be fanciful. The reality in the case of the United States and the Soviet Union is of two large industrial nations. Both, it has been amply shown, can achieve success by their very similar economic tests of success at the same time. Theirs is anything but implacable conflict, anything but a zero sum game as it is actually being played.

There is a large and unquestioned difference in the two systems in the role of politicians, writers, artists and scientists. None may minimize the difference made by the First Amendment. But it is less clear that the contrast in the systems of economic management is so great. Both systems are subject to the imperatives of industrialization. This, for both, means planning. And while each uses different techniques for dealing with the individual who contracts out of the planning, planning in all cases means setting aside the market mechanism in favor of the control of prices and individual economic behavior. Both countries, quite clearly, solicit belief for what serves the goals of the planning mechanism. Instead of contrast leading to implacable conflict, a more evident economic tendency is convergence.

The notion that the arms competition is ultimately benign likewise has small foundation. There is no inconsiderable chance of accident. There is always a chance that someday some true believer will react to the liturgy of conflict, defeat the safeguards and provoke the ultimate confrontation.

That the risks of agreed disarmament are greater than those of a continuing and unresolved weapons competition is also remarkably unproven. It is not clear why agreements can be negotiated in good faith with the Communists on all subjects except disarmament. To eliminate civilized life for all time in response to a short-run calculation that liberty might otherwise be endangered is also irrational. And those who would make such a decision are themselves strongly subordinate to a particular system of belief. They are not themselves free men.

It is extremely important in itself to know that our imagery is, in part, derived from the needs of the planning system. This leads to introspection and scrutiny that would not, otherwise, be forthcoming. For the same reason it helps us to know that part of our view of the world and of its politics originates not in our minds but in the needs of the planning system.

But two other steps are also necessary. One is to ensure that skeptical scrutiny of official belief is an important political function. The other is to meet the technological and planning needs of the planning system by ways that are less mortal than the weapons competition.

5

In the past, imagery favorable to the entrepreneur was assured of close scrutiny because, among other reasons, of the opposed pecuniary interest of the trade unions. If the entrepreneur, in the name of promoting enterprise, sought a tax system which fell resoundingly on the poor, the unions could be counted upon to come up with a countering doctrine. There is no hope that they will serve a similar function in relation to the images of foreign policy. For, apart from their general enfeeblement, their needs on these matters are far too closely aligned with those of the technostructure. The support that was accorded by the unions to the Vietnam war, as by most now to military spending, is proof of the point.

The principal hope for such scrutiny, in conjunction with the political power to make it effective, lies with the educational and scientific estate. In the past this community has been ambiguous as regards the imagery of the planning system. In economics, on such matters as the control of the firm by the market or the origin of wants with the sovereign individual, its formal tendency, we have seen, has been to underwrite the needed beliefs of the planning system, the economists of orthodox mind being especially helpful in this regard.[6] On larger questions of foreign policy this tendency has been less clear. In the early years of the Cold War there

[6]Others much less so. And there is an increasing skepticism, which extends to younger economists, of this service to the approved belief.

was a fairly full acceptance of its tenets. And for very good reason. Stalinist oppression, later to be affirmed by the Soviets themselves, was no contrivance. Impressive also was the overt attack in Korea, then seen, like the Chinese Revolution, as part of the Soviet grand design. In the wake of those developments university specialists in Cold War strategy and the associated arms competition proliferated. Doctrines of deterrence, war games, coalition architecture and economic warfare became fashionable subjects for university research, reflection and instruction. At the highest levels of sophistication, scholars calculated the acceptable limits of loss in the event of nuclear war and weighed the comparative disadvantages of forty as against eighty million casualties. University centers for the study of international relations, which had once concerned themselves with peace, became preoccupied with the Cold War. Close relations were maintained with the services; a small aristocracy of scholars did periodic duty with RAND. Scientists and engineers had similar association with the services or defense firms. It was easy to imagine that the educational and scientific estate would, by identification and adaptation, come to have the same relation to the state in these matters as the technostructure itself. Any hope of a different view of the imagery by which all alike were sustained would be lost.

On the whole, it has not happened. The larger educational and scientific estate has not been strongly receptive to the imagery that sustains the arms competition. Its mood has, on the whole, been one of growing skepticism. And in time the Cold War specialists within the scholarly community have become an increasingly alienated group. To have an intimate and committed association to official war planning is to invite suspicion of one's scholarly rectitude. With passage of time (this observation was first made in 1967, before the Vietnam war added an immense new dimension), this suspicion has greatly increased.

There are a number of reasons for this. The scientists have been peculiarly situated to see the dangers of the weapons competition, including the possibilities of conflict by accident or the high emotions generated by some essentially transient crisis. It was they, not the university specialists on international relations or the professional diplomats, who instituted the steps leading to the partial test ban and similarly on to other discussions with the Soviets[7] on weapons control and disarmament. There has been a general and growing suspicion of the doctrine of implacable conflict based on a bilateral confrontation of good and evil. More and more the conflict is being seen in such quarters as a ghastly trap in which each side stimulates the responding action of the other side and leads on to the next cycle of initiative and response. The educational and scientific estate has also been open to the evidence on the growing pluralism of the Communist world, with its adverse effect on the doctrine of monolithic and hostile conspiracy. There has been a similar response to liberalizing trends, however halting, in the Communist world, with the accompanying implication that the appropriate policy is not one of conflict but one of patience. Finally, the educational and scientific estate has been open to the view that Communist protestations on behalf of a policy of peaceful coexistence and détente may not be a trick but could reflect a disinterest in nuclear annihilation. The image of a unified conspiracy requires an automatic reaction to any Communist initiative. Otherwise, after exploiting one opportunity, it will be encouraged to proceed to the next. This has been deeply questioned by the educational and scientific estate. It is, on the whole, an encouraging development.

As the educational and scientific estate grows in numbers and self-confidence; and as it comes to realize that foreign policy is based on an imagery that derives in part from the needs of the planning system; and as it realizes further that this tendency is organic; and as it sees that the only corrective is its own scrutiny and involvement and that this involvement is not a matter of choice but an obligation imposed by its position in the economic and political structure, we can reasonably expect it to be more effective. Nothing in our time is more important.

6

In the field of international relations, going back especially to the days of the Cold War, high public officials have invariably been more diligent in instructing other governments than their own. Though often cautious and deferential in their relations with the Congress, Secretaries of State have been

[7]Soviet scientists, perhaps similarly motivated, have assumed similar leadership.

bold and forthright in informing the Soviets of their error.
The late John Foster Dulles rarely missed an opportunity to
advise the Russians on the merits of liberty and the rule of
law and the sanctity of freedom of speech. He was much
more cautious as regards Senator Joseph McCarthy, although
the latter, on frequent occasions, attacked freedom of expression and due process and did not omit to concern himself
with Mr. Dulles's own department. Mr. Dean Rusk, a circumspect man in dealing with domestic critics, especially
those who might charge undue liberalism in relations with
China, showed contrasting boldness in telling the Communist
powers of their great and varied shortcomings. In the forma-
tive months of the Carter Administration there was an ex-
plosion of concern for human rights in the Soviet Union that
was not similarly manifested as regards areas of more immediate American power and concern such as South Korea. It
may be laid down as a rule of foreign relations that the lower
the probability that advice will be taken, the more firmly it
will be proffered. Our officials are more circumspect in advising the Congress of its error than in admonishing the British.
They are much more cautious in telling the British what to do
than the French. They are least inhibited in instructing the
Soviets, and it is rare that the leaders of the Soviet Union will
encounter a State Department speech which fails to inform
them of their faults and point the way to improvement. The
tendency of Soviet leaders in instructing the United States is
the same. The action in response to the advice so exchanged
is slight but does not discourage it.

Only limited progress can be made in reducing the com-
mittment to the arms competition without the concurrent action of the Soviet Union.[8] On this it is well to be clear. Still,
there is merit in departing from the rules and addressing advice in this matter to the United States. It is the country that
one can advise with possible effect as distinct from comfortable immunity. It is also richer than the Soviet Union, has
greater scientific and technological resources and tends, in
consequence, to be the pace-setter in the weapons competition. If we understand that we are subject to the imagery of

---

[8]In the mystique of the Cold War, the Chinese for a time played an
important role, and their behavior was sometimes highly favorable to
the image of enduring conflict. However, it was not, in the end, practical to argue that China was scientifically and technologically a serious
threat to the United States in the weapons competition.

the planning system in these matters and seek to act in accordance not with the image but with the reality of our situation, then it may be possible to make a bargain with the Soviets. It may also prove impossible. We do not know for sure to what images the Soviets are subject. We may wisely assume that, as in other matters, there are parallel tendencies here and that the weapons competition has an organic role and power in Soviet society. Yet it also remains that the arms race has elements of a self-fulfilling prophecy, for it has cultivated the reciprocal mistrust which it assumes. Only if we understand our situation and the nature of our commitment is there a chance that matters will improve.

It is also extremely important that we be aware of what, given the needs of the planning system, is the most practical course of action. Escape from the weapons competition, with its attendant dangers, need not follow the path of maximum resistance. In the past we have proposed Calvinist solutions and made no progress. We shall do better with less painful solutions which, if less deeply satisfying to the Calvinist soul, could serve to keep it longer in this world.

7

In the conventional view, as earlier noted, we could escape our commitment to the weapons competition without insuperable economic difficulty. We would need to offset the decline in arms expenditures by increasing other public outlays or by cutting taxes or by both, and we would need to help those affected retrain, re-educate and relocate themselves. These would be formidable but feasible undertakings. And without minimizing the required action, the orthodox discussion of disarmament almost invariably concludes by saying how welcome would be this challenging task. This pious expression of hope is also partly liturgical. Given the remarkable destructiveness of modern weapons, it is necessary to assure ourselves that we are not dependent on their production. Any other view of the economy is unsettling. Additionally, the ancient Marxian contention, still reflected in some modern Soviet propaganda, holds that a capitalist economy suffers from an inherently limited market. Arms expenditure, like imperialism, is one of the necessary correctives. No circumspect scholar wishes to have it said that he has served, wittingly or unwittingly, the purposes of Communist propaganda. Indeed, one of the more extreme tenets of behavior in the Cold War years was that no scholar should do so. So grave was this conflict that it was accepted, tacitly, that embarrassing truth should be constrained for *raisons d'état*.

There is, in fact, nothing to the Marxian contention. The market is not limited, as Marx held; the management of aggregate demand, a possibility which he did not foresee, can be served by different types of public spending. And it has now been amply shown that, by such management, the size of the market can be increased as employment or other considerations require.[9] Arms expenditures have no unique value for increasing aggregate demand.

But the orthodox statement of the problem of disarmament, as the present analysis also amply shows, is deficient in two other respects. One cannot replace the spending for armaments with private outlays for private consumption and investment, such as would be encouraged by a massive reduction in taxes. The regulation of aggregate demand requires that the public sector of the economy be large. It must be so if personal income and corporation taxes are to be large enough to have their indispensable stabilizing effect.

And while all expenditures, whether for arms or health care or housing or control of air pollution, add to demand, not all play the same role in underwriting technology. Military spending, we have seen, is highly serviceable in this regard. It also pays for innovation that may be useful for civilian production. Risks that would otherwise be unacceptable can be assumed in the civilian economy if they are protected by the much more nearly riskless weapons economy. General Dynamics was helped to survive its disastrous misadventure in jet air transports earlier mentioned,[10] and the Studebaker Corporation was able to survive the loss of its automobile business[11] because of a large (and in the case of Studebaker) expanding participation in military procurement. The Lockheed Corporation was bailed out of its civilian aircraft misadventure because, as a major arms producer, it was thought vital for national security, and profitable weapons or-

[9] The point is now conceded at least by the younger generation of Soviet economists.
[10] Richard Austin Smith, *Corporations in Crisis* (New York: Doubleday, 1963), p. 67 et seq.
[11] The effect of military orders in saving the company is described by Duscha in *Arms, Money and Politics*, pp. 14–15.

ders were ultimately as important as loan guarantees for the rescue. These advantages of the weapons competition to the planning system will not readily be sacrificed.

There are, however, pressures on the modern industrial society for expenditures which are in strong competition with those for arms and which, in a general way, serve the needs of the planning system. Urbanization is proving far more expensive as to pubic services than anyone hitherto imagined. People are winning release from the prescriptive restraints that once specified that blue-collar workers, manual workers, blacks or other minorities were meant by nature to consume less. This is leading to an enhanced demand for both private and public services. In consequence, those who argue the case for arms expenditures are encountering an increasing competition from civilian claimants. Civilian claims in the Soviet Union seem also to be strong. This competition, all must hope, will continue, become stronger and force or help to force restraint on the arms race and the agreement that will preclude reciprocal suicide.

8

It is the nature of competition that the rewards of winning need not be examined. To excel, or to hope to excel, is sufficient to justify the contest, and this is equally the case for football, chess, sexual prowess, moneymaking or scientific achievement. A scientific and engineering competition in any field is thus quite as capable of enlisting the serious energies of man as a weapons competition. And akin to an athletic competition, while it is capable of generating a substantial amount of reciprocal ill will, it could be much more benign as to pollution of atmosphere, possibility of accident and ultimate outcome than a weapons competition.

It is also clear that we have already come some distance along this path in our relations with the Soviet Union. The competition in space exploration was largely—although not totally—devoid of military implication. It aroused the competitive passions of both countries. It was devoid of danger of accident except to the passengers. And, as compared with earlier competition in transoceanic aviation, this was small. In relation to the needs of the planning system, the space competition was nearly ideal. It required very high spending or complex and sophisticated technology. It underwrote the same highly developed planning as does the weapons competition and, hence, was an admirable substitute for it.

The imagery of the planning system strongly supported the space race. It was held to be of the utmost importance to the international prestige of the United States that its vehicles be first to the moon and on to the other parts of the solar system.

There has been some tendency to question the validity of this imagery. Why is it uniquely important that the United States be first to Saturn? Is it likely that the imperial prospect will be especially rewarding? Is not the area of cultivable land likely to be small? Are there not better uses for the resources so employed? There is no rational answer to these questions, as there is none to a query as to why negotiated disarmament is inherently more dangerous than a continuance of the weapons competition. Truth in both instances is subordinate to need and the needed belief. But this does not affect the value of the space competition in meeting the needs of the planning system in a comparatively harmless instead of in an extremely dangerous way. A similar case could be made for competitive underwriting of the widest area of general scientific research—in exploring the ocean floor; in getting into the regions below the earth's crust; in any other competition that suitably combines advanced technology with great expense.

The planning system has not become identified with the weapons competition by preference or because it is inherently bloody. Rather this has been the area where the largest amount of money to support planning was available with the fewest questions asked. And since armies and cannon have always been in the public sector, government underwriting in this area had the fewest overtones of socialism. But the space race shows that underwriting outside the area of weaponry is equally acceptable.

The path to salvation for the two great planning systems is now clear. Whether it will be followed is less certain. There must be maximum support for civilian needs. In their increasing urgency they appear as a welcome and well-timed substitute. And there must be agreement on arresting and eliminating the competition in lethal technology. On this, survival of both the industrial and the nonindustrial populations of the world depends. There is no rhetoric in such a statement. It is of prime importance to this effect that it be realized how much of past action has been based not on reality but on imagery and the sources of the latter. Nor may it be supposed that this imagery is confined to one side. Discussion of disarmament must now result in action. It can no longer serve, as it does now, as the surrogate for action.

But agreement can be made easier and less painful if competition continues and is encouraged and widened in non-lethal spheres. This competition serves an organic need for the planning system as now constituted. And it does not culminate in explosions of immeasurable effect.

The Further Dimensions

". . . for the first time since his creation man will be faced with his . . . permanent problem—how to use his freedom from pressing economic cares, how to occupy the leisure, which science and compound interest will have won for him, to live wisely and agreeably and well."

—John Maynard Keynes

"We should not fall prey to the beautification extremists who have no sense of economic reality."

—Fred L. Hartley, President of the Union Oil Company, shortly before a big Santa Barbara oil spill in which his company was disastrously involved.

THE PLANNING SYSTEM identifies itself with the goals of society. And it adapts these to its needs. The adaptation would not be so successful were those who comprise society aware of it—did they know, in effect, how they are guided. It is the genius of the planning system that it makes the goals that reflect its needs—production of goods, a steady expansion in their output, a steady expansion in their consumption, a powerful preference for goods over leisure, an unqualified commitment to technological change, autonomy for the technostructure, an adequate supply of trained and educated manpower—coordinate with social virtue and human enlightenment. These goals are not thought to be derived from our environment. They are assumed to be original with human personality. To believe this is to hold a sensibly material view of mankind. To question it is to risk a reputation for eccentricity or asceticism.

Or so it has been. Few things are so appealing as reflection on the novelty or originality of one's own position. In recent times there has, in fact, been a persistent questioning of conventional economic and social goals. Economic values have been especially questioned. Alienation has been evident among the young. It has manifested itself to a differing extent at different times in rejection of conventional attitudes on work, career, clothing and foreign policy. But this unease is not confined to youth. It has been widespread in the educational and scientific estate. And it has invaded even the great philanthropic foundations, where it has led to grants to groups duly constituted to re-examine the purposes of the society. Such re-examination has invariably led to a strong affirmation of the goals that serve the needs of the planning system.[1]

These pages have shown, one trusts, the considerable social and economic foundation for our unease. They also make clear the nature of the forces by which we have been captured. What, now, are the mechanics of emancipation?

The most important step has already been accomplished by the diligent and responsive reader, for knowledge of the forces by which one is constrained is the first step toward freedom. But another is to have clearly in view the dimensions of life which the planning system, by its nature, does not or cannot serve and which, because of its disabilities, it will tend to minimize.

A further step, no less important, is to identify a mechanism which will assert and promote the neglected dimensions of life against the powerful adaptive motivation of the planning system. In less formidable language, there must be some political force for accomplishing what the planning system ignores and, indeed, holds to be unimportant. I come to this in the final chapters.

---

[1] Cf. *Prospects for America, The Rockefeller Panel Reports* (Garden City, New York: Doubleday, 1961), and *Goals for Americans: The Report of the President's Commission on National Goals* (New York: Prentice-Hall, 1960).

The last mentioned provided what stands as the classically conventional list. "The economy should grow at the maximum rate consistent with primary dependence upon free enterprise . . . Technological change should be promoted and encouraged as a powerful force for advancing our economy . . . The development of the individual and the nation demand that education at every level and in every discipline be strengthened . . . Communist aggression and subversion . . . threaten all that we seek to do both at home and abroad . . . Disarmament should be our ultimate goal." Pp. 3–20.

2

The planning system generally ignores or holds unimportant those services of the state which are not closely related to the system's needs. National defense, support to research and technological development, such collateral needs of industrial growth as highways and air traffic management are not neglected. Nor is education. With the passage of time, support for education reflects not alone the needs of the planning system but also the increasing political power of the educational and scientific estate. Educators, in pursuit of professional self-interest, differ from others principally in the impression of exceptional purity of motive which they are able to convey.

Services of the state that are not directly related to the needs of the planning system are much less favored. Two factors operate here. Services that are unneeded by the planning system and which, unavoidably, the state must render, suffer from a negative discrimination. Soap and dentifrices are accorded importance by the planning system by the advertising by which it manages demand. Public clinics, which may do more for health, are the beneficiaries of no similar promotion. They suffer accordingly. Still other activities of the state are inimical to the planning system or to the goals it avows and the priorities it enjoys. They encounter the active opposition of the planning system. Both cases require brief examination.

Such services of the state as the care of the ill, aged and physically or mentally infirm, the provision of health services in general, the provision of parks and recreation areas, the removal of rubbish, the provision of architecturally decent public structures, assistance to the impoverished and many other services are not of particular importance to the planning system. And they are in competition for funds with the wants that result from the aggressive management of the consumer by the planning system. In consequence, they do badly in competition for public funds. Street cleaning does badly in competition with the automobiles parked on the streets. Expenditures for parks for outdoor play do poorly in competition with those for chromatic and violent television. And so forth.

And belief is extensively, although imperfectly, accommodated to this discrimination. Private virtue consists in producing more for more money. Public virtue still lies, on the whole, not with the politician who proposes to accomplish more for the same expenditure but with the one who proposes to do more for less. And the voice of the man who wishes government to do less for less is still heard in the land. By especially accommodating philosophers it is still held that the state should minimize its services. Otherwise it abridges the right of the individual to decide his purchases for himself.

Doctrine thus supports the organic tendency to create a natural imbalance between the goods produced and the services supplied by the planning system and those which are supplied by the state and which do not serve the needs of the planning system. But these are matters on which I have written elsewhere and at length.[2] With no views is it so pleasant to agree in detail as with one's own. But the temptation must be put down.

I turn now from the negative discrimination against public services to the much stronger opposition that arises from the association of the state with goals that are alien or inimical to the planning system.

3

Beyond the area of goods and services, however supplied, and the demand for them, however contrived, is the further world of aesthetic experience. This is served not by factories or engineers but, in one manifestation or other, by artists. Enjoyment of the experience owes something to preparation; no more than the response to a lighter, smoother, blended whiskey is it original in the soul of man.

The aesthetic experience was once a very large share of life—unimaginably large, given the meager resources of earlier societies and the wealth of the modern planning system. The traveler from the United States or the industrial cities of Europe or Japan goes each summer to visit the remnants of preindustrial civilizations. That is because Athens, Florence, Venice, Seville, Agra, Kyoto and Samarkand, though they were infinitely poor by the standards of modern Nagoya, Düsseldorf, Dagenham, Flint or Magnitogorsk, included, as

---

[2] In *The Affluent Society*, 3rd ed., rev. (Boston: Houghton Mifflin, 1976).

part of life, a much wider aesthetic perspective. No city of the postindustrial era is, in consequence, of remotely comparable artistic interest. Indeed, no traveler with a predominantly artistic concern ever visits an industrial city, and, a few especially designed capitals apart—Washington, Brasilia, Canberra, New Delhi—he visits very few of any kind which owe their distinction to architecture and urban design postdating the publication of Adam Smith's *Wealth of Nations* in 1776.

One of the terms of disapprobation in the planning system is aesthete. This is because aesthetic achievement is beyond the reach of the planning system and, in substantial measure, in conflict with it. There would be little need to stress the conflict were it not part of the litany of the planning system that none exists.

The conflict derives partly from a conflict in goals and partly because aesthetic goals are beyond the reach of the technostructure, which is to say that it cannot identify itself with them. So, if they are strongly asserted, they will be viewed as a constraint.

Thus, in an obvious case, if aesthetic goals are strongly asserted, this will affect the location of industrial plants. These will be placed not where they are most efficient but where they are least offensive. Their mode of operation, including the odors they dispense into the atmosphere and the wastes they deposit into streams, lakes and subsoil, will also be controlled. This means higher cost, smaller output or both. Questions will be asked about products—about the shape, number and construction of automobiles that are consistent with a pleasant urban aspect or an agreeably neutral air.

Such constraints are inconvenient. Social thought on behalf of the planning system does not allow of inquiry as to whether increased or more efficient production of a particular product is a good thing. It is, *per se,* a good thing.

Aesthetic goals contest the claims of power lines over landscape, of power development over natural streams or national parks, of highways over urban open spaces, strip mining over virgin mountainsides, modern shopping centers over ancient squares and high-speed air travel over tranquillity below. In the first edition of his book (in 1967) the case that aesthetic consideration had a claim against the values of the planning system was asserted with some sense of novelty, even of fleeting courage. It was conceded that if the countering claims of the planning system—adverse effect on output, income and cost—were strongly asserted, these, in the usual case, would be decisive. On few matters has the change in social attitudes been more marked; environmental claims are now asserted as a matter of course. The goals of the planning system, though put forward with vigor and controlled indignation, are no longer assuredly decisive. People have come fully to understand that the goals of the planning system, though regularly presented as those of the society, are not identical with them. This perception is far from welcomed by the planning system but it is accepted as a fact of life.

To assert aesthetic goals is also to interfere seriously with the management of the consumer. This, in many of its manifestations, requires dissonance—a jarring of the aesthetic sensibilities. An advertising billboard that blends gracefully into the landscape is of little value; it must be in sharp contrast with its surroundings. This jarring effect then becomes competitive. The same principles of planned dissonance are even more spectacularly in evidence in the radio and television commercial. They also characterize the design or packaging of numerous industrial products. And this dissonance is even justified on occasion by resort to the conventional canons of economic theory. It reflects consumer preference, gives the consumer what he or she wants. If the consumer did not approve, he would not respond. A man who comes to a full stop because he is hit over the head with an ax proves similarly by his response that the blow was what he was yearning for. However, here too, public understanding and resistance are also emerging—although they still have much distance to go.

4

The planning system has a yet further and more fundamental conflict with the aesthetic dimension. As we have sufficiently seen, the planning system depends urgently on organization. Fragments of information, each associated with a person, are combined to produce a result which is far beyond the capacity of any one of the constituent individuals. But while this is a procedure which lends itself admirably to technological development and to the less inspired levels of scientific research, it does not lend itself to art. Artists do not come in teams. The greatest industrial achievement, myth to the contrary, emerges from committees. But not the greatest painting, sculpture or music. The artist may be more of a social being than the legend holds. It is noticeable that he regularly eschews, in practice, the cruel isolation which, as a deeply creative being, he is supposed to suffer in principle. His flocking and nesting tendencies are rather more convivial than those of accountants, engineers and high executives. But he does, in his work, enfold the whole of his task within himself. He cannot work on or with a team. We have here a principal explanation of why the high technical and productive achievements of the planning system are so regularly combined with banal or even offensive design.

The aesthetic dimension being beyond the ready reach of the planning system, members of that system are led naturally to assert its unimportance. Juveniles who do not like Latin, economists who do not like mathematics and men who do not like women manifest precisely the same tendency.

But this is not all. Cultivation of the aesthetic dimension accords a new and important role to the state and one to which, by virtue of its handicaps, the planning system is unrelated. Part of this role has already been implied. Where there is a conflict between industrial and aesthetic priorities, it is the state which must assert aesthetic priority against the industrial need. Only the state can defend the landscape against power lines, advertisers, lumbermen, coal miners and, on frequent occasions, its own highwaymen. Only it can rule that some patterns of consumption—the automobile in the downtown areas of the modern city is a prominent example—are inconsistent with community goals. The state alone can protect radio and television from contrived dissonance—or provide alternatives that are exempt. And were aesthetic priority asserted, the state would be required to come to its defense not, as now, episodically and in response to some exceptional outrage of aesthetic sensibilities. It would have to do so normally and naturally as the defender of goals in which aesthetic considerations were consistently important. Such goals, it must be added, will not occasionally but usually be achieved at some cost to industrial expansion—to economic growth. That one must pause to affirm that beauty is worth the sacrifice of some increase in the Gross National Product shows how effectively our beliefs have been accommodated to the needs of the planning system.

5

But the role of the state on the aesthetic dimension is not merely protective; it is also affirmative. While art is an expression of individual personality, important branches of the arts can only flourish within a framework of order. This must be provided by the state. Specifically, painting, sculpture and music, although not within the ambit of the planning system, do reasonably well on the patronage that its participants provide. There is need for instruction in appreciation and enjoyment. (In keeping with the ethos of the system, this is considered a much inferior employment of educational funds to their devotion to science, mathematics and engineering.) But, while there is much that the state can do by way of encouragement here, its role is not decisive.[3]

In the case of architecture and urban and environmental design, its role *is* decisive. Art is one manifestation of order. And it is the first casualty of disorder. Florence, Seville, Bloomsbury and Georgetown are beautiful because each part is in orderly relation to the whole. The modern commercial highway, the sprawling fringe of any city, the route into town from any airport, are hideous because no part is related to a larger design. This order is rarely if ever achieved permissively; it must always be imposed by the state or by social pressure.

Good architecture is also mostly meaningless unless it is within a consistent framework. The Taj Mahal would lose much of its queenly elegance if surrounded by modern service stations. This has been the fate of quite a few distinguished modern buildings. Nineteenth-century Paris owes its excellence not to the brilliance of the individual buildings but to the consistency of the overall design.

Further, there is much architecture of which the state must always be the patron. It is the natural source of handsome buildings, interesting monuments, agreeable gardens and fountains, long vistas, imposing squares, soaring towers and rich façades. Only as nations have become very rich and the

---

[3] Once again there has been progress since the early editions of this book. The United States government has emerged, in recent years, as a modest but not insignificant patron of the arts. There has been movement also on the matter of public television.

planning system has made economic growth identical with life, have we ceased to suppose that such patronage is a fit function of government. Quite commonly it is said that it cannot be afforded.

6

It would be foolish to insist that government in the United States—whether of cities, states or the federal government—is a good custodian of aesthetic goals. Politicians may well have a special penchant for banality. Those who do not urge it out of personal preference will think it necessary as a concession to the popular taste. Although the world owes a greater debt to public architecture than to private, it owes more to the taste of talented despots—Shah Jahan, Cosimo and Lorenzo, Peter the Great, Louis XIV—than to that of democrats. It is part of the case against public sponsorship of aesthetic goals by modern democratic governments that they will be strongly biased in favor of what is bad.

This cannot be denied. It is only that for asserting aesthetic priorities and providing the essential framework for artistic effort there is no alternative to the state. Those who say that, in consequence of its shortcomings, the state must forgo all concern for art thereby reject aesthetic priority. They become advocates of environmental disorder.

For even when the state exercises artistically imperfect control over the environment, the result will be better than when there is none at all. In the late twenties and early thirties the planners and architects of Washington, D.C., swept clear an area between Pennsylvania and Constitution Avenues to build a vast block of buildings called the Federal Triangle. The Triangle is unimaginative, derivative and pretentious. Artists rightly condemned it. But it is far better than the cabbage patch of buildings it replaced or abuts. In its general cohesiveness it has come to be admired in comparison with those parts of the city where no similar effort was ever made.

And the state can be expected to do better in support of the aesthetic dimension in the future than in the modern past. For this will be recognized as a high public responsibility. What is done as an afterthought is rarely done well. Something better can be expected when a task is seen to be central, not marginal, to life. It is worth hoping that the educational and scientific estate, as it grows in power, will encourage and enforce more exacting aesthetic standards. Nothing would more justify its intrusion on public life.

7

For many years politicians completing a term of office and seeking another have taken, as the measure of their deservedness, whether their constituency is more prosperous than when they began. If it is, and larceny has not been palpable, they consider themselves to have a good claim for re-election. It is a test which it has been hard for even the most negligible statesman to fail. All, the intelligent and stupid, diligent and idle, have been swept along on a current of increased output that, in the usual case, owed nothing whatever to their efforts.

The aesthetic dimension introduces a new and much stronger test. It means that mayors completing a term at city hall, governors at the state capital, Presidents in the White House, Prime Ministers at 10 Downing Street will be asked whether they have left their city, state or country more beautiful than before. This test will not be easy. None of note in this century would have passed. The fact of universal failure is another reason for insisting on the unimportance of the aesthetic dimension. No one likes an examination which he surely flunks. But far more than the test of production, which is far too easy, the test of aesthetic achievement is the one that, one day, the progressive community will apply.[4]

[4]In the third volume in this series, *Economics and the Public Purpose* (Boston: Houghton Mifflin, 1973) I return once more to the artistic dimension and seek to place it more fully in the larger context of the planning and market systems.

XXXI

The Planning Lacunae

THE GENIUS of the planning system lies in its organized use of capital and technology. This is made possible, as we have duly seen, by extensively replacing the market with planning. The notable accomplishments of the planning system are all the result of such planning: there would be no vehicles journeying to the planets and not many flying to Los Angeles were market incentives relied upon to bring into existence the required equipment. The same is true of other services, amenities and artifacts of the planning system from telephone communications to Chevrolets to dentifrices. In all cases there are careful projections of output; careful control of prices; careful steps to see that the projections of output are validated in the greatest possible measure by consumer response; and careful steps to see that the things needed for production—labor, components, machinery—are available in the requisite amounts at the anticipated prices at the right time. To leave these matters to the market would be regarded by those principally involved as the equivalent of leaving them to chance.

Yet, as we have seen, the myth of the system is quite different. That holds, and a large, expensive though not universally successful educational effort teaches, that all credit belongs to the market, which is a force of transcendent power. It alone motivates and regulates performance. There are agnostics who do not place their trust in God. But a deeper, more indignant faith reposes trust in the market. The community that does so cannot go wrong.

There is an inherent implausibility about this faith—apart from the impossibility of reconciling it with the practice of the planning system. In all other aspects of business organization, profoundly rational and determinist attitudes are held to rule. As little as possible is left to faith and hope. But then at the ultimate and decisive point, where the great and important decisions are made on what and how much and at what price things are to be produced, there is assumed to be abdication to the impersonal magic of market forces. This is improbable as well as wrong. But, however remarkably, it still solicits belief.

One consequence is a great deal of physical discomfort. The planning system performs its tasks with technical competence. That is why it seeks to make the competent production of goods the only social purpose and the sole test of social performance. But for a variety of reasons the planning system does not perform all necessary tasks. Since there is a presumption that the planning system functions in response to the market rather than through its instruments for planning supply and demand, it is naturally assumed that the market will also work its unplanned wonders where the writ of the planning system does not run.

In quite a large area outside the planning system—the world of the small retail entrepreneur, repairman, independent craftsman, barber, market gardener, bookmaker—the market does work sometimes inadequately, sometimes adequately, sometimes well. The generally inferior performance of such services or their absence is one of the notable features of the fully planned economies of Eastern Europe. However, there are also products and services, some of them of the highest convenience or necessity, which cannot be called into being by the market. The society recognizes the failure of the market in these areas. But since the market is assumed generally to be a success, the planning in these areas of failure is conceived to be abnormal. It is approached half-heartedly and with a sense of being unfaithful to principle. Nor are all of the requisites of effective planning identified and provided. In consequence, these tasks are badly performed to the general public's discomfort or worse. Were it recognized that they require planning, and in the context of a largely planned economy have been left unplanned, there would be no hesitation or apology in the use of all the necessary instruments for planning. Performance would be much better.

These abstractions may now be fleshed out with specific examples.

2

The clearest case is urban and close interurban surface transportation of people. This, it is clear in retrospect, required that there be one corporation, that is to say one planning instrument, covering the cities of an entire region, including the lines between. The local systems would then have been developed in relation to the intercity and interregional system with joint use of rights-of-way, terminals and other facilities as appropriate. The prospective growth of the entire system would have been largely independent of local influences and pressures in setting fares. Prices, in other words, would have been wholly or largely under its planning control. It could have held its own with the automobile industry and the airlines in managing, i.e., promoting, the demand for its services. It could have held its own with the automobile industry and the highway users in getting requisite public underwriting of its facilities—were costs and risks too great for it to carry, it could have pleaded military necessity as did the automobile industry and highway users in the case of the interstate highway system. Pleading further the doctrine of military necessity, it could have sought state underwriting of technical development. The need for faster surface movement of troops could have been made especially compelling. This would have placed it more or less on a parity with the airlines, which, in the last thirty years, have had many billions of dollars of subsidy in the form of military development of aircraft (ultimately usable as passenger vehicles) and in the development and installation of navigational facilities. The planning unit, assuming success, would have had internal sources of capital from earnings. This would have exempted it from petty interference by local governments or other sources of funds. It would have been able to make its own decisions on growth and technical innovation and would have tended to measure its success by its virtuosity in this regard. Its size and capacity for technical change, including automation, would have given it leverage in dealing with unions. Not least important, such a unit would have had a developed technostructure in which group decision would have replaced the vagaries of individual competence.

None of this has happened. Local transit systems have developed under public and private auspices and subject to local political influences and regulation. The railroads, under a different system of regulations, followed their own rather special pattern of development.[1] Each part provided a frac-

---

[1] Most American railroads have had a pattern of development different from that of the firms of similar size in the planning system. There is no similarly developed technostructure; for most of their history

tion of the total services of moving people locally and region-
ally; none, in consequence, could plan the entire service.
None had appreciable authority over prices, use of service,
capital supply or labor supply. None had a developed technostructure. In an industry which required planning, none of
the requisites of planned performance were available. It is not
surprising that the results have been singularly bad.

3

Although no parallels are exact, it is interesting to contemplate the different development of telephone service. This
makes use of an old form of electronic communication. As in
the case of the railroads and urban transit, alternative technology has been massively subsidized by the federal government for military purposes. But in the telephone industry one
giant corporation had planning authority coordinate with the
whole task. It embraced both local and long-distance service.
It had resources for competitive technical development and
also for seeking government underwriting of such development where, as is usually the case, this could be justified by
military application. The scale of A. T. & T. accorded it substantial authority over rates; it could enter actively on the
management of the demand for its services; it had control
over its capital supply; size, combined with technological advance, has enabled it to plan its labor requirements, keep
them within the prospective supply and maintain authority
over its labor force.

Had local telephone service been provided by one or more
companies in each city, town and hamlet; had all these rates
been subject to local regulation and influence; had long-dis-

---

there has been no similar technical dynamic; there has been no similar
capacity for taking control of prices, demand for the services, labor
and capital supply and the other requisites of successful planning. Regulation, prohibitions on mergers and diversification of activities and a
tradition of routine, highly ritualized management of low technical aspiration and competence have all been factors. In Japan, France,
Canada and other countries where there has been one national system
or one or two dominant systems, the industry has had greater control
over the requisites of its planning, and its comparative performance
and survival value have been much better. Belatedly and halfheartedly,
with Conrail and Amtrak, both shame-faced concessions to the inevitability of planning, a step has now been taken on the proper and,
indeed, only course.

tance service been supplied by numerous separate companies, only loosely coordinated with the local service; had there been little or no research or technical development anywhere in the system; had the local units been strongly dependent on external authority—municipal government or local banks—for capital; and had there been no planned provision for labor supply or substitute technology, it seems unlikely that telephonic communications could have survived in any very useful form.[2] That they flourished, none can doubt, is owning not to a mindless response to a free market but to the subordination of the market at all points to comprehensive planning.

In recent years, by support to technical development in interurban transit and diverse subsidies to local transit systems, steps have been taken to offset the patent incompetence of past performance in the field of surface transportation. This action has been typical of the apologetic planning which assumes that such action is the exception rather than the rule. The plausible course, reflecting the rule, would be to constitute one autonomous company with ample capital to take over all mass surface movement of people in the United States, say, east of the Appalachians. This would have running rights over the railroads and full control over other facilities. It would have a wide latitude in setting rates and promoting use. Massive technological innovation would be encouraged and subsidized, and urgent defense need would of course be invoked. It is entirely possible, by such a step, that urban and interurban movement of people might continue, and with elements of comfort and dispatch.[3]

4

Urban and interurban transit is one of the most visible and dramatic of the planning lacunae. It is not the most important. The most painful consequences from assuming the competence of the market are in urban and suburban housing, commercial and other real property development.

[2] As a partial demonstration of the point, it has been suggested that, in the absence of automatic transmission of calls, it would long since have required the entire female working force of the country—this having been thought peculiarly a job for women—to handle the traffic.

[3] See the earlier footnote on Amtrak and Conrail. Since the previous editions of this book there has been movement in this direction. I have allowed the original suggestion to stand.

In the slums, it has long been recognized, there is no socially useful market response. Rents, partly because of demand for limited space, tend to be at the highest level the traffic will bear. Being at the maximum, they will be no higher if the property is replaced, improved or even decently maintained. The most profitable course is to minimize outlay and, where possible, to pack more people in.

Commercial urban development is responsive to the market. But it is also responsive to the greatest opportunity for gain for the individual owner. This will frequently be inconsistent with the best economic opportunity for the community—a profitable slaughterhouse will have a more than offsetting effect on the earnings of an adjacent shopping center or the rents of an adjacent housing development. And the best commercial opportunity, in the manner of the vertical greenhouses on modern Manhattan, will often be either aesthetically inferior or offensive. Only as an act of charity will space be left for pedestrians.

The suburban residential market response is also frequently perverse. Nothing can be sold so cheaply as a house that is unprovided with sewerage, trash collection, police protection and schools. An isolated house without such amenities transgresses only upon itself. A community of such houses is incestuously offensive. The contemporary classic is the strip town which is by way of connecting all urban centers in the United States. This is the pattern of development which the market encourages.

These shortcomings are recognized. Again, however, they are assumed to be isolated failures of the market. In consequence, the corrective is the patchwork planning provided by weakly financed housing authorities of limited power and autonomy; housing and building codes which seek to enforce less profitable but socially more desirable behavior; zoning regulations which seek to deny to the owners of land what seems to them their normal right to the best return; and subsidies to offset the financial advantages of bad use and promote redevelopment. Or, as also happens, nothing is done, and the adverse consequences are suffered in the belief or hope that market responses, however bad in the present, will eventually become benign.

The remedy is a twofold one. The first step is to minimize or neutralize the adverse market influences. The second is to develop a planning authority of adequate power. Only strong and comprehensive planning will redeem and make livable the modern city and its surroundings.

Since the focus of market forces is the return to, and capital gains from, land, this solution means that there must be public land acquisition wherever market influences are palpably adverse. Planning, which under urban and metropolitan administration will never be strong, will not then have to contend in each decision with the resistances of the market. Those with a vested interest in bad land use are unlikely to welcome such a solution. But, in the end, there will prove to be no other.

The best instrument for urban and related land acquisition and administration is the strong planning, housing and development authority. And, no less than for the manufacture of automobiles or the colonization of the moon, it requires the scale, financial autonomy, control over prices and opportunity to develop a technostructure which are the requisites of effective planning.

The remedy also carries a price. Only liberal politicians on first coming to office imagine that there can be social gain with no cost. Although money is important, as elsewhere in the planning system, power and organization are almost equally important. And as elsewhere, individuals will have to surrender to the goals of organization. It is thus that planning, like the planning system in general, accomplishes its tasks. The horsebreeder and the buggy-maker were far less subject to organization than the General Motors man. They were also far less successful in imposing their values on their customers. But they were also less efficient in moving people about. The wretched freedom of the slums is the counterpart of the individualism of the buggy-maker.

5

Viewing the whole economy in purely technical terms, no natural superiority can be assumed either for the market or for planning. In some places market responses still serve. But over a very large area such responses cannot be relied upon; the market must give way to more or less comprehensive planning of demand and supply. Otherwise performance will be poor and perhaps appalling. The conservation of natural resources, the development of outdoor recreation, forestry in the eastern United States and, most urgent of all, the health industries are all further examples. The error is in basing action on generalization. There is no natural presumption in favor of the market; given the growth of the planning system, the presumption is, if anything, the reverse. To rely on the market where planning is, in fact, required, is to invite serious trouble.

To see these problems as they are requires, once again, a sharp break with the established economics. This and consumer sovereignty give high sanction to whatever the system produces. If the mix of goods at any given time seems unsatisfactory, consumer sovereignty holds, very simply, that this reflects the dominant consumer will. The tendency of the economy is to an equilibrium of maximized consumer satisfactions. The person who disapproves of this outcome is seeking, in undemocratic, elitist fashion, to substitute his taste for that of a majority. In consequence of a quite wonderful exercise in intellectual befuddlement that is fully sanctioned by the textbooks, he does not recognize the sovereign right of the consumer to be dissatisfied with his housing or his health care. But if the revised sequence is assumed, the mix of goods being produced will be the expression of comparative producer competence and power. If there appear to be too many automobiles and insufficient intercity or commuter rail service or urban rapid transit, this will be a plausible consequence of the superior power of the automobile industry to plan and persuade. Consumer sovereignty, by making questions about too many automobiles, too few houses, an elitist and undemocratic interference with consumer choice, excludes questions about the power of the automobile industry to impose its preferences on the public. This, in effect, is the result of existing economic theory. It gives high moral and scientific sanction to social indifference.

XXXII

Of Toil

Don't mourn for me, friends, don't
  weep for me never,
For I'm going to do nothing forever
  and ever.
    —Traditional epitaph
    of an English charwoman

THE PLANNING SYSTEM has long held out one rather striking promise to its participants. That is the eventual opportunity for a great deal more leisure. The workweek and the work year will be radically reduced. There will be much more free time. Over the last quarter century a reputation for cerebration beyond the reach of run-of-the-mill minds has been most easily achieved by speculation on how, when this day comes, men will employ what is invariably called their new-found leisure. It is agreed that the question deserves the most careful study. There are grave if highly unspecific dangers for which all must be braced. Over the last thirty years the average workweek in industry has remained almost constant. The standard workweek has declined but this has been offset by increased demand for overtime work and the companion willingness to supply it.[1] "Employed American adults have had no net gain in their leisure time in 30 years—since the end of World War II."[2] During this period average weekly earnings, adjusted for price increases (but not allowing for

---

[1] In 1941, the average workweek in manufacturing was 40.6 hours; in 1973, it was 40.7 hours; in 1976, 40.1 hours. *Economic Report of the President, 1962*, p. 238; *Economic Report of the President, 1977*, p. 226.

[2] John D. Owen, "Workweeks and leisure: an analysis of trends, 1948–1975," United States Department of Labor, Bureau of Labor Statistics, *Monthly Labor Review*, Vol. 99, No. 8 (August 1976), p. 3.

taxes), have increased by about fifty percent.[3] On the evidence, one must conclude that, as their incomes rise, men seek more income but do not wish for more leisure.

The notion of a new era of greatly expanded leisure is, in fact, a conventional conversation piece. Nor will it serve much longer to convey an impression of social vision. The tendency of the modern economic system is not in this direction.

Specifically, in the early stages of the planning system, toil was dreary, repetitive and physically painful. It was also very long. Severe prison sentences featured the inclusion of hard labor. Heaven was a place, above all, of eternal rest. Until curbed by the enlightened intervention of (among others) Warren Gamaliel Harding, the steel industry in the United States worked a twelve-hour day and an eighty-four-hour week. There were no holidays; in the steel towns all days were alike. When the shift changed, a man worked twice around the clock; as a reward, in return, he had twenty-four hours off a fortnight later. The management of wants was still in its infancy, and the steelworker—without radio or television, often illiterate, and his needs made evident by appetite and cold weather—was well beyond its reach. As important therefore as making money, and perhaps more important, was to make it with fewer hours of this hideous toil. Men worked to meet a minimum—to make a living. Few nonworkers have been able since to suppose that progressive reduction in hours can be other than a prime goal of the working stiff.

Outside of the planning system, as in the cotton and vegetable fields, work can still be hard and tedious. But within the planning system, though always with exceptions, work is unlikely to be painful, and it can even be pleasant. And the worker has now been brought within the fully deployed power of modern demand management. He too is subject to the revised sequence. So, where his precursor in the steel towns worked to make a living, he works to satisfy his constantly expanding wants. The result is obvious. With more pleasant work and expanded wants, a man is as likely to choose more work as more leisure, maybe more so.

As one moves into and up through the technostructure, men increasingly exercise the option of more work and more income. And more and more pride themselves on an unlimited and competitive commitment to toil—one that, at the

[3] *Economic Report of the President, 1977*, p. 227.

highest levels, can easily outrun even the most imaginative possibilities for the acquisition and use of goods and services.

2

It follows that to argue for less work and more leisure as a natural goal of industrial man is to misread the character of the planning system. There is no intrinsic reason why work must be more unpleasant than nonwork. Presiding over the console that regulates the movements of billets through a steel mill may be as pleasant as sojourning with a connubial fishwife. To urge more leisure is a feckless exercise so long as the planning system has the capacity to persuade its people that goods are more important. Men will value leisure over work only as they find the uses of leisure more interesting or rewarding than those of work, or as they win emancipation from the management of their wants, or both. Leisure is not wanted, *per se*, but only as these prerequisites are provided.

The two ends—the cultivation of interests that are an attractive alternative to work and the greater or less emancipation from demand management—are both, it is reasonable to assume, the result of education. Men of substantial mental accomplishment have not usually lacked interesting ways of employing their time apart from toil. And it seems likely that they are somewhat less susceptible to the management of demand. The ethos of the educational and scientific estate is illuminating in this connection. Especially in its higher orders, the academic community ostentatiously resists demand management and insists on extensive exemption from a formal commitment to toil. Excessive attention to goods is considered gauche; an elderly automobile or a slightly bruised Volkswagen, casual and shabby clothing, undistinguished but obviously comfortable furniture, self-designed entertainment, unluxurious travel, well-explained resistance to color television and functionally clothed women are sources of distinction. Academic prestige is associated with a minimum of formal teaching; anything in excess of six or nine hours weekly is a serious abridgement of academic freedom. Long vacations, sabbatical years and further leaves of absence are established rights. All are assumed to enable the individual to cultivate interests not served by his formal hours of toil. As the capitalist of an earlier era thought himself entitled to the homage of the community by natural and even divine right, so the aforementioned privileges are regarded by the academic community as appropriately unique to itself. Only men whose minds are tooled to a similarly fine response could require such protection from routine—and use it well. This may not be so. More likely, it is merely one of the fringe benefits of education and associated opportunity.

Most people will believe that the greatest possible emancipation of the individual from the management to which he is subject, the considerable cost to the planning system by its own standards notwithstanding, is a worthy objective. And it follows that the greatest chance for achieving such emancipation lies with education. This requires, in turn, that the educational and scientific estate have a clear view both of its powers and its responsibilities. I come to these matters in the next two chapters. Additionally, and as a quite practical matter, there is need for a much larger range of options for the individual person in the planning system. This will allow those who are able to emancipate themselves to do so. This opportunity for choice between toil and its alternatives, not leisure *per se*, is the immediate need. It is something that could well engage the residual energies of the trade unions.

3

Few things are more fully adapted to the convenience and the values of the planning system than the arrangements to which the labor force is subject. It is assumed that all men should work a standard number of hours a week. Those who wish may, by overtime or moonlighting, work more; none may work less. Negotiation is ordinarily for increased income or its equivalent. If more leisure—for example, paid vacations—is sought, it is obtained in equal amount for all alike. The ethos of the planning system is evident at all points. A basic minimum of toil is required from all. All have a normal preference for money. All have the same desire and capacity for leisure. All should be treated alike.

None of this is necessary. The employed person should be accorded a much wider set of options than at present as between work and goods on the one hand and leisure on the other. The way should be open for the individual who wishes to satisfy his needs for food, clothing and simple houseroom with ten or twenty hours of labor a week to do so. We should look with interest and even with admiration on inventive use of the remaining time.

But the options should not be confined to the workweek. This is a poor unit around which to organize the effective use of leisure time; it has long been a perquisite of high social, educational or financial position that life—holidays, travel, tasks—is planned in terms of months or years. All individuals, in return for a lower annual pay, should have the option of several months' paid vacation. And all should similarly have the option of extended leaves of absence. The employees exercising these options would not be favored in compensation per hour worked. What they are offered is the opportunity of choosing absence and exemption from toil in various forms as an alternative to earnings. There would be some inconvenience. But to fail to allow such choice—to be guided by the belief that everyone should work a standard week and year—is to make the needs of the planning system, not the opportunity of the individual to fashion his own existence, the ruling social concern. Men who speak much of liberty should allow and even encourage it.[4]

4

In the United States as in other industrial countries, the natural objects of social concern are the wage worker and, subject to local circumstance, minorities, small farmers, the mentally deficient, the aged and the endemically indigent. Others are thought able to look after themselves. While businessmen and the rich occasionally appeal for compassion, it is usually with reference to some specific act of public oppression such as a tax. And they regularly argue that the ultimate incidence of their affliction is on some manual toiler who is denied the benefits of the capital they would otherwise invest or the incentives by which they otherwise would be driven. They suffer for the worker as a surrogate. The scholar who devotes himself to the woes of the well-to-do is usually

[4]Again, since the earlier editions of this book, there has been appreciable movement in the direction here urged. There has been some bargaining for a more flexible workweek, work year and retirement age. And, perhaps most interesting of all, a number of companies have accorded clerical workers much greater liberty in the selection of the particular hours that will comprise their working day.

thought by the captious to have a special concern for the
hand that feeds him or that might.

Yet it could be that the planning system and its ethos impose the greatest burden on its leaders—on those who are at
the center of the technostructure. This is not because they
subordinate their personality to organization; that is inherent
and could be remedied only by dispensing with the planning
system. And, in any case, the surrender is voluntary; it occurs
because men find the goals of organization superior to their
own.[5]

But the technostructure has compulsions that are in addition to the demands of organization. And, far more than for
the workers, these shape the lives of its members or those of
the inner circles. It begins with education. Success in the
technostructure calls for mastery of one or more of the arts
associated with planning, technology or organization or the
management of demand. In some of its scientific and technological branches this study has considerable intrinsic interest.
But it seems likely that in a culture where education was pursued for its own sake, few men would study personnel management, media analysis, market research or cost and quality
control.

In the inner circles of the technostructure the commitment
of mental energy and moral purpose must, for all practical
purposes, be total. The purposes of the planning system being
identical with all life, those so serving it must make it identical with life. The blue-collar worker who supplies forty hours
of service each week is morally acceptable. A senior executive who sets any such limits on his effort is morally deficient.
He must have recreation. He cannot be indifferent, at least
vocally, to juvenile delinquency, cancer, drug addiction, heart
disease or civic growth. But all of this must, generally speaking, be in support of his primary business function.

And the outcome is not attractive. Having been measured
through his lifetime by the single-mindedness with which he
subordinates all normal tastes and enjoyments to the needs of
the corporation, he is then, at the age of sixty-five, firmly retired. This is essential. In an occupation which depends on
group activity and oral interchange, no one is so feared as the
putatively senile. The habit of total commitment having been
fully established, he has now nothing to do—or only what is

[5] See Chapter XI.

obviously made-work. Having become wholly habituated to group activity, he is now alone. It is not a beautifully sculptured arrangement. Millions since the dawn of man have led a less inspired existence but never have they done so on comparable income.

Ultimately one of the problems of the planning system may be in reproducing the technostructure. And there may already be signs of difficulty in doing so. Once the schools of business, the most general training ground for the technostructure, were among the most prestigious branches of American higher education. They are still highly regarded by foreign students. And they still attract numerous and industrious Americans in times when other academic opportunity seems lacking. But an appreciable number now hold that they prepare for a life that is excessively disciplined, damaging to individuality, not worth the high pay or dull.

We come to an interesting if speculative result. Emancipation could be the salvation of the planning system. Its discipline will be worse but only thus will it attract people who are of a quality that will serve it well. However, this is, indeed, speculation. There are enough harder truths to occupy our attention.

XXXIII

Education and Emancipation

BOTH THE BASIC tendencies of the planning system and the thrust of needed policy are now clear. As an organic characteristic of its operation, the planning system reaches out comprehensively to win the belief that validates its planning and which wins acceptance of its goals. Therewith it ensures the success of the organization on which it so greatly depends. There is, most will think, an uncomfortably collectivist and monolithic aspect to this. The countering action is whatever helps the individual escape this subordination. The requirements are twofold: the first is comprehension and skepticism, which ensure that there will be systematic questioning of the beliefs impressed by the planning system. The second is a political pluralism which voices the ideas and goals of those who, intellectually speaking, choose to contract out of the planning system.

For this emancipation, education—higher education in particular—is obviously strategic. It is, among other things, an apparatus for affecting belief and, we must hope, inducing more critical belief. The planning system, by making trained and educated manpower the decisive factor of production, requires a highly developed educational system. If the educational system serves generally the beliefs of the planning system, the influence and monolithic character of the latter will be enhanced. By the same token, should it be superior to and independent of the planning system, it can be the necessary force for skepticism, emancipation and pluralism.

Modern higher education is, of course, extensively accommodated to the needs of the planning system. The schools and colleges of business administration mentioned in the last chapter are preparatory academies for the technostructure. The great prestige of the pure and applied sciences and mathematics in modern times and the support accorded them reflect the needs of the technostructure. The ample sums available for research and related graduate training in these areas reflect specific adaptation to such need, whereas the lesser prestige and lesser support for the arts and humanities suggest their inferior role. No modern university administration would insist, in fact as distinct from speech, that the study of the theater, fine arts or *Beowulf* had the same claim to funds in the same amounts as an electronic accelerator or the computer center. Such is the influence of the planning system.

This influence has not gone unchallenged. Too complete an orientation to the needs of the planning system is resisted, at least in the more mature and self-confident educational communities. The business and engineering schools are valued for their reassuring aspect of utility, as are the scientists and mathematicians for their association with pregnant and often alarming change. But the service of the university to the aesthetic, cultural and intellectual enjoyments of the individual is still asserted. Indeed, such assertion comprises, by a wide margin, the largest part of the ceremonial literature of modern higher education. No university president is inaugurated, few speak, only rarely is a commencement address given, no anniversary is celebrated and no great educator is retired without a reference to the continuing importance of liberal education for its own sake. In part, this reflects only the paucity of noncontroversial topics available to men with a high reputation for wisdom but slight specific information. But it reflects also the deep conviction of the modern college president that any unsatisfactory educational tendency can be exorcised by sufficiently solemn oratory. To transfer actual funds from engineering to fine arts would be more difficult. Yet even the oratory, however vacuous, suggests the problem. The growth of the planning system has induced an enormous expansion in education. This can only be welcomed. But unless its tendencies are clearly foreseen and strongly resisted, it will place a preclusive emphasis on education that most serves the needs, but least questions the goals, of that system.

2

The proper course of action is clear. The college and university community must seek or retain paramount authority for the education it provides and for the research it undertakes. Support for research and scholarship must be in accordance with some natural distribution of human curiosity and competence. It will be urged that this is a counsel of perfection. That we see it as such shows how readily we assume that education and research must be subordinate to the needs of the planning system. But they need not be subordinate if it is realized that the educator is a figure of power in this context. He is the source of the factor of production on which industrial success depends; he must realize this and exert his power, not on behalf of the planning system but on behalf of the entire human personality.

The first, and very practical, step is for educational institutions to ensure control of their own budgets. For many years this control has been undergoing steady erosion. Funds are accepted from the federal government and, in lesser measure, directly from industrial firms, for research, for teaching and for scholarships for specified purposes or areas. The funds reflect the areas of industrial need. In effect, it means that the planning system, acting on its own behalf or through the agency of the federal government, has bypassed the university administration to adapt education to its requirements. The nineteenth-century entrepreneur who, from his position on the university board, intervened to suppress faculty heresy and insist on proper respect for the basic tenets of Christianity and acquisitive capitalism, exercised only the most trivial influence as compared with the power thus deployed. It is a measure of its subtlety, and of its absence in the conventional college president, that the latter, declaiming on his commitment to academic freedom, is often unaware of how much of it he has himself surrendered.

If individual university disciplines are directly subsidized by the state or the business enterprise and continue to have and expand contractual relationships with these sources of funds, the result is nearly certain. Not only will the subjects so favored have a distorted growth in response to the needs of the system but those involved will tend to identify themselves increasingly with the goals of the contracting agencies and enterprises. They will not be immune to the tendencies here analyzed; they will come more or less fully into the orbit of the planning system. The university will become a shell with which they have only a residential association. If, however, universities can regain and retain power in the distribution of their resources, not only is there a chance that these will be allocated in accordance with humane and intellectual, as opposed to industrial, need, but, moreover, the identification of the constituent members will be with the corporate entity of the university and with its goals. Both the possibility of this, and its importance, the present analysis sufficiently shows.

3

In the distribution of educational resources it ought to be the rule that the student preparing for a career in personnel management, television advertising or computer programming as a servant of the planning system would find the requisite educational facilities and have access to the needed financial support. Concern for a remunerative career will ensure an adequate number of applicants. But the individual whose concern is with poetry or painting and but slightly with his financial prospects would have equal opportunity, including equal chance for a scholarship. Similarly with provision for research and scholarly effort. The price that the planning system must pay for the education of *its* people and the conduct of *its* research is the support of general enlightenment.

To support and encourage those concerned with aesthetic and intellectual experience is to support the requisite scrutiny of the planning system and to sustain the requisite pluralism. The cultivation of these attitudes and interests is by no means a hopeless or even difficult task. The young have a reassuring tendency to take a fresh view of life. Education that accords with the needs of the planning system does not have a natural aspect of interest, plausibility or novelty. Much of it is dull. The learning that enables an individual to participate effectively in the development of the monogramming toaster described heretofore does not have an intrinsic air of social urgency. Nor does preparation for the manufacture of automobiles in a world gorged with vehicles, or of a more potently, precisely and diversely destructive missile in a world which has already arranged extensively for its own incineration. Against this, education that serves purely intellectual and aesthetic interests and encourages the resulting detachment from the goals of the planning system is by no means unattractive.

Commitment to these alternative goals, and the associated questioning and pluralism, will also characterize the larger intellectual and artistic community. But the commitment can be directly cultivated only by the proper educational policy. This is a matter about which no serious educator can be indifferent, for to be indifferent is to give passive support to a preclusive role for the goals of the planning system. Though these serve that system well, they do so by diminishing the aesthetic and intellectual dimensions of life. To this no one who takes himself seriously as a teacher or as an intellectual can consent. And the planning system also constructs images of public and foreign policy which, though they serve admirably the needs of the planning system, could, if unchallenged, be mortal.

4

These changes, important though they are, will not come easily to American education. For one thing, next only to businessmen, educators have acquired the habit of lecturing each other on their social responsibilities and, as a necessary counterpart, since reaction to this flood of adjuration would be impossible, of ignoring it. The first inclination of most educators will be to dismiss these pages as another hortatory exercise.

Additionally, American colleges and universities were long fed on the crumbs from the rich man's plate or accorded public funds only after those for genuinely important matters such as roads, the courts, public hygiene, jails and insane asylums were provided. They were frequently watched for heresy by the entrepreneur or his appointed agents. Many maintained their independence less by courage than guile, although one must not minimize the astonishing intransigence of those whose vanity lies not in wealth or power but in the right to think. All college and university administrations and many professors developed habits of extreme obsequiousness where money was concerned. Many scholars persuaded themselves, in one way or another, that they had no political or public responsibilities of any kind. Some came to believe that, as scholars, they were required to eschew all public responsibility. Politics was for the intellectually inferior or depraved.

Educators have yet to realize how deeply the planning system is dependent upon them. That public and private funds are supplied in comparative abundance as a result of this dependence still evokes surprise. After living so long on charity, the habits of obsequiousness continue. That the purposes of the university should be strongly asserted, even where money is at stake, still seems a trifle irresponsible.

Such attitudes of mind are both out of date and dangerous. Colleges and universities can serve the needs of the techno-structure and reinforce the goals of the planning system. They can train the people and cultivate the attitudes which ensure technological advance, allow of effective planning and ensure acquiescence in the management of consumer and public demand. And they can affirm the policy images, including those on foreign policy, that the latter requires. This is the line of least resistance; it will be the consequence of a purely passive response by educators to the development of the planning system. And it will be the consequence of the orthodox view by the educator of his role. Or colleges and universities can strongly assert the values and goals of educated men—those who serve not the production of goods and associated planning but the intellectual and artistic development of man. It is hard to believe there is a real choice.

The educational and scientific estate has the power to exercise its option. It holds the critical cards. For in committing itself to technology, planning and organization, the planning system has made itself deeply dependent on the manpower which these require. The banker, in the days when capital was decisive, was not unaware of his bargaining power. The educator should not be more innocent today.

The growth and influence of college and university communities are in response to the needs of the planning system. But this does not necessarily create a primary obligation to its needs. Gratitude and debt do not exist as between social institutions. The only reality is the right social purpose.

5

There can be little doubt that higher education, which has been most extensively and expensively accommodated to the needs of the planning system, is the point where effort must be concentrated. Secondary and primary education have been less accommodated and lend themselves less to accommodation to the needs of the planning system and to its beliefs. Adolescents, accordingly, emerge in comparatively malleable condition. Here too there is benefit and safety in recognizing how our social belief, and what is taught or assumed, tend to reflect the needs of the planning system. But, *prima facie* at least, no dangers or correctives seem urgent. As compared with the pressures of the earlier industrialism, there can only be satisfaction at the influence which the planning system exerts for improved primary and secondary education.

The planning system has little direct power over channels of written communication. Much of this already reflects approved belief. But this congeniality is the result of indoctrination, persuasion or absence of persuasively argued alternatives rather than of repression. The dissenter to the needed beliefs of the planning system has little problem or risk in expressing his dissent. If nothing else, the fact that most instruments of literary communication—newspapers, magazines, book publishers—must be manned by intellectuals ensures that the goals of the intellectuals will be respected. This also accounts, one imagines, for a good part of the leverage exercised by intellectuals on behalf of more liberal expression in the Soviet Union and the Eastern European states.

Those who complain that they have been censored in the United States usually turn out, on examination, to have had nothing much to say.

In one area the planning system is uniquely powerful, although less in the propagation of ideas than in general mental conditioning. This is radio and especially television broadcasting. As we have seen, these are essential for effective management of demand and thus for industrial planning. The process by which this management is accomplished, the iterated and reiterated emphasis on the real and assumed virtues of goods, is powerful propaganda for the values and goals of the system. It reaches to all cultural levels. In the United States there is no satisfactory noncommercial alternative.

It would be good if there were. The desideratum is not educational radio and television but radio and television offering a wide range of enjoyment which is not committed by its nature to the service of the planning system. Halting steps are now being taken in this direction in the United States. They are in response to a need, the solid foundations of which will now be clear.

XXXIV

The Political Lead

ONLY THE INNOCENT REFORMER and the obtuse conservative imagine the state to be an instrument of change apart from the interests and aspirations of those who comprise it. The interests or needs of the planning system are advanced with subtlety and power. Since they are made to seem coordinate with the purposes of society, government action serving the needs of the planning system has a strong aspect of social purpose. And, as we have seen, the line between the planning system and the state becomes increasingly artificial and indistinct. The technostructure of the large corporation tends to become an extension of those parts of the federal bureaucracy—notably the armed services, NASA, the Nuclear Regulatory Commission and the other agencies concerned with technological development—on which it most depends. It identifies itself with the purposes of the agency and adapts these to its needs.

The last chapters have told something of what we must do if we are to have a safer and more durable as well as a more eclectic, agreeable and intellectually and aesthetically progressive society. Some of the needs, notably a safer basis for underwriting technology and an understanding between industrial societies on this point (between the United States and the Soviet Union in particular), are obviously important for the survival of the planning system as well as of all other organizations requiring the continued use of human beings. Other steps—the improvement of public services that are not sponsored by the planning system, the assertion of the aesthetic dimension of life, widened choice as between income and leisure, the emancipation of education—require that the monopoly of the planning system on social purpose be broken. This will not, one imagines, be welcomed by all participants in that system. They will see, correctly, that it is designed to reduce their role and that of the planning system in life. But it is not inconsistent with the continued existence of that system. As the next chapter suggests, that will be decided by other circumstances.

Still, none of these changes can be brought about save by some agency that is powerfully determined to make them. What is this agency?

2

The needed changes, including those in the images by which military and foreign policy are shaped, all involve the sensibilities and concerns of the mind. Their natural, although by no means exclusive, interest therefore is to those who are called intellectuals. The largest number of intellectuals with an occupational identification are those in the educational and scientific estate. It is to the educational and scientific estate, accordingly, that we must turn for the requisite political initiative. The initiative cannot come from the planning system, although support can be recruited from individuals therein. Nor will it come from the trade unions. Apart from their declining power, they are under no particular compulsion to question the goals of the planning system or the tendency to make all social purpose identical with those goals.

In a study of this sort, one must ration carefully one's generalizations concerning the fate of man. No currency is so quickly devalued. Those one would least trust to decide man's fate are invariably the first to pronounce upon it. Yet it is safe to say that the future of what is called modern society depends on how willingly, rationally and effectively the intellectual community in general, and the educational and scientific estate in particular, assume responsibilities for political action and leadership.

For this they have numerous advantages. There is a tradition, limited but significant, of their political involvement in the United States as well as elsewhere. The intellectual, as he is loosely described, is a commonplace figure in American politics. The type-cast professional politician with his florid speech, unvalidated self-confidence, ineffable affability, skill at evading issues and undemanding mind is highly regarded by journalists and novelists to whom he gives a rewarding sense of their own superiority. Both regularly give credence to the professional's estimate of the ineptitude of the intellectual in politics. Withal, it is the intellectual, or at least the man who is intelligently committed to social purpose, who survives. At the moment when political pundits are according him the greatest praise for his acuity, the accomplished professional politician is regularly going down to well-merited defeat.

Unlike members of the technostructure, the educational and scientific estate is not handicapped in political action by being accustomed to function only as part of an organization. It gains power in a socially complex society from its capacity for social invention. And while its power must rest on its ability to attract the support of attached and unattached individuals, in the future its numbers will command respect. In several states—Michigan, Wisconsin, Minnesota, California—the educational and scientific estate has long had substantial power in the state and local organization of the Democratic Party. And the university and college community has been expressing itself with special insistence on issues of foreign policy. Although bureaucratic and military attitudes have not been perceptibly affected, political leadership has not been indifferent. As noted, one of the indices of the growing power of the educational and scientific estate has been the reaction which such intervention on foreign policy has provoked. Like the middle class a century ago and the unions a generation back, it has been regularly advised that it should eschew such interference and confine itself rigorously to its proper tasks. It is perhaps sensed that numerous of our present images of foreign policy and national security are vulnerable to competent scrutiny.

Finally, since World War II, scientists have emerged as an independent force, especially where science impinges on foreign policy. General public and political awareness of the dangers of nuclear conflict, and desirability of détente with the Soviet Union and the technical possibilities for disarmament owes a great deal to the scientific community. It owes very little to the military, diplomatic and industrial community.

3

The educational and scientific estate, with its allies in the larger intellectual community, has formidable difficulties to overcome. Like any new political force it lacks self-confidence. This includes a lack of confidence in its own objectives. There is wide skepticism in the educational and scientific estate about the images that underlie the arms race. The ethos of the planning system—its measurement of success by its capacity to increase production in response to wants of its own creation—evokes skepticism. There is considerable agreement in the educational and scientific estate on the need to assert the other dimensions of life and on the use of social authority on their behalf. It would not be difficult to arouse support for wider options in regard to work and leisure on an educational system more strongly oriented to aesthetic and intellectual values, as distinct from the vocational needs of the planning system. But not all will believe that there is any chance of persuading the larger national community of their importance or even that the educational and scientific estate has any responsibility in the matter. It still has a strong tendency to surrender to the goals of the planning system before the battle is joined.

There are also dangers in the lead that is assumed, more or less as a right, by economists in these matters. Not all economists accept the goals of the planning system; speculation on the origins and sanctity of conventional belief is professionally encouraged in principle, so long, at least, as it does not alter conclusions. And that beliefs are extensively accommodated to the needs of the planning system is accepted by many economists. Economists, younger ones in particular, have not been resistant to the present argument.

But the economic stereotypes—the production models that lend themselves to assembly-line instruction—insist on the approved sequence. And, for the protection of intellectual investment and convenience, they will continue to do so. Their defenders will hold that wants are original with the individual; that the success of the society is measured by the amount that it supplies to satisfy these wants; that this test, so convenient for the planning system, is the only sensible one to apply. These beliefs are inherent in man's nature and the result of no social conditioning of any kind. Other goals being unimportant and other beliefs being frivolous, they hardly call for political effort.

In past years it often appeared to those outside the discipline that the economists were in heavy conflict with the business world. This especially concerned the regulation of aggregate demand. The economists proposed more spending by the state for a wide variety of things; they advocated tax reduction and deliberate deficits. Businessmen recoiled in alarm. To the rest of the educational and scientific estate the economists seemed thus to be the defenders of the broader social purposes of employment and expansion against the smaller, more parochial objectives of their business critics. This is an illusion. The economists were partly at odds with the entrepreneurs who, unlike the technostructure, were not major beneficiaries of these policies. The general capacity of economists for social discussion and innovation had put them somewhat in advance of the technostructure in the policies they urged. Thus they seemed disturbing. And they differed on methods and on the vigor with which the goals of full employment and growth should be pursued. But these differences, and the associated polemics, did not involve goals as such. There has been full agreement between economists and the planning system on the preclusive importance of high and expanding production and, therewith, high employment. To the extent that the rest of the educational and scientific estate surrendered responsibility for social purposes to the economists, they surrendered to the goals of the planning system.

Were economic goals of central importance, economists, always assuming competence, would be a safe guide to social action. As economic goals have diminished in relative importance, they have become, progressively, a less safe guide. Allowing for numerous exceptions, they are prone to identify economic goals with all of life. They are not, accordingly, the best proponents of the public, aesthetic and intellectual priorities on which the quality and safety of life increasingly depend. They are, in their establishment manifestation, the implicit allies of the planning system.[1]

4

Both the educational and scientific estate and the intellectual community are handicapped by the belief, diminishing but still extensive, that their role is professionally passive—that it is to feel and think but not to act. Righteousness, as well as convenience, defends this passivity. Politics is not the business of the intellectual or the artist. Nor of the educator nor of the scientist. Theirs is the purer domain of the spirit and the mind. This can only be sullied by concern for practical affairs. In the last milli-second before the ultimate nuclear fu-

[1] Again I refer the reader to the Addendum following the next chapter.

sion, a scientist will be heard to observe that the issue of nuclear control and military security is really one for politicians and their military and diplomatic advisers. And as the last horizon is lost behind the smoke, gas, neon lights and detritus of the industrial civilization, men of self-confessed artistic sensitivity will be heard to observe that, unfortunately, none of this is the business of the true artist. In fact, no intellectual, no artist, no educator, no scientist can allow himself the convenience of doubting his responsibility. For the goals that are now important there are no other saviors. In a scientifically exacting world scientists must assume responsibility for the consequences of science and technology. For custody of the aesthetic dimension of life there is no substitute for the artist. The individual member of the educational and scientific estate may wish to avoid responsibility; but he cannot justify it by the claim of higher commitment.

In the earlier stages of economic development, when the academic community was a small, weak and partially decorative appendage of the industrial society, it was natural that many should see their best role as being seen and not heard. Commanding power lay with the capitalist and entrepreneur. It made sense not to affront him. If a righteous commitment to science or art could be adduced as the justification for this discretion, it was ideal—the equivalent of a priestly indulgence for cowardice. Those who would suffer from a more active role by the educational and scientific estate, as it grows in numbers and power, will naturally hope that it will continue to find such reasons for abstaining from political concern. And they will applaud as saintly persons those who do.

The educational and scientific estate, like the intellectual community in general, has tended also to be diverted by the surrogates for political action. Writing, lecturing and even determined conversation bulk large in this regard. They are the tools of the intellectual's trade; since they are what he possesses, he must, like an air force general arguing during the Vietnam war the value of bombers for stopping men from walking through a jungle, assume that they are of value. He ends either by persuading those who are already persuaded; or he asserts personality and invents or sharpens disagreement on the small, neat points that are so cherished in academic debate and are so damaging to political effectiveness.

Here, perhaps, is the most important point of all. Effective political action requires cohesive effort. This means there must be willingness to subordinate individual to larger group goals for the purposes of the given political result. There is no escape from this. To combine on behalf of the good rather than to divide (and lose) in pursuit of the perfect is not intellectually disreputable or demeaning. It is simply good sense.

With political cohesiveness and discipline must also go persuasion—which, oddly enough, also comes hard to the educational and scientific estate. And here, also, the costs of failure have been very great. Condescension, impatience and the suffering ungladly of seeming political obtuseness have all been damaging. Much worse has been the failure of novitiate members of the educational and scientific estate, students in particular, to see that political persuasion is a slow process and one that is not served by jumping rapidly from one issue to another—from civil rights to the environment, to the military-industrial complex, to the liberation of women—but requires continued, patient and persistent effort on all error. And, most of all, persuasion has been damaged by those who have made violence a catharsis for impatience. The popular preference for peaceful process may be regretted but it cannot be denied.

There is no alternative to political effort. All of the matters here urged—redirection of the weapons competition, social control of the environment, a wider range of choice by the individual, emancipation of education—require some form of political action. Political action requires that legislators be persuaded or replaced by those who do not need persuasion. There is no alternative to having effective friends of these ideas occupy the relevant elective and appointive public offices and to having them held firmly to their duty by a watchful and determined constituency.

5

But in other respects the prospect for such political action is better. The educational and scientific estate and the associated intellectual community have—as repeatedly noted—grown to formidable proportions. And this growth has taken place, as also noted, at a time when there is a strong tendency to question established goals. In both foreign and domestic economic policy there is suspicion of what is believed, not inaccurately, to be the unexamined or automatic position of what has come to be called the Establishment. Such attitudes await the political lead here urged.

This questioning of goals comes because a long current of liberal reform has now run its course. In the past liberals have been economic liberals; reform has meant economic reform. The goals of this reform have been reproduced in hundreds of platforms, speeches and manifestoes. Production must rise; income must rise; distribution of income must improve; unemployment must fall. This, for decades, has been the platform of the liberal reformer; not even the Ten Commandments are so familiar, and certainly they are far from being as well realized. Except as the reformer may (or should) stress more equitable distribution of income, the old economic goals are identical with those of the planning system. Except as he concerns himself specifically with the poor, the erstwhile reformer has become the political voice of the planning system. It is an effortless role; no loud controversy is involved, there are no unseemly quarrels, no one need be persuaded. It is merely necessary to stand modestly at attention and take a bow as the Gross National Product goes up again. Reformers who so spend their time are, in effect, unemployed. And it cannot be doubted that many realize that this is their case.

Progress on the present agenda will be much less measurable than that which associates all progress with percentage increases in Gross National Product or lowered percentage levels of unemployment. It is because the goals of the planning system are so narrow that they lend themselves to precise statistical assessment. But life is meant to be complex. There will be dispute over the definition of success. And there will be considerable controversy over both the legitimacy of the alternative goals and the means of achieving them—over aesthetically motivated control of environment, for example. There will be opposition from both entrenched interest and inert intellect. And there will be need to persuade. In short, there are tasks here, once more, that are worthy of a modern reformer's mettle.

XXXV

The Future of the Planning System

IN THE LATTER PART of the last century and the early decades of this, no subject was more discussed than the future of capitalism. Economists, men of unspecific wisdom, Chautauqua lecture, editorial writers, knowledgeable ecclesiastics and socialists contributed their personal revelations. It was taken largely for granted that the economic system was in a state of development and, in time, would transform itself into something better, it was hoped, but certainly different. Socialists drew strength from the belief that theirs was the plausible next stage in a natural process of change.

The future of the planning system, by contrast, is not discussed.[1] The prospect for agriculture is subject to debate—it is assumed to be in the course of change. So are the chances for survival for the small entrepreneur or the private medical practitioner. But General Motors, General Electric and U.S. Steel are an ultimate achievement. One does not wonder where one is going if one is already there.

Yet to suppose that the planning system is a terminal phenomenon is, *per se,* implausible. It is itself the product, in the last eighty years, of a vast and autonomous transformation. During this time the scale of the individual corporation has grown enormously. The entrepreneurial corporation has declined. The technostructure has developed, removed itself from control by the stockholders and acquired its own internal sources of capital. There has been a large change in its relations with the workers and a yet larger one in its relations with the state. It would be strange were such a manifestation of social dynamics to be now at an end. So to suggest is to deny one of the philosophical tenets of the system itself, one that is solemnly articulated on all occasions of business rit-

[1] I exclude from consideration a certain amount of general talk on the left about the overthrow of the "System." It is not to a large audience; the participants cannot have very high expectations and are rarely specific on what then transpires.

ual—conventions, stockholders' meetings, board meetings, executive committee meetings, management development conferences, budget conferences, product review meetings, senior officer retreats and dealer relations workshops. It is that change is the law of economic life.

The future of the planning system is not discussed partly because of the power it exercises over belief. It has succeeded, tacitly, in excluding the notion that it is a transitory, which would be to say that it is a somehow imperfect, phenomenon. More important, perhaps, to consider the future would be to fix attention on where it has already arrived. Among the least enchanting words in the business lexicon are planning, government control, state underwriting and socialism. To consider the likelihood of these in the future would be to bring home the appalling extent to which they are already a fact. And it would not be ignored that these grievous things have arrived, at a minimum with the acquiescence and at a maximum on the demand of the system itself.

2

Such reflection on the future would also emphasize the convergent tendencies of industrial societies, however different their popular or ideological billing; the convergence being to a roughly similar design for organization and planning. A word in review may be worthwhile. Convergence begins with modern large-scale production, with heavy requirements of capital, sophisticated technology and, as a prime consequence, elaborate organization. These require control of prices and, so far as possible, of what is bought at those prices. This is to say that planning must replace the market. In the Soviet-type economies the control of prices is a function of the state. The management of demand (eased by the knowledge that their people will mostly want what Americans and Western Europeans already have) is partly by according preference to the alert and early-rising who are first to the store; partly, as in the case of houseroom, by direct allocation to the recipient; and partly, as in the case of automobiles, by making patience (as well as political position or need) a test of eligibility. With us this management is accomplished less formally by the corporations, their advertising agencies, salesmen, dealers and retailers. But these, obviously, are differences in method rather than purpose. Large-scale industrialism requires, in both cases, that the market and consumer sovereignty be extensively superseded.

Large-scale organization also requires autonomy. The intrusion of an external and uninformed will is damaging. In the non-Soviet systems this means excluding the nonparticipating capitalist from effective power. But the same imperative operates in the socialist economy. There the business firm seeks to minimize or exclude control by the official bureaucracy. To gain autonomy for the enterprise is what, in substantial measure, the modern Communist theoretician calls reform. Nothing in our time is more interesting than that the erstwhile capitalist corporation and the erstwhile Communist firm should, under the imperatives of organization, come together as oligarchies of their own members. Ideology is not the relevant force. Large and complex organizations can use diverse knowledge and talent and thus function effectively only if under their own authority. This, it must be stressed once more, is not autonomy that subordinates a firm to the market. It is autonomy that allows the firm authority over its planning.

The planning system has no inherent capacity for regulating total demand—for ensuring a supply of purchasing power sufficient to acquire what it produces. So it relies on the state for this. At full employment there is no mechanism for holding prices and wages stable. This stabilization too is, or will one day become, an accepted function of the state. The Soviet-type systems also make a careful calculation of the income that is being provided in relation to the value of the goods available for purchase. Stabilization of wages and prices in general is, of course, a natural consequence of fixing individual prices and wage rates.

Finally, the planning system must rely on the state for trained and educated manpower, now the decisive factor of production. So it is also under socialist industrialism. The flight of the first Sputnik precipitated a great and fashionable concern in the United States over the state of scientific and technical education. Many not previously disposed to find virtue in socialism were heard to argue that the Soviet system, with its higher priority for state functions, among which education is prominent, had a natural advantage in this regard.

Thus convergence between the two ostensibly different planning systems occurs at all fundamental points. This is an exceedingly fortunate thing. In time, and perhaps in less time than may be imagined, it will dispose of the notion of inevitable conflict based on irreconcilable difference. This will not be soon agreed. Marx did not foresee the convergence, and he is accorded, with suitable interpretation, the remarkable, even supernatural, power of foreseeing all. Those on the other side who speak of the unbridgeable gulf that divides the free world from the Communist world and free enterprise from Communism are protected by an equally ecclesiastical faith that whatever the evolution of free enterprise may be, it cannot conceivably come to resemble socialism. But these positions can survive the evidence only for a time. Only the most committed ideologist or the most fervent propagandist can stand firm against the feeling that an increasing number of people regard him as obsolete. Vanity is a great force for intellectual modernization.

To recognize that planning systems are convergent in their development will, one imagines, help toward agreement on the common dangers in the weapons competition, on ending it or shifting it to more benign areas. Perhaps nothing casts more light on the future of the planning system than this, for it implies, in contrast with the present images, that, along with the market system and associated public institutions, it could have a future.

3

Given the deep dependence of the planning system on the state and the nature of its motivational relationship to the state, i.e., its identification with public goals and the adaptation of these to its needs, the planning system will not long be regarded as something apart from government. Rather it will increasingly be seen as part of a much larger complex which embraces both the planning system and the state. Private enterprise was anciently so characterized because it was subordinate to the market and those in command derived their power from ownership of private property. The modern corporation is no longer subordinate to the market; those who run it no longer depend on property ownership for their authority. They must have autonomy within a framework of goals. But this allows them to work easily in association with the bureaucracy and, indeed, to perform for the bureaucracy tasks that it cannot do, or cannot do as well, for itself. In consequence, as we have seen, for tasks of technical sophistication there is a close fusion of the planning system with the state. Members of the technostructure work closely with their public counterparts not only in the development and manufacture of products but in advising them of their needs. Were it not so celebrated in ideology, it would long since have been agreed that the line that now divides public from so-called private organization in military procurement, space exploration and atomic energy is so indistinct as to be nearly imperceptible.[2] Men move easily across the line. On retirement, admirals and generals, as well as high civil servants, go more or less automatically to the more closely associated industries. One highly experienced observer has called these firms the "semi-nationalized" branch of the economy.[3] It has been noted that "the Market mechanism [is replaced by] . . . the administrative mechanism. For the profit share of private entrepreneurs, it substitutes the fixed fee, a payment in lieu of profits forgone. And for the independent private business unit, it substitutes the integrated hierarchical structure of an organization composed of an agency . . . and its contractors."[4] A former Yale law professor once summarized the interdependence of corporation and state in even more specific terms: "In the seven years from 1961 through 1967 Lockheed was awarded nearly $11 billion in defense contracts, equal to 88 percent of its total sales. General Dynamics has $9 billion in contracts making up two thirds of its gross receipts. For McDonnell Douglas ($8 billion from 1961 to 1967, 75 percent of its sales), Boeing ($7 billion and over half its revenue), Grumman (a major Navy supplier, with $2.5 billion, or 67 percent), and Ling-Temco-Vought (almost $8 billion, or 70 percent of its total sales), the story is essentially the same. For these companies, and for many others in fields like communications and electrical equipment, chemicals (all of Thiokol's sales are to the government), and ship

---

[2]Perhaps, indeed, it is becoming agreed. Recurrently, spokesmen for the great weapons firms protest their private character. This, I am persuaded, no longer invites belief from the intellectually viable. Those who make the assertion may quite possibly see it as an exercise in liturgy, not persuasion.

[3]Murray L. Weidenbaum, "The Defense-Space Complex: Impact on Whom?" *Challenge: The Magazine of Economic Affairs*, Vol. 13, No. 4 (April 1965), p. 46. Professor Weidenbaum was formerly employed by Boeing and later, in the Nixon Administration, was Assistant Secretary of the Treasury for economic policy.

[4]From a study by Richard Tybout, *Government Contracting in Atomic Energy* (Ann Arbor: University of Michigan Press, 1956), p. 175. Professor Tybout is referring especially to cost-plus-fixed-fee contracts.

construction, the Federal defense-space agencies are not just customers—they are the lifeline and guarantor of continued corporate existence."[5]

The foregoing refers to firms which sell most or all of their output to the government. But firms which have a smaller proportion of sales to the government are more dependent on it for the regulation of aggregate demand and equally for the underwriting of especially expensive or risky technology and the supply of trained and educated manpower.

So comprehensive a relationship cannot be denied or ignored indefinitely. Increasingly it will be recognized that the mature corporation, as it develops, becomes part of the larger administrative complex associated with the state. In time the line between the two will disappear. Men will look back in amusement at the pretense that once led less inspired executives and their public relations men to refer to General Dynamics, Lockheed and A. T. & T. as *private* business.

Though this recognition will not be universally welcomed, it will be healthy. There is always a presumption in social matters in favor of reality as opposed to myth. The autonomy of the technostructure is, to repeat yet again, a functional necessity of the planning system. But the goals this autonomy serves allow some range of choice. If the mature corporation is recognized to be part of the penumbra of the state, it will be pressed more strongly to the service of social goals. It cannot plead its inherently private character or its subordination to the market as cover for the pursuit of different goals of particular interest to itself. The public agency has an unquestioned tendency to pursue goals that reflect its own interest and convenience and to adapt social objectives thereto. But it cannot plead this as a superior right. There may well be danger in this association of public and economic power. But it is less if it is recognized.

Other changes can be imagined. As the public character of the mature corporation comes to be recognized, attention will focus on the position of the stockholder in this corporation. This is anomalous. He (or she) is a passive and functionless figure, remarkable only in his capacity to share, without effort or even without appreciable risk, in the gains from the growth by which the technostructure measures its success. No grant of feudal privilege has ever equaled, for effortless re-

[5]Richard J. Barber, *The American Corporation* (New York: E. P. Dutton, 1970), pp. 191–192.

turn, that of the grandparent who bought and endowed his descendants with a thousand shares of General Motors, General Electric or I.B.M. The beneficiaries of this foresight have become rich by no exercise of effort or intelligence beyond the decision to do nothing, embracing as it did the decision not to sell. But these matters need not be pursued here. Questions of equity and social justice as between the fortuitously rich have their own special expertise.

4

Most of the individual developments which are leading, if the harshest term may be employed, to the socialization of the mature corporation will be conceded even by men of the most conservative disposition. The control by the mature corporation over its prices, its influence on consumer behavior, the euthanasia of stockholder power, the regulation by the state of aggregate demand, the effort to stabilize prices and wages, the role of publicly supported research and development, the role of military, space and related procurement, the influence of the firm on these government activities and the modern role of education are, more or less, accepted facts of life.

What is avoided is reflection on the consequences of putting them all together, of seeing them as a system. But it cannot be supposed that the principal beams and buttresses of the economic system have all been changed and that the structure remains as before. If the parts have change, so then has the whole. If this associates the mature corporation inextricably with the state, the fact cannot be exorcised by assertion, however stubborn, of an economic and political theory that holds that they are separate.

It will be urged, of course, that the planning system is not the whole economy. Apart from the world of General Motors, Exxon, Ford, General Electric, U.S. Steel, Chrysler, Texaco, Gulf, Western Electric and Du Pont is that of the independent retailer, the farmer, the shoe repairman, the bookmaker, narcotics peddler, pizza merchant and that of the car and dog laundries. Here prices are not controlled. Here the consumer is sovereign. Here pecuniary motivation is unimpaired. Here technology is simple and there is no research or development to make it otherwise. Here there are no government contracts; independence from the state is a reality. None of these entrepreneurs patrol the precincts of the Massachusetts Institute of Technology in search of talent. The existence of all this I concede. And this part of the economic system is not insignificant. It is not, however, the part of the economy with which this book has been concerned.[6] It has been concerned with the world of the large corporation. This too is important, and it is more deeply characteristic of the modern industrial scene than the dog laundry or the small manufacturer with a large idea. One should always cherish one's critics and protect them where possible from error. The tendency of the mature corporation in the planning system to become part of the administrative complex of the state ought not to be refuted by appeal to contrary tendencies outside that system.

Some who dislike the notion that the planning system merges into the state in its development will be tempted to assault not the tendency but those who adumbrate it. This, it must be urged, is not in keeping with contemporary ethics and manners. Once the bearers of bad tidings were hanged, disemboweled or made subject to some other equally sanguinary mistreatment. Now such reaction is regarded as lacking in delicacy. A doctor can inform even the most petulant client that he has terminal cancer without fear of adverse physical consequences. The aide who must advise a politician that a new poll shows him to be held in all but universal distaste need exercise only decent tact. Those who find unappealing the present intelligence are urged to exercise similar restraint.

They should also be aware of the causes. It is part of the vanity of modern man that he can decide the character of his economic system. His area of decision is, in fact, exceedingly small. He could, conceivably, decide whether or not he wishes to have a high level of industrialization. Thereafter the imperatives of organization, technology and planning operate similarly and, we have seen, to a broadly similar result, on all societies. Given the decision to have modern industry, much of what happens is inevitable and the same.

5

The two questions most asked about an economic system are whether it serves man's physical needs and whether it is con-

[6]It is, however, the one to which, in its relation to the planning system, I return in *Economics and the Public Purpose* (Boston: Houghton Mifflin, 1973).

sistent with his liberty. There is little doubt as to the ability of the planning system to serve man's needs. As we have seen, it is able to manage these needs only because it serves them abundantly. It requires a mechanism for making men want what it provides. But this mechanism would not work—wants would not be subject to manipulation—had not these wants been dulled by sufficiency.[7]

The prospects for liberty involve far more interesting questions. It has always been imagined, especially by conservatives, that to associate all, or a large part, of economic activity with the state is to endanger freedom. The individual and his preferences, in one way or another, will be sacrificed to the needs and conveniences of the apparatus created ostensibly to serve him. As the planning system evolves into a penumbra of the state, the question of its relation to liberty thus arises in urgent form. In recent years, in the Soviet-type economies, there has been an ill-concealed conflict between the state and the intellectuals. In essence, this has been a conflict between those for whom the needs of the government, including above all its needs as economic planner and producer of goods, are pre-eminent and those who assert the high but inconvenient claims of uninhibited intellectual and artistic expression. Is this a warning?

The instinct which warns of dangers in this association of economic and public power is sound. It comes close to being the subject of this book. But conservatives have looked in the wrong direction for the danger. They have feared that the state might reach out and destroy the vigorous, money-making entrepreneur. They have not noticed that, all the while, the successors to the entrepreneur were uniting themselves ever more closely with the state and rejoicing in the result. They were also, and with enthusiasm, accepting abridgment of their freedom. Part of this is implicit in the subordination of individual personality to the needs of organization. Some of it is in the exact pattern of the classical business expectation. The president of McDonnell Douglas is no more likely in public to speak critically, or even candidly, of the Air Force than is the head of a Soviet *combinat* of the ministry to which he reports. No modern head of the Ford Motor Company will ever react with the same pristine vigor to the

---

[7] As indicated in Chapter XXI (and as I have urged at length on other occasions), it excludes the unqualified and the unfortunate from its beneficence.

presumed foolishness of Washington as did its founder. No head of Montgomery Ward will ever again breathe defiance of a President of the United States as did Sewell Avery, who was once carried by the police from the company offices for resisting a demand that he do business with a union. Manners may be involved. But it would also now be said that "too much is at stake."

The problem, however, is not the freedom of the businessman. Business orators have spoken much about freedom in the past. But it can be laid down as a rule that those who speak most of liberty are least inclined to use it. The high executive who speaks fulsomely of personal freedom carefully submits his speeches on the subject for review by the experts in public imagery for elimination of controversial words, phrases and ideas, as befits a good organization man. The general who tells his troops and the world that they are in the forefront of the fight for freedom is a man who has always submitted happily to army discipline. The pillar of the foreign policy establishment who adverts most feelingly to the values of the free world is the man who extravagantly admires the orthodoxy of his own views.

The danger to liberty lies in the subordination of belief to the needs of the planning system. In this the state and the planning system will be partners. This threat has already been assessed, as also the means for minimizing it.

6

If we continue to believe that the goals of the planning system—the expansion of output, the companion increase in consumption, technological advance, the public images that sustain it—are coordinate with life, then all of our lives will be in the service of these goals. What is consistent with these ends we shall have or be allowed; all else will be off limits. Our wants will be managed in accordance with the needs of the planning system; the policies of the state will be subject to similar influence; education will be adapted to industrial need; the disciplines required by the planning system will be the conventional morality of the community. All other goals will be made to seem precious, unimportant or antisocial. We will be bound to the ends of the system. The state will add its moral, and perhaps some of its legal, power to their enforcement. What will eventuate, on the whole, will be the benign servitude of the household retainer who is taught to love her mistress and see her interests as her own, and not the compelled servitude of the field hand. But it will not be freedom.

If, on the other hand, the planning system is only a part, and relatively a diminishing part, of life, there is much less occasion for concern. Aesthetic goals will have pride of place; those who serve them will not be subject to the goals of the technostructure; the planning system itself will be subordinate to the claims of these dimensions of life. Intellectual preparation will be for its own sake and not for better service to the planning system. Men will not be entrapped by the belief that apart from the goals of the planning system—apart from the production of goods and income by progressively more advanced technical methods—there is nothing important in life.

The foregoing being so, we may, over time, come to see the planning system in fitting light as an essentially technical arrangement for providing convenient goods and services in adequate volume. Those who rise through its bureaucracy will so see themselves. And the public consequences will be in keeping, for if economic goals are the only goals of the society, it is natural that the planning system should dominate the state and the state should serve its ends. If other goals are strongly asserted, the planning system will, one can hope, fall into its place as a detached and autonomous arm of the state but one responsive to the larger purposes of the society.

We have seen wherein the chance for salvation lies. The planning system, in contrast with its economic antecedents, is intellectually demanding. It beings into existence to serve its intellectual and scientific needs the community that, all should hope, will reject its monopoly of social purpose.

An Addendum on Economic Method and the Nature of Social Argument

> "It has generally held true that the accredited learned class and the seminaries of the higher learning have looked askance at all innovation."
>
> —Thorstein Veblen

IT IS NOT, in general, my instinct to avoid controversy or criticism. Those who seek to do so have, not infrequently, reconciled themselves to irrelevance. But it is probably unwise to invite criticism that assumes innocence when, in fact, one is writing after what may well have been excessively solemn deliberation. Economics, like other disciplines, has its canons by which behavior is judged. These, in general, call for careful specialization on particular issues; for having one person deal with one subject at a time; for according a very high priority to purely economic judgments; and, on the whole, for being suspicious of change. All of these canons have been violated in the preceding pages. Some professional wrath may be forestalled and some will certainly be understood if this is known to be highly deliberate and if the reasons for not worshipping at these accepted altars are adumbrated. Let me deal first with specialization.

Economists, on the whole, think well of what they do themselves and much less well of what their professional colleagues do. If a scholar probes deeply into a small section of the subject, he is fairly certain to mistrust, as superficial, the man who ranges more widely. The latter, in turn, will think the specialist lacking in vision or what is called reach. By knowing ever more about ever less, he will seem to risk becoming quite ignorant. Those who are mathematically inclined see others as in retreat from rigor. The others think those who manipulate symbols impractical. The statisticians believe those who prove points deductively to be dangerously intuitive. But, by their colleagues, those who are controlled by numbers are often thought unduly cautious or even dull. It is exceedingly fortunate for the psychic health of members of the profession that inadequacy is thought to lie so uniformly with others. The situation in the other social sciences is said to be equally satisfactory.

This book has not, it will be agreed, been confined to narrow points. But I have singularly little quarrel with those who so restrict themselves. I have drawn on their work, quantitative and qualitative, at every stage; I could not have written without their prior efforts. So I have nothing but admiration and gratitude for the patient and skeptical men who get deeply into questions, and I am available to support their applications to the Ford Foundation, however minute the matter to be explored. I expect them to judge sternly the way their material has been used in this book.

But we must remind ourselves that specialization is a scientific convenience, not a scientific virtue. It allows, among other things, the use of a wider spectrum of talent. Fifty years ago, at the University of California, there were specialists not on economic theory, not on price theory, not on agricultural prices, not on fruit prices, but on prune prices and citrus prices. These were not great men but they did useful work and were highly respected by the prune growers and the cooperatives. They would have been less useful if exposed to more cosmic questions or even diversified to artichokes. Specialization also permits an indispensable division of scientific labor and allows for the development of subcultures of scholarship in which participants are known to each other, communicate readily, and from cooperation, competition, criticism and scholarly recrimination deepen their knowledge of their own subject matter. But, at least in the social sciences, specialization is also a source of error. The world, to its discredit, does not divide neatly along the lines that separate the specialists. These lines were drawn in the first instance by deans, department chairmen or academic committees. They were meant to provide guidance in appointing professors, establishing courses and supporting research. Excellent though the architects were, they cannot be credited with a uniquely valid view of the segments into which society naturally divides itself. And if they could, there would still be danger that the specialist, in concentrating on his specialty, would deny himself knowledge that could only be had from outside.

In economics, economic theory—the subject which deals with the way prices, output and incomes for individuals, firms and the economy at large are decided—is one area of

specialization. The corporation is another. Decision theory—
how decisions are reached in complex organizations—is yet
another and more modern field. For many years those who
specialize on the problems of the corporation have been
much concerned with the way control in the large firm has
been passing, without recourse, from stockholders to the hired
management. The latter, as sufficiently noted in this study, selects itself and its successors as an autonomous and self-perpetuating oligarchy. In the past reasons have been sought by
the specialists in their own area of concern—in the control of
proxy machinery by management, in failure to keep stockholders informed, in the practice, once much favored, of
holding annual meetings in obscure New Jersey hamlets
where none but the most intrepid stockholder would pene-
trate. Remedy has been sought (with no visible effect on the
way corporations are controlled) in these same areas, i.e.,
within the field of corporate practice. We have seen that a
highly plausible reason for the shift in control of the corporations is the declining importance of capital in relation to
trained manpower and the increasing complexity of decision-
making in the modern corporation. There is less power
gained from having supplied capital; there are fewer decisions
on which the stockholder can hope to intervene. Those who
make decisions have greatly increased bargaining power. But
questions concerning the supply of capital and labor belong
to the economic theorist, and the problems of decision-making belong to the specialist on decision theory. In general,
their knowledge has not been brought to bear on the changing constitution of the corporation.[1]

Thus to deal with the larger matrix of change is to complement and very possibly to illuminate the work of the specialist on his own specialty. Since it does not follow that the
work on smaller points is any less necessary, the conclusion
that emerges seems clear. In economics, and social sciences
generally, one may justly distinguish between competent and
incompetent work. As between kinds of work, judgment, save
as it may be necessary to support the self-esteem of the man
who is praising his own line, is less wise.

[1]To make error reciprocal, the economic theorists of the firm have
assumed (and most still do) that the men who ran the business received the profits. All specialists in corporation matters knew the managers to be recipients (in the main) of salaried income and to be
normally quite independent of those who own the enterprise and receive the profits. But their knowledge did not accrue to the teacher of
microeconomic theory; theirs was a different field.

2

According to the experience of all but the most accomplished jugglers, it is easier to keep one ball in the air than many. To deal simultaneously, or even in close sequence, with all of the interrelated changes which have shaped the planning system and the modern organized economy is more difficult than to deal with one change or a few. The problem of exposition is especially taxing. All who write on economic matters must decide how much of the burden of exposition to shoulder themselves and how much of the task they should leave to the reader. Justice requires, no doubt, that much be left to the reader. Writing is hard enough work without having to make it comprehensible, and scholarship endorses a division of labor between those who write and those who read.

I have, on occasion, found the problem of exposition more taxing than that of analysis. And doubtless the reader has found passages that he has considered worthy of his mettle. But it has not been my purpose to test it. There are few, if any, useful ideas in economics that cannot be expressed in clear English. Obscurity rarely if ever denotes complexity of subject matter; it never denotes superior scholarship. It usually signifies either inability to write understandable prose or—and more commonly—muddled or incomplete thought.

And though to deal with change comprehensively is a source of difficulty, it is also a great simplification. In real life change in one place does beget change in other places, and the latter changes react on the first and elsewhere. Accordingly, to deal with the complex of change is to deal with the world as it is. A change in one place alerts one to likely change elsewhere. In searching for causes, one has before him the companion changes that are the most likely causes.

Also, since one is dealing with things as they are, one can check conclusions for their consistency with what exists or seems to exist. The reader of these pages will have seen, I venture to think, how usefully this test can be employed. To see change comprehensively, or as much so as may be possible, is also to be prepared for what otherwise may seem odd. The unwashed and unlettered men who came out of the fens and down from the north to Runnymede in 1215 derived their power from their control of land. The Great Charter, accordingly, is mostly concerned with the just and unjust liabilities of the landed. The protection it was subsequently to accord to the liberties of the landless was foreseen, if at all, only by the philosophical, if any. To King John this intrusion of landed power upon divine right seemed arbitrary, impertinent and uncouth, and of highly questionable legitimacy. It greatly justified him in his intention not to honor his signature.

In the last century capital became more important than land. Power associated itself with this. To the older ruling classes the new capitalists again seemed obtrusive, uncivilized and of questionable legitimacy.

In recent times, through the agency of the union, substantial economic power accrued to labor. Political power once again went with it. Union exercise of political power seemed of highly questionable legitimacy. Labor leaders were widely advised to leave politics alone.

In yet more recent times, complex technology and highly developed organization have become important for economic success. One would expect power to pass to those who are skilled in guiding or serving organization. One would also expect the sources of such specialized manpower to win prestige and authority. One would also be prepared to learn that this new exercise of power appeared to many to be impertinent and obtrusive and of questionable legitimacy.

The legitimacy of the nonowning management of the modern corporation has been deeply questioned. The displacement of the owning stockholder has been viewed with alarm. So have the growing power and assertiveness of the universities which supply this manpower. Faculty members and students have played a significant, and in some cases strategic, role in civil rights legislation, educational policy and, most important, in foreign policy, where they have ended, one hopes decisively, a long habit of public acquiescence in whatever was officially proclaimed by military and civilian bureaucrats and their establishment acolytes to be the policy of the United States. Their political role is important in some states. By professional politicians with a comfortable identification with business and labor, and by the traditional archons of foreign policy, this academic intrusion has seemed impertinent and irregular and a highly illegitimate use of scholarly energy. All concerned have been strongly advised to confine themselves to the campus.

To view the new power of the managers or the more assertive role of the universities in isolation from other change is to see almost nothing of their significance. They are minor eddies in the pattern of life, the sort of thing that attracts attention for a season. But viewed in the whole context of change, as part of a new and further transfer of power to organization and to those who supply it with talent, it becomes a development of durable importance, as this book has duly urged.

3

The advantages of dealing comprehensively with change are thus considerable. Those of dealing with change that extends beyond economics are also great and, with passage of time, become more so. That is because, with improvement in popular well-being, economics becomes progressively more inadequate as a basis for social judgment and as a guide to public policy. This too calls for a brief comment.

If people are hungry, ill-clad, unsheltered or diseased, nothing is so important as to remedy their condition. Higher income is the basic remedy; their problem is thus an economic problem. It will be time to worry about leisure, contemplation, the appreciation of beauty and the other higher purposes of life when everyone has a decent meal. Even personal liberty is best defended and spiritual salvation best pursued on a full stomach. In a poor society economics is not all of life but, as a practical matter, it is most of it.

With high income, questions beyond the reach of economics obtrude. These require consideration of how much beauty should be sacrificed for increased output. Or how many civilized values in order that goods can be more effectively sold—for no experience suggests that sober and quiet truth is as valuable for this purpose as meretricious and raucous violence. Or how extensively should education be accommodated to the needs of production as opposed to the needs of enlightenment? Or how much discipline should be enforced on men to ensure greater output? Or how much military risk should be run to win new technology? Or how completely should the individual subordinate his personality to the organization which was created to supply his wants?

That these questions, or some of them, are important has long been conceded by economists; textbooks, teachers and economists in high office regularly warn that economic judgments are not the total judgment on life. This warning having been given, economics is then, routinely, made the final test of public policy. The rate of increase in income and output in National Income and Gross National Product, together with the level of employment, remain the all but exclusive measure of social achievement. This is the modern morality. Saint Peter is assumed to ask applicants only what they have done to increase the GNP.

There are good reasons for this insistence on the totality of economic goals. It arrests what otherwise would be a disconcerting obsolescence in the profession of economics. For so long as social achievement is coterminous with economic performance, economists are the highest arbiters of social policy. Otherwise not. Theirs is an eminence not to be sacrificed casually.

There is a further advantage in economic goals. The quality of life is subjective and disputable. Cultural and aesthetic progress cannot easily be measured. Who can say for sure what arrangements best allow for the development of individual personality? Who can be certain what advances the total of human happiness? Who can guess how much clean air or uncluttered highways are enjoyed? Gross National Product and the level of unemployment, on the other hand, are objective and measurable. To many it will always seem better to have measurable progress toward the wrong goals than unmeasurable and hence uncertain progress toward the right ones. But this would hardly have served the purposes of this book.

4

The supremacy of economic goals is also vital for the division of labor within the field of economics. For specialization is only possible if the specialists are united by a common and accepted goal. As matters now stand, a man can work on the economics of the textile, steel or chemical industry or he can concern himself with agriculture, labor or transportation and be secure in the knowledge that if a course of policy makes possible a larger output with given resources, it is socially sound. Were it open to a man working on textile, steel or chemicals to conclude that social virtue lay on the side of smaller production of these things with more relaxed conditions of toil or less air or water pollution, there would be chaos. He would have, however gently, to be retired. The situation of a labor economist who concluded that too many men were already at work producing things of marginal, submarginal or carcinomatous significance would be sadly similar. That of a specialist on fiscal policy who urged a particular tax because he sought a lower rate of growth, more sharing of work and a larger amount of leisure would be the most difficult of all. A serious, as distinct from a purely oral, concern for larger social goals would have an exceedingly disturbing effect on economics as it is professionally practiced.

Some adverse reaction can even now be detected. The espousal of noneconomic goals has an aspect of menace from which the professionally sensitive automatically recoil. They dismiss such extra-economic concerns as "soft," which is to say that they are professionally substandard.

Yet professional convenience and vested interest are not the safest guides in social thought. The questions that are beyond the reach of economists—the beauty, dignity, pleasure and durability of life—may be inconvenient but they are important.

5

In a book that has much to do with change, it is perhaps particularly useful to say a word about the economist's reaction to change. His reaction tends to be conservative, and this is true not only of the few who call themselves conservatives but of quite a number who unhesitantly describe themselves as liberals.

The reasons trace to the twofold character of change in economics. In the physical sciences—chemistry, physics, biology—change is associated only with discovery, with the improving state of knowledge. The matter being studied does not change. In economics, as in the other social sciences, there is change both in the state of knowledge and in what is being studied. There is improvement in the knowledge of the way prices are established. There is also change in the *way* prices are established. This will happen as the small proprietorship with no control of its market gives way to the giant corporation which has such control, or as both make way for government price-fixing.

Economists are not inherently resistant to novelty but they

react very differently to the two types of change. New knowledge or new interpretations of existing knowledge are much welcomed. Changes in the underlying institutions are much more slowly assimilated.

Thus at any time in the last sixty years, a new view of wage determination in competitive markets would have been quickly taken up. Some were. But the existence of the trade union was, for a long time, unrecognized in the theory of wages. Although the labor economist took unions for granted, the more prestigious economic theorist continued to assume "an absence of impediments" in the labor market.[2] Similarly the theory of the firm, and how it maximizes its revenue in the market, has undergone endless refinement in recent decades. This theory assumes that the man who maximizes the revenue gets that revenue or a compelling share. So he does on a Wisconsin dairy farm. But this is not so in the modern large corporation where the management is on a salary and the beneficiaries are stockholders whom the managers have never seen. Although the large corporation, like the union, is far from new, it has never been really assimilated into the main body of economics.[3]

Extensive government procurement in areas of high technology; extensive government intervention on wages and prices; widespread affluence, with its evident effect on the economic problem that it partly solves, have still to work their passage into the main body of economic theory.

Conservatism in these matters is not without justification. The fringes of economic discussion have long been afflicted by aborted revolutions or ones that turned out to be inconsequential. The demonetization of silver, the NRA codes, the effects of minimum wage legislation, court decisions bringing oligopoly within the ambit of the Sherman Act, the passage and amendment of the Taft-Hartley Act were all such nine-day wonders. In the end, they changed little. This has caused

[2] E.g., F. H. Knight, "Wages and Labor Union Action in the Light of Economic Analysis," in *The Public Stake in Union Power*, P. D. Bradley, ed. (Charlottesville: University of Virginia Press, 1959), p. 21 et seq.

[3] ". . . [T]he functioning of the corporate system has not to date been adequately explained, or, if certain explanations are accepted as adequate, it seems difficult to justify." Edward S. Mason in *The Corporation in Modern Society*, Edward S. Mason, ed. (Cambridge: Harvard University Press, 1959), p. 4. The author is the acknowledged dean of authorities on the modern corporation.

economists to take a conservative view of institutional change.

But economics also resists consequential and durable change because it seems more scientific to do so. Physics, chemistry, geology and biology are indubitably sciences; they are mounted on an unchanging subject matter. If economics is to be equally scientific, it presumably should have a similarly stable platform. If this does not exist, it can be assumed. To accept underlying change is to be dubiously respectful of the scientific aspirations of economics. To deny that it has relevance is to assume a much better scientific posture.

These attitudes also accord well with vested interest. Knowledge for the intellectual is what skill is for the artisan and capital for the businessman. In all, the instinct is to fear obsolescence. But the intellectual is in a far better position to resist obsolescence than the craftsman or businessman. The machine that replaces the craftsman is wholly tangible. His only line of resistance is overt—a strike or a sledgehammer to smash the thing. Both encounter social disfavor. Any effort by a businessman to protect obsolete plant, to regulate or suppress competitive innovation, is equally reprehensible. But the intellectual can always deny that there *has* been any change. The factors making for his alleged obsolescence, he can insist, are the figment of an undisciplined imagination. He can be a Luddite without violence and even without knowing it. It would be surprising, indeed, were such opportunity to remain unexploited.

For a book which is concerned with change and its consequences, it is obviously desirable that the reader and the critic be disposed to accept both the fact and the importance of change. Thus this argument.

But one is aided by the fact that the change here examined is not unobtrusive. The work of modern science and technology is highly visible. It will be assumed by most that it must have its effects on economic organization and social behavior. The great corporation is not easily concealed. Not many will imagine that the social impact of General Motors—on employees, markets, customers and the state—is the same as that of the Wisconsin dairy farm. The state clearly is a vastly greater force in economic affairs than it was sixty years ago. That science, technology and organization have placed new demands on educational institutions or that they have changed the balance of power as between capital and organization will not seem improbable.

Indeed, many will agree that the burden of proof is on those who aver that these changes have left conclusions concerning economic life unchanged. And that, precisely, is where I wish to have that burden placed.

Index

Abrams, Frank, 117

Accepted sequence, 194–198; consequences of, 198–200

Adams, Walter, 165n

Adaptation, 80; as motivation, 122–123, 126–127; and compulsion, 123, 124; and identification, 125–126; in the technostructure, 129, 143–145; in Soviet Union, 133; in the mature corporation, 134, 149–150; of public goals to technostructure's, 281, 282, 283, 286; and political hostility, 286–287

Adelman, M. A., 26n

Advertising, 3–4, 70, 185–190; radio and television, 190–191; and the creation of wants, 247–248, 248n; disdained by intellectual community, 267–268; truth in, 295–296

Aesthetic experience, 314–316

Aesthetic goals: and planning system, 314–316; and the state, 316–320; assertion of 343–344, 348 *Affluent Society, The* (Galbraith), ix, 185n, 236n, 248n, 314n

Agnew, Spiro, 107

Agriculture: and land ownership, 47–48; price control in, 174n

Air Force, 282–283

Air India, 95n

Airlines, 85n, 95n

Airplanes: World War I, 16; World War II, 17; development of, 23–24, 283; supersonic, 92

Aldrich, Winthrop W., 73

American Capitalism (Galbraith), 185n

American Telephone and Telegraph Company (AT&T), 68–69, 138, 324–325, 356

American Tobacco Company, 169n

Amtrak, 323n, 325n

Antitrust laws, 168–172, 179–180

Archbold, John D., 83n

Architecture, 315, 318

Armada, Spanish, 16, 17

Arms race, xviii; and image-building, 296–304; and the Soviet Union, 298, 301–302, 303–304, 305–306; and the educational and scientific estate, 302–304; substitute for, 306–308

Arrow, Kenneth J., 55n

Artists, 316–317; alienation of, 261n

Arts: patronage of, 318–319

Associated Gas and Electric, 110

Assumption, role of in setting goals, 150–151, 160

Atlantic and the Pacific Tea Company, Great (A&P), 76

Automation: and worker identification, 139–140; use of term, 215n

Automobile industry, 273

Autonomy: threats to, 74–77; in Great Britain, 92–93; in Ceylon, 94–95; in India, 94–95; and the technostructure, 96, 100–101, 153; in Soviet firms, 96–101; and the planning system, 353

SIGNET and MENTOR Books of Special Interest

☐ **THE AGE OF REVOLUTION 1789-1848 by E. J. Hobsbawm.**
The dual revolution—industrial and political—in England and France, and its global consequences. "A brilliant account of Europe in its revolutionary age."—*New Statesman*
(#ME1740—$2.50)

☐ **THE AGE OF CAPITAL by E. J. Hobsbawm.** Brilliantly analyzing the many facets of the age—commerce, industry, science, politics, art, morals, and manners—this major work by the renowned author of THE AGE OF REVOLUTION offers important new understanding of an era of history when individual initiative seized ruthless hold of the reins of progress, and capital was king.
(#ME1763—$2.95)†

☐ **CAPITALISM: THE UNKNOWN IDEAL by Ayn Rand.** A powerful advocacy of capitalism on the moral grounds that it is "the only system consonant with man's rational nature." By the best selling author and founder of Objectivism. Recommended Bibliography, Index.
(#J8271—$1.95)

☐ **UNDERSTANDING THE ECONOMY: For People Who Can't Stand Economics by Alfred L. Malabre, Jr.** The U.S. economic scene made easily comprehensible and intensely interesting . . . "Millions of readers can learn from this lively book."—Paul Samuelson, Nobel Prize-winning economist.
(#ME1570—$1.75)

☐ **THE COMMON SENSE WAY TO STOCK MARKET PROFITS (Revised and Edited) by Claude Rosenberg.** A famous investment advisor shows you how to play the market the sure, safe and easy way. "A first-class, practical investment primer—one of the best I've ever read . . . Unique and valuable."—Barton M. Biggs, *BARRON'S National Business and Financial Weekly.* (#J8397—$1.95)*

* Price slightly higher in Canada
† Not available in Canada

To order these titles, please
use coupon on the next page.

Books of Interest from the MENTOR Executive Library

☐ **WORK AND THE NATURE OF MAN by Frederick Herzberg.** Why do most workers in our society fail to realize their full human potential? How industry can alter its orientation toward work and workers, to make work a meaningful and enriching activity, forms the heart of this probing and extremely timely book. (#MW1239—$1.50)

☐ **FOUR DAYS, FORTY HOURS and Other Forms of the Rearranged Work Week (Newly Expanded and Updated** edited by Riva Poor. Foreword by Paul A. Samuelson. Twelve leading experts assess the pros and cons of the four-day work week, answering such questions as: How does this new work week affect labor? Management? The consumer? Foreign competition? Leisure activities and contemporary lifestyles? "Businessmen rely on this book as new mothers rely on Dr. Spock."—*The National Observer.* (#MJ1232—$1.95)

☐ **MODERN MANAGEMENT & MACHIAVELLI by Richard H. Buskirk.** An executive's guide to the psychology and politics of power, based on Machiavelli's classics THE PRINCE and THE DISCOURSES. Machiavelli's practical advice on how to achieve success in a competitive world is applied directly to the day-to-day problems and challenges of modern management. (#ME1703—$2.25)

☐ **MANAGERS FOR TOMORROW by the staff of Rohrer, Hibler, and Replogle, edited by Charles D. Flory.** A team of highly qualified industrial psychologists and management consultants examine the characteristics of the successful executive in industry's increasingly complex managerial positions. Foreword by Clarence B. Randall, former president of Inland Steel. (#ME1732—$2.25)

THE NEW AMERICAN LIBRARY, INC.,
P.O. Box 999, Bergenfield, New Jersey 07621

Please send me the SIGNET and MENTOR BOOKS I have checked above. I am enclosing $_____(please add 50¢ to this order to cover postage and handling). Send check or money order—no cash or C.O.D.'s. Prices and numbers are subject to change without notice.

Name _____

Address _____

City_____ State_____ Zip Code_____
Allow at least 4 weeks for delivery
This offer is subject to withdrawal without notice.